SALONUL DE PROÏECTE

Archive Books

BRANCUSI

An Afterlife

A research by Alexandra Croitoru

Foreword by Cristian Nae

2015
Salonul de proiecte, Bucharest
Archive Books, Berlin

Brancusi. An Afterlife

Text: Alexandra Croitoru
Foreword: Cristian Nae
Translation: Alistair Ian Blyth
Editing: Cristian Nae, Alexandru Polgár
Proofreading: Alistair Ian Blyth, Alexandru Polgár
Graphic Design: Nona Inescu, Lenke Janitsek

Insert & Cover
Selected Works: Alexandra Croitoru
Texts: Cristian Nae
Translation: Alistair Ian Blyth
Editing & Proofreading: Alistair Ian Blyth, George State
Graphic Design: Nona Inescu

Published by:
Salonul de proiecte Association, Bucharest & Archive Books, Berlin
www.salonuldeproiecte.ro
www.archivebooks.org

Printed at: Idea Design & Print, Cluj
Print run: 350

ISBN 978-3-943620-40-5
28 lei

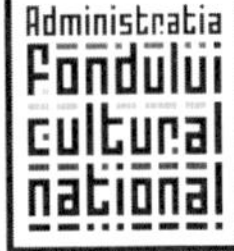

Editorial project co-financed by The Administration of the National Cultural Fund, Romania.

This project does not necessarily reflect the position of The Administration of the National Cultural Fund. The Administration of the National Cultural Fund is not responsible for the content of this project or the ways in which the results of this project might be used. These are solely the responsibility of the beneficiary of the funding.

Supported by: FUNDATIA**PLAN B**   tranzit.ro/ Iași
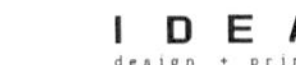

CONTENTS

Necessary Irreverence:
Brancusi and the Imaginary of the Nation

by Cristian Nae

More often than not, in the common parlance nationalism occurs as a form of extreme politics. We associate it with intolerance, chauvinism and social violence. However, as Michael Billig observes, nationalism does not represent a marginal phenomenon specific to minority communities and "peripheral" states; it is not the reserve of far-right discourse and of those who wish to construct a new nation state; and nor does it manifest itself in extreme forms, which are sooner the exception.[1] On the contrary, it is constitutive of mature nations, set within the everyday routine, through symbols that have become established in the popular culture and are consequently banal. Such ideological customs ensure the reproduction and perpetuation of already established nations.[2]

The idea according to which the global political configuration since 1989 has of itself brought about a demonetarisation of nationalism is both empirically contestable (we need only think of the Gulf War, waged in the name of national freedom, and the inter-ethnic wars that led to the breakup of Yugoslavia) and conceptually erroneous. It is based on an understanding of the nation as pure modern fiction (therefore devoid of any reality that might underlie the nationalist discourse) and projects onto world history a chronology that situates postmodernism as the inevitable end of modernity. The persistence of nationalism can also be remarked in the case of post-communist Romania, where it manifested itself in excessive forms in the public space of the city of Cluj during Gheorghe Funar's tenure as mayor. Recently, its symbols have re-emerged in less megalomaniacal versions, particularly in a religiously tinged commemorative form. The fact that since 1989 religion has seen a comeback in the former Eastern Bloc, being associated with a collective identity crisis, has already been underlined. For example, Katherine Verdery views the cult of the dead, materialising in Romania in the 2000s in the form of a resurgence in pilgrimages and the worship of relics, as a recurrent historical phenomenon in periods of social instability and identity crises.[3] Irrational worship was facilitated by the dissolution of the atheist ideology of communism and its specific forms of collective ritualisation. However, what has not been sufficiently highlighted by researchers who have dealt with the Romanian context is the surprising and particular confluence between ethno-nationalism, political populism, mysticism, Christian Orthodox discourse and cultural hybridisation resulting from massive emigration of the workforce to the West, manifested at the level of the everyday discourse in the form of a "banal nationalism." This recent social phenomenon has been examined in the artistic research of Alexandra Croitoru, who has focused on an exemplary case of ideological instrumentalisation of an artis-

---

1. Michael Billig, *Banal Nationalism*, London, Sage, 2005, p. 5.

2. *Idem*, p. 6.

3. Katherine Verdery, *The Political Lives of Dead Bodies: Reburial and Postsocialist Change*, New York, Columbia University Press, 1999.

tic corpus: the transformation of the life and work of Constantin Brancusi into a national cult in the popular discourse in pre- and post-1989 Romania.

Brancusi and the Ethno-nationalist Discourse

A brief review of the cultural theories of nationalism might clarify the particular structure of this discursive construct in our situation. Nationalism can be approached as an ideology before all else. No idea is born fully formed. The romantic idea of a timeless community, in which the individual expresses herself/himself within the framework of a culturally defined collective, arose as a response to the rationalism and individualism of the Enlightenment, and therefore represented an irrational form of attachment.[4] For Marxist historians, the process of social modernisation, illustrated through the professionalisation of the state, industrialisation and capitalism, made a decisive contribution to the formation of nations. Myths, traditions and historical narratives had to be invented in order to justify the new social configurations. The rise of the printing press and, as a result, the distribution of such legends via vernacular languages specific to the educated middle class also made a decisive contribution to the formation of "imagined communities," simultaneous with the erosion of trust in the divine right of kings and the concomitant transformation of cosmic space into "empty, homogenous time."[5] The nation thus arises as a "discursive formation of linguistic and symbolic practices."[6] To these can also be added, in the opinion of Eric Hobsbawn, a series of traditions invented by the elites.[7] This constructivist perspective on the nation, which views it as a modern invention of a discursive order, was dominant in political studies in the 1980s and 1990s, to the detriment of theories that postulated ethnicity and territory as a basis for national constructs. It was also supported by cultural theories that questioned the effects of globalisation, emphasising the hybridisation and fragmentation of the notion of national identity.

However, sociologically informed analyses examine the persistence of ethnic identities mobilised in the construction of modern nations. Ethnicity may be defined

4. Charles King, *Extreme Politics: Nationalism, Violence and the End of Eastern Europe,* Oxford, Oxford University Press, 2009, p. 23.

5. Benedict Anderson, *Imagined Communities: Reflections on the Origin and Spread of Nationalism,* London, Verso, 1991.

6. Anthony D. Smith, *Ethno-Symbolism and Nationalism: A Cultural Approach,* London and New York, Routledge, 2009, p. 12.

7. Eric Hobsbawn, Terence Ranger (eds.), *The Invention of Tradition,* Cambridge, Cambridge University Press, 1983.

in brief as "politicised social action."[8] Holding to the "realism" of the notion of nation, this school of thought believes that nationality represents a strong (re)source of group solidarity, providing a collective identity constituted through already established behaviours and beliefs, including attachment to language, territory, culture, ethnicity and other such data that existed prior to the formation of the modern states. In the opinion of John Armstrong, the persistence of these is connected to the existence of a symbolic language capable of solidifying the feeling of belonging to a certain identity, which includes spoken language and symbolic images, but also elements of architecture and dress codes, inscribed in ritual matrices that support mythic structures.[9] The importance of visual symbols in the nationalist discourse and their mobilisation in relation to various ethnographic codes can be observed in the use of the modernist elements from Brancusi's work (such as the serialism of *The Endless Column*) in Romanian popular culture, as well as in the replication of national effigies within the framework of the commemorative manifestations organised by Laurian Stănchescu in particular—the writer who in the late 2000s began to militate vehemently for the national rehabilitation of the artist.

Despite the fact that constructivist elements such as the imaginary nature of the nation, supported through invented traditions and public rituals, are obvious in the present situation and prove useful for a correct understanding of it, the introduction of a fiction of ethnic homogeneity into the cultural discourse via the work of Brancusi, as well as the myths invented or perpetuated through the symbolic recontextualisation of his oeuvre are not to be neglected. The argument of "Romanianness" put forward by nationalists such as Laurian Stănchescu relies on both territorial and ethnic essentialisation of national identity. Unity of language (undermined by Brancusi when he voluntarily went to France, where, as an artist, he was absorbed by Western modernism) is replaced with the language of folk forms. It is a mute visual language, which thereby allows Brancusi to be repatriated within an archaic and at the same time national language. Furthermore, from a "micronationalist" perspective of study, focused on everyday and folk expressions, nationalism not solely represents an effect of the discursive construct realised by the cultural elites and employed to instrumentalise the masses, but also a result of their naturalisation in the form of pre-existing religious beliefs and customs. From this standpoint, it is possible to explain the seductive power Laurian Stănchescu's discourse exerts on intellectuals such as the president of the Romanian Academy, as well as the complicity between the nationalist and religious appropriation of

---

8. Sinisa Malesevic, *Identity as Ideology: Understanding Ethnicity and Nationalism*, New York, Palgrave MacMillan, 2006, p. 27.

9. John Armstrong, *Nations before Nationalism*, Chapel Hill, University of North Carolina Press, 1982.

Constantin Brancusi as a "national, Christian Orthodox artist," expressed for example by the Patriarch of the Romanian Orthodox Church, who thus unwillingly evokes the Iron Guard discourse of interwar Romania. It is true that some of these ethnic fictions have been passed down to popular culture by historians legitimised by the communist regime in the period of the political isolationism practised by Nicolae Ceaușescu after 1974, who supported theories such as Dacian protochronism.[10] But they are perpetuated today at the level of cultural discourse via popular culture. The resurrection of ethno-nationalism in post-1989 Romania can therefore be compared with that of Irish nationalism, where the revival of the ethnic community was brought about through a reinterpretation of ancient symbols and myths[11]—in Brancusi's case these are attributed to the Dacians, particularly in the collective discourse originating in the diaspora since 1989.

ARTISTIC RESEARCH: A SOCIAL ENGAGEMENT

In brief outline, this is the social, cultural and political background that motivated the artistic research that Alexandra Croitoru conducted into the reception of Brancusi in Romania. As opposed to the scientific one, artistic research is characterised by the singularity of the methods it employs and the particularity of the conclusions it reaches, which cannot be generalised.[12] It cannot be used as a predictive element in general theories of society, economy, politics or culture. Works of art borrow methods of investigation from the field of social sciences (and not only) in order to construct alternative models of social life, to put forward utopias, to expose the fault lines and omissions in the dominant discourse, to visualise what is not publicly placed in view. Art constructs imaginary spaces, tests the convergence of seemingly incompatible discourses, fissures certainties and intensifies knowledge of the particular. Furthermore, it can be engaged in the transformation of society and openly acknowledges a political engagement passed over in silence by

---

10. Initially, the term denoted the seeds of subsequent developments in the history of culture. Later on, it came to denote the glorious inventions of the Romanian people prior to the modern construction of the nation, which existed *in nuce* before their achievement by other cultures. See Edgar Papu, "Protocronismul Românesc" [Romanian Protochronism], *Secolul 20*, 1974, and Edgar Papu, *Din clasicii noștri. Contribuții la ideea unui protocronism românesc* [From Our Classics. Contributions to the Idea of a Romanian Protochronism], Bucharest, Eminescu, 1977. For its instrumentalisation in the communist discourse, see Lucian Boia, *Istorie și mit în conștiința românească* [History and Myth in the Romanian Consciousness], Bucharest, Humanitas, 1997.

11. John Hutchinson, *The Dynamic of Cultural Nationalism*, London, Allen & Unwin, 1987.

12. Henk Slager, "Methodicy" in W. Balkema, Henk Slager (eds.), *Artistic Research*, Volume 18, Amsterdam, Rodopi, 2004, p. 13.

many academics under the pretext of scholarly neutrality. In the present situation, the artistic practice is aimed at exposing ethnic fictions active in the construction of this discourse and at counteracting its effects at the level of common sense.

Alexandra Croitoru's works reflect an impressive investigation specific to cultural studies, in which the central element is the social construction of the Brancusi "myth," as well as the processes by which this myth is reproduced and conserved in Romanian popular culture. The myth is here interpreted as a naturalised ideological construct, which ultimately comes to be identified with a national superstructure of identity. Within the framework of this research, the artist traces the genealogy of a number of cultural mechanisms that contributed to the mediatisation of Constantin Brancusi's name and work both inside and outside the art world: the appropriation of modern art (and its codes) in popular visual culture; the emergence of an art history field of study marked by an obsessive interest in the life and work of Constantin Brancusi ("Brancusiology"), as well as by an academic dilettantism excused by documentary passion; the conservation of the cult of Brancusi in the communist period via commemorative rituals aimed to reveal what, in another study,[13] I have called, using a paradoxical phrase, the "historical transcendentalism" of Brancusi's work—its universal, timeless but at the same time local value, a value rooted in Romanian folklore and legends; and finally the construction of an imaginary, heroic and mythological figure in Romanian literature. The element shared by these discourses is without a doubt fiction—that narrative construct fundamental to defining a nation as an imagined and imaginary community.

A short analysis of the artistic strategies of cultural criticism mobilised by Alexandra Croitoru in her works is able to highlight the particularity of her intellectual approach, which constantly comes back to an interrogation of the condition of the artist. Unlike many academic researches that are content to describe and explain the genesis or structure of a given historical phenomenon, the urgency of a public response, arising from a necessary civic engagement, seems to have generated this extended history of the reception of Brancusi in Romania. Alexandra Croitoru launches into the articulation of a consistent artistic critique, which aims to counterbalance the potential ideological deviations of civil society and temporarily to limit the nationalist aberrations they can generate. She is not interested in the collective, strident and often violent forms of nationalist extremism, which appear as obvious threats against social stability. On the contrary, making use of specific and symptomatic situations, she aims to bring to light its less visible aspects, the beliefs that are naturally accepted at a personal level and which

---

13. Cristian Nae, "Divergent Modernisms: Abstraction, Temporality and Cultural Politics in the Interpretation of Brancusi's Pedestals" in Irina Cărăbaş, Olivia Niţiş (eds.), *After Brancusi*, Bucharest, Unarte, 2014, pp. 46–62.

are thereby all the more dangerous. In her works, real people embody ideas, become conceptual figures—such as the figure of "nationalism"—and brief, seemingly banal moments excised from everyday life demonstrate (and dismantle) the banality of evil, to use Arendt's famous phrase. Wagering on the tacit rationality of the majority of viewers, on congenital common sense, the cynical realism with which the artist operates in her documentary works is surgical in its action, like a keyhole operation on the social tissue. The incision achieved through photography and video recordings aims to identify and extirpate the pathological elements that are camouflaged as normality merely by exhibiting them, by situating them in the public debate.

A second strategy, favoured by the artist, is to stage performative situations. Resorting to subversive affirmation of certain dominant attitudes and concepts within a given cultural context, Alexandra Croitoru aims to hijack the symbolic capital of such associations by presenting them hyperbolically, by hypertrophying them. Regarded as a contemporary version of over-identification with ideological symbols and ritual practices specific to the state apparatus in the communist period, subversive affirmation represents a tactic of resistance to the cultural mythology of the capitalist economy.[14] The extreme acceptance of such symbols wagers on causing an implosion of the syntax of the communicational structures that put them into circulation in the everyday discourse. It is possible to draw a useful parallel between Foucault's archaeology of discourse and the tacit use of subversive affirmation: in both situations, the limits of discourse are highlighted, the practices of exclusion that legitimise what can be said and determine what cannot be visualised are exposed. For example, tracing the parallel history of Brancusi's aphorisms and their influence on recent generations of artists, Alexandra Croitoru exposes the limits of the official discourse within which Brancusi as an author-function is constituted.[15] If the effects of Brancusi's works have extended outside the framework of the art world, as they have been appropriated by popular culture and have become, since the 1980s, a national symbol, the performative dimension of Alexandra Croitoru's works aims to deconstruct the sculptor's authority within the Romanian cultural discourse—a position significant also because it can be read from the standpoint of gender politics. Her interventions are situated at the terminus of a history of the reception of Brancusi that has included epigone-like copying, pious reproduction and creative pastiche in Romanian sculpture of the 1960s to 1990s. The patriarchal authority of the sculptor as modernist genius is counterbalanced by the punctual tactics of a woman artist, who operates via recycling,

14. Inke Arns, Sylvia Sasse, "Subversive Affirmation: On Mimesis as Strategy of Resistance" in Irwin (ed.), *East Art Map*, London, Afterall, p. 444–455.

15. See Michel Foucault, „What is an author?" in *Language, Counter-memory, Practice*, Donald F. Bouchard (ed.), Ithaca, Cornell University Press, 1977.

recodification and distortion of such visual codes, focusing on the context in which the elements appropriated from the work of Brancusi are exhibited and received rather than on their intrinsic meaning. For Croitoru, art is defined as a system of institutionalised representations and practices, in other words as a discursive practice, rather than as an artistic language attached to a specific medium. From the outset, this position allows her to interrogate not only Brancusi's "influence" in the art world, which is restricted to a formal and/or stylistic vocabulary, but also, more importantly, the discursive effects of Brancusi's work in cultural fields that interpenetrate and contaminate each other without fusing —and consequently its inevitable politicisation. This is why I prefer to talk about the Brancusi effect, in other words about its visually materialised echoes and reverberations, as well as a certain attitude, an ensemble of commemorative practices and rituals that have maintained his aura of sacrality and ultimately contributed to the monumentalisation of the artist.

In the latter respect, both in her textual interventions and in her conceptual installations and performance rituals recorded on video, Alexandra Croitoru constructs counter-monuments dedicated to Constantin Brancusi. The sculptural object commissioned from sculptor Napoleon Tiron illustrates a broad category of cultural products that have sprung up since Brancusi's death and his transformation into an artistic brand—the result of the contemporary expansion of culture industry. But at the same time it evokes the vernacular use of Brancusi motifs in the urban architecture of the 1980s, as well as their appropriation at the level of popular culture in the form of advertising campaigns of greater or lesser aesthetic value. In short, the *Walking Stick* work explores kitsch as a "secondary discourse," the result of interference between folklore and popular culture, as well as between high art and mass culture. From the sociological perspective, kitsch is not merely an aesthetic category that expresses the result of a negative value judgement, removing certain artefacts from the sphere of art, but the result of a social classification, which denotes a particular symbolic function of the objects. Associated with the souvenir (a recent and more accessible version of the cabinet of curiosities), kitsch is a modern phenomenon, arising from the intermixing of the social classes after the emergence of the bourgeoisie and from the erosion of firm social stratifications. This tendency has become generalised in postmodern culture through the acceleration of consumerism, the intensification of desire, the manipulation of affects, the instrumentalisation of knowledge, and the transformation of art into merchandise and both art and merchandise into signs. The kitsch object perhaps expresses most clearly the fetish character of merchandise in the contemporary period—and Brancusi does not escape this fundamental transformation of Romanian society.

All these posthumous interpretations of the work of Constantin Brancusi, as employed by Alexandra Croitoru, are part of what can be understood as the Brancusi effect in post-Stalinist Romanian culture. Unlike the established concept of influence, which denotes a relationship of causality between an active agent and a passive receptor, the term effect, the same as afterlife, has the advantage of affirming a plurality of cultural agents that contribute to a given cultural construct. It also allows the affirmation of a retrospective influence on the meaning of Brancusi via terms such as re-contextualisation, re-modelling, etc.[16] The cultural signifier Brancusi has inevitably expanded its range of significations, just as from the viewpoint of the art world the museum reproduction of his studio within the Centre Georges Pompidou inevitably transforms our current perception of the original Montparnasse studio; and the reading of Brancusi, as well as his cultural meaning, can today no longer be naive or indifferent or purely aesthetic: it is inevitably contaminated by the plurality of replicas and visual fragments that utilise his image, by decorative and vernacular appropriations, by kitsch legitimised by museums and the entertainment industry, and by the discourses into which his work has in the meantime been inserted. In all this amalgam of signs and codes that symbolically capitalise on modern art, the myth of "Brancusi—son of Romania" is perhaps the most dangerous. Not only that it replicates a history of art from the national perspective, and it promotes a nostalgic country branding, but it can also become a meta-sign, easily liable to be rendered banal, and its inherent ideology naturalised. This is why irony and the irreverent attitude specific to the works of Alexandra Croitoru is today all the more necessary.

---

16. For a discussion of the term historical effect in art theory, see Martha Buskirk, Mignon Nixon (eds.), *The Duchamp Effect*, Cambridge and London, The MIT Press, 1996.

INTRO

Against the backdrop of left-wing movements opposing capitalism and globalisation, one of the most interesting topics under discussion in the context of contemporary art has become the precariousness of the artist, of the cultural worker.
The artistic discourse seems to be in as insecure a state, increasingly instrumentalised
as it is in institutional policies whatever their nature. It seems that not even the most
critical approaches can eradicate the mechanism whereby radical discourse and
politically engaged art are appropriated by institutions connected to power and
capital. In the situation in which culture has been privatised, with many cultural
institutions coming to rely on corporations and private money, there is increasingly frequent discussion of the need for a sustained protest against the co-opting of
cultural activity by corporate sponsors and the "negative" use of credibility gained
within the field of the arts. At the same time, although the left-wing cultural critique focuses mostly on art's relationship with private sponsors, public institutions
have just as dangerous an agenda, which is further complicated by the pressure of
national representativeness. In this context, there is talk of the dangers to the artist's
professional integrity when her/his cultural product is manipulated in an ideological discourse alien to her/his original intention.

The international artistic community is making efforts to inform artists about these
problems, in order to bring the situation to awareness, to crystallise a structure—a
union—to defend the rights of cultural workers and to put forward solutions for an
existence that would not depend on the state, sponsors or patrons, to find ways of
fighting the abusive use of cultural production to ideological and economic ends.[1]
In parallel with such initiatives, equally important is to expose and question these mechanisms of manipulation in research projects such as the one undertaken here.

We also need to take into consideration the nuances between manipulation and
interpretation, between copyright and copyleft. Equally important for the discussion are the role and authority of the author as debated by W. K. Wimsatt and
Monroe Beardsley, Umberto Eco, Roland Barthes or Michel Foucault. While
manipulation is obviously negative in its connotations, interpretation is connected to an activation of the reader that reaffirms a certain democratisation of the art
field, but which at the same time opens a Pandora's box of the interpretations.

Such manipulations/interpretations can be regulated by a professional ethics
or by given institutions within the artistic context, but outside this context they often
lose their authority. When it comes to the institutions that may be involved in the
politically (or financially) correct dissemination of an artist's work, there are, on
the one hand, museums and public institutions that deal with copyright consequent

---

1. A recent example is *ArtLeaks*, a collective platform initiated by an international group of artists,
   curators, art historians, and intellectuals in response to the abuse of their professional integrity
   and the open violation of their labour rights. *Artleaks* activity is available online at <www.art-
   leaks.org>.

to the Berne Convention, and, on the other hand, private foundations that manage artists' estates. In regard to the private institutions that regulate the dissemination of artists' work after their death, one interesting case is the Estate of Diane Arbus, administered by her daughter. After the artist's death, it was the family that looked after her work, preventing access to her correspondence and frequently refusing to exhibit or publish the photographs in contexts that were considered to be unsuitable. As a result of this situation, in 1993 the editors of *October* magazine went so far as to publish a text harshly criticising the family's control of Arbus's work, as well as their attempts to censor articles and debate about her work.[2] In 2007, the whole archive was purchased by New York's Metropolitan Museum of Art, an institution which, it may be supposed, would guarantee responsible circulation of Arbus's work: "The Museum will collaborate with the Estate to preserve Arbus's legacy and to ensure that her work will continue to be seen in the context of responsible scholarship and in a manner that honours the subjects of the photographs and the intentions of the artist."[3]

Another interesting case is that of Richard Wagner: his family and the Bayreuth circle were responsible for the Nazi contextualisation of his work. It was not until after Wagner's death that the romantic nationalist movements acquired an aggressive and militaristic note, and Bayreuth became a meeting place for German nationalists attracted by the Teutonic pathos of Wagner's work. Although a short time after the composer's death Nietzsche saw him as a flatterer of every German vanity, obscurity and arrogance and wondered whether he might be regarded as the expression of the synthesis of the German soul,[4] it was the Bayreuth circle that was responsible for Wagner's "Nazification", supported by the composer's wife, Cosima Wagner, his son-in-law, Houston Stewart Chamberlain, whose writings influenced the official philosophy of German nationalism during the Hitler regime, and his daughter-in-law, Winifred Wagner, who was a close friend of Hitler's and who ran the festival from 1930 to 1945.

Setting out from the Wagner case and discussing the mechanisms whereby the work of an artist can be contextualised within an ideological discourse, we might also talk about the "nationalisation" of an artist's work, its confiscation and exploitation by the state. A more recent example in this respect is the work of Jackson

---

2. The editorial text explains why the article about Diane Arbus was published without any images, as a protest against this type of censorship: in order to grant the right to publish the requested images, besides exorbitant sums, the estate demanded alterations to the text, rejecting "everything of what little there was that could possibly be taken as a negative judgment about Arbus and her subjects." *October*, 66, Autumn 1993, pp. 28, 30.

3. "Metropolitan Museum Acquires Diane Arbus Archive" (press release), 18 December 2007; <http://www.metmuseum.org/about-the-museum/press-room/news/2007/metropolitan-museum-acquires-diane-arbus-archive>.

4. Ironically, Nietzsche's work was also later associated with Nazism.

Pollock, which was deeply politicised at the beginning of the Cold War. In the 1950s, the press read into Pollock's work creative expression and individual freedom, which it presented as being in opposition to Soviet socialist realism, while MOMA—with financial support from the Congress for Cultural Freedom, an organisation to promote American culture and values that was backed by the CIA—organised travelling Pollock exhibitions in Europe.[5] Rosalind Krauss draws a parallel between this cultural export and the Marshall Plan,[6] while other more radical critics, such as Eva Cockcroft, call Pollock a "weapon of the Cold War."[7]

As an extension of these ideas, I put forward in the present research the term *reciprocal appropriation* (the opposite of what we are accustomed to address, namely the process whereby art appropriates elements from the social sphere) in order to discuss the mechanisms by which an artist or her/his work can be appropriated in discourses that relate more to the sphere of ideology or economy than to that of art. When I use the word *appropriation*, I am considering the wider sense of the word, the cultural appropriation by which we understand the borrowing or even theft of material or immaterial cultural properties which, taken out of context, can acquire meanings different to those they originally possessed. The idea of making use of the concept of reciprocal appropriation took shape proceeding from Marcel Duchamp, who said in a lecture given at MOMA in 1961: "wanting to expose the basic antinomy between art and readymades, I imagined a 'reciprocal readymade': use a Rembrandt as an ironing board!"[8]

Another theoretical reference point for this approach is Roland Barthes and his concept of myth, viewed as a system of communication: "Every object in the world can pass from a closed, silent existence to an oral state, open to appropriation by society, for there is no law, whether natural or not, which forbids talking about things."[9] Barthes believed that in regard to myth the signifier can be discussed from two standpoints: as the final term of a linguistic system or as the initial term of a mythic system. In this semiotic chain, taking into account the terms put forward by Barthes, we may regard the artist and her/his work—the signifier—as the

---

5. Ideas developed by Frances Stonor Saunders in *The Cultural Cold War: The CIA and the World of Arts and Letters*, New York, The New Press, 1999.

6. In the chapter "Roundtable: Art at Mid-Century" in Hal Foster, Rosalind Krauss, Yves-Alain Bois, Benjamin H. D. Buchloh (eds.), *Art since 1900. Modernism, Antimodernism and Postmodernism*, New York, Thames and Hudson, 2004, p. 328.

7. Eva Cockcroft, "Abstract Expressionism: Weapon of the Cold War," *Artforum*, no. 10, June 1974, pp. 39–41.

8. Marcel Duchamp, "Apropos of 'Readymades'" in Michel Sanouillet, Elmer Peterson (eds.), *The Writings of Marcel Duchamp*, Oxford, Oxford University Press, 1973, pp. 141–2.

9. Roland Barthes, *Mythologies*, New York, Noonday Press, 1991, p. 107.

final term in the artistic context, as well as the initial term of the mythic construct in a wider social context.

Finally, this two-directional appropriation can be traced setting out from Theodor Adorno, who notes how "the culture industry, to the detriment of both, forces together the spheres of high and low art, separated for thousands of years."[10] The transfers between the culture of the elite and popular culture may also be regarded as productive ones. Andreas Huyssen also points to "the attempts launched from either side to bridge the gap or at least to appropriate elements of the other: from Courbet's appropriation of popular iconography to Brecht's immersion in the vernacular of popular culture, from Madison Avenue's conscious exploitation of avant-gardist pictorial strategies to postmodernism's uninhibited learning from Las Vegas there has been a plethora of strategic moves tending to destabilize the high/low opposition from within."[11] In addition, these transfers need to be traced not only in the sphere of art, but also in its connections with capitalism and nationalism.

Thus, I have examined the international context in a search for the strategies whereby a leading artist is transformed into a national symbol, and I have traced the stages of the construction of such a myth and its connections with ideology, capital and the tourism industry. From this viewpoint, I examined the case of Constantin Brancusi, questioning the way in which his achievements in the international artistic context have been imbued with meanings connected to the nationalist and protochronist discourse and transformed into a Romanian high-performance. The present research focuses on the cult of Brancusi in Romania, following the connections between the artist and the national discourse, tracing how the legend was born, how the myth was established, discussing the underlying causes of the phenomenon and the way in which it materialised in the Romanian context.

This research is not yet another interpretation of the life and work of Constantin Brancusi, but rather an analysis of the artist's national representativeness as it appears in academic texts, works of fiction, governmental and commercial strategies, or crusades such as the one to repatriate the artist's earthly remains. From one chapter to the next, the research outlines the cultural, historical, political and social framework that made it possible to propagate this cult, and brings into question its aberrations in the artistic context, as well as in the wider context of contemporary Romanian society.

In order to discuss the relationship between Brancusi and Romania, I made use of the concept of *banal nationalism* introduced by Michael Billig to observe how the

10. Theodor W. Adorno, "The Culture Industry Reconsidered" in J. M. Bernstein (ed.), *The Culture Industry. Selected Essays on Mass Culture*, London and New York, Routledge, 2001, pp. 98–99.

11. Andreas Huyssen, "Adorno in Reverse: From Hollywood to Richard Wagner," *New German Critique*, No. 29, Spring–Summer, 1983, p. 8.

artist was caught up in the mechanisms whereby the nation/the nation state communicate and reproduce themselves beyond times of crisis, in which nationalism is explicitly invoked. From the outset, the work of Brancusi was situated between native spirituality/folkloric tradition and universality, and his "canonisation" occurred against the problematic backdrop of the relationship with the West, which I considered from the point of view of Alexander Kiossev's concept of *self-colonisation*. Thus, as early as the interwar period, international legitimation appears to be the principal driving force of the transformation of Brancusi into a national hero. This process, which is also later to be found within the framework of the "socialist-humanist" rehabilitation of Brancusi in the 1960s and 1970s and the protochronist rehabilitation of the 1970s and 1980s, has developed and been refined right up until the present context of competitive nation states, where, against the backdrop of globalisation and European policies of national identity, Brancusi even becomes a mainstay of Romania's branding strategies. This cult of the sculptor has been maintained over the course of time by the exegetic overproduction of Romanian Brancusi specialists, who have ultimately influenced both works of fiction and the way in which Brancusi is appropriated in governmental strategies, in popular culture and in various nationalist discourses, such as those of the Dacologists and Orthodox fundamentalists, or in trans-national discourses such as those of yoga practitioners and freemasons.

During the course of this research, I explored the pros and cons of the appropriation of artistic production: some believe that the phenomenon succeeds in destabilising the hierarchical relationship between the elite and popular culture, thereby blurring the boundaries between art and the social sphere; others argue that only experts in the arts—participants in the *illusio*, to use Pierre Bourdieu's term—are entitled to handle artistic production. They regard popular culture as an inferior register (but a threatening one, because it is dominant in the contemporary context) that exploits art to various commercial or ideological ends. Although both positions are justified, I was not interested in pronouncing verdicts in this regard. Nor was I interested in discussing such appropriations/interpretations of Brancusi in relation to the author's original intentions. On the contrary, I took the phenomenon to be one that was "productive," on the boundary between art and society, intrinsic to any system of representation or interpretation, and I developed the research as a deconstruction/documentation of the cult of Brancusi in the Romanian context, from the viewpoint of a visual artist for which an understanding of the contemporary cultural framework is vital.

In close connection with the text, the artistic research metabolises all these ideas in a series of autonomous works and can be seen as an extension of my interest in the area of national identity and representativeness. This interest previously generated works such as the *ROM_* series of photographs from 2004, the *Solutions for Building a Common Future* installation from 2005, the *Immigrant* installation and *The*

Art of Hygge video from 2006, in which I brought into discussion the notion of national identity in the contemporary context of the European Union and of the debates linked to xenophobia and nationalism. In 2009, together with Ștefan Tiron, I started a project titled *A Fresco for Romania*, in which this interest was developed in a work discussing the writing of history and the role of the artist in this process, and entered the competition for the Romanian Pavilion at the Venice Biennale with a curatorial project that questioned the cultural legacy of Constantin Brancusi. Since then, the subject of Brancusi grew increasingly important to me, finally becoming the subject of the present research.

As an artist educated in Romania, I grew up with the image of Brancusi as a paragon seated on the topmost step of the pantheon of art history, and the very overexposure to this type of laudatory discourse generated in the end a need to deconstruct the Brancusi myth, but without it affecting my perception of his work per se. The absence of any aesthetic consideration of Brancusi's work might seem unusual in a research project such as this one and I want to make clear at this point that I am absolutely not contesting the value of his work. At the same time, I believe that a purely aesthetic response to Brancusi's œuvre has become impossible in the Romanian context, where the sculptor's work has so violently been invested with meanings connected with national achievements. Here we may recall the vote organised by Saatchi Art in 2009 to name the world's best artists, which mobilised many fellow artists to urge a vote for Brancusi in order to prove that we are still "patriotic Romanians."[12]

In the text I was interested in the history of Brancusi's "canonisation" and "nationalisation" and I argued in favour of regarding the artist's international legitimation as the principal driving force of these processes, which unfold—against the backdrop of the problematic relationship with the West—both within the sphere of high art and in that of popular culture. Following the structure of the text, a part of the artworks relate to the "canonisation" of Brancusi within the artistic context: the project for the Romanian Pavilion at the Venice Biennale, the object commissioned from Napoleon Tiron, the intervention on the façade of the Paintbrush Factory in Cluj, and the project realised in the Brancusi Studio in Paris; the other part ques-

---

12. Viral email: "BRANCUSI NEEDS US! The Saatchi Art Gallery is compiling a list of the greatest artists of the twentieth century. BRANCUSI was in second place, just three hundred votes' distance from Picasso, but according to an email sent to ARP publications he lost two thousand points on the grounds that he WASN'T voted for from Romania. Copy the contents of this message and send it to all your friends! Let us show that we are still Romanian patriots, that we care about our artists! It will take you just a few seconds to vote to lift Brancusi from the eighteenth place, where he has been relegated, to his place of honour, two thousand points equals two thousand Romanians, equals two thousand computers. (It isn't possible to vote from the same computer more than once.) Vote for Brancusi! Of the five hundred artists that are there, in the list of the best, only Constantin Brancusi is from Romania... he deserves our vote... it takes only one click."

tions the popular appropriation of the artist in the nationalist discourse: the poetic recital, the anthem, the cemetery actions, etc. One constant throughout these years is represented by my encounters with Laurian Stănchescu and the recording of his activities, which were a source of constant inspiration for many of my artistic projects. Quite often, the artworks were reactions to specific situations and events encountered during the research. In the past year alone, one could come across Brancusi in extremely different contexts: on the web page of the Artmark auction house, in a text that appeals to our need for a "national cultural identity" urging us to vote to keep a Brancusi masterpiece in Romania; as a character in a recent feature film directed by Adrian Popovici—*Brancusi from Eternity*; as the subject of a lecture about "peasant values" given by Matei Stîrcea-Crăciun at the Museum of the Romanian Peasant; as a symbol of perennial Romanian values and traditions in an advertisement celebrating 150 years of the CEC Bank.

I think it is extremely important that we maintain a critical attitude and constantly question the socio-political context in which we are active and I hope that through this research I will have opened up a way to perceiving Brancusi in a more complex way, beyond the specifics of art history, as symbolic capital exploited by various social agents. Moreover, this type of research could become a tool that we might employ to observe the ways in which cultural production more generally is instrumentalised in contemporary discourses related to capital and power.

This book started from the doctoral research that I completed in the autumn of 2014 at the National University of the Arts in Bucharest. Throughout my years of research I constantly benefitted from the guidance, understanding and suggestions of my supervisor Ruxandra Demetrescu and Professors Anca Oroveanu and Adrian Guță. During this time I had access to the Barbu Brezianu Centre for Brancusi Studies, part of the "George Oprescu" Institute of Art History, via Ioana Vlasiu and Irina Cărăbaș, to the Brancusi Archive of the Kandinsky Library of MNAM—Centre Pompidou, via Doina Lemny and Mica Gherghescu, and to the Brancusi archive of artist Vlad Nancă. I thank the aforementioned and also all those who, over the years, encouraged me in this research and pointed out to me various instances of the Brancusi cult in the Romanian mass media and public space. Finally, I would like to thank Ioana Vlasiu, Irina Cărăbaș, Magda Radu and Mihnea Mircan for their advice regarding this publication, and Cristian Nae for the patience, time and attention he granted this project.

PART 1

The Battlefield:
From Appropriation to "Nationalisation"

If we see the art world as an autonomous entity, included within the social one, but separated from it by a membrane, we may imagine that this membrane is permeable in two directions: just as artists appropriate elements from the social sphere, so too society appropriates elements from the sphere of the art. Just as there is a reason behind each appropriation made by an artist, so too we may observe various ideological or economic reasons in the process whereby society appropriates the artist/artwork. In this chapter I shall discuss cultural appropriation and its ethics, reciprocal appropriation (appropriation of the artist/artwork in the social sphere), and the political or economic motivation behind this process. A number of modes of reciprocal appropriation may be detected, some of them carried out in complicity with the artist, some of them abusive, throwing into question the idea of the artist/artwork as a trademark seen through the prism of marketing and branding.

Discussing appropriation in the wider sense of the concept, we understand by the term the relocation, annexation or even theft of cultural properties, objects or ideas, associated with European colonialism, the expansion of global capital, the emergence of disciplines such as anthropology or museum studies and their connected methodologies: description, collection, comparison, evaluation. There is even speculation that this culture of appropriation, specific to the West, might originate in the greatest act of material expropriation in the history of Europe: the annexation and absorption of European and Mediterranean cultures by the Roman Empire. Debates about cultural appropriation branch off in a number of different directions, ranging from intellectual property and government restitutions to the rights of ethnic minorities, and refer to appropriation in art, music, symbols, narratives, and scientific information, on the one hand, and appropriation of properties, objects and territories, on the other.

How did the field of the arts gain its autonomy from the social field? In *The Rules of Art*, Pierre Bourdieu draws a parallel between the cultural producer and Max Weber's agricultural labourer, commenting on the transition from domestic worker in the employ of a client or patron of the arts to the free worker who has to brave market competition on his own.[1] Thus, in the nineteenth century, the literary and artistic field was constructed in parallel with the ascendant bourgeoisie, and was divided between three positions: bourgeois art (the press, popular literature, theatre), social (or realist) art, and "art for art's sake". Later, these positions became polarised: the pole of mass production, subordinate to the wider public, and the pole of "pure" production, in which the producer's main clients were other producers. In time, the field of pure production expanded and professionalised, animated by what Bourdieu

---

1. He goes on to introduce the idea according to which the modern artist's social destiny is similar to that of the prostitute (a free worker in the market of sexual exchanges). Pierre Bourdieu, *The Rules of Art: Genesis and Structure of the Literary Field*, Stanford, Stanford University Press, 1995, pp. 55, 358.

calls *illusio*: an invisible complicity, "the collective adhesion to the game that is both cause and effect of the existence of the game."[2] Museums, galleries, travelling exhibitions, magazines, catalogues came into being, thereby facilitating an unprecedented relationship between interpreters (art critics, curators, dealers, gallery owners) and artworks. Bourdieu argues that "the discourse on the work is not a simple side-effect, designed to encourage its apprehension and appreciation, but a moment which is part of the production of the work, of its meaning and its value."[3]

Whereas within the art world, within the *illusio*, we can talk about the invention of the professional modern artist[4] as being something "natural," outside the *illusio* there occurs what we might call the social creation of the creator as fetish[5] or myth.

The autonomy of the art field, gained at the price of a rupture with the social field, led to this empire within an empire, which was relatively independent of economic and political powers external to it and possessed the characteristic of being its own privileged market that operated with symbolic capital: recognition within the field.

Not only is the artist the creation of the field of art, but in the conception of a number of theorists, art itself would not be possible outside the field. In his essay "The Artworld," Arthur C. Danto notes that "to see something as art requires something the eye cannot descry—an atmosphere of artistic theory, a knowledge of the history of art: an artworld."[6]

That which within the art world is perceived as legitimate, the process of cultural "borrowing" or the concept of "influence" (taken by Michel Foucault as functioning to preserve the continuity and integrity of history, tradition and discourse) —terms employed prior to "appropriation," the process of "creative misreading" of previous artistic production, of which literary critic Harold Bloom speaks,[7] becomes debatable in the social field, for, as Bourdieu notes, "the fundamental adhesion to the game, the *illusio*, recognition of the game and of the utility of the game, belief in the value of the game and in its stakes," is behind "all the allocations of meaning and of value."[8]

---

2. *Idem*, p. 167.

3. *Idem*, p. 170.

4. Or rather his work: "the artist who makes the work is himself made, at the core of the field of production, by the whole ensemble of those who help to 'discover' him and to consecrate him as an artist who is 'known' and recognized." *Idem*, p. 167.

5. Jean Baudrillard argues that in fetishism, what is essential is the code that governs both subject and object, subordinating them, leaving them prey to abstract manipulation.

6. Arthur C. Danto, "The Artworld" in Mark Francis (ed.), *Pop*, London and New York, Phaidon Press Limited, 2005, p. 257.

7. "Poetry is the anxiety of influence, is misprision, is a disciplined perverseness. Poetry is misunderstanding, misinterpretation, and misalliance." Harold Bloom, *The Anxiety of Influence: A Theory of Poetry*, Oxford, Oxford University Press, 1973, p. 95.

8. Bourdieu, *op. cit.*, p. 173.

Bourdieu also brings into discussion the "battlefield" at the boundary between the two empires, the artistic and the social, talking about institutions such as the museum that constantly reaffirm the rupture between the two: by extracting the works from their original context, the museum dispossesses them of their various religious or political functions, reducing them to their artistic function. In regard to reciprocal appropriation, the artworks are ripped from their original context, from the art world, in order to be invested with new economic or ideological functions, and this without affecting the aforementioned rupture in any way. Returning to the "battlefield," where elements are extracted from one sphere (be it the artistic, be it the social) in order to be reinvested with new meanings and functions in the other sphere, we can identify various strategies whereby such more or less violent transfers became possible.

In the late 1930s, Clement Greenberg spoke of the "the avant-garde's emigration from bourgeois society to bohemia," which also brought "an emigration from the markets of capitalism,"[9] giving rise to the opposition between the culture of the elite and popular culture: "Where there is an avant-garde, generally we also find a rear-guard. True enough—simultaneously with the entrance of the avant-garde, a second new cultural phenomenon appeared in the industrial West—popular, commercial art and literature."[10] Discussing the separation of the modernist artist (seen as apolitical), from bourgeois society, Greenberg pointed to the existence of an "umbilical cord of gold"[11] that nonetheless bound the two entities, in the sense that the artist depended on society to make a living. Similarly, Benjamin Buchloh comments on the isolation of the modernist artist from the socio-political sphere, and regards it as legitimated by concepts such as aesthetic autonomy or formalism.[12] What in the nineteenth century had been a positive value, the autonomy the art world had gained, acquires negative connotations in the second half of the twentieth century; it is renamed "isolation" and contested even from within, by artists who appropriate means of production or reception, materials and references from the much broader sphere of mass culture.

According to Buchloh, all cultural practices appropriate elements of alien, exotic or marginal discourse, the motivations and criteria for the selection of these elements being closely bound to the interests of the moment that animate each culture. They may range from explicit imperialist appropriation of cultural arte-

---

9. Clement Greenberg, "Avant-Garde and Kitsch" in Joseph Tanke, Colin McQuillan (eds.), *The Bloomsbury Anthology of Aesthetics*, New York and London, Bloomsbury Academic, 2012, p. 431.

10. *Idem*, p. 433.

11. *Ibidem*.

12. Benjamin H. D. Buchloh, "Parody and Appropriation in Francis Picabia, Pop and Sigmar Polke" in David Evans (ed.), *Appropriation*, London, Whitechapel Gallery; Cambridge, The MIT Press, 2009, p. 178.

facts to the more subtle methods of geographical, historical or scientific exploration. Buchloh believes that whenever art appropriates elements of mass culture, it publicly exposes its elitist isolation and outdated modes of production. The aspiration to a fusion of art with real life—romantically expressed by Robert Rauschenberg as "bridging the gap between art and life"—merely confirms this division. Every act of appropriation constructs a simulacrum of a dual position: elite/masses, exchange value/use value, individual/society, it perpetuates the separation of cultural practices and reaffirms the isolation of individual producers from the collective interests of the society within which they operate.

Buchloh brings into discussion Duchamp and representatives of Pop Art, who have come to be historicised with their original intentions having been inverted. They wanted to abolish the boundaries between high art and the rest of the world, but their works became new masterpieces of art celebrated by the world's great museums. In addition, the radicality of Duchamp's solution—"a petit bourgeois radicality" according to Daniel Buren[13]—concealed this process of reaffirmation of artistic institutions, of the market and artistic commodities, in other words, of the art world. Outside the art world, the readymade cannot be perceived as artistic production.

More often than not, appropriation in artistic practice has been interpreted as critical or subversive per se, but it can also be affirmative, and the artist's relationship towards the object of appropriation can be based on obsessive fascination. Douglas Crimp discusses appropriation, pastiche and quotation as strategies that extend throughout the sphere of culture, from the most calculated products of the fashion and entertainment industries to critical artistic products. Consequently, appropriation in itself cannot signify a specific—critical—reflection on culture.[14]

One relevant example of the circuit of appropriations between elite culture and consumer culture, a circuit we shall discuss below, is that of Mel Ramos. In 1962, he began a series of paintings, appropriating the figure of Batman. Just a few years later, in the June 1966 issue of the comic book, there is a scene in which Bruce Wayne attends "a sensational Pop Art show," which features life-size portraits similar to paintings by Mel Ramos.[15]

---

13. Cited in Buchloh, *op. cit.*, p. 178.

14. As an example, he presents the appropriation carried out by Sherrie Levine as being a meditation on strategies of appropriation: Weston's appropriation of the classic sculptural style, Mapplethorpe's appropriation of Weston's photographic style, art institutions' appropriation of Weston, Mapplethorpe and photography in general, and finally the appropriation of photography as a tool of appropriation. Douglas Crimp, "Appropriating Appropriation" in David Evans (ed.), *op. cit.*, p. 189.

15. Lawrence Alloway, "Popular Culture and Pop Art" in Mark Francis (ed.), *op. cit.*, p. 241.

Discussing the way in which an artistic product is appropriated in popular culture, Umberto Eco observes that "what happens to a message that is interpreted by means of an overcharged code is very similar to what happens to the *objet trouvé* that the artist pulls out of context and frames as a work of art: in this case, the artist selects certain aspects of the object as the possible signifiers of signifieds that have been elaborated by his cultural tradition. By arbitrarily superimposing a code on a message that has none (a natural object, for instance) or has a different one (some industrial product), the artist in fact reinvents, reformulates that message."[16]

In the contemporary context there are two views of cultural appropriation: the first, which seems innocent and fatalistic, presents it as a natural phenomenon—that of consuming cultural difference—generated by globalisation, with the market of cultural consumption thus being seen as a force that encourages and refines the phenomenon of appropriation. Here, appropriation is de-politicised and produces financial profit as part of a universal, non-hierarchical harmony, in which all cultures steal from one another, whatever their position, dominant or subordinate. The second view, which is that taken in the present research, is specific to the post-colonial discourse and holds that appropriation should be seen in the context of a hierarchy of cultures and is operated top-down by the dominant cultures.

Employing the methodologies of post-colonialism, in *Cultural Appropriation and the Arts* James O. Young examines the ethical and aesthetic problems that arise when cultural appropriation occurs in the context of the arts. In addition to obvious cases of appropriation of objects by individuals or institutions, it is also interesting to look at the appropriation of content, the process whereby an entity takes over and employs elements from another culture in the creative process: styles, motifs, subjects. In the post-colonial discourse, all these appropriations of objects and content on the part of individuals, institutions or industries from dominant cultures may be regarded as theft. From the theft of objects and content, the discussion has also extended to the theft of voices and even audiences. Minority cultures are entitled and also the most competent to communicate their cultural content by themselves, but if a dominant culture takes over this content and communicates it more aggressively, since it has access to more effective means of dissemination, the information market can reach saturation and the voices of the minority cultures will no longer be heard. It is a highly sensitive area: if a dominant culture does not include in its official discourse the products of the minority culture, it is accused of discrimination, but when it does include them, there are always questions regarding the position from which it does so and the impossibility in itself of presenting them "correctly" from an outsider position. And incorrect representation can "morally" damage the members of the minority culture, giving rise to the phe-

---

16. Umberto Eco, *The Open Work*, Cambridge, Harvard University Press, 1989, p. 199.

nomenon of assimilation: if the members of a minority culture are consistently exposed to "incorrect" representations, there is a risk that new generations will come to regard such representations as "correct."

Extrapolating from Young's text and recalling Flaubert and his portrait of the artist as *ouvrier de luxe*, we may consider an ethics of appropriation inspired by "subaltern" studies. In his texts on cultural hegemony, Antonio Gramsci speaks of a cultural war, in which the working class is oppressed by the dominant class precisely because the latter has control over the distribution of information in the mass media and, by extension, over popular culture. Gramsci's worker is equivalent to the contemporary cultural worker, who is just as lacking in rights and just as isolated from society as in the time of Flaubert. If we take into account the balance of forces between the art world and the social field, the appropriations made by artists seem justified strategies in a cultural war, unlike those made by the dominant discourse of consumer culture, which are received as being abusive precisely because the two fields are separate entities engaged in a hierarchical relationship. The field of popular culture is regarded as dominant because of the monopoly it holds not only over the means of production, but also over the means of communication. To the extent that the artist and her/his work are the product of the artistic field, they are also the collective property of the artistic field and deserve "as much respect and protection as the trademarks of a corporation."[17] Here, we can bring into discussion the capacity to contextualise correctly an artist/cultural product viewed as having been generated by participation in the *illusio* of which Bourdieu speaks. This argument, based on cultural experience/expertise is important given that when somebody outside the field contextualises an artist/artwork simulating belonging to the field of art, this can lead to distortions in the interpretation, evaluation and appreciation of the artist/work in question.

In an essay on appropriation, Robert S. Nelson discusses the connection between art and individual, corporate, civic and national identity, setting out from a copy of the sculpture of the four horses from San Marco in Venice installed at the entrance to a cemetery in Texas. He notes that appropriation is never passive, objective or disinterested, but always active and subjective, and draws an analogy with Barthes' myth, appropriating it and renaming it appropriation.[18] For Barthes, myth is a type of speech, a speech that is largely defined through its intention rather than its letter, a system of communication, a message. He extends the concept of sign and defines myth as a secondary system of communication. In myth, the sign, the relationship between signifier and signified, becomes the signifier of a new signified forming a second sign. Myth's function is to distort meaning, as the myth is neither a lie nor a confession,

17. James O. Young, *Cultural Appropriation and the Arts*, Chichester, Wiley-Blackwell, 2010, p. 122.
18. Robert S. Nelson, "Appropriation" in *Critical Terms for Art History*, Chicago and London, The University of Chicago Press, 2003, p. 163.

but an inflection. Roland Barthes believes that "the best weapon against myth is perhaps to mythify it in its turn, and to produce an artificial myth: and this reconstituted myth will in fact be a mythology." He then asks: "Since myth robs language of something, why not rob myth?"[19] This leads to a discussion of the ultimate "prostitution" of myth: it can affect anything, corrupt anything.

Nelson encourages us always to integrate the mythic structure into a more general context and to observe how myth responds to the interests of a given society at a given time. For example, he argues: "like a radioactive isotope, appropriation or myth breaks down over time, either fading away or mutating into a new myth. Because appropriations, like jokes, are contextual and historical, they do not travel well, being suppressed or altered by new contexts and histories."[20] He notes that "myth or appropriation is fundamental to modern advertising and to the abstracting and expropriating strategies of capitalism itself," presenting advertising agencies as "the true semiotic magicians of our world."[21] Indeed, there are countless instances in which advertising steals content from the art world without specifying the source, but in the present research I was particularly interested in cases where the name/work of an artist are employed to give plus value to a product targeting more sophisticated buyers.

A study on advertising and psychoanalysis[22] puts forward the idea that whenever a subject becomes interested in an advertising, cinematic or publishing offer, he is captivated by the fundamental questions of life and seeks to unravel the answers to such questions. The answers might be subversive (of an artistic kind) or simplistic (of an advertising or ideological kind). An artistic proposal makes us think, while an advertising proposal makes us buy (products or ideas). In advertising campaigns aimed at a more educated target audience, the symbolic capital earned by somebody within the art world can be transformed into branding capital—including that of having objects branded with a trademark—and can be exploited to confer value and to extract profit from the association between the two worlds: art and advertising. In the contemporary context it is becoming more and more obvious that it is not only the artist who is dependent on society. The system itself relies on artists in activities that generate increases in capital.

In the heyday of Pop, the visual arts were presented as depending "on the popular arts for their vitality, and the popular arts depended on the fine arts for their respectability". Even then, the elite believed that "things hardly 'exist' before the fine artist has made use of them, they are simply part of the unclassified background

---

19. Barthes, *Mythologies*, New York, Noonday Press, 1991, p. 134.

20. *Idem*, p. 163.

21. *Idem*, p. 164.

22. Doris-Louise Haineault, Jean-Yves Roy, *Unconscious for Sale: Advertising, Psychoanalysis, and the Public*, Minneapolis, University of Minnesota Press, 1993.

material against which we pass our lives."[23] At present, this idea has been adopted by corporations that implement it in their marketing strategies aimed at more sophisticated audiences. As Andreas Huyssen remarks: "just as art works become commodities and are enjoyed as such, the commodity itself in a consumer society has become image, representation, spectacle. Use value has been replaced by a packaging and advertising. The commodification of art ends up in the aestheticisation of the commodity. The siren song of the commodity has displaced the *promesse de bonheur* once held by bourgeois art."[24]

One interesting example is the Louis Vuitton company, for which association with famous contemporary artists has already become a tradition, particularly after designer Marc Jacobs was appointed creative director of the label in 1997. Icons of Japanese art, such as Takashi Murakami, since 2003, and Yayoi Kusama, in 2012, have been intelligently used in LV collections, reaching the extreme point where the French press claimed that the Printemps department store, whose windows Kusama decorated for Louis Vuitton, "has replaced the Reina Sofia Museum in Madrid, the Pompidou Centre in Paris, the Tate Modern in London, and the Whitney in New York."[25]

This confusion between museum and store works also the other way around, in the case of Murakami—a declared admirer of Andy Warhol—who in his artistic practice appropriates symbols from Japanese popular culture and who in turn was appropriated by Louis Vuitton, to the point where, in 2007, in a solo exhibition of the artist at MOCA Los Angeles, the label set up a shop inside one of his installations, selling LV accessories.

It is interesting to trace how artists who have built up a career from appropriating elements of consumer culture finally end up being appropriated themselves by multinational corporations. Richard Price was one of the artists who, from the late 1970s, used the strategy of appropriation in the most radical way—as visual piracy—artists whose works gave rise to a significant part of the critical theory of postmodernism. In series such as *Untitled (living rooms)* and *Cowboys*, he photographed printed advertisements, which he presented—without altering them in any other way than by reframing them—as his own works, thereby bringing into question the very subject of the originality of the artwork.[26] Thirty years later, a recent

---

23. Alison and Peter Smithson, "But Today We Collect Ads" in Mark Francis (ed.), *op. cit.,* p. 194.

24. Andreas Huyssen, "Adorno in Reverse: From Hollywood to Richard Wagner," *New German Critique,* No. 29, Spring–Summer, 1983, p. 14.

25. "Graphic Fashion: la rencontre Yayoi Kusama/Louis Vuitton s'expose au Printemps"; <http:// culturebox.francetvinfo.fr/graphic-fashion-la-rencontre-yayoi-kusama-louis-vuitton-sexpose-au-printemps-114880>.

26. This interpretation has its critics, see Isabelle Graw, "Dedication Replacing Appropriation: Fascination, Subversion and Dispossession in Appropriation Art" in Philipp Kaiser (ed.), *Louise Lawler and Others*, Ostfildern, Hatje Cantz, 2004, pp. 45–67.

series by the artist, *Nurses*, was used in a Louis Vuitton Spring/Summer collection, proving yet again that all anti-capitalist subversion will sooner or later be integrated into the system. In an interview, Marc Jacobs declares that Louis Vuitton specially chose to work with Richard Price, "an artist who uses appropriation in his works, which is exactly what LV does too—and that is okay, as long as there are always three differences from the starting point!"[27]

Another similar case is that of Cindy Sherman, who, in *Untitled Film Stills*, a series she started in the late 1970s, staged cinematic images questioning the female stereotypes generated and maintained by the popular culture. It is interesting to observe how an artist so important to the critique of gender clichés ends up placing her practice in the service of nothing less than the fashion industry, the most aggressive industry when it comes to laying down the norms of femininity, in magazines such as *Vogue* (1984) and *Harper's Bazaar* (1993) or in advertising campaigns for Comme des Garçons (1993) and Marc Jacobs (2005).

In aesthetic practice, appropriation can be the result of an authentic intention to question the historical validity of a local contemporary code through association with a different set of codes—previous heterogeneous styles or iconographies—or with different modes of production and reception. Buchloh remarks on the fact that only in the fashion industry (but to extrapolate, we may regard the phenomenon as being specific to mass culture more generally), which employs appropriation as "a strategy of commodity innovation," does the function of appropriation find its fulfilment—that of granting "a semblance of historical identity through ritualised consumption"—and he opens up an interesting discussion on the social behaviour of the contemporary individual, who is defined by "depoliticized consumption" and "consumerised politics."[28]

Andy Warhol was undoubtedly a historical figure emblematic of the erasure of boundaries between the art world and the corporate world, as he himself declared: "I started as a commercial artist, and I want to finish as a business artist. After I did the thing called 'art' or whatever it's called, I went into business art. I wanted to be an Art Businessman or a Business Artist. (...) Making money is art and working is art and good business is the best art."[29]

Discussing Warhol's "brazen dismissal of aesthetic autonomy," David E. James presents him as "an entrepreneur, carelessly crossing the ideological and functional boundaries of art itself, thus repudiating one of its most crucial criteria, its self-definition against advertising" and argues that Warhol's example demonstrates that

---

27. "SPRING 2008 READY-TO-WEAR Louis Vuitton"; <http://www.style.com/fashionshows/review/S2008RTW-LVUITTON/>.

28. Buchloh, *op. cit.*, p. 178.

29. Andy Warhol, *The Philosophy of Andy Warhol*, New York and London, Harcourt Brace Jovanovich, 1975, p. 92.

"there was no longer a position outside corporate capital for art to inhabit."[30] By the end of the 1950s Warhol was recognised in the advertising world as a commercial artist specialising in advertisements for luxury shoes,[31] and in 1961, when he was invited to decorate the window of the Bonwit Teller store, he took advantage of the opportunity to combine the commission with an exhibition of his recent works. Soon thereafter, he gave up commercial commissions to focus on his own artistic production, but kept as his main subject American consumer culture, appropriating its icons, using them to contract a successful artistic career.[32] In the 1980s he returned to pure advertising in a different way, appearing in person in various campaigns for BMW, New York Airlines, Diet Coke, Drexel Burnham, and others.

In the introduction to *Corporate Mentality*,[33] a publication that sets out to analyse the function of art in late capitalism—scanning the cultural context of the intersection between art and business and presenting critical artistic practices—Warhol is named the "founding father" of the phenomenon of art's subordination to capital. There is a specific discussion of the case of Swedish vodka company Absolut, which in 1985 was contacted by Warhol, who offered to redesign their bottle, thereby renouncing the form of autonomy (in relation to consumer culture) that the act of appropriation had guaranteed him hitherto. This step may be regarded as a return to his experience in the world of advertising, but this time enjoying a privileged position.

Talking about his early period, Warhol expressed frustration at the fact that the objects he drew for advertisements were regarded as being "artistic," while his drawings were not,[34] and so he probably felt vindicated as a result of his collaboration with Absolut Vodka, in which his name appears in letters as large as the brand itself. An important law of marketing says that after an image has been associated with a name for a long time, the image can replace the name. But it is also the name that lends power to the brand.[35] For the Absolut Vodka company it was not enough to be associated with Warhol's artistic practice; what was more important was the association with his name, which was already recognised as a famous brand and which would function on the market even when the real person no longer existed,

---

30. David F. James, "The Unsecret Life: A Warhol Advertisement," *October*, 56, Spring 1991, pp. 21, 41.

31. It may be observed that as early as 1955, one of the advertisements for I. Miller was made in the same style as the silkscreen from the same year: *À la recherche du shoe perdu.*

32. In 1985 he produced a series of silkscreens named *Ads.*

33. Aleksandra Mir, John Kelsey (eds.), *Corporate Mentality*, New York, Lukas and Sternberg, 2003, p. 10.

34. Roy Lichtenstein, Andy Warhol and Robert Indiana, "What is Pop Art? Interviews with Gene Swenson" in Mark Francis (ed.), *op. cit.*, p. 230.

35. Al Ries, Laura Ries, *The 22 Immutable Laws of Branding*, New York, Collins Business, 2002.

as Barbara Kruger observes in an essay written after the artist died, in which she speaks about the end of a physical body and the perpetuation of the proper name, of his afterlife as a historicised and venerated product.

There has been much discussion about proper names having a separate status, as "identity statements" that denote but do not connote. In *Naming and Necessity*, Saul A. Kripke puts forward the idea according to which, in the case of proper names, an "initial baptism" takes place, and when they are transmitted, the receiver has to learn to use them with the same reference used by the person from which she/he heard them.[36]

Setting out from Searle's question—"Do proper names have meaning?"—we must rather ask ourselves: how, by whom and with what intention are such meanings constructed or modified? To return to the even more specific situation of an author's name, Michel Foucault argues that it oscillates between description and designation, but without being determined by these functions, as it is not a mere element or speech or a function of a man's civil status, but nor is it a fictional construct. Foucault believed that the name of an author "points to the existence of certain groups of discourse and refers to the status of this discourse within a society and culture."[37] In addition, the name of an author invests a discourse with value, its reception and status consequently being regulated by the cultural instances in which it circulates at a given moment. As Claude Gandelman also remarks in a text about the semiotics of the signature in painting: "when one abstracts it from the signature which indicates it and 'contains' it, it loses its 'index' character and becomes a 'trademark'. Indeed, like the trademark, the name is of symbolic order."[38] In a recent interview discussing the contemporary artistic circuit, Boris Groys concludes that "nothing apart from the name stirs interest any more."[39] This was something Warhol also realised as early as 1966, when he composed the following ad for *The Village Voice*: "I'll endorse with my name any of the following: clothing AC-DC, cigarettes small, sound equipment, ROCK 'N' ROLL RECORDS, anything, film, and film equipment, Food, Helium, Whips. MONEY!! Love and kisses ANDY WARHOL."[40]

---

36. Saul A. Kripke, *Naming and Necessity*, Cambridge, Harvard University Press, 2001.

37. Michel Foucault, "What is an author?" in Donald F. Bouchard (ed.), *Language, Counter-memory, Practice*, Ithaca, Cornell University Press, 1977, p. 123.

38. Claude Gandelman, "The Semiotics of Signatures in Paintings: A Piercian Analysis," *American Journal of Semiotics*, 3, 1985, pp. 73–108.

39. "Arta trăieşte cu stigmatul absenţei legitimării democratice" [Art lives with the stigma of the absence of democratic legitimation], interview with Boris Groys by Ekaterina Degot; <http://www.criticatac. ro/3370/%E2%80%9Earta-traieste-cu-stigmatul-absentei-legitimarii-democratice%E2%80%9D/>.

40. Ad in *The Village Voice*, 10 February 1966, reprinted in Wayne Koestenbaum, *Andy Warhol*, London, Weidenfeld and Nicolson, 2001, pp. 99–100.

To return to Absolut Vodka, Warhol's silkscreen was the company's first commission of this kind and subsequently gave rise to the *Absolut Art* initiative, via which hundreds of artists were invited to associate their names and artistic practice with Absolut products and, by extension, their country of origin: when the company was acquired by Pernod Ricard, the Swedish state took over the collection, after it was declared "an important part of Sweden's cultural heritage."[41]

One cannot deny what Michael Fried argues, namely that "an art like Warhol's is necessarily parasitic upon the myths of his time, and indirectly then upon the machinery of fame and publicity that market these myths."[42] But we should also be aware that the "machinery," as he calls it, is in its turn parasitic upon artists and their practice, speculating on their symbolic capital in order to increase profits. Marketing and branding constantly elaborate strategies to this end. One of the unwritten laws holds that in the world of marketing there exist only the perceptions that buyers or potential buyers have about products—the perception is the reality,[43] while in the PR department, also informally known as perception management, the fabrication and maintenance of companies' public images is regarded as a complex, long-term process.

Particularly remarkable are the strategies whereby corporations associate themselves with artistic initiatives/events in order jointly to construct a national image. Such was the case of the Pepsi and Coca-Cola companies in the years following the Second World War, when the United States, as part of an imperialist drive, was building a new image to be exported.

In 1944, Pepsi launched its *Portrait of America* campaign, a competition organised in partnership with Artists for Victory, an association founded in 1942 by artists who wanted to place their artistic practice in the service of the United States' war effort. The Pepsi company, posing as "the protector of American art," actually profited from the benefits of a "patriotic" image.[44] The winning works were published in a calendar that had extremely large visibility, and the company's profits increased enormously thanks to the minimal investment.

Ten years later, Coca-Cola allied itself with US governmental policies to promote *The Family of Man*, a photographic exhibition organised by Edward Steichen at MOMA and then exported to twenty-eight countries, attracting more than seven million visitors. As Allan Sekula notes, it may be regarded as "the epitome of American cold war liberalism, promoting a benign view of an American world

---

41. Introductory page on <http://www.absolutartcollection.com>.

42. Michael Fried, "New York Letter: Warhol" in Mark Francis (ed.), *op. cit*, p. 219.

43. Al Ries, Jack Trout, *The 22 Immutable Laws of Marketing: Violate Them at Your Own Risk!*, New York, Harper Business, 1994.

44. Serge Guilbaut, *Voir, ne pas voir, faut voir. Essais sur la perception et la non-perception des oeuvres*, Paris, Éditions Jacqueline Chambon, 1993, p. 109.

order stabilized by the rule of international law." In the exhibition organised with the support of the United States Information Agency and corporations such as Coca-Cola, "the discourse was explicitly that of American multinational capital and government—the new global management team—cloaked in the familiar and musty garb of patriarchy."[45]

Hitherto I have discussed the appropriation of artists and their artistic practice in corporate strategies that make use of association with a trademark already recognised in the art world in order to consolidate their position on the market. The same marketing strategies also apply in the case of positioning within the political context and in the construction of country brands. In this final section, I shall present a number of cases in which artists and their practices were appropriated in the national discourse and I shall bring into discussion the decline in the authority of the author, setting out from the "innocent" concept of active audience and moving on to manipulation and abusive politicisation of authors.

The theory of perception presupposes that every system of communication is made up of a message, a transmitter, and a receptor. Setting out from the communicational model put forward by Roman Jakobson, Stuart Hall proposed a more nuanced system, in which the message is caught in the middle of two distinct codes, one belonging to the transmitter, and the other to the receptor. He presents the position of the transmitter as being privileged and hegemonic and argues that there are three formats of decodification: a reading that accepts the dominant message as such, one that negotiates an interpretation of the message, and one that positions itself in opposition to the message. To relate cultural production to this system, the author is perceived as occupying the hegemonic position of the creator, hence the parallel between the death of the author proclaimed by Barthes and the death of God proclaimed by Nietzsche, to which William Gass lends nuance as follows: "The death of the author signifies a decline in authority, in theological power, as if Zeus were stripped of his thunderbolts and swans, perhaps residing on Olympus still, but now living in a camper and cooking with propane."[46]

We cannot help but wonder whether there is a connection between the literary critical theories which hold that the author's intention is unimportant to interpretation, or which activate the work or the audience to the detriment of the author, and cases in which an artist/artwork is instrumentalised in a public discourse. In a text that opens up the possibility of such a discussion, "The Intentional Fallacy," W. K. Wimsatt and Monroe Beardsley argue that the interpretation of a work should

---

45. Allan Sekula, "The Traffic in Photographs in Modernism and Modernity" in Benjamin H.D. Buchloh, Serge Guilbaut, David Solkin (eds.), *The Vancouver Conference Papers*, Halifax, The Press of Nova Scotia College of Art and Design, 2004, p. 121.

46. William H. Gass, "The Death of the Author," *Salmagundi*, No. 65 (Fall 1984), p. 3.

be independent of the author's intention and draw a distinction between commentary on the work in itself and "author psychology, which (...) takes the form of inspirational promotion," warning of "the danger of confusing personal and poetic studies."[47] They believe that rigorous analysis of the work is the only acceptable interpretation and are against consulting the author, even if she/he is still living: "Critical inquiries, unlike bets, are not settled in this way. Critical inquiries are not settled by consulting the oracle."[48] Finally, they also touch upon the idea according to which poetry belongs neither to authors nor critics, but rather to the public: "it is embodied in language, the peculiar possession of the public, and it is about the human being, an object of public knowledge."[49] Barthes, who considered that "the image of literature to be found in ordinary culture is tyrannically centred on the author, his person, his life, his tastes, his passions,"[50] goes even further and symbolically kills the author, in order to liberate the text from his authoritarian control. In his opinion, the public is thereby activated: "to give writing its future, it is necessary to overthrow the myth: the birth of the reader must be at the cost of the death of the Author."[51] He argues that "to give a text an Author is to impose a limit on that text, to furnish it with a final signified, to close the writing."[52] Once the author has been eliminated, the critic, whose role was to fix meanings, also disappears, and the premises for a genuinely revolutionary context are thereby laid, "since to refuse to fix meaning is, in the end, to refuse God and his hypostases – reason, science, law."[53]

There are voices[54] that from this standpoint contest even copyright regulations, regarding copyright as being justified only within an economic paradigm, but not in regard to moral rights. Thus, the author is viewed as being incorrectly protected based on the argument of creation: "The weakness of this argument as a justification for copyright can be seen by contrasting it with the theological claim that it seems to parallel. First, unlike the God of the monotheistic religions, no human being creates *ex nihilo*. Every work, even leaving aside the claims of the post-modern critics, is in some part creation and some part imitation. It at least draws upon

---

47. W. K. Wimsatt, Monroe C. Beardsley, "The Intentional Fallacy" in W.K. Wimsatt, *The Verbal Icon: Studies in the Meaning of Poetry*, Lexington, The University Press of Kentucky, 1954, p. 10.

48. *Idem*, p. 18.

49. *Idem*, p. 5.

50. Roland Barthes, "The Death of the Author" in *Image Music Text*, London, Fontana Press, 1977, p. 143.

51. *Idem*, p. 148.

52. *Idem*, p. 147.

53. *Ibidem*.

54. See Michael Spence, "Justifying Copyright" in Daniel McClean, Karsten Schubert (eds.), *Dear Images. Art, Copyright and Culture*, London, Ridinghouse/ICA, 2002, pp. 389–403.

the traditions of the genre in which it is working."[55] Moreover, Michael Spence argues that "the harm from the unauthorized use of a work is of a type to which all expressive acts are subject—all our words are constantly being read and misread—and it is arguable that the state ought not to intervene to prevent use of this type,"[56] and finds it debatable that the state intervenes to regulate such situations in the author's favour.

In the attempt to redefine the notion of the author, like Barthes who presents the author as a figure of modernity, Michel Foucault considers that, before becoming a product caught up in a circuit of intellectual property, every discourse was "a gesture charged with risks,"[57] the birth of the author occurring at the intersection between the emergence of punishments for undesirable discourses and the emergence of the benefits resulting from regulations connected to copyright. The same idea also occurs in the writings of Barthes, who regards the author as "the epitome and culmination of capitalist ideology."[58] The emergence of the printing press inevitably led to an increase in the potential to disseminate ideas, and the first attempts to regulate this new domain were made by the authorities, which were in fact interested in controlling the content of printed materials. It was not until the beginning of the eighteenth century that there was a transition from control of content to regulations concerning commercial interests. It was also at this time that authors' rights began to be recognised, "for the encouragement of learned Men to compose and write useful Books" or, as the United States Constitution puts it, "to promote the progress of science and useful arts." Thus, regulations connected to copyright appeared simultaneous with the birth of the "profession" of author in the Romantic period. As Gass observes, "it should be recognized that the elevation or removal of the author is a social and political gesture, and not an aesthetic one."[59]

Concomitant with debates about the death of the author (according to some experts, the post-structuralist critique of the author seems to have had no significant influence on copyright law, which has continued to employ the Romantic image of the author[60]), at the beginning of the 1970s the Berne Convention regulated the moral rights of the author: "Independent of the author's economic rights, and even after the transfer of the said rights, the author shall have the right to claim authorship of the work and to object to any distortion, mutilation, or other modification of, or other

---

55. *Idem*, p. 397.

56. *Idem*, p. 395.

57. Foucault, *op. cit.*, p. 124.

58. Barthes, *op. cit.*, p. 143.

59. Gass, *op. cit.*, p. 11.

60. Lionel Bently, "Copyright and the Death of the Author in Literature and Law," *The Modern Law Review*, Vol. 57, No. 6 (Nov., 1994), p. 977.

derogatory action in relation to the said work, which would be prejudicial to his honour or reputation."[61] In order to prevent a blockage of cultural production and the circulation of information, at the end of the 1970s a certain type of use of existing cultural production—fair use—was legalised. This concept is relative and based on a number of factors being taken into account: the purpose and the character of the use, the nature of the copyrighted work, the amount and substantiality of the portion used, and most importantly, "the effect of the use upon the potential market for or value of the copyrighted work."[62]

To return to the author-function, Foucault problematizes the transition from a simple proper name to the concept of the author whose function is "to characterize the existence, circulation, and operation of certain discourses within a society" and argues for a historical analysis of discourse, alongside analysis connected to expressive value and its formal transformations, an analysis of "the modifications and variations, within any culture, of modes of circulation, valorisation, attribution, and appropriation" of discourse.[63]

All these interrogations of the author's authority, originating in literary theory and the philosophy of culture, draw attention to the reader, who, having become active thanks to the dethroning of the author and the professional critic, can produce interpretative aberrations or deliberate instrumentalisation/politicisation of a cultural discourse within the wider context of social discourse.

Marcel Broodthaers believes that although the artist conceives a work by relating to certain ideas and events, this work "begins to live its own life, to grow and to produce new cells. This is how a biological process, that not even the artist can control any more, appears in art. (...) Ideas begin to multiply, like living cells."[64] Of course, these cells can be benign or malignant, with the greatest risks arising in the sphere of consumerism, which, as Gass notes in his attempt to resurrect the author, "will fasten the reader to a rock and leave him to be eaten up by trademarks and localisms and proper names."[65] Thus, if the innocent eye was never an option, we have to wonder whether we can speak of a guilty gaze that profits from the death of the author in order to appropriate the floating discourse.

---

61. Article 6bis of the Berne Convention, revised in Paris in 1971, quoted in Ruth Redmont-Cooper, "Moral Rights" in Daniel McClean, Karsten Schubert (eds.), *op. cit*, p. 70.

62. Martha Buskirk, "Commodification as Censor: Copyrights and Fair Use," *October*, 60, Spring 1992, pp. 83–110.

63. Foucault, *op. cit.*, pp. 124, 137.

64. "Fragment d'un entretien avec Broodthaers, Entretien de Jürgen Harten et Katharina Schmidt" in Anna Hakkens (ed.), *Marcel Broodthaers par lui-même*, Gent, Ludion and Paris, Flammarion, 1998, p. 81.

65. Gass, *op. cit.*, p. 24.

Speaking of the open work, Umberto Eco argues that the beauty of the poetic/artistic message comes precisely from the fact that it is open-ended, and if we want it to be possible for brilliant decodings to arise within the field of elite culture, then we should also reconcile ourselves to its "corruption" in the decodings made by *Masscult* and *Midcult*: "Because of its complex structure, the poetic message retains the power to elicit a variety of decodings. The life of messages caught in the whirlwind of mass production and mass consumption, including the life of the poetic message whenever it is sold as a commodity, is much more varied and unpredictable than we might think in our moments of greatest discouragement. Even the most indiscriminate and naive superimposition of codes and decodings inevitably involves an exchange between message and addressee that cannot be reduced to a simple scheme—an exchange that will remain forever open to investigation, exploitation, and renewal."[66]

The modern figure of the artist arose at the same time as the printing press that put into circulation images of famous artworks, thereby creating a delimitation between artist and artisan. On the other hand, the publication of artists' biographies and portraits helped to construct the figure behind the work. In the Romantic period there was an increase in the fascination for the artist as a person, who was seen as exceptional, as a genius displaying superior spirituality and creative originality, detached from the pragmatism of ordinary everyday life. Discussing the writings of a major Romantic figure, Moshe Barasch notes: "what the spectator looks for, and indeed finds, in a painting are not the material or formal components of the painting itself; the true subject of the spectator's vision is the personality of the artist. The work of art is only a stepping stone to the artist, a medium through which we can meet him."[67]

To return to the name of the artist viewed as brand, Martha Buskirk discusses the relationship between the author-function and brand loyalty, making reference to Walter Benjamin's essay "The Work of Art in the Age of Mechanical Reproduction," in which he talks about the film star who "preserves not the unique aura of the person but the 'spell of the personality', the phony spell of a commodity."[68] In the contemporary context, the author is also subject to this spell, and as such is exploited by the market. The advertising industry developed in the nineteenth century in parallel with the fields of production and transportation. Buskirk notes that brand differentiation became necessary as large-scale manufacturing developed. Brandy loyalty became a central concept for this system, which was based only on

---

66. Eco, *op. cit.*, p. 200.

67. Moshe Barasch, *Theories of Art: From Winckelmann to Baudelaire*, London and New York, Routledge, 2000, p. 295.

68. Buskirk, *op. cit.*, p. 93.

public perception of products: "Trademarked names and images have assumed an increasingly prominent place in twentieth century society and their importance is directly related to their commercial value; the concept of the trademark and the reign of the image are inseparable, and their link is advertising."[69]

A brand can be a name, a sign or a symbol that produces given associations in the consumer's mind and which is used to identify and distinguish products on the market. Brands are considered intellectual property and, even if immaterial, they represent "a highly valuable form of commodity: they are precious because of the associations they carry—associations that can be broadly categorized with reference to another precious intangible, the corporate asset known as consumer goodwill."[70]

In the art world, which Buskirk views as a sub-culture with its own unwritten laws, an artist's name becomes a registered trademark: "the value of the individual work of art is dependent on the name of the artist connected with it; and though the importance of the artist's name is based on the quality associated with his or her previous work, once the artist's name becomes a label given to an œuvre it can acquire an increasingly abstract value unto itself."[71]

One interesting case discussed by Celia Lury in such terms is that of Damien Hirst, "a thriving brand whose name adds immense value to a product." Lury argues that Hirst's claim that he is a brand name can be seen as "a transformation of the author-function in which the relation between subject and object is no more, and no less, than a relation of assertion"[72] and draws attention to the fact that in the relationship between art and popular culture we also need to take into account reverse instances, the use of artworks in various forms of mass culture. In addition, she believes that such two-directional movements are not accidental, but are in fact constitutive of the art world, and she presents the example of the relationship between Hirst and Charles Saatchi, who explicitly embodies the relationship between art and advertising, demonstrating the extent to which the boundaries of art are permeable. Lury notes that Damien Hirst's image is connected also with that of Britain in the mind of the wider public: the country "is developing macro-brands—whole industries where the word 'British' raises the value of the product. British film, British fashion, British art and British architecture are more fashionable then ever."[73]

---

69. *Idem*, p. 95.

70. *Idem*, p. 84.

71. *Idem*, p. 106.

72. Celia Lury, "Portrait of the Artist as a Brand" in Daniel McClean, Karsten Schubert (eds.), *op. cit.*, p. 325.

73. *Idem*, p. 314.

Having discussed the phenomenon of transformation of the author into a brand and its association with the corporate discourse, we shall now observe how this phenomenon is reflected within the national discourse. Corporate branding strategies are now also applied in political communication, with a new generation of experts constructing country and location brands. In one of the texts that introduce this discipline, Wally Olins even re-reads universal history through the terminology of marketing. For example, in his view, Napoleon rebranded France and even Europe, with Jacques-Louis David playing the role of the advertising agency, while Pol Pot downsized Cambodia. He sees no difference between political and corporate communication: "Business people have to exploit and attempt to manipulate human emotions just like political leaders. Businesses have to create loyalties; loyalties of the workforce, loyalties of suppliers, loyalties of the communities in which they operate, loyalties of investors and loyalties of customers. In creating these loyalties they use very similar techniques to those of nation builders. They create myths, special languages, environments which reinforce loyalties, colours, symbols, and quasi historical myths."[74] Similarly, he sees Spain as the first example of successful contemporary rebranding: after the death of Franco, the government initiated a campaign to improve Spain's public image, which was implemented through a partnership between "opinion makers" in the fields of business and art and government representatives. In an article celebrating the twentieth anniversary of the country's new logo, Ignacio Vasallo, one of the governmental bureaucrats responsible for promoting tourism in the 1980s, recalls his collaboration with Joan Miró, the artist who was invited to design the logo that was to mark Spain's rise in Europe: "Joan Miró's final work is not to be found in a public or private collection, it is not an oil painting nor a watercolour, it is not even an original. But nevertheless it is undoubtedly his most universal work, recognised by ninety per cent of Europe's population."[75] It seems that Miró was honoured to place himself in the service of his country and refused payment for the logo conception, thereby becoming an example for strategies of nationalising a cultural product with the author's consent.

Moving ahead from country to location branding, here too the role of the artist is viewed as important, either because he is an essential gentrification factor, contributing involuntarily to the process of constructing a new identity of a location,[76] or because the very act of representation can contribute to such a branding or to

---

74. Wally Olins, "Branding the Nation: The Historical Context" in Nigel Morgan, Annette Pritchard, Roger Pride (eds.), *Destination Branding*, Oxford, Elsevier Butterworth-Heinemann, 2004, p. 24.

75. Ignacio Vasallo, "La última obra de Joan Miró," *El Pais*, 23.02.2003; <http://elpais.com/diario/2003/02/23/domingo/1045975961_850215.html>.

76. The authors studied the role of artists in the context of constructing the new identity of a Finnish village. The results confirmed that "artists are extremely important to the construction of the

the feeling of national belonging. To define a nation through images representing the natural landscape also means the exclusion (whether intentional or not) of those places that are not represented. In Europe and America, landscape painting was one of the many strategies for constructing the modern nation state, symbolically appropriating the earth, because it was essential that a nation state have a territory, real or imaginary.

In regard to the artists employed in location branding, Vincent Van Gogh deserves particular attention since he has been instrumentalised very aggressively in the touristic promotion of Amsterdam and the Netherlands. A press release of the Van Gogh Museum[77] reveals that its Trade, Marketing and Sales Department has stimulated the tourist market using new "marketing products and activities, such as combined tickets and the promotion of the Van Gogh Museum as a cultural 'must see' while on holiday in Amsterdam." Many of these activities were organised in partnership with transport and hotel companies, and the proof that the strategy worked is the fact that in 2012 eighty-five per cent of the one and a half million visitors of the museum were foreign tourists. In a study about the museum, Van Gogh is presented as being in every top ten: most popular painters, greatest artists of all time, most famous paintings, most expensive paintings, best viewed paintings on Google Art, etc. Given that "Van Gogh has a larger than life reputation around the globe, it would be a wonderful achievement for the Van Gogh Museum"—and by extension for Amsterdam and the Netherlands as tourist destinations—"to enjoy a similarly grand reputation."[78] Here, it should be noted that the museum shop supplies a variety of items that recycle images of the artist's works, products designed also as mementos of the Dutch experience. In a way, the subversive strategies employed by Broodthaers in the 1970s appear to be integrated, developed and refined by the industry of museum shops. As Lawrence Alloway noted in the 1960s, "as art is reproduced (in magazines, on album covers) it becomes itself pop culture, just as Van Gogh and Picasso, through endless reproduction have become mass produced items of popular culture." He believed that "Van Gogh would have welcomed it because he had the greatest respect for clichés, which he regarded as the autho-

<hr>

identity of a place; their roles unfold as stories, artefacts and atmosphere as well as entrepreneurs." Tuula Mittilä, Tanja Lepistö, "The Role of Artists in Place Branding: A Case Study in Place Branding and Public Diplomacy," *A Quarterly Review of Branding and Marketing for National, Regional and Civic Development*, Volume 9, Issue 3, August 2013.

77. Annual Report of the Van Gogh Museum / 2009; <http://www.vangoghmuseum.nl/download/vgm_jaarverslag_annualreport2009klein.pdf>.

78. Laurine van de Wiel (Van Gogh Museum), Saskia Brocx (TNS NIPO), "Emotion and Inspiration at the Van Gogh Museum. How Emotion-Based Visitor Research Can Create Engaging Brand Experiences" (presentation at *2013 ESOMAR Annual Congress*, Istanbul); <http://www.slideshare.net/TNSspain/emotion-and-inspiration-at-the-van-gogh-museum>.

rised expression of mankind, a kind of common property that especially binds us together."[79] As the Van Gogh/the Netherlands connection has already been established, in the recent period there have begun to appear on the market other products that make use of the artist's image/name in order to reaffirm Dutch identity. One example is Van Gogh Vodka, which was launched on the market in the 2000s. This is how Tim Vos, the company's master distiller, explains the choice of the name: "Van Gogh was the name of a famous Dutch artist, a creator of important and colourful paintings. We believe we are creators of Dutch vodkas with a broad palette of tastes and colours, it is a name that makes sense for us."[80] We can find another example even in Bucharest: the Dutch investors who opened the Amsterdam Café changed its name to Grand Café Van Gogh when they moved to a different location.

Setting out from such cases in which artists and/or their practices are instrumentalised in country branding strategies closely connected to the tourist industry, as part of a capitalist logic in which the symbolic capital from the cultural field is transformed into financial capital, we may further explore the subject and identify cases of instrumentalisation in ideological contexts more explicitly linked to the national discourse.

In the volume *Pop or Populus. Art Between High and Low*, Bettina Funcke discusses the case of Jackson Pollock and Abstract Expressionism, analysing the various interests vested in the public figure and the work of Jackson Pollock by different entities—from *Life* magazine and MOMA to the cultural strategies of the Cold War and Hollywood—and examines the artist's exposure in relation to the political sphere and consumer culture.[81] She argues that in the context of the 1940s, when in popular culture the artist was presented as a misunderstood genius, a rebel isolated in his studio, and the elite was deepening its contacts with the European avant-garde, the press constructed around Pollock an image that confirmed this stereotype of the bohemian artist. This image of Pollock was perpetuated also by Hans Namuth's photographs, which ultimately came to have a larger audience than Pollock's paintings and which contributed to creating his myth in popular culture, even influencing more recent representations, such as the Hollywood film in which Ed Harris plays the role of the artist. Setting out from Clement Greenberg's theory that only "a fully matured cultural tradition" can be recycled as kitsch in popular culture,[82] she notes: "only when an artist is marketable to a broader public, that is, already established within high culture, and there is a

---

79. Lawrence Alloway, "Popular Culture and Pop Art" in Mark Francis (ed.), *op. cit.*, p. 241.

80. <http://www.vangoghvodka.com/master-distiller/>.

81. Bettina Funke, *Pop or Populus. Art between High and Low*, Berlin and New York, Sternberg Press, 2009.

82. Clement Greenberg, "Avant-Garde and Kitsch" in Joseph Tanke, Colin McQuillan (eds.), *op. cit.*, p. 434.

potential within the art market, can he or she attract the interest of popular culture."[83]

Pollock's work was also used in the American political propaganda at the beginning of the Cold War, when Abstract Expressionism was exported to Europe as a symbol of creativity, vitality and artistic freedom, the opposite of Soviet socialist realism. As Eva Cockroft argues, MOMA played an important role in this instrumentalisation. A museum founded and supported by important families that controlled American industry and finance, MOMA was also funded by the CIA. It took on the task of exporting American cultural imperialism during the Cold War, at a time when government policies were still paralysed by McCarthyism and its abuses and ridiculous censorship. Cockroft concludes that "the functions of both CIA's undercover aid operations and MOMA's international programmes were similar: to provide well-funded and more persuasive arguments and exhibitions needed to sell the rest of the world on the benefits of life and art under capitalism."[84] Serge Guilbaut brings into discussion Clement Greenberg as a precursor of this strategy of promoting American Abstract Expressionism in Europe: "For the first time in the history of American art, a major critic was aggressive enough, confident enough, and devoted enough to American art to confront openly the supremacy of Parisian art and to try to replace it with the art of New York, the art of Pollock."[85] In an article from 1948,[86] Greenberg was presenting the supremacy of the movement, not in opposition to Socialist Realism, but as an attempt to topple Paris from its central position in the art world.

To return to the United States of the 1950s, in order to be politicised, art had to be apolitical. A movement such as Abstract Expressionism, which had no political agenda and placed the emphasis on individual expressivity, became a symbol of a democratic society that promoted freedom of expression. Artists were thereby instrumentalised in a national propaganda war. As Eva Cockroft notes: "the artist creates freely, but his work is promoted and used by others for their own purposes."[87] And when the state supports an artistic movement, we need to be aware that "it does so for political reasons because the promotion of art must be understood in a broader sense as a part of a nation's political program."[88]

---

83. Funke, *op. cit.*, p. 87.

84. Eva Cockroft, "Abstract Expressionism, Weapon of the Cold War," *Artforum*, June 1974, p. 40.

85. Serge Guilbaut, "Les Nouvelles aventures de l'avant-garde en Amérique: Greenberg, Pollock, ou du trotskysme au nouveau libéralisme du Vital Center" in Chantal Pontbriand (ed.), *Parachute. Essais choisis 1975–1984*, Bruxelles, Lettre volée, 2004, p. 86.

86. His conclusion was that the centre of Western art had shifted to America "at the same time as that of industrial production and political power." Clement Greenberg, "The Decline of Cubism," quoted in Guilbaut, *op.cit.*, p. 85.

87. Cockroft, *op. cit.*, p. 41.

88. Funke, *op. cit.*, p. 88.

If Abstract Expressionism was appropriated in US political propaganda precisely because it was apolitical, in the case of Richard Wagner, it was the Germanic mythology and Romantic *volkisch* ideology of his works, as well as his nationalist and anti-Semitic discourse, that led to them being adopted by Hitler and employed in Nazi propaganda. Wagner's works were thereby "Nazified," which has led to the problematic reception of his music in Israel. Hitler used Wagner's music during his meticulously staged public appearances. The music also featured in films such as *The Triumph of the Will* and propaganda reels such as *The Eternal Jew*, which even included a quotation from Wagner's essay *Judaism in Music* (1850).

Much has been written about Wagner's connection with German nationalism, starting with Nietzsche, who saw in the composer's music a "certain catholicism of feeling, and a predilection for some ancient indigenous (so-called national) ideals and eccentricities"[89] and ending with Slavoj Žižek, who in his "Why is Wagner worth Saving?" asks: "Why not leave behind this search for the 'proto-Fascist' elements in Wagner and, rather, in a violent gesture of appropriation, reinscribe Parsifal in the tradition of radical revolutionary parties?"[90] Alain Badiou even speaks of the "philosophical 'quarrel' with Wagner" as becoming a literary genre, which has attracted various leading cultural figures, including Nietzsche, Heidegger, Adorno and Lacoue-Labarthe, and observes that in relation to Nietzsche the situation is complicated by the "image of a Nietzsche that was constructed during the Nazi regime, in which he appears reconciled, or even complicit with Wagner, given that the latter was one of the major artistic figures revered by the regime."[91]

Although identification of the proto-fascist elements of Wagner's operas is still a subject of interest in the contemporary context, we should not forget that their association with Nazi ideology took place after his death, with his family and the intelligentsia of the time being responsible for the dissemination of his work within that specific political context. Initially, "Wagner as the advocate of the *Volk*" was an image propagated by his wife Cosima, leading to the musician being perceived as a prophet of Germanism in the Bayreuth circle. This tradition was continued by his daughter Winifred, who after 1933 transformed the Bayreuth Festival into a "National Socialist ritual."[92]

---

89. Friedrich Nietzsche, *The Case Of Wagner, Nietzsche Contra Wagner, and Selected Aphorisms*, Project Gutenberg EBook, 2008, p. 114; <http://www.gutenberg.org/files/25012/>.

90. Slavoj Žižek, "The Politics of Redemption. Why is Wagner Worth Saving?," *Journal of Philosophy and Scripture*, Fall 2004; <http://www.lacan.com/zizred.htm>.

91. Alain Badiou, "De la dialectique négative dans sa connexion à un certain bilan de Wagner" (lecture given at L'École Normale Supérieure, Paris, January 2005); <http://www.lacan.com/badwagnertwo.htm>.

92. George L. Mosse, *The Crisis of German Ideology. Intellectual Origins of the Third Reich*, New York, Schocken Books, 1981, pp. 92–93.

In keeping with the contemporary tendency that subordinates ideology to capital, more recent publications present Wagner as a genius of branding: "Richard Wagner was his own press agent, his own manager, his own public-relations consultant. He pioneered his image as a leading cultural figure, creative genius, true German, inventor of a brand new form of aesthetic product. The Wagner industry today continues to rely on the astounding wealth of themes conceived, images shaped, and issues developed by Wagner in order to assert and retain the exclusivity of his brand."[93] In the same spirit, Wally Olins argues that Wagner contributed to the development of the German country brand: "The newly invented country celebrated a range of newly reinvented myths, folklore and traditions. Wagner's celebration of Teutonic myths and legends in his operas, supported by a panoply of other artists and writers, reinforced Germany's industrial, economic and military power with a massive cultural presence and helped to make Germany the most admired and by some the most feared new brand of the 19th century.[94]

It is within this paradigm of the transgression of the boundary between the fields of art and the social that I shall discuss the case of Constantin Brancusi in the next chapters, tracing the processes through which he was transformed into a national brand and the strategies whereby his image was appropriated in the Romanian context in various ideological and commercial policies.

---

93. Nicholas Vazsonyi, *Richard Wagner. Self-Promotion and the Making of a Brand*, Cambridge, Cambridge University Press, 2010, p. 7.

94. Olins, *op. cit.*, p. 21.

PART 2

Brancusi and Romania

In this chapter, my intention is not to rehash the various theories of nationalism, but to discuss the ways in which the nation and the nation state are communicated and reproduced beyond moments of crisis in which nationalism is explicitly invoked. This reproduction occurs not only within state institutions such as the police, the army, or the education system, but also in popular culture and intellectual production. To be more precise, in the present research I am interested in the ways in which the figure of Constantin Brancusi and his artistic work have been caught up in this mechanism. Cultural production can be contextualised in a national discourse precisely because of its historicity, which according to Boris Buden is twofold: "the historicity of the means and ends of art, as well as the historicity of the world which can use or misuse art for its own means and ends."[1]

In contemporary studies, nationalism appears as a political phenomenon, which many theorists have tried to define in recent decades without having reached any consensus as to its definition or its origins, past and future. The only point in which they agree is the age of nationalism, namely that it has existed for at least two centuries, which, according to Benedict Anderson, would under normal circumstances have been long enough for the phenomenon to be understood.[2] Other theorists such as Katherine Verdery suggest that rather than looking for definitions, it would be more productive to regard the nation as being an aspect connected to the political and symbolic-ideological register, as well as to social and emotional interaction, which has come to legitimise various social actions and movements with often divergent agenda. In her view, the concept of nation functions as a symbol because, on the one hand, it has an ambiguous meaning, which allows the mobilisation of a heterogeneous public that merely imagines that it is employing the same definition of the concept, and because, on the other hand, it evokes sentiments that were shaped within the same process of national construction. Thus, from this viewpoint, nationalism may be understood as "the political utilization of the symbol nation through discourse and political activity, as well as the sentiment that draws people into responding to this symbol's use."[3]

Beyond these multiple meanings and interpretations, most voices present the nation/the nation state and nationalism as cultural artefacts, constructs with either negative (fabrication/manipulation in Ernest Gellner) or positive connotations (imagining/creation in Benedict Anderson[4]), as invented traditions, as in the case

---

1. Boris Buden, "Why Not: Art and Contemporary Nationalism?" in Minna Henriksson, Sezgin Boynik (eds.), *Contemporary Art and Nationalism*, Pristina, Institute for Contemporary Art "EXIT", Centre for Humanistic Studies "Gani Bobi", 2007, p. 16.

2. Benedict Anderson in the introduction to Gopal Balakrishnan (ed.), *Mapping the Nation*, London, Verso, 2000, p. 1.

3. Katherine Verdery, "Whiter 'Nation' and 'Nationalism'?" in Gopal Balakrishnan (ed.), *op. cit.*, pp. 226–227.

4. In Anderson's opinion, Ernest Gellner "is so anxious to show that nationalism masquerades under

of Eric Hobsbawm,[5] or even as narratives. In the introduction to *Nation and Narration*, Homi K. Bhabha presents the nation as "an agency of ambivalent narration that holds culture at its most productive position," as a force for—in the words of Edward Said—"subordination, fracturing, diffusing, reproducing, as much as producing, creating, forcing, guiding."[6]

Nationalism's dual, Jekyll-and-Hyde condition[7] has been remarked upon by many theorists. For example, the context in which Franz Fanon encouraged the production of "nationalist" art and culture was one of colonial oppression and domination, with nationalism being regarded as justified in such cases and consequently "good", especially when it is also contextualised within revolutionary internationalism. In order for nationalism not to become "bad", as Edward Said reminds us, it is important that it develops within a social consciousness that is, in his eyes, very different from the national consciousness.[8] In a text about the European nation state, Jürgen Habermas explains why national feelings can easily be manipulated: it is precisely because national identities have been fabricated through the intellectual efforts of writers and historians, and the national consciousness has been shaped/disseminated through the mass media. Thus, in modern democracies, nationalism has come to be "a rather cheap resource"[9] which political leaders exploit through every media channel.

In attempting to explain the connection between Brancusi and nationalism, I have not set out to operate within the good/bad[10] paradigm accepted by many theorists, rather I have made use of the concept of *banal nationalism* introduced by

---

false pretences that he assimilates invention to fabrication and falsity, rather than to imagining and creation". Benedict Anderson, *Imagined Communities: Reflections on the Origin and Spread of Nationalism*, London, Verso, p. 6.

5. Hobsbawn believes that the national phenomenon should be researched in relation to that of the invention of tradition, precisely because "so much of what subjectively makes up the modern 'nation' consists of such constructs and is associated with appropriate and, in general, fairly recent symbols or suitably tailored discourse (such as 'national history')". Eric Hobsbawm, "Inventing Traditions" in Eric Hobsbawm, Terence Ranger (eds.), *The Invention of Tradition*, Cambridge, Cambridge University Press, 2000, p. 14.

6. Homi K. Bhabha in the introduction to Homi K. Bhabha (ed.), *Nation and Narration*, London and New York, 1990, p. 3.

7. Michael Billig, *Banal Nationalism*, London, Sage Publications, 1995, p. 7.

8. "Art & National Identity: A Critics' Symposium," *Art in America*, September 1991, p. 80.

9. Jürgen Habermas, "The European Nation-State – Its Achievements and Its Limits. On the Past and Future of Sovereignty and Citizenship" in Gopal Balakrishnan (ed.), *op. cit.*, p. 288.

10. Although even the author of the concept of *banal nationalism* believes it is "wrong to assume that it is 'benign' because it seems to possess a reassuring normality, or because it appears to lack the violent passions of the extreme right" and reminds us of what Hannah Arendt wrote in the 1960s: banality is not synonymous with harmlessness. Billig, *op. cit.*, pp. 6–7.

Michael Billig in order to discuss the ways in which nation states daily reaffirm themselves through "a whole complex of beliefs, assumptions, habits, representations and practices" that are banally reproduced on the familiar ground of everyday life.[11] He believes that these ideological rituals whereby nations daily reproduce themselves often go unobserved, as they are not associated with nationalism, the same as loyalty to the nation state, which more often than not passes for patriotism. In the nation states, national identity is daily maintained, through familiar and shared rituals, in a manner so subtle that this type of banal nationalism passes unobserved, transforming every backdrop into a national backdrop. Thus, national identity comes to be perceived as natural and, in the increasingly homogenous cultural context of globalisation, it seems threatened by the multiple trans-national identities generated by the consumer rituals of the new communities shaped by lifestyle criteria.

Thus, on this free market of identities, globalisation generates nationalist reactions among those who feel what Anthony Giddens calls "ontological insecurity," with national symbols being reinvested with even greater passion and feeling. To return to Constantin Brancusi, he is one of the national symbols in which Romanians have invested a great deal of emotional energy over the decades, and the artist has now come to be contextualised in explicitly nationalist situations that to a large extent have to do with the phenomenon of self-colonisation and protochronism. Self-colonisation is a concept introduced by Alexander Kiossev in order to discuss cultures that import civilisational values and models, giving up their own authenticity in favour of foreign models.[12] Some cultures are not important enough to be considered central, but not marginal or backward enough to feel that they are not part of Europe, and this situation leads to a certain type of national identity modelled entirely on the West. Such is the case of Romania, which in the nineteenth century was constantly caught in the middle of conflicts between Turkey and Russia and chose to adopt the Western cultural and political model, even importing a foreign prince in order to gain greater stability and prestige. Romania thus became, "to a partial extent in reality, and even more in the realm of the imaginary, an extension of Western Europe."[13]

Kiossev observes that such cultures generate two symmetrical and conflicting doctrines: the doctrine of Westernisation or Europeanisation, which strives to catch up and to identify with Western civilisation, and that of Nativism, which seeks, often

---

11. Billig, *op. cit.*, p. 6.

12. Alexander Kiossev, "Notes on Self-Colonizing Cultures" in Bojana Pejić, David Elliott (eds.), *After the Wall: Art and Culture in Post-Communist Europe*, Stockholm, Moderna Museet, 1999, pp. 114–118.

13. Lucian Boia, *Romania: Borderland of Europe*, London, Reaktion Books, 2001, p. 12.

invents, and idealises the "authentic" national substance as it was prior to corruption by imported Western values, and thereby gives birth to vehement nationalist ideologies.

Historians confirm that in the development of the Romanian national character too, the West has always been a major reference point relative to which the national intellectual tradition has positioned itself, whether in agreement or conflict. This constant reference to the West can be traced since the Romantic period, passing through the anti-Romantic, positivist/organicist phase of Junimism, the cultural neo-nationalism of the *fin de siècle*, the interwar attempts to create an ethnic ontology, and the national-communist ideology of the 1980s.[14] After the events of 1989, the reorientation towards the West gathered speed, and the voluntary import of cultural values coincided with the implementation of supranational political structures. The theorists of postsocialism discuss democratisation and privatisation as processes specific to Western cultures, imposed on the rest of Europe as a symbol of the end of the Cold War. They wonder whether the emphasis placed on the implementation of these economic and social measures was aimed at transforming these cultures into an outdated image of Western cultures, the same as in the case of modernisation.[15] At the same time, they take into account the geopolitical and social effects of the Cold War in regard to the development of the market and various institutions, observing a hybridisation of the two systems.

To return to the two symmetrical doctrines Kiossev identifies in self-colonising cultures, both succeed in instrumentalising Brancusi in ideological intellectual productions and political discourses. Viewed from this perspective, the "canonisation" of Brancusi in Romanian culture is by no means surprising: as early as the interwar period his work was always situated between the native tradition and universality, albeit a universality[16] also couched in a nationalist equation. This is what Cioran was talking about when he said: "a people becomes a (great) nation only when (...) it imposes its own particular values as universally valid."[17] In this type of discourse, the equation works as follows: if Brancusi has crystallised the spirituality of the Romanian people and if Brancusi is a universally acknowledged genius, then the spirituality of the Romanian people has a universal value.

---

14. Balázs Trencsényi, "Conceptualizarea caracterului național în tradiția intelectuală românească" [The Conceptualisation of National Character in the Romanian Intellectual Tradition] in Victor Neumann, Armin Heinen (eds.), *Istoria României prin concepte* [The History of Romania in Concepts], Iași, Polirom, 2010, pp. 341–342.

15. Sharad Chari, Katherine Verdery, "Thinking between the Posts: Postcolonialism, Postsocialism, and Ethnography after the Cold War," *Comparative Studies in Society and History*, 51(1), 2009, p. 30.

16. Universality should here be read from Kiossev's perspective as belonging to Western culture.

17. Emil Cioran, *Schimbarea la față a României* [The Transfiguration of Romania], Bucharest, Humanitas, 2006, p. 48.

In 1904, Brancusi chose to move to Paris, the absolute centre of artistic emancipation at the time, and the sacrifices he made in order to arrive at his destination have since been transformed into legend. Once he arrived, he integrated into the circles of the Parisian avant-garde. From 1910 he exhibited in the Salons des Indépendents, and from 1913 he gained worldwide fame through connections with the US art world. In Romania there was real,[18] albeit sporadic, interest in the sculptor prior to the confirmation of his major role in Western culture.[19] His name is mentioned in a number of press articles, and in 1910 he was even caught up in a generational conflict in Bucharest's official art scene: in the exhibition of *Tinerimea artistică* [Artistic Youth], *The Wisdom of the Earth* was part of a group of works exhibited separately that had a negative reception and the artists in question were excluded from the show by the exhibition committee. Theodor Enescu identifies this moment as being essential to the paradigm shift and the acceptance of Euro-centric modernism in Romania. He believes that in the context of a favourable climate, in which "the latest trends that had come to the fore in European art were embraced," a climate that already existed within the *Tinerimea artistică* group, influenced by young artists who, returning to Romania, had facilitated the import of values specific to European art, the "decisive shock" was brought about by Brancusi, "who provoked violent reactions and precipitated the process of introducing expressive modern values into Romanian art."[20] Along the same lines, Ruxandra Demetrescu points out that it was not until "after modernity had taken root that it was possible for a debate to arise regarding the national specificity versus synchronism with the various Western art movements," which led to a "strategy of legitimation within the avant-garde itself, such as the recuperation of Brancusi as a genuine native model."[21]

---

18. For details see Barbu Brezianu's extraordinarily detailed study: "Brâncuşi în cultura şi critica românească. 1898–1914" [Brancusi in Romanian Culture and Criticism. 1898–1914] in *Pagini de artă modernă românească* [Pages of Romanian Modern Art], Bucharest, Editura Academiei Republicii Socialiste România, 1974, pp. 59–106.

19. At this point we also need to take into account the fact of Romanian culture being "out of phase": "the temporal distance between the first contacts with innovative art movements from the West and their effective assimilation being from ten to twenty years." Ruxandra Demetrescu, "Modernitate, tradiţie, avangardă. Repere în literatura artistică românească 1908–1946" [Modernity, Tradition, Avant-Garde. Landmarks in the Romanian Artistic Literature 1908–1946] in *(Dis)continuităţi. Fragmente de modernitate românească în prima jumătate a secolului al 20-lea* [(Dis)continuities. Fragments of Romanian Modernity in the First Half of the 20th Century], Bucharest, Simetria, 2010, p. 189.

20. Theodor Enescu, "Momentul 1910 în istoria artei moderne româneşti" [The 1910 Moment in the History of Romanian Modern Art] in *Studii şi cercetări de istoria artei* [Studies and Searches in Art History], Seria Artă plastică, Tomul 38, Bucharest, Editura Academiei Române, 1991, pp. 60–62.

21. Demetrescu, *op. cit.*, pp. 150–151.

If in 1914 there was a need for Tudor Arghezi[22] to publish in *Seara* a series of articles supporting Brancusi, "an artist originally from Romania, who has made a name for himself in France and has been rejected at home," and if in issue no. 52 of *Contimporanul* Brancusi is presented as "almost unknown in his own country, already famous throughout the world," towards the end of the interwar period Brancusi began to be included in the national artistic Pantheon, enjoying special attention in the Romanian avant-garde journals. Paul Cernat identifies a "visible shift in attitude, probably stimulated by the artist's world renown and his unadulterated native ethnic origins,"[23] referring to speculations according to which Brancusi was recuperated over time in a manner different to other expatriate avant-gardists, who were of Jewish origins.[24]

Like Barbu Brezianu,[25] Cristian-Robert Velescu is of the opinion that Brancusi already enjoyed fame and respect in Romania even before the First World War and suspects the representatives of the Romanian avant-garde of "petty calculation," since "by exhibiting alongside Brancusi the avant-gardists hoped that his fame would rub off on them, even if only infinitesimally, that it would rub off on them as artists and on their art." He speaks of "the avant-gardists' unshakable belief that they 'discovered' the sculptor before any other Romanians," a discovery which to them had "the value of a 'patent,' of a 'registered trademark,'" transforming his work into "a flag which, ostentatiously, they waved only to their own advantage,"[26] while Ruxandra Demetrescu notices the attempt to demonstrate that the avant-garde works in *Contimporanul's* International Exhibition of 1924 "were merely innovative ramifications

---

22. Arghezi presents Brancusi as an "authentic peasant who has nothing of the national parvenu about him," towards whom "the state and private individuals have shown themselves to be indifferent," and expresses his regret that at the end of the *Tinerimea artistică* exhibition none of his works were purchased: "That which could not be appreciated in Romania will find a place in a foreign collection alongside the classics." Tudor Arghezi, "Tabula rasa – artă și artă" [Tabula Rasa – Art and Art], *Seara*, 23 iunie 1914.

23. Paul Cernat, *Avangarda românească și complexul periferiei* [The Romanian Avant-Garde and the Complex of the Periphery], Bucharest, Cartea Românească, 2007, p. 311.

24. It is also speculated that unlike Dada production, the works of Brancusi came to sell for large sums of money, and therefore the sculptor was perceived as being more important than the other expatriate avant-garde artists.

25. Brezianu surveys Brancusi's admirers, beginning with the upper-class clientele of the tavern in Craiova where the artist worked as a youth, the teachers of the Trade School and of the National School of Fine Arts (where he received no less than fifteen rewards), and so on. Brezianu, *op. cit.*, pp. 59–106.

26. Cristian-Robert Velescu, "Corespondența Brâncuși – document personal ori sursă pentru istoriografia de artă?" [The Brancusi Correspondence – A Personal Document or a Source for Art History?] in *Brâncuși inedit: Însemnări și corespondență românească* [The Undiscovered Brancusi: Notes and Romanian Correspondence], Bucharest, Humanitas, 2004, pp. 119–127.

of Brancusi's art, with the great Romanian sculptor being taken advantage of even then and used as an alibi for 'authentically Romanian' artistic renewal."[27]

In addition to the Romanian avant-garde's need for legitimacy in the native cultural space, we should also note its need for legitimisation abroad. In his study on the Romanian avant-garde, Paul Cernat identifies "a diffuse local inferiority complex compounded by frustration at lack of foreign recognition,"[28] which was sublimated in the case of Brancusi, the purely Romanian artistic genius legitimised by the West. Also in the interwar period, discussing the tragedy of small cultures, Emil Cioran argued: "for Romania, history means Western culture and cannot mean anything else (…) the becoming of the Western world should be our sole preoccupation." He also spoke of the same inferiority complex which "characterises the minor forms of life, whose becoming cannot be conceived without examples, without prototypes."[29]

According to Paul Cernat, the entire interwar debate about national identity, tradition and specificity rests under the sign of the periphery complex,[30] with "foreign legitimisation playing a determining role in the process of the domestic recovery/re-canonisation of the historic avant-garde."[31]

Against the background of debates about the national specificity, whose protagonist became Lucian Blaga and his radical nativist-philosophical project, there began to be a re-valorisation of traditional culture and the spirituality of the Romanian archaic substratum, even going as far as discussing "folk metaphysics."[32] Thus, Brancusi's art also began to be appreciated along the lines of Romanian folk tradition, with origins in universal archaic mythologies. Mircea Eliade lends universal meanings to such national traditions and speaks of "the continuity of the Romanian spirit—in institutions, in spiritual life, in the creations of the mind": "From folklore to Eminescu and Lucian Blaga; from folk art (with roots in prehistory) to Brancusi and George Enescu; from apocrypha and folk legends to Creangă and Liviu Rebreanu—the 'Romanian' succession is uninterrupted."[33]

---

27. Demetrescu, *op. cit.*, p. 201.

28. Cernat, *op. cit.*, p. 214.

29. Cioran, *op. cit.*, pp.169, 106, 10.

30. He defines this complex as the sum of the cultural complexes identified by Mircea Martin in relation to Romanian literature, complexes of European integration and, at the same time, of the affirmation of difference: "the complex of humble origins, of peripheral existence, of belatedness, of historical discontinuity and the absence of a classical tradition, of rurality, of the continual beginning, of being doomed to imitate foreign models, of the absence of any frontrunners, of the lack of an audience (domestic or foreign), of provincial isolation, of lack of durability and monumentality." Cernat, *op. cit.*, p. 400.

31. *Idem*, p. 404.

32. Trencsényi, *op. cit.*, p. 361.

33. Mircea Eliade, *Profetism românesc 2 – România în eternitate* [Romanian Prophetism 2 – Romania in Eternity], Bucharest, Roza Vînturilor, 1990, p. 98.

It is obvious from the press of the time that Romanian intellectuals had already sanctified the sculptor in the interwar discourse, and the official/public strategies of the period also reflect a positive attitude towards the artist. Even in the period prior to his departure to Paris, Brancusi had received public commissions (the bust of General Dr. Davila for the Military Hospital in Bucharest), and others of his works were purchased by public institutions, such as the plaster bust of Nicolae Dărăscu and the *Écorché*, both purchased by the Ministry of Public Education and Religions, which reproduced the second and distributed it to various educational institutions. Brancusi received a bursary to study in Paris from the Ministry of Education, via the Schools Department, and a "letter of introduction" from Romania's Plenipotentiary Minister in Paris. From 1910 he was a member of *Tinerimea artistică*, a society that was under the honorary patronage of Queen Maria. In 1912, he won the first prize at the Official Salon in Bucharest, presided over by the Ministry of Education. In 1923, he was decorated with the Star of Romania. In 1931, Nicolae Iorga, the president of the Council of Ministers and Secretary of State in the Department of Religions, proposed him for the Order of Cultural Merit for Art.

In the opinion of Cristian-Robert Velescu, the fact that Brancusi enjoyed genuine appreciation in Romania is also proven by the repeated and insistent invitations for him to create public monuments in Romania, even if the greater part of these commissions never materialised.[34] Velescu finds the explanation for this in the cultural level of Romanian society, which valued realistic representation and was not really prepared for the sculptor's radical proposals, rather than in opacity on the part of decision-making bodies, as Barbu Brezianu suggests. For example, in 1913 Brancusi received a commission from the future Minister of Public Education, Vasile G. Morţun, for a monument to Spiru Haret, which would have been erected in Piaţa Universităţii in Bucharest, but which in the end was never realised, because the unexpected solution proposed by Brancusi, a fountain, was rejected by the commissioner.

The correspondence in the Brancusi Archive of the Georges Pompidou Centre reveals that besides the Târgu Jiu Monumental Ensemble commissioned in 1935 by Arethie Tătărescu, the wife of the then Prime Minister of Romania and the Chairwoman of the National League of Gorj Women, there were also other commissions for public monuments in Peştişani (1920), Caracal (1926–1928), Sibiu (1920) and Ploieşti (1931). Likewise, there are documents regarding a proposal for an editorial project made by the "King Carol II" Foundation for Literature and Art (1938) and a project to improve the crypt of the Romanian Orthodox Church in Paris (1942).

Commissioned in 1935, the only public monument that Brancusi realised in Romania was not officially inaugurated in Târgu Jiu until October 1938, during the

---

34. Cristian-Robert Velescu, "Proiecte şi comenzi publice în România" [Public Projects and Commissions in Romania] in *Brâncuşi inedit: Însemnări şi corespondenţă românească*, p. 385.

dictatorship of King Carol II. The artist did not come to the very low-key ceremony, which was attended by only a few local politicians, and there were very few echoes of the event in the political and cultural press. Ioana Vlasiu explains that King Carol II was cultivating a specific artistic and ideological style, close to the style of sculptor Ivan Meštrović, who received official commissions for the regime's public monuments (Brătianu, Carol I, Ferdinand).[35] In the same period, although Brancusi had been promised an entire room, his contribution to the Romanian Pavilion at the Universal Exhibition of 1937 ended up being very limited. The shadow that fell over Brancusi's work in Romania during the regime of Carol II continued during the Second World War, when the artist became a recluse in his Paris studio, and deepened after the war, during the People's Republic of Romania. In the 1990s, Barbu Brezianu put forward a theory according to which the donation of Brancusi's studio had been rejected by Romanian officials and published in *Revista 22*[36] a procès-verbal of the Academy of the People's Republic of Romania from 1951, which criticised Brancusi, although it did not mention any donation. The theory gained credence against the backdrop of virulent anti-communism of that period,[37] and a copy of the procès-verbal was exhibited at the Memorial of the Victims of Communism and of the Resistance, in the "Art behind Bars" room of the Sighet Museum.[38] As Katherine Verdery also explains, in Eastern Europe the rewriting of history arose from "powerful pressures to create political identities based expressly on rejecting the immediate past," pressures that come "not just from popular revulsion with communism, but also from desires to persuade the Western audiences to contribute the aid and investment essential to reconstruction." She argues that such revisionist histories were ultimately "central to dramatising the end of Communist Party rule."[39]

---

35. Ioana Vlasiu, "Public Art and Political Context in Romania during the Authoritarian Reign of Carol II (1938–1940)" in Irina Cărăbaş, Olivia Niţiş (eds.), *After Brancusi*, Bucharest, Unarte, 2014, pp. 39–46.

36. "Sfârşit de secol cu Brâncuşi. Interviu de Rodica Palade" [The End of the Century with Brancusi. An Interview by Rodica Palade] (according to the bibliography posted on the site of the Brezianu Archive of the Romanian Academy's "George Oprescu" Institute of Art History, in this interview Barbu Brezianu launched the unconfirmed hypothesis of the rejection on the part of the Academy of the People's Republic of Romania of a putative Brancusi donation), *Revista 22*, no. 43, 22 Oct. 1995, pp. 10–11.

37. Another legend speaks of an attempt to demolish the *Endless Column* in Târgu Jiu using tractors. It seems that it was a local initiative, in 1951, which was countermanded by the Oltenia region's organs of the Party and State, according to the account of Ştefan Georgescu-Gorjan in *Amintiri despre Brâncuşi* [Memories about Brancusi], Craiova, Scrisul Românesc, 1988, pp. 122–123.

38. Recently reproduced in *Memoria, revista gîndirii arestate*, No. 78–79 (1–2/2012), pp. 16–17.

39. Katherine Verdery, *The Political Lives of Dead Bodies: Reburial and Postsocialist Change*, New York, Columbia University Press, 1999, p. 52.

At present there are voices that note the lack of any documents to support Brezianu's theory and which present the attitude towards Brancusi of the state apparatus at that time as rather one of indifference, as the whole of the official attention was then focussed on the aesthetics of socialist realism. Pavel Țugui[40] identifies the period 1948–55 as a period of negative judgements regarding the artist, although such judgements were in a minority, against the backdrop of a "guilty silence." It was a period marked by reticence on the part of the state institutions and by "the absence of any homage to the artist in the form of personal exhibitions or recognition of the national and universal value of his work or election to the Romanian Academy or the award of important academic titles."[41] The first steps towards official recognition of Brancusi were the inclusion of two of his sculptures in the National Gallery of Bucharest's Museum of Art in 1950, followed by a decision of the Union of Artists to make Brancusi a member with full rights. In the period that followed discussion began on the possibility of organising an exhibition in Bucharest to mark the artist's eightieth birthday. The exhibition opened in 1956 at the Art Museum of the People's Republic of Romania. It was designed as a "manifestation strictly cultural and artistic in nature, conceived by its initiators outside any political or party ideology, with the explicit aim of 'reconsidering' the work of a Romanian artist of genius, seen in its entirety to be a substantial contribution to the development of the art and culture of the Romanian Nation."[42] In the same period, the Romanian state included in the national heritage the sculptures now housed in the collections of art museums in Bucharest and Craiova. Pavel Țugui speaks of the "cultural-artistic battle" waged between 1954 and 1965, as a result of which there was a shift in the authorities' attitude towards Brancusi's art, and of the "artistic and civic manifestations[43] that augmented the public atmosphere of admiration and esteem for Romania's artist of genius."[44] We find the same type of discourse in Petre Gigea,[45] who describes in detail

---

40. Pavel Țugui was the head of the Literature and Art Sector of the Propaganda and Agitation Section of the Central Committee of the Romanian Workers Party from 1951, holding various official positions within the state apparatus and becoming in 1954 the locum tenens of the Minister of Culture, and in 1955 the head of the Science and Culture Section of the Central Committee.

41. Pavel Țugui, *Dosarul Brâncuși* [The Brancusi Dossier], Cluj, Dacia, 2001, pp. 20, 96.

42. *Idem*, p. 126.

43. They include the public sculpture *Homage to Brancusi* realised by Constantin Lucaci in 1957 and now located in Craiova's Romanescu Park.

44. Țugui, *op. cit.*, pp. 142, 158.

45. Petre Gigea began his career in the Financial Section of Oltenia Region, rising through the hierarchy until he became head of the section (Director General of Public Finances). He then held the positions of Mayor of Craiova, First Vice-President of the People's Council of Dolj County, Minister of Finances, Adviser to the President of Romania, President of the Romanian Financial-Banking Council, Governor of Romania at the International Monetary Fund, Governor of Romania at

the efforts of the local administration in Craiova to pay homage to Brancusi, efforts stretching from 1965 to 1977, the period in which Gigea was mayor of Craiova and, from 1968, First Vice-President of the People's Council of Dolj County. These démarches were initiated by V. G. Paleolog, in order to purchase the woodwork of Brancusi's Paris studio and bring it to Romania after it was dismantled in 1972, with a view to erecting a *Brancusi Memorial* and opening a Brancusi Memorial House. In 1976, the planned Memorial was rejected by the State's Central Commission for National Cultural Heritage, one of the reasons being that the Memorial might "overshadow the memory of the sculptor,"[46] for which reason the "sacred vestiges," as Paleolog called them, were deposited in the courtyard of what is now the "Constantin Brancusi" Technical College of Art and Trade, where they remain today.

Official recognition of Brancusi in Romania—which commenced in the art world with the exhibitions of 1956[47] and continued at the "highest level" (in 1966 when Ceaușescu visited Oltenia, his itinerary included the Târgu Jiu Monumental Ensemble, where he gave a speech in front of the *Endless Column*)[48]—became increasingly present in the public consciousness, perpetuating itself after 1989 and coming down to the present in extremely various and creative forms. As Irina Cărăbaș notes in her study, this official homage occurred at the juncture between art, art history and political propaganda, and she argues that its research will bring "new ways of understanding the cultural policy of the regime and the relationship between art and power which involved not only contemporary production and artists but also revisions of local art history."[49]

Although the homages paid to the sculptor served different agendas,[50] the result was the same, namely the birth of the cult of Brancusi as a national artist. His rehabilitation was based on the connection between his work and Romanian folklore, a connection that was presented to the public via every means possible, even in the obituaries published when the artist died,[51] and repeated on every possible occasion through every media channel. For example, various international academic con-

---

the World Bank, Romanian Ambassador to U.N.E.S.C.O., and Extraordinary and Plenipotentiary Romanian Ambassador to Paris, until 1989, when he was recalled to Romania.

46. Notice published in Petre Gigea-Gorun, *V. G. Paleolog și Brâncuși – Un dialog etern* [V. G. Paleolog and Brancusi – An Eternal Conversation], Craiova, Scrisul Românesc, 2003, pp. 235–236.

47. Besides the one in Bucharest, another exhibition in homage to Brancusi was held in the Hall of Mirrors of the Craiova Museum of Art.

48. *Working Visit to the Oltenia Region – Second Day*, report broadcast on Romanian Television on 12 June 1966; <http://euscreen.eu/play.jsp?id=EUS_A624BC585BCF4386A52A9C999F45AFD6>.

49. Irina Cărăbaș, "Commemoration without shores. Celebrating Brancusi in post-Stalinist Romania" in Irina Cărăbaș, Olivia Nițiș (eds.), *op. cit.*, p. 65.

50. One of them being to demonstrate an opening up of the regime to the West.

51. Reproduced in Pavel Țugui, *op. cit.*, pp. 206–232.

ferences, colloquia and symposia were held,[52] which brought together Brancusiologists of every stripe. Artistic events were organised, providing an opportunity for contemporary artists to reflect on Brancusi's aesthetics.[53] There was intensive publication of writings about the sculptor (academic texts, but also articles in the popular press), thereby encouraging heterogeneous overproduction of exegesis.[54] An ornamental style inspired by Brancusi was even developed in architecture. In the 1970s, the theme of national specificity became important also in architecture, finding its fulfilment above all in ornaments applied to the prefabricated concrete elements that were the basis for standardised architectural projects. The module of the *Endless Column* and the bisected circle on the *Gate of the Kiss* were recycled in these ornaments precisely in order to "refer to traditional architecture, while at the same time providing an example of essentialisation (and consequently modernism), also validated by recognition [of Brancusi] at the international level."[55] Such recycling of Brancusi's motifs also occurred in various official images of state communication: the five-lei coin, a series of postage stamps, the logo of the Scientific and Encyclopaedic Publishing House, etc.

In 1970, the Museum of Art in Bucharest organised a Brancusi retrospective, at the opening of which Ion Frunzetti declared: "Brancusi the Romanian is a universal value. Brancusi the universal is Romanian. He would not have existed without his great forerunner which is the Romanian village,"[56] and in 1971 the Constantin Brancusi Memorial House was inaugurated in the village of Hobița, in a house regarded as representative of the architecture specific to the region in the nineteenth century, which was bought from another villager and relocated to the plot of land that had belonged to the sculptor's family. As Irina Cărăbaș notes, the

---

52. The "Brancusi" Colloquium organised by the Union of Artists Commission for Literature and Art in collaboration with AICA to mark the tenth anniversary of the artist's death (1967); the "Brancusi" Colloquium organised by the Union of Artists' Criticism Section in collaboration with the Department of National Cultural Heritage (1975); the "Brancusi and the Art of the Twentieth Century" Colloquium, part of the Brancusi Centenary (1975–76).

53. The artistic contributions include the public monuments dedicated to Brancusi by Ion Irimescu, the first produced for the 1967 colloquium, now situated in Bucharest's Herăstrău Park, the second for the 1976 centenary, now situated in front of the Trade Unions Culture Club in Târgu Jiu.

54. Two indicative publications that marked the Brancusi Centenary: *Carte de inimă pentru Brâncuși* [Book of the Heart for Brancusi], edited by Nina Stănculescu at the Albatros publishing house, and *Omagiu lui Brâncuși* [Homage to Brancusi], published by *Tribuna* magazine.

55. Marius Marcu-Lapadat, "Proiectul tip și panoul prefabricat în deceniul șapte. Rapeluri brâncușoide și degradarea execuței" [The Standardised Project and the Prefab Panel in the 1970s. Brancusioid Rappels and the Deterioration in Workmanship] in *Fețele ornamentului. Arhitectura bucureșteană în secolul 20* [The Faces of the Ornament. The Architecture of Bucharest in the 20th Century], Bucharest, Univers Enciclopedic, 2003, p. 128.

56. Quoted from a video recording of the exhibition opening; <http://euscreen.eu/play.jsp?id=EUS_2BEA874F4BF44599AEC76B8B327B7A2C>.

ethnographic image of the Memorial House merely reinforced the idea of a connection between Romanian traditional culture and universal modern art.[57]

From the 1970s, the "reclamatory" discourse constructed around Brancusi's
connection with Romanian folklore went hand in hand with protochronist strategies that aimed to impose Romanian values nationally and internationally, based on
their originality and the idea of Romanians being precursors in various areas of universal civilisation and culture. Although the term was not established until 1974,[58]
such strategies can be found in Romania as early as the nineteenth century and are
interpreted as "clearly symptomatising the plight of subaltern cultures dominated by
metropolitan centres."[59] As Paul Cernat argues: "the thesis of 'Romanian export modernism' and absolute European precursordom (Brancusi, Janco, Tzara)—repeated-
ly articulated by Vinea in the interwar period—was to be officially resized in the
1970s and 1980s, along the ideological lines of national-communist protochronism."[60]
Brancusi thus came back to the public attention as "the first man who, within the
framework of *European* civilisation, not only *searches for*, but also *finds* a different path,
on which he tears himself away from the psychology and condition of 'the world's
twilight' (...), transcends an avant-garde that did not yet exist and makes the leap
into a future whose paths we are only now beginning to decipher."[61] In her study of
protochronism, Alexandra Tomiță also speaks of "the acts of appropriation characteristic of nativist rhetoric, a rhetoric in a continual crisis of legitimacy," and of the
campaigns to annex "illustrious cultural figures from the pre-communist period."[62]
Moreover, she argues: "the extent to which the nativist formative strategies bore fruit
is also revealed to us by the nationalist stereotypes still present in post-1989
Romania,"[63] adopted from figures such as Constantin Noica and combined with the
neo-Orthodox discourse of Father Stăniloaie. Noica, regarded as the most important "mediator between the intellectual culture of the interbellum and that of communist Romania"[64] and currently perceived as a major landmark in Romanian

---

57. Cărăbaş, *op. cit.*, p. 69.

58. According to Alexandra Tomiță, Edgar Papu's article "Protocronismul Românesc" [Romanian
    Protochronism], commissioned by *Secolul 20* magazine in 1974, contributed to "the birth of pro-
    tochronism as an ideological weapon of nationalist communism." Alexandra Tomiță, *O istorie
    „glorioasă". Dosarul protocronismului românesc* [A "Glorious" History. The Dossier of Romanian
    Protochronism], Bucharest, Cartea Românească, 2007, p. 45.

59. Katherine Verdery, *National Ideology Under Socialism: Identity and Cultural Politics in Ceauşescu's Romania*,
    Berkley and Los Angeles, University of California Press, 1991, p. 168.

60. Cernat, *op. cit.*, p. 410.

61. Dan Zamfirescu, "De la sincronism la protocronism" [From Synchronism to Protochronism],
    Luceafărul, no. 40 (805), 1 October 1977, p. 18.

62. Tomiță, *op. cit.*, pp. 231, 222.

63. *Idem*, p. 294.

64. Trencsényi, *op. cit.*, p. 370.

intellectual history, occasionally also wrote about art and a number of times about the art of Brancusi himself, which, unsurprisingly, he interpreted via his model of national ontology, of "becoming within being."[65]

Such nationalist and protochronist stereotypes have been perpetuated to the present day in the public discourse connected to Brancusi, from the specialist discourse[66] to that found in popular culture. They have even been integrated with greater or lesser critical distance by a respected historian such as Lucian Boia, who includes the sculptor in the Romanian pantheon as an "artistic revolutionary, and one of the most important at that"[67] and by mathematician, philosopher, diplomat, futurologist and historian Mircea Malița, who in a book whose title is derived from a Brancusi sculpture, *The Wisdom of the Earth: Strategies for Survival in the History of the Romanian People*, presents the artist as a representative of the "Romanian character" and one of the "fathers of the Romanian nation": "Of all those who have taken [the nation] into universal orbits, he soared the highest and shone the brightest. One of the strategies of survival is to be well placed in such orbits, to emit messages from there constantly and to be received as a good of mankind."[68]

---

65. See Cristian Teleuca, "Constantin Noica: Gânduri despre arta românească" [Constantin Noica: Thoughts on Romanian Art]; <http://cerculnoica.wordpress.com/2013/02/15/constantin-noica-ganduri-despre-arta-romaneasca/>.

66. Besides the classic theory perpetuated to the present day which presents Brancusi as the inventor of modern sculpture, according to which "the struggle between old and new, that difficult bout, was waged in sculpture by Brancusi almost single-handedly" (Brezianu, *op. cit.*, p. 62), there are a number of other examples of protochronist citation of Brancusi: the "small rumour" created in 1914 about the "unprecedented presence of a female nude in the local cemetery" in Buzău, on the installation of *The Prayer*, precedes "the two famous incidents that followed the exhibitions of 1920 and 1927, unpleasant incidents that were dealt with by the French police and the American courts" (Brezianu, *op. cit.*, p. 62); "the first customs incident in the sculptor's career" occurred in Bucharest in 1912, preceding the one in New York in 1926: "the works dispatched from Paris (for the official Salon) could not be removed from the Filaret Warehouses on Calea Rahovei because in accordance with the "instructions in force" exemptions were granted only for paintings, while sculptures had not been stipulated in the table" (Brezianu, *op. cit.*, p. 88); in 1910, after being exhibited at the *Tinerimea artistică* exhibition, *The Wisdom of the Earth* "provoked violent reactions that led to the process of the introduction of modern values of expression into our art just as three years later it was also the works of Brancusi (alongside those of Matisse, Braque and Duchamp) that would stir the most violent anti-modernist reactions at the famous Armoury Show in NY" (Enescu, *op. cit.*, p. 62); even Brancusi's failure to find commissions in Romania is ascribed to the refusal of patrons who were at least as "enlightened" as the "New Yorkers who had seen the sculptures of Brancusi in 1913 at the Armoury Show and mocked them" or as "the representatives of official American art that had testified against Brancusi in the trial brought against him by the customs authorities of the United States" (Velescu, *op. cit.*, p. 386).

67. Boia, *op. cit.*, p. 260.

68. Mircea Malița, *Cumințenia Pământului: strategii de supraviețuire în istoria poporului român* [The Wisdom of the Earth: Strategies for Survival in the History of the Romanian People], Bucharest, Corint, 2010, p. 225.

After the events of 1989, the annexation of Brancusi's image to Romania became more and more visible in practices of reconstructing the country's identity, whether in relation to the West, whether domestically or even locally. In 1990 Constantin Brancusi was elected postmortem a member of the Romanian Academy, with the new regime quickly trying to compensate for this past oversight. If in 1977 the *Endless Column* adorned the five-lei coin, in the early 1990s the artist's portrait emblazoned two series of banknotes issued by the new political regime, and in 2001 two commemorative coins struck by the National Bank of Romania and the National Bank of Republic of Moldova.

In an interview, the designer of Swiss francs, which at the time featured only cultural figures,[69] explained why currency is a very important element of national identity: "Every new country does its money first. All the former Soviet states started by designing new money. Even EU took care of the Euro first. Money physically represents the value of a country; it connects the immaterial with the material."[70] In the same spirit, Michael Billig regards money as an example of what he calls a "banal reminder of nationhood," with the national emblems represented on money passing unobserved in daily financial transactions.[71]

Besides such national emblems, banknotes more often than not feature the portraits of figures regarded as representative of the country in question, with such being the case of Brancusi. In his preface to *The Music of European Nationalism: Cultural Identity and Modern History*,[72] Philip V. Bohlman discusses from this standpoint the design of the European currency that was launched in 2002 and which, in order to represent European unity, had to eliminate its traditional enemy, nationalism. Thus, from Euro banknotes national symbols and heroes vanished, be they politicians or cultural figures, although as Bohlman argues music/art and money "have long been companions in Europe." He talks about the figures of musicians and artists that have adorned the banknotes of many European countries, including George Enescu and Constantin Brancusi in Romania, and believes that the cultural figures represented on money have not only a national, but also a nationalist meaning: "Whatever its political stance, whatever its geographical position on the map of Europe, the iconic representation of musicians made specific statements about European nationalism."

---

69. Le Corbusier, Arthur Honegger, Sophie Taeuber-Arp, Alberto Giacometti, Charles Ferdinand Ramuz, Jacob Burckhardt.

70. Nienke Terpsma, Rob Hamelijnck, "Switzerland, platform for the world. Conversation with Jorg Zintzmeyer, designer of Switzerland's banknotes," *Fucking Good Art*, #20/2008, p. 83.

71. Billig, *op. cit.*, p. 41.

72. Philip V. Bohlman, *The Music of European Nationalism: Cultural Identity and Modern History*, Santa Barbara, ABC-CLIO, 2004, p. xv–xvii.

To return to the "nationalisation" of Brancusi, whereas in the 1970s the motif of the *Endless Column* became an ornament for the new housing blocks, in the late 1990s and early 2000s it became an ornament on a Boeing 737 operated by Tarom,[73] named the "Brancusi Aeroplane," which was reserved for official presidential flights, and in the 2000s the National Housing Agency, a department of the Ministry of Transport, Constructions and Housing, named its biggest real-estate investment in Romania the "Constantin Brancusi" District. Whereas in 1967, the opening speech at the "Brancusi" Colloquium was delivered by the Chairman of the State Committee for Culture and Art, in 2001 the "Brancusi at the Apogee: New Perspectives" International Colloquium opened with messages from the President of Romania, Ion Iliescu, and the Prime Minister, Adrian Năstase. To celebrate the one hundred and twenty-fifth anniversary of the sculptor's birth, 2001 was declared International Brancusi Year in Romania, which predictably gave rise to countless official and unofficial, academic and popular events, as well as a series of celebratory publications and articles in the press. The following selection of book titles is indicative: *Brancusi the Romanian*, published by the Thausib publishing house in partnership with the Romanian Government's Department of Public Information (1996); *Brancusi—Today* by Zenovie Cârlugea, published by the Ministry of Internal Affairs in partnership with the "Pasărea Măiastră" Policemen's Foundation from Târgu Jiu (2000); *Constantin Brancusi: The Posthumous Destiny*, also published by the Ministry of Internal Affairs after a session of talks organised in 2001 at the Bucharest Police Academy by the Ministry's Public Relations, Traditions, Education and Sport Department in partnership with the Romanian Academy's "George Oprescu" Institute of Art History (2002). Also in the tradition of the commemorations of 1967 and 1976, Horia Sabău realised a monument to the memory of Brancusi, erected in front of the Trade Unions Culture Club in Oradea.

At the local level,[74] the "Constantin Brancusi" Municipal Cultural Centre, active in connection with the Târgu Jiu Town Hall, commemorates the sculptor by organising an extremely diverse series of events called *Brancusiana*: national sculpture camps and symposia (yearly since 2001); sessions of Brancusiological talks (2001, 2003, 2011–2014); the "Gate of the Kiss" National Folk and Ballad Festival

---

73. There is a well-known connection between states and national airlines; even Frederic Jameson mentions it, using an amusing turn of phrase in "The National Situation" seminar: "A nation is something that has a flag and an airline." James Elkins, Zhivka Valiavicharska, Alice Kim (eds.), *Art and Globalization*, University Park, Pennsylvania State University Press, 2010, p. 17.

74. The instrumentalisation of national values in local politics is not a new phenomenon. Speaking about the re-burials of Lenin and the Tsar of Russia, Katherine Verdery argues that the groups who wanted this to take place in Sankt Petersburg were involved in the rivalry between the city and Moscow for spiritual primacy in Russia. Note 58 in Katherine Verdery, *The Political Lives of Dead Bodies: Reburial and Postsocialist Change*, p. 133.

(yearly since 2002); "Worship in the Name of Christian Orthodox Sculptor Constantin Brancusi" (yearly since 2004, held on the Day of the Dead according to the Orthodox tradition); the *Brancusi* journal (first published in 1995, with a new series beginning in October 2013).[75]

Making political capital of the *Endless Column* motif, Victor Ponta, the deputy for Gorj since 2004 and later Prime Minister of Romania, used it as a backdrop in the USL electoral campaign for the parliamentary elections of 2012 and as a logo in the PSD campaign for the European Parliament elections of 2014, combined with the slogan: "Proud that we are Romanians!"

In the drive to obtain the title of European Capital of Culture 2021, Craiova has joined forces with Târgu Jiu, with the Mayor of Craiova, Olguța Vasilescu, wagering on "the brands of Oltenia," Constantin Brancusi and Maria Tănase. The local press reports that the partnership between the Gorj and Dolj authorities was signed at the *Table of Silence*, on which occasion Olguța Vasilescu declared: *"I am positive that Craiova will win because we have invested the most money in culture. Today we are producing the ace from up our sleeve and the Brancusi Monumental Ensemble will be the winning card."*[76] Plans for local investments were not limited to culture alone. In 2013, a plan for a "Brancusi" motorway was launched, which would link the two cities, and a "Brancusi" mini-airport at Stănești, to make "the road to Brancusi easier and more attractive for tourists."[77] More recently, in June 2014, although the Romanian Senate rejected the law proposal put forward by a cross-party group of deputies and senators aimed at establishing a "Constantin Brancusi" National Museum of Art in Târgu Jiu,[78] it was decided to build a Brancusi museum in Craiova, in the form of an International Centre, which Dolj County Council will build next to the city's Art Museum—an investment of seven million euros. The Chairman of Dolj County Council, Ion Prioteasa, said in a press conference that the project *Constantin Brancusi International Centre—An Interactive Tourist Centre* is *"an unprecedented investment in Romania which comes at a time when in no other town, including Bucharest, has anything important been done for the most famous Romanian in the world. (...) In Craiova something outstanding will happen, for which we will be envied throughout Romania. I am convinced that it will become a place of pilgrimage."*[79] Târgu Jiu also aimed to become a place of pilgrimage after

---

75. Information taken from the Centre's web page: <http://centrulbrancusi.ro/>.

76. Costin Soare, "Proiect ambiţios pentru olteni! Autostrada 'Brâncuşi' între Târgu Jiu şi Craiova" [An Ambitious Project for Oltenians! The 'Brancusi' Highway between Târgu Jiu and Craiova], *Impact în Gorj* (local newspaper), 15 July 2013; <http://www.impactingorj.com/actualitate/autostrada-brancusi-intre-targu-jiu-si-craiova.html>.

77. *Ibidem.*

78. The Târgu Jiu Museum would have operated as a public institution subordinated to the Romanian National Museum of Art and administered by Gorj County Council.

79. Ion Prioteasa quoted by Mediafax; <http://www.mediafax.ro/cultura-media/un-muzeu-dedicat-lui-constantin-brancusi-va-fi-infiintat-la-craiova-cu-o-investitie-de-7-mil-euro-12690653>.

its "Brancusi Axis" won the "Golden Apple" from the International Federation of Journalists and Travel Writers. Its candidacy was organised by the Association to Promote Gorj Tourism in partnership with the National Tourism Authority and the local authorities, which realised that winning the Golden Apple for Brancusi's town would increase the range of tourist products that Romania exports, with the award being the starting point for creating tourist interest in the area. This is how the invitation to make a pilgrimage sounded: "Romanians from all over the world, from the homeland or outside its borders: come to Târgu Jiu to touch with your own hands the legacy left by Brancusi! Bring your children and show them they have reasons to be proud. You now have an extra reason to do this! The Brancusi monumental axis in Târgu Jiu, a matrix of our Romanianness, has become part of the circuit of universal heritage values and will carry the name of Romania all over the world!"[80]

At the international level, it should not be forgotten that Romanians from the diaspora made huge efforts to keep alive the memory of Brancusi, the symbolic connection with the sculptor providing them with a better self-image, legitimised by Western culture. From the 1960s, Ionel Jianu was involved in various actions to promote Brancusi in France, later followed by Doina Lemny, a researcher at the Centre Georges Pompidou. Radu Varia was another controversial Brancusiologist in exile, who in 1991 founded the "Constantin Brancusi" International Foundations in New York and Bucharest, with the aim of raising funds to restore the Monumental Ensemble in Târgu Jiu. More recently, writer Laurian Stănchescu, the man behind the campaign to repatriate Brancusi's remains, founded the International "Constantin Brancusi" Society in Canada, along with actress Claudia Motea, via which he organised in 2013 the event to mark the 137th anniversary of the artist's birth, in partnership with the Autonomous Administration of Film Distribution—RADEF Romaniafilm.[81]

As a continuation of such private initiatives on the part of the diaspora, in the new international climate generated by the culture of competing states, it is becoming more and more obvious that the government is also making efforts to exploit the image of Brancusi as a national brand. But Brancusi is not an isolated case. Paul Cernat analyses Urmuz from the same angle in a chapter of his book on the avant-garde, titled "The Urmuz Effect and the Myth of the Avant-gardist Forerunner. Adventures in Reception. From the 'Centre of the Margins' to the

---

80. Adriana Caranfil, "Axa Brâncuşi din Târgu-Jiu obţine Oscarul turismului mondial!" [The Brancusi Axis from Târgu Jiu obtains the Oscar of Global Tourism], *Adevărul*, 6 April 2014; <http://adevarul.ro/life-style/travel/axa-brancusi-targu-jiu-obtine-oscarul-turismului-mondial-1_53415caa0d133766a88c6d8e/index.html>.

81. For more information on the actions initiated by Jianu, Lemny and Varia, see the chapter on Brancusiology, and for those initiated by Laurian Stănchescu, see the chapter on Popular Appropriation.

'Periphery of the Centre.' A Case Study on the Critical Canonisation of the Romanian Avant-Garde." Drawing a parallel between Urmuz and Brancusi, he argues that "the value of Brancusi's sculpture (praised both by the avant-gardists of *Contimporanul*, *Integral* and *unu* and by the mystic nativists of *Gândirea*) was not truly acknowledged in Romania until two decades after it became prominent abroad." Likewise, he claims that "both the 'humanist-socialist' reclamation of the historical avant-garde (which took place partially and tardily in the 1960s and 1970s) and above all the 'protochronist' reclamation of the 1980s ought to be reinterpreted, through the lens of the aforementioned periphery complex, in terms of symbolic profitability, in keeping with the state policy of the Ceaușescu regime."[82] He goes on to argue that *"foreign legitimation* played a determining role in the process of *domestic* reclamation/re-canonisation of [the] historical avant-garde," also noting that "the interest—increasingly prominent in recent years—in the local avant-garde is due, at least in part, to the 'profitability' of the phenomenon, as part of a cultural strategy to promote Romania's image abroad."[83] Such image capital becomes highly important in the context of policies of national identity developed under pressure from globalisation or the cultural diversity policy of the European Union.

In *Contemporary Art and Nationalism*, a collection of texts that examine policies of national and cultural identity in the European context, the events of 1989 are discussed as proof that at the time, although it was assumed that there no longer existed any major narratives in which the nation was the main character, the nation states still played a historically important role. Boris Buden even asks: "Who, if not the nation, was the actual subject of the democratic revolutions of 1989?"[84] The same idea also occurs in the "Art and National Identity" symposium and the special issue of *Art in America*, which was conceived as a result of those events and discussed the way in which national strategies are reflected in institutional strategies (Guy Brett) and the way in which institutions "dramatically enact the nation through performing its 'culture'" (Barbara Kirshenblatt-Gimblett), as well as the way in which national identity can become aesthetic rather than geographical or political (Tadayasu Sakai).[85]

Another essential concept in the present context, which also becomes the main subject of state cultural policies, is that of *identity*. Cultural policies become identical with policies of national identity, thereby generating a mutation from "national politics to (nationalist) cultural policies,"[86] a mutation evident in particular within

---

82. Cernat, *op. cit.*, p. 404.

83. *Idem,* pp. 392, 404.

84. Buden, *op. cit.*, p. 13.

85. "Art & National Identity: A Critics' Symposium," *Art in America*, September 1991, pp. 80–83.

86. Simon Sheikh, "Battle Lines Are Being Drawn – The Cultural Politics of Identity in Denmark" in Minna Henriksson, Sezgin Boynik (eds.), *Contemporary Art and Nationalism*, p. 58.

the institutions that deal with cultural exports. Thus, the post-nation state, legitimised through ideological mechanisms of identity building, is perceived as mediating between global pressures and local resistance in order to reach a compromise that will make it competitive in the global system.[87] Culture is employed to generate international recognition and prestige, and is caught up in the mechanism of national promotion alongside folkloric production and tourist attractions.

But this phenomenon is not new, as Judith Huggins Balfe argues. She sees artworks as "as symbolic carriers, as mediators of politics and as propaganda for secular and religious ideologies (including, of course, the 'aesthetic religion' of 'art-for-art's-sake')."[88] Thus, in the international context, works of art are employed as "cultural ambassadors" whenever political, economic or religious interests demand.

To return to Constantin Brancusi, we may observe that he has been caught up in this mechanism that transforms art into an element of competitive national identity. In European Union strategies, speculating on the universality of the aesthetic experience and visual language, art's main function becomes to shape national identities and, at the same time, the sense of European belonging.[89] Thus, in 2011, to mark Romania's National Day, the Romanian delegation of the EPP group in the European Parliament organised the *Guests of Brancusi* event, at which were exhibited miniature replicas of Brancusi's sculptures along with the interior of a traditional Oltenian house, folk costumes and traditional ceramics. In an interview, deputy Marian-Jean Marinescu, vice-president of the EPP group, expressed his pride at having managed to bring to the European Parliament in Brussels "the *Endless Column*, the *Gate of the Kiss* and the *Table of Silence*, alongside the other exhibits representing both the artist's source of inspiration and an expression of the spiritual riches of the Romanian people."[90]

The following year, PSD MEP Victor Boştinaru, along with the president of the French socialist delegation to the European Parliament, Catherine Trautmann, organised with the help of Doina Lemny an exhibition dedicated to Constantin Brancusi, this time in the European Parliament in Strasbourg. According to MEP Victor Boştinaru, "the purpose of the exhibition was to mark the importance of

---

87. Ratko Močnik, "Identity and the Arts" in Minna Henriksson, Sezgin Boynik (eds.), *op. cit.,* p. 45.

88. Judith Huggins Balfe, "Artworks as Symbols in International Politics," *International Journal of Politics, Culture, and Society*, Vol. 1, No. 2, The Sociology of Culture (Winter, 1987), p. 195.

89. *United in diversity* has been the motto of the European Union since 2000. It signifies "how Europeans have come together, in the form of the EU, to work for peace and prosperity, while at the same time being enriched by the continent's many different cultures, traditions and languages."; <http://europa.eu/about-eu/basic-information/symbols/motto/index_en.htm>.

90. Marian-Jean Marinescu quoted in <http://nouapresa.ro/ultima-ora/operele-lui-brancusi-in-parlamentul-european>.

Romanian sculptor Constantin Brancusi, not only as an established artist, but also as a symbol of the two nations: Romanian and French." He sees Brancusi as "representing the soul of the Romanian people, of the Romanian countryside, in a unique body of modernist work of international prestige," whereas the MEPs from other countries kept closer to the official discourse of the European Union. Catherine Trautmann speaks of "the sculptor's role in uniting the two nations, Romania and France," while Hannes Swoboda, the president of the S&D group of the European Parliament speaks of the "diversity" that Constantin Brancusi symbolises: "The artists who have come from Romania to France show how a cross-border activity is a very good example, something that Europe ought to emulate. Likewise, Constantin Brancusi demonstrates the fact that art is not bounded by frontiers and that art should be part of our lives."[91]

Unlike spectacular cultural exports that sophisticatedly present art works at the intersection of economic and diplomatic interests, the homages to Brancusi exhibited in the lobbies of European Union headquarters have a makeshift look, reminiscent of a display in a provincial tourism fair. One explanation for this may be Romania's postsocialist context, in which superficial adoption of models of promotion and neo-liberal strategies organically mixed with local fictions and fanaticisms regarding national traditions and identity, the end product being such populist narratives. But not even successful recipes involving the export of national festivals with huge budgets and heterogeneous activities employed as cultural diplomacy can truly succeed in breaking free of the nationalist paradigm and exoticism. As Brian Wallis discusses in his article "Selling Nations," such festivals merely remind us of culture's role in inventing/defining the nation.[92] They construct national identity in order to be consumed by a foreign audience, in the process being forced to dramatise the most conventional versions of past glory, or national allegories, thereby perpetuating stereotypical national representations. In such contexts, the nation can be viewed "as an empty and elastic container into which can be fit any variety of art objects."[93]

Thus culture comes to be supported only as an export whose role is to consolidate the image of the nation state within the international community. Globalisation perceived as a national threat generates a competitive nationalism based on the concept of location of performance, which contributes to the instrumentalisation of culture in various national marketing and branding strategies. As Michael E. Porter predicted as early as the 1990s, in the context of global competition, nations will

---

91. Information taken from the web page of PSD MEP Victor Boştinaru; <http://victorbostinaru.ro/2012/07/eurodeputatii-victor-bostinaru-si-catherine-trautmann-au-organizat-o-expozitie-dedicata-lui-constantin-brancusi-in-parlamentul-european/>.

92. Brian Wallis, "Selling Nations," *Art in America*, September 1991, pp. 85-91.

93. *Idem*, p. 88.

become even more important than they were in the past: "Competitive advantage is created and sustained through a highly localized process. Differences in national values, culture, economic structures, institutions, and histories all contribute to competitive success."[94] Success at the international level is also the main goal of country branding strategies, which ultimately aim to promote the image of a state in order to attract foreign investment and tourist traffic. Effective country branding not only strengthens positive images where they exist, but also helps to eliminate negative images by implementing new images and associations. Whether it be a question of the strategies of public diplomacy implemented by cultural institutions such as the Romanian Cultural Institute, the British Council, the Goethe Institut, etc., or whether a question of advertising campaigns in the media designed to attract tourists, culture plays an essential role in constructing the national brand and its long-term sustainability.

From the marketing perspective, the name of a country is viewed as a brand, and the image a country has influences consumers' perceptions of the products it exports (the country of origin effect). But this perception at the international level also works the opposite way—the image of a product brand affects our image of the producer country. The figure of Brancusi, an artist internationally recognised and appreciated, has been used as a brand that might positively influence perceptions of Romania, both at official events such as those mentioned above and in national branding campaigns. The Ministry of Foreign Affairs, also responsible for promoting Romania's image abroad, launched two major projects in 2005: the implementation of Cultural Institutes abroad and the declaration of the Decade of Romanian Culture, to include various cultural events paying homage to figures such as Eminescu, Brancusi and Caragiale. In 2007, to mark Romania's integration into the European Union, the ministry launched the *Fabulouspirit* national branding campaign, aimed at presenting Romania as a national production company that had achieved success stories: flight (Henri Coandă), the infinite (Constantin Brancusi), balance (Nadia Comăneci), and natural monuments (the Bucegi Sphinx). Lucian Georgescu, who conceived the campaign, said that "*Fabulouspirit* was an opportunity to talk about success stories, with known and as yet unknown features. About the creative, innovative, ancestral spirit and the mythic allure of genesis."[95]

The specialists suggest that in constructing Romania's image for a foreign audience it is vital to take advantage of the positive symbols that already exist in the Western public awareness, and Brancusi is one of those symbols, alongside Nadia

---

94. Michael E. Porter, "The Competitive Advantage of Nations," *Harvard Business Review*, March-April 1990, p. 73.

95. Lucian Georgescu quoted in Irina Cristea, "Campanie – Fabulouspirit cu Brancuși" [Campaign – Fabulouspirit with Brancusi], *Jurnalul Național*, 1 March 2007; <http://jurnalul.ro/stiri/externe/campanie-fabulospirit-cu-brancusi-1004.html#>.

Comăneci, Gică Hagi, Eugène Ionesco, Mariana Nicolesco, beautiful women, the House of the People, and Dracula's Castle.[96]

More recently, in the "Choose a Symbol for Romania" campaign initiated by *Adevărul* newspaper in 2011, the *Endless Column* was voted the symbol of Romania. Art critic Pavel Şuşară declared himself deeply moved by the choice, claiming that the image of the Romanian people, dominated by Eastern elements, but also Western manifestations and tendencies, perfectly combines with Brancusi's sculpture: "The choice of the *Endless Column* shows that the moral substance and the dynamic of local intelligence are not wholly compromised in the Romanian context."[97] We may observe how the association of the Brancusi brand with Romania occurs both within governmental strategies and in the popular context of *Adevărul* newspaper readers, and even in poems that circulate on the Internet, such as *Country Brands*, by Dumitru Delcă:[98]

The Romanian has in his blood / The Dacian-Roman gene.
Death cannot defeat / His Dacian-Roman stock.
He has eminence in his soul / As high as the Carpathians.
He exports intelligence / Through the Column of the Dacians.
The Brancusian column / Shows to the whole world
How vertical is /Romania, eternally.
The country brand is the people. / It is the Romanian nation.
It is the branch and the spring, / It is ancestral history.
The tricolour is the country brand. / The red is the throbbing blood.
The yellow the endless wheat, / The blue lays its peace.
They are brands that define / The whole Romanian people.
They have dwelled an eternity / On my ancestral soil.

If in the interwar period the modest reception of Brancusi had to do with Romania's level of visual culture and, in the 1950s, with the ideological mechanisms that promoted socialist realism, in the protochronist discourse of the Ceauşescu regime he became a highly popular figure. Since 1989, in the context of competing states, the sculptor has been transformed into a true national brand that con-

---

96. Luminiţa Nicolescu, Cristian Păun, Irina Alina Popescu, Alina Drăghici, "Romania Trying to be a European Brand," *Management & Marketing*, 1/2008, p. 70; <http://www.management-marketing.ro/home.php?var[1]=1&var[3]=2008&var[2]=93>.

97. Information taken from the web page of the *Adevărul* newspaper; <http://adevarul.ro/locale/ targu-jiu/coloana-infinitului-fost-desemnata-simbolul-romaniei-1_50aeea017c42d5a663 a1a2ff/index.html>.

98. Poem posted in 2013 on <http://www.citatepedia.ro/comentarii.php?id=187277>.

tributes to what has been called country equity,[99] a term extrapolated from marketing which refers to the positive emotional value resulting from the association between a brand and a country. Thanks to his international recognition, Brancusi represents a precious image capital that Romania exploits by annexing him to the national culture and identity in the process of transforming symbolic value into financial profit.

---

99. Brand equity evaluates a brand according to brand loyalty, name awareness, perceived quality, brand associations.

Am ținut să aducem, de asemenea, un omagiu lui Brâncuși, acestui mare sculptor al poporului nostru, de valoare mondială, care prin opera lui a lăsat veacurilor o expresie a gîndirii și sensibilității poporului nostru, făcîndu-l cunoscut în întreaga lume.

NICOLAE CEAUȘESCU

Din cuvîntarea rostită la Tîrgu-Jiu
(„Scînteia", 14 iunie 1966)

First page of the volume *Testiomonies about Brancusi* published by The Committee for Culture and Socialist Education of Dolj County in 1975

[*We likewise insist on paying homage to Brancusi, this great sculptor of our people, a sculptor of world value, who through his work has handed down to the ages an expression of the thought and sensibility of our people, making it known throughout the world.* From the speech delivered by Nicolae Ceaușescu in Târgu Jiu (*Scînteia*, 14 June 1966)]

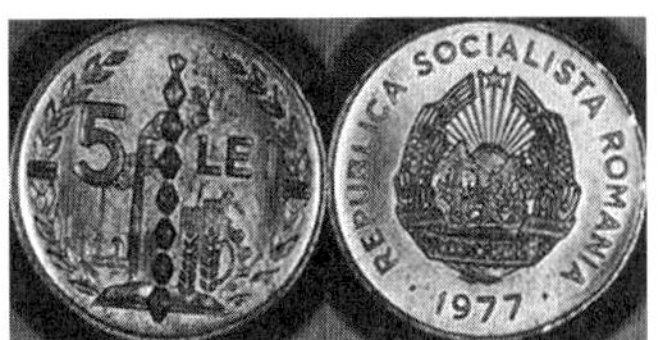

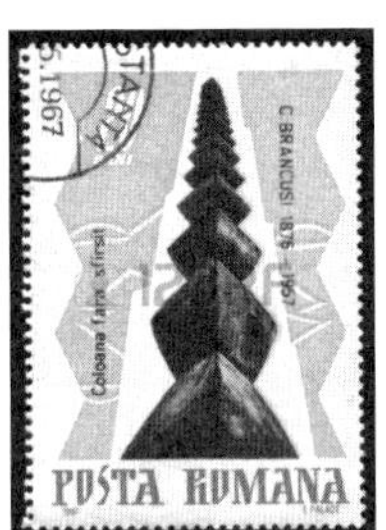

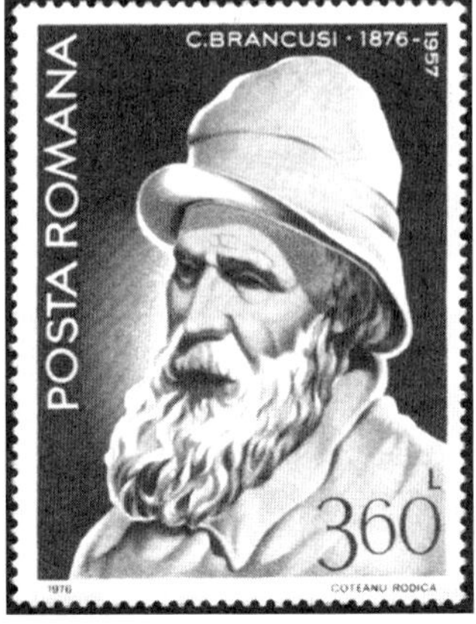

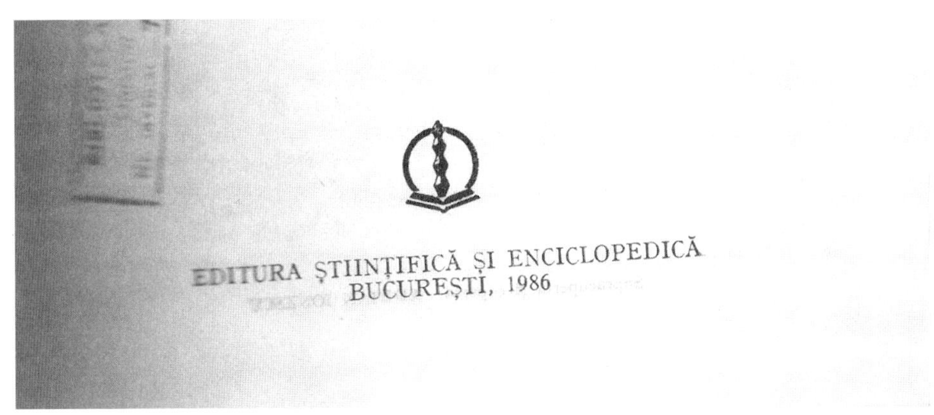

Usages of Brancusi in Romanian official communication of the 1960s–1980s

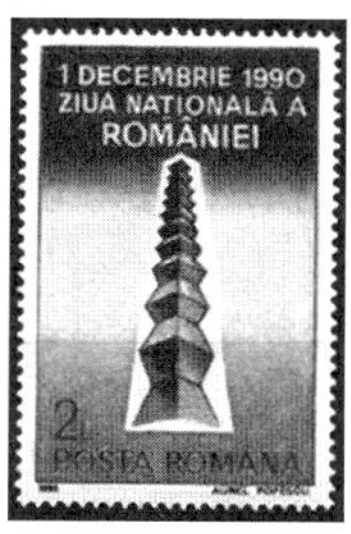

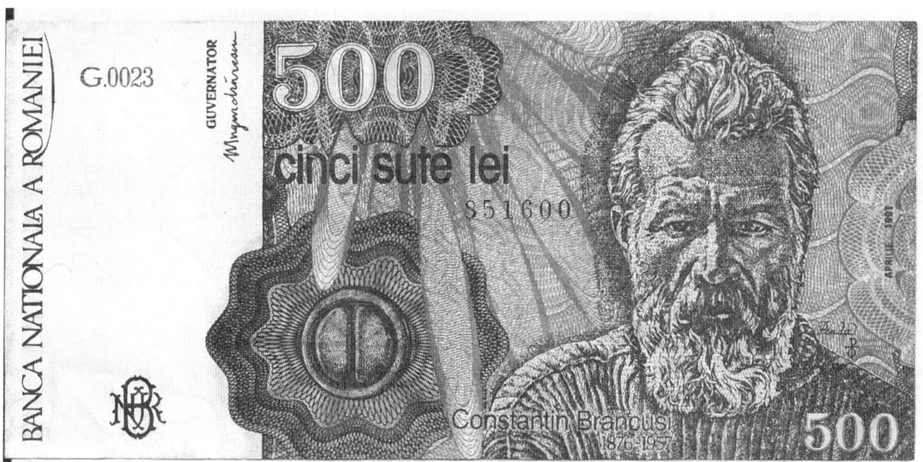

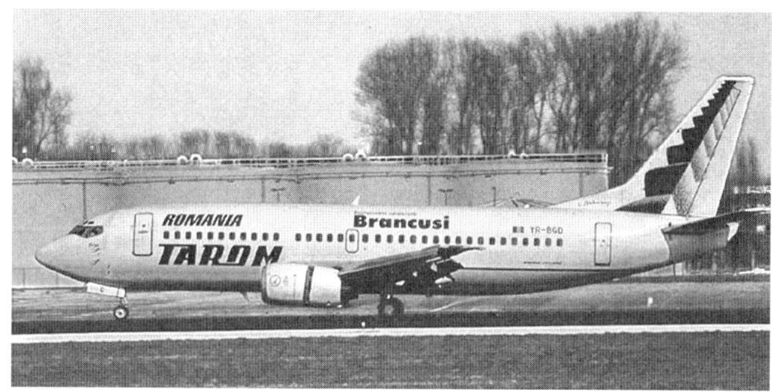

Usages of Brancusi in Romanian official communication of the 1990s and 2000s

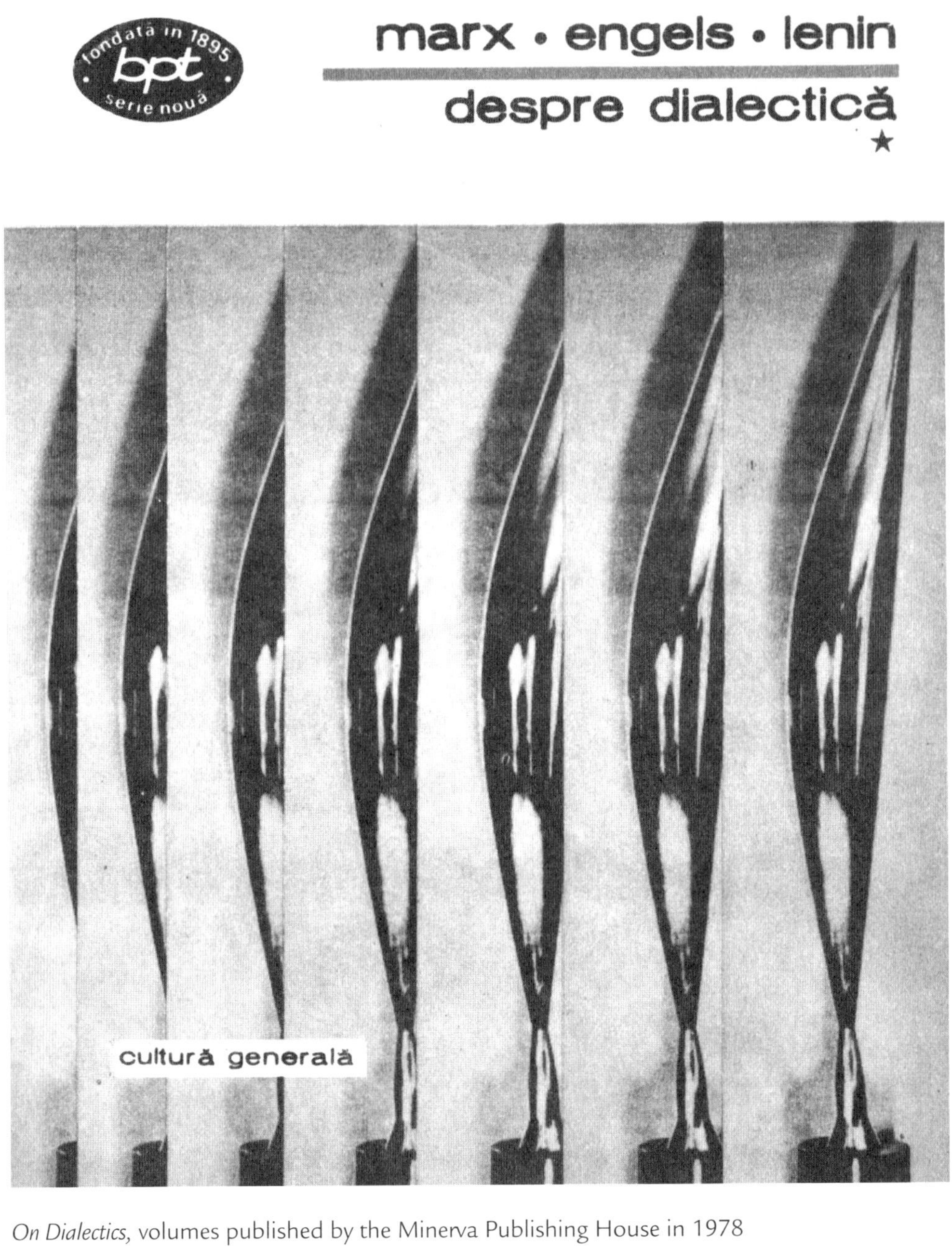

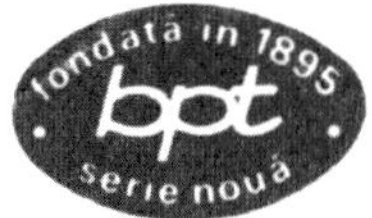

marx • engels • lenin
despre dialectică
★

On Dialectics, volumes published by the Minerva Publishing House in 1978
(from the archive of Vlad Nancă)

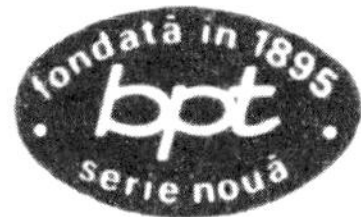

marx · engels · lenin
despre dialectică
★ ★

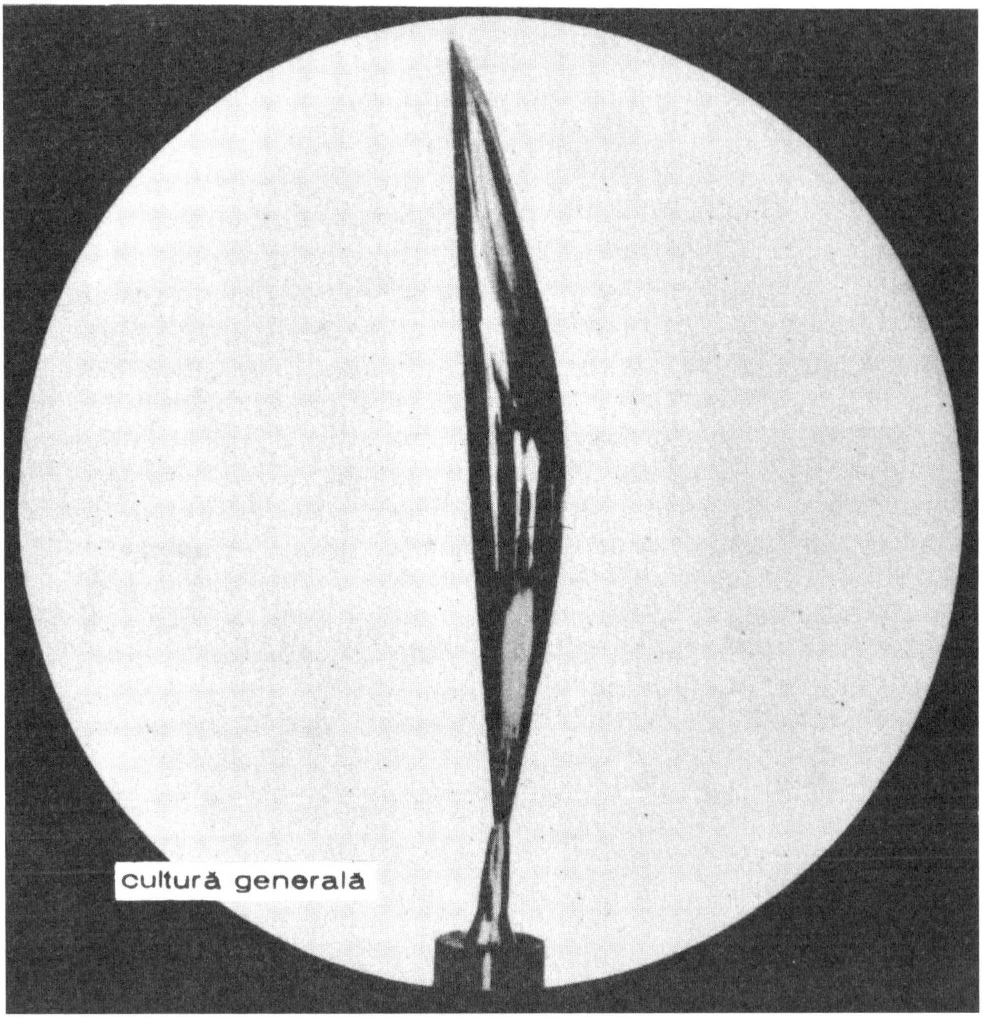

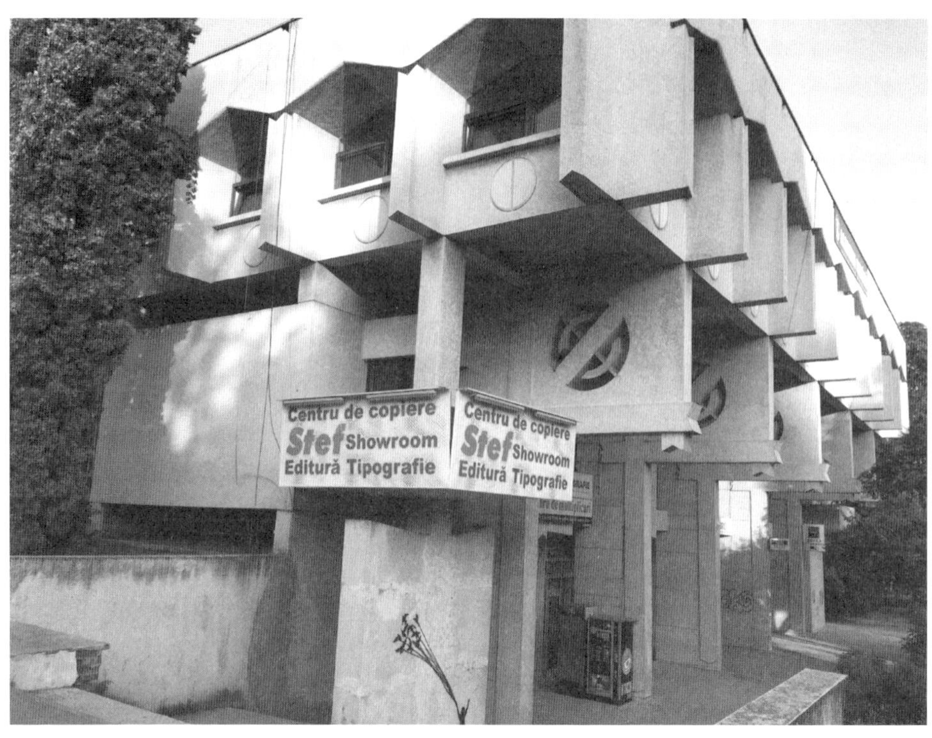

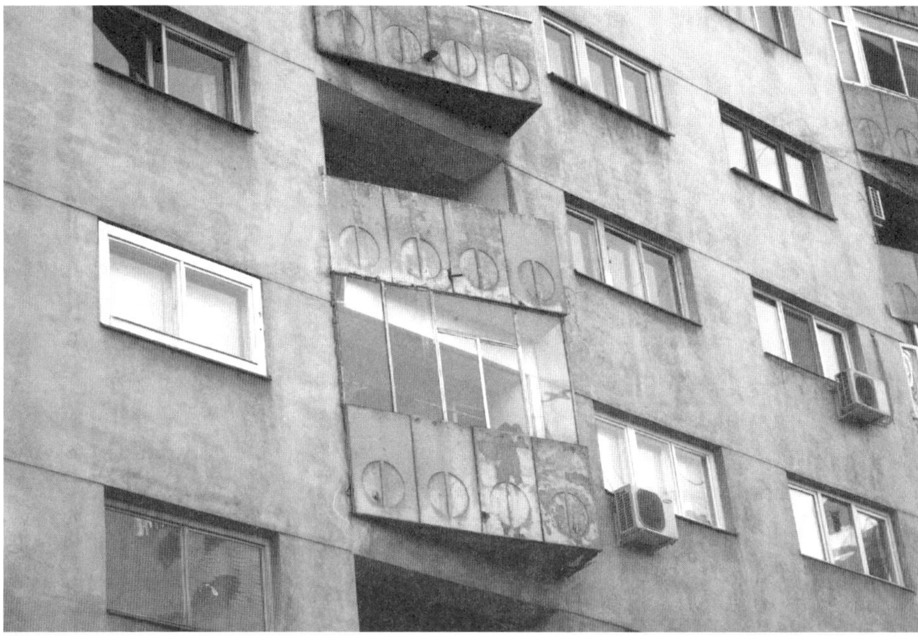

Usages of Brancusi in the 1980s in Iaşi/Bucharest (from the archive of Vlad Nancă)

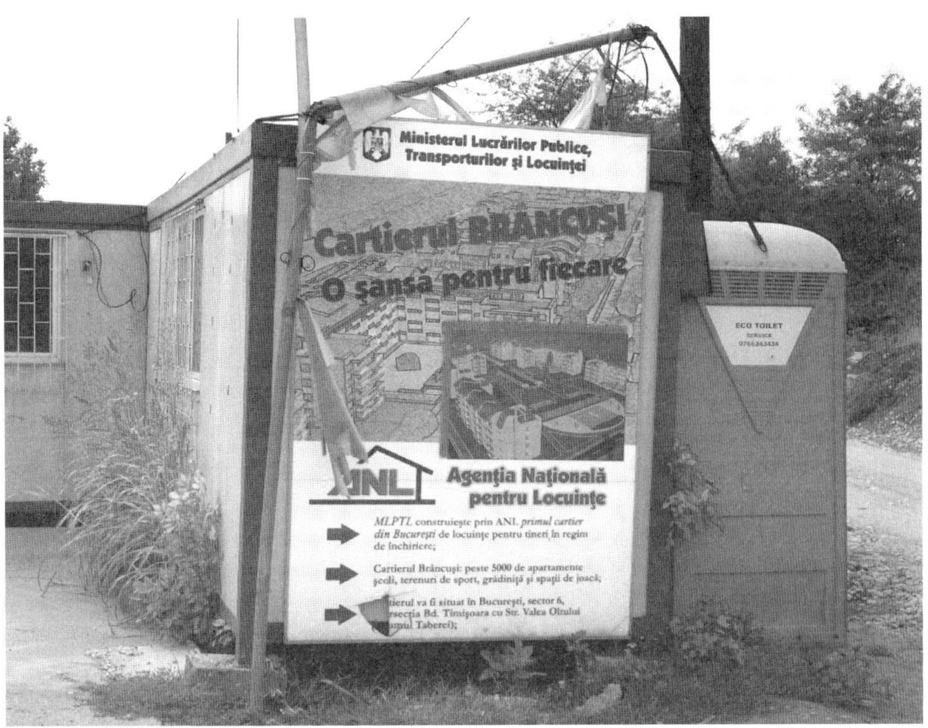

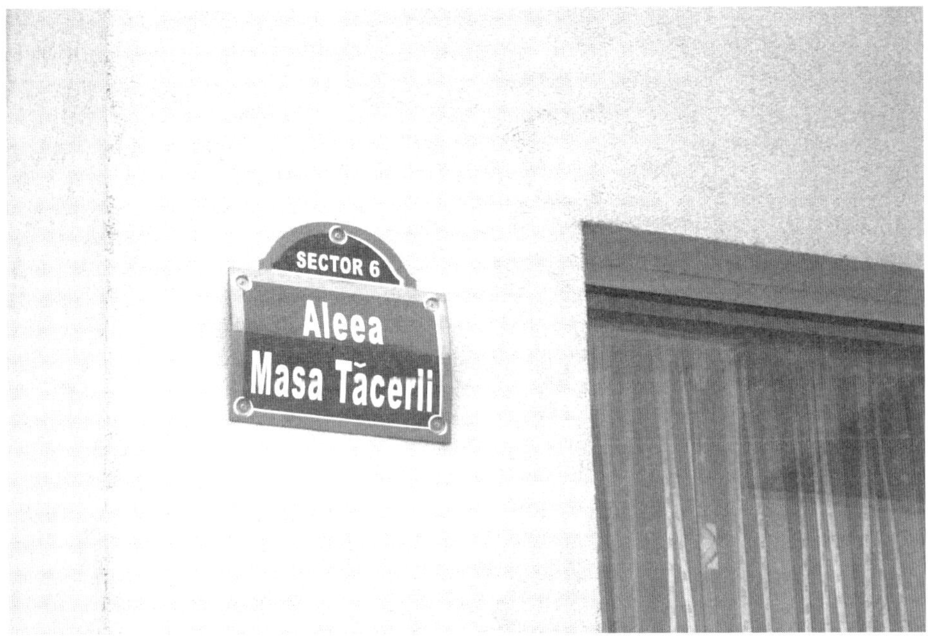

Usages of Brancusi in the 2000s in Bucharest (from the archive of Vlad Nancă)
[The Brancusi District. A Fair Chance for All] Construction site of the National Housing
Agency / [The Table of Silence Lane]

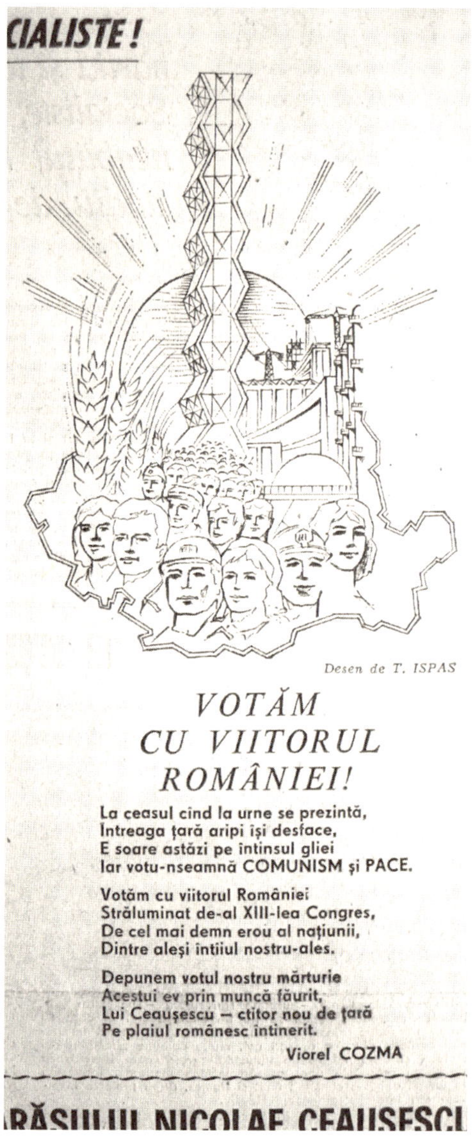

Usages of Brancusi in Romanian official communication pre- and post-1989
(from the archive of Vlad Nancă)

[*We Vote for the Future of Romania!* When the time comes to go to the polls, / Our nation arises and spreads its wings / The sun shines down on our ancestral soil, / We vote COMMUNISM and PEACE our goal. / We vote for the future of Romania, / Illumined by the Thirteenth Party Congress / And by the nation's worthiest hero, / Whom above all others we do profess. / We cast our vote, a living testimony / To this epoch our toil has brought to birth, / To Ceaușescu, new founder of a nation / On rejuvenated Romanian earth.]

Ouvrage remis par le Président de la République de Roumanie
à Jean-Jacques Aillagon, Président du CGP, lors de sa visite
de l'Atelier Brancusi le 7 novembre 1997. Il porte son
paraphe plus bas soit la signature de Emil CONSTANTINESCU.

Românul
BRÂNCUŞI

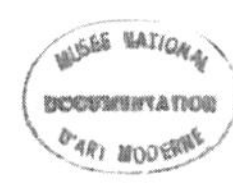

First page of the volume *Brancusi the Romanian*
published by Romanian Government's Department
of Public Information, signed by President of
Romania Emil Constantinescu on the occasion of
his visit at the Brancusi Studio/MNAM Paris, 1997

Album
realizat de
EDITURA THAUSIB
în colaborare cu
Departamentul Informaţiilor Publice al Guvernului României

Sibiu, 1996

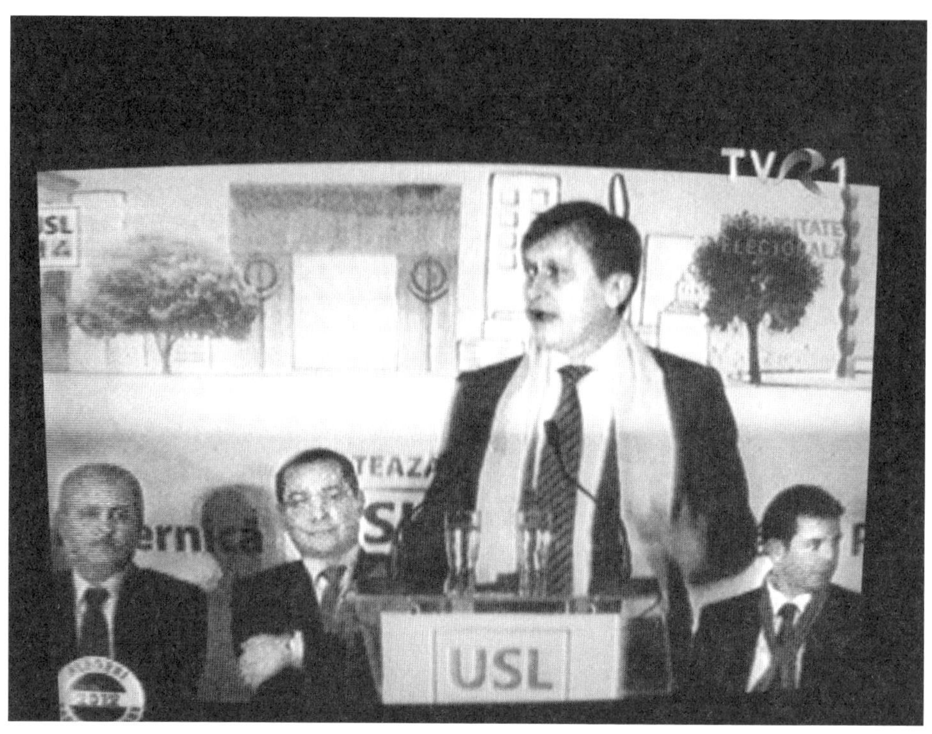

USL electoral campaign for the parliamentary elections of 2012

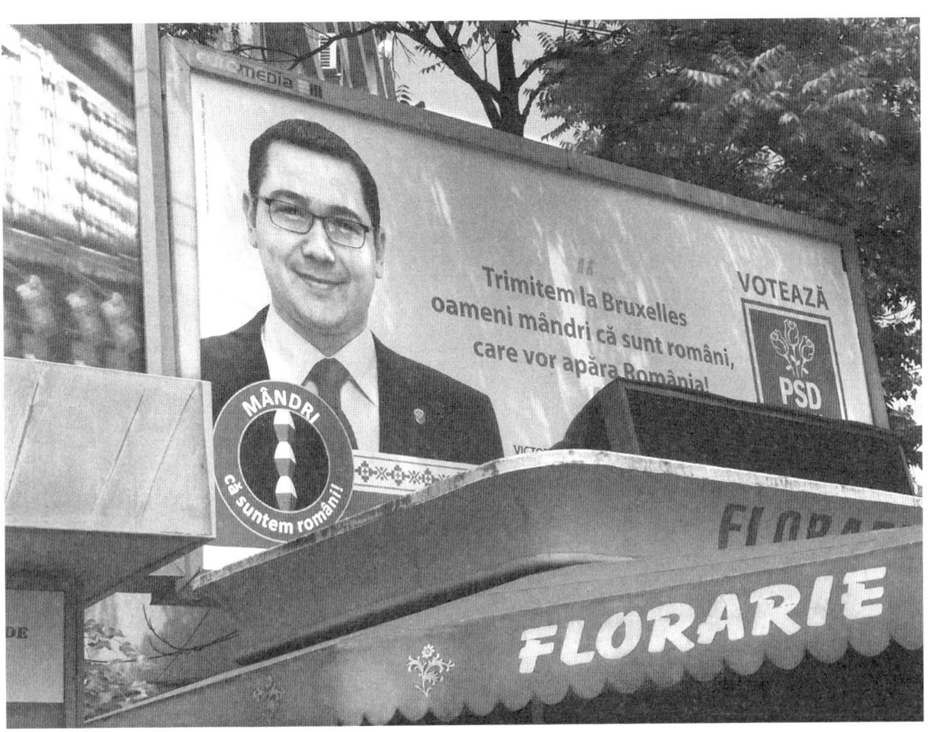

[Proud That We Are Romanians!] PSD campaign for the European Parliament elections of 2014

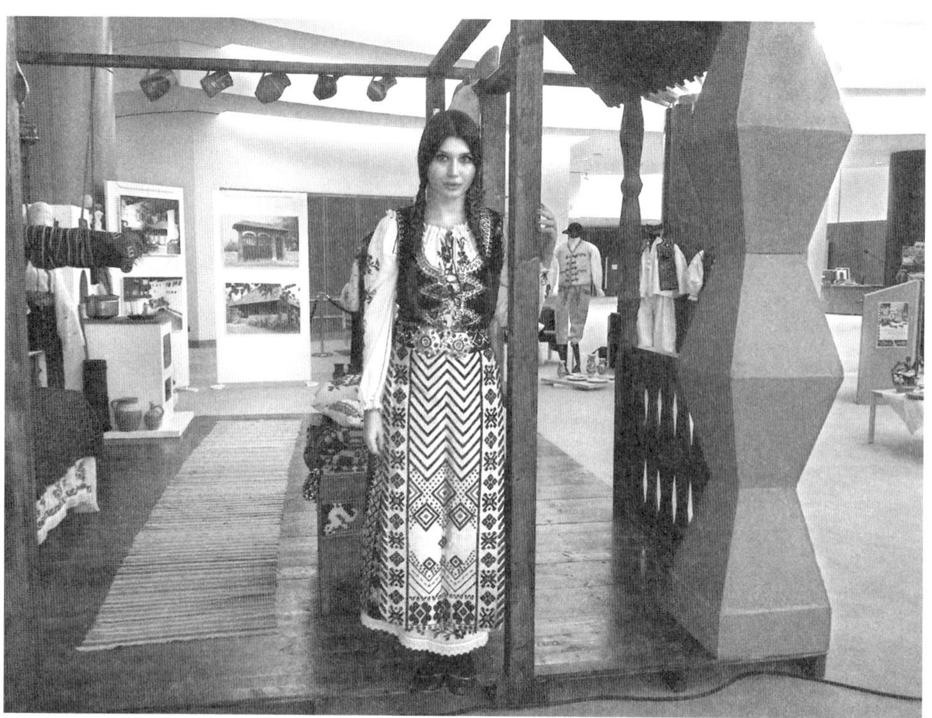

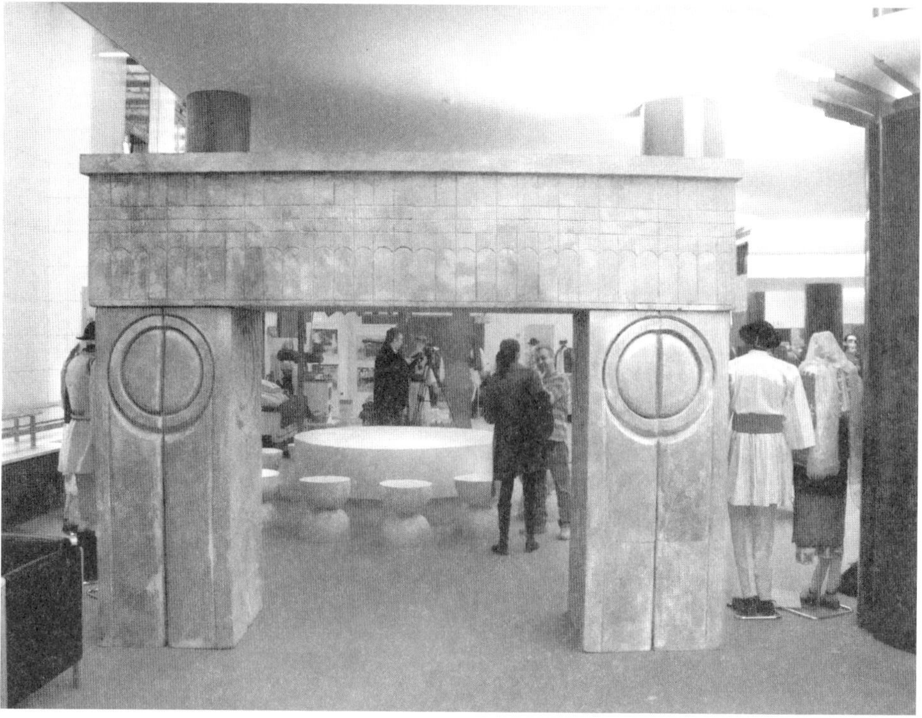

Guests of Brancusi, celebration of Romania's National Day organised by the Romanian delegation of the EPP Group at the European Parliament in Brussels, 2011 (from the archive of Doina Lemny)

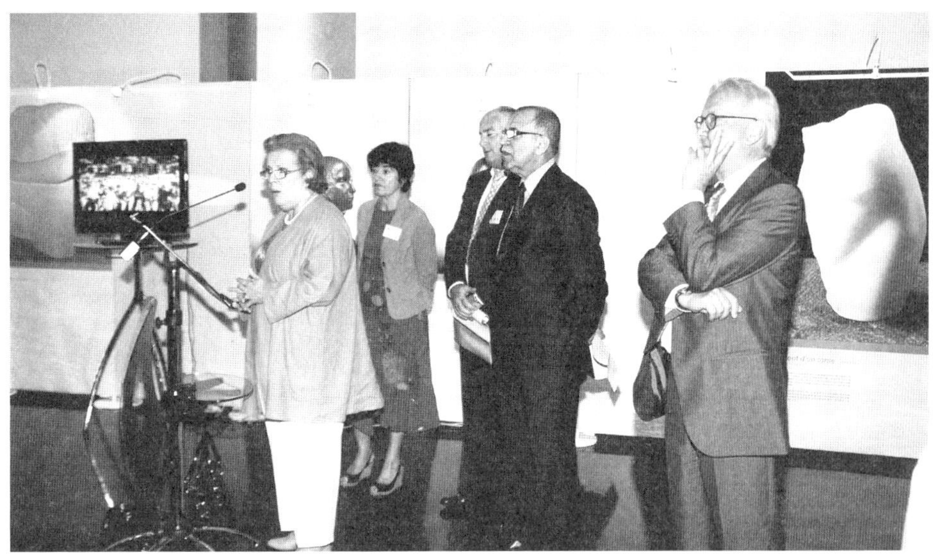

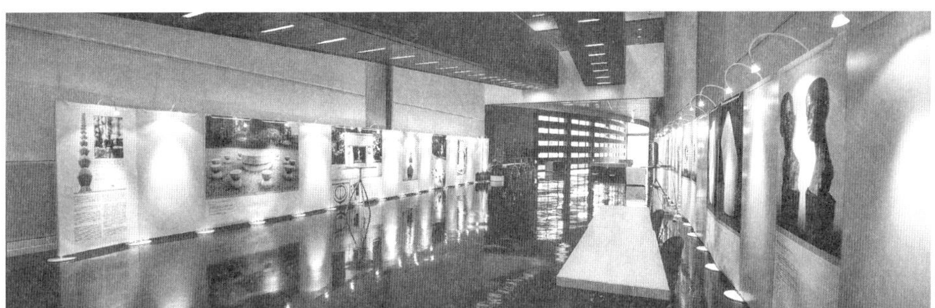

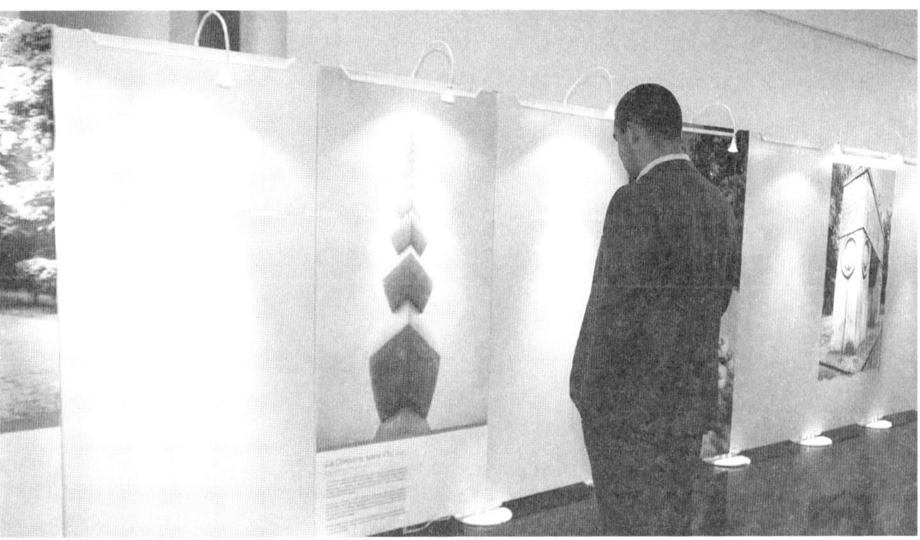

Homage to Brancusi, exhibition organised by the S&D Group at the European Parliament in Strasbourg, 2012 (from the archive of Doina Lemny)

BRANCUSI EST

ROUMAIN

PAS

FRANCAIS !

....Vous êtes fou....

Brancusi est roms / Adi

PART 3

Brancusiology and
Brancusiologists of National Renown

The starting point for this chapter is the definition of Brancusiology that opens Constantin Zărnescu's book *The Code of Brancusi's Work*: "For whoever is accustomed to the bibliographies and the *revuistique* of the museums of France, as well as with those of the European and American modern arts, the notion of Brancusiology will be familiar, denoting everything represented by the criticism and exegesis of the art that was constituted around the reforming work left to posterity by the great Romanian sculptor Constantin Brancusi."[1]

As we can see, through the mention of the "museums of France," the main point of reference is the Western discourse. Zărnescu continues: "To the extent that albums and studies about Brancusi have multiplied, especially since 1957, it has (also) been possible to classify the scientific status of a discipline named with increasing frequency… Brancusiology, representing knowledge of the life, revolution and exemplary sacrifice of Brancusi, of their propagation in the sphere of national and international education, especially of the young, the conservation of his artistic legacy, kept in state or private collections, on every meridian; the thoroughgoing study in university education of the reforming character of his work and thought, his innovative influence on modern architecture, on technical-scientific and industrial design; (…) and not least his fertile influence on the postmodernity of today's urban structures, of 'architectural' sculpture or of sculpted architecture."[2] Hence, for Brancusiology it is important not only to establish Brancusi within the specialised discourse of the art world, but also to recognise his influence on the whole of the contemporary context, "in the aerodynamic forms of automobiles and cosmic rockets," or in the new "visions of religious or political postmodern temples and edifices" and even economic buildings: "chrome, glass and stainless steel banks."[3]

Continuing this discourse on the importance and influence of Brancusi, Nina Stănculescu argues that "Brancusi's works are not only those that he fashioned with his own hands and poured into all the museums of the world," emphasising "the continuous dilation, like ripples of water, of this miraculous seed" from which "today spring all the works of our sculpture camps throughout the country" and through which "the treasury of Romanian wisdom and beauty bears fruit for the entire world."[4]

But most important is the fact that this new "uomo universale"[5]—as Zărnescu calls him—is Romanian, and his achievement becomes the achievement of the entire

---

1. Constantin Zărnescu, *Codul operei lui Brâncuşi* [The Code of Brancusi's Work], Cluj, Dacia, 2007, p. 5.

2. *Idem*, pp. 5-6.

3. *Idem*, p. 6.

4. Nina Stănculescu, *Izvoare şi cristalizări în opera lui Brâncuşi* [Sources and Crystallisations in Brancusi's Œuvre], Bucharest, Editura Ştiinţifică şi Enciclopedică, 1984, pp. 62-80.

5. Zărnescu, *op. cit.*, p. 5.

nation. He is the one who causes Romanians finally to glimpse "the springtime of small cultures"[6] of which Cioran spoke.

In regard to the history of Brancusiology, although articles about Brancusi appeared in the Romanian press from the 1900s, the beginnings of Brancusiology per se are linked to the Ramuri publishing house in Craiova. In 1938, Ramuri published a work by V. G. Paleolog, *C. Brancusi*, which was republished in French and with a large number of illustrations by the Forum publishing house from Bucharest in 1947, becoming the first major book about Brancusi to circulate internationally. In the early 1950s, Brancusi's work entered a cone of shadow, being officially regarded as decadent, but in 1956 there was a Brancusi exhibition at the Museum of Art in Bucharest. The organisers were Mircea Deac, the head of the Arts Department of the Ministry of Culture, and H. M. Maxy, the museum's director. Although it opened without invitations, posters or a catalogue, the exhibition was the first event to counterbalance the official negative reception of Brancusi in Romania (a negative reception visible also in *Romanian Statuary Sculpture*, a book written by George Oprescu, Remus Niculescu and Eugen Schileru and published in 1954).

From 1957, the year of the artist's death, a series of texts on Brancusi were published internationally: in 1957, Christian Zevros in Paris, David Lewis in New York, Ezra Pound in Milan; in 1958, George Uscătescu in Madrid; in 1959, Carola Giedion-Welcker in Neuchâtel. In Paris in 1962, to mark the inauguration of the Brancusi Studio at the Palais de Tokyo (relocated to the Centre Pompidou in 1977), Ionel Jianu organised a commemorative event. He thereby became an important proponent of Brancusiology. In 1963 Jianu published in Paris a work entitled *Brancusi* and in 1967 he was the co-author, with Mircea Eliade and Petru Comarnescu, of *Testimonies about Brancusi*.

In 1964, when Romania opened up to Europe politically, Brancusi's work began to be re-evaluated, and the Târgu Jiu Monumental Ensamble was restored in the same year. Petru Comarnescu, another major proponent of Brancusiology, was the first to draw the attention of the international art world to the monumental works at Târgu Jiu, in a study published in *Le Journal de Genève*. In 1965, the first book on Brancusi was published since the war: *Constantin Brancusi* by Mircea Deac, and in 1967, ten years after Brancusi's death, in parallel with commemorations in Paris, Rome, Rimini, New York and Budapest, the first "Brancusi" International Colloquium was held in Bucharest, organised by the State Commission for Literature and Art in partnership with AICA.

In 1969, a Brancusi retrospective was organised by the Philadelphia Museum of Art, which travelled to the Guggenheim Museum in New York, the Art Institute

---

6. Emil Cioran, *Schimbarea la față a României* [The Transfiguration of Romania], Bucharest, Humanitas, 2006, pp. 148–149.

of Chicago, the Museum of Art in Bucharest, and the Gemeentemuseum in the Hague. In 1970 a symposium was held in Bucharest, on the subject *Brancusi in the World*, and in 1971 the Memorial House was inaugurated in Hobița. More and more publications on Brancusi began to appear, written by Petru Comarnescu, Barbu Brezianu, V. G. Paleolog (in Romania) and Sidney Geist and Athena Tacha Spear (in the United States), among others. By 1976, the centenary of the artist's birth, cultural policies had already changed, and Brancusi began to be valorised as an artist who embodied the national specificity.[7] In Bucharest, the Romanian Academy organised a scholarly session, the Union of Artists organised a colloquium, a symposium was held in Târgu Jiu, and in Cluj *Tribuna* magazine published a volume entitled *Homage to Brancusi*. Just a few years later, in 1982, Dan Hăulică organised an exhibition and a colloquium dedicated to Brancusi at the Venice Biennale.

After 1989, Brancusi was established as the Romanian genius who reinvented modern sculpture, and the Ministry of Culture declared 2001 International Brancusi Year, an occasion that marked the beginning of obsessive publication of new titles dedicated to Brancusi. The "Constantin Brancusi" Municipal Cultural Centre in Târgu Jiu began to hold an annual *Brancusiana* symposium and a sculpture camp dedicated to Brancusi, and in 2011 it relaunched the campaign to have the monumental ensemble *Calea Eroilor* [Avenue of Heroes] listed as a UNESCO World Heritage site.[8]

With regard to the researchers who have studied the life and work of Brancusi, it should be noted that although there are a number of famous international names, such as Sidney Geist, Carola Giedion-Welcker or Friedrich Teja Bach, in the present work, which focuses on the image of Brancusi as a national artist, I shall refer only to Brancusiologists of Romanian origin.

V. G. PALEOLOG is regarded as the first genuine Brancusiologist, if not the founder of Brancusiology. In a résumé drawn up by an inspector from Dolj County Committee for Culture and Art, it emerges that there is no evidence he had any higher education, but rather "V. G. Paleolog's scientific activity begins in the period of his trips to Italy, France, England, Austria, Switzerland, Belgium, etc., when he visited many museums. (…) For a deeper knowledge of literature and arts he penetrated artistic circles of the time and maintained relations with famous artists and

---

7. For more details on this rehabilitation, see the previous chapter, "Brancusi and Romania."

8. In June 2015, the UNESCO World Heritage Committee recommended not to submit the candidacy file for the *Avenue of Heroes* Monumental Ensemble in Târgu Jiu. According to a recent press release of the Romanian National Heritage Institute, the UNESCO World Heritage candidacy file was withdrawn by the Romanian state for the documents to be compiled more thoroughly and resubmitted; <http://www.mediafax.ro/cultura-media/inp-ansamblul-brancusi-a-primit-din-partea-unesco-recomandare-de-neinscriere-va-fi-repropus-14589973>.

writers."[9] After returning to Romania, between 1924 and 1947 he engaged in agricultural activities, before settling in Craiova, where he dedicated his entire existence to the study of the life and work of Brancusi. He defined himself as "toiler for the memory of Brancusi" and argued that it was his "sacred duty to do everything possible in order that the great sculptor be known and studied so that he remains in the awareness of present and future generations."[10] Marin Sorescu calls him "the seigneur of exegesis of the illustrious sculptor; the image of a wizard unbridled in his interminable phrases and periods, in his dazzling suggestions and intuitions."[11] Besides weekly articles in the *Înainte* newspaper and books on Brancusi, in Craiova V. G. Paleolog was responsible for the "C. Brancusi Bio-Bibliographical Information" section of the Academy of Political Sciences and Socialist Education, the "Brancusi" Room in the Museum of Art, the project for a Brancusi Memorial House, and the project to reconstruct the Brancusi Studio (a copy of the Paris studio), for which he arranged the purchase of the façade beams salvaged after demolitions in Impasse Ronsin, "vestiges of national symbolic importance (…) and which will become sacred to the future."[12]

As for the volumes he published, the first dedicated to Brancusi appeared in 1938 following a lecture given the previous year at the Friends of Science People's University. His *Second Book on Brancusi* was published in 1944 and, together with a collection of essays originally published in French in the *Arcades* journal, constitutes the nucleus of *Brancusi-Brancusi*, edited in 1976 by his son, Tretie Paleolog. From the foreword of this book we discover that "it is a question of three progressive visions of Brancusi's work and thought, three visions by which we gradually ascend to more and more elevated planes of knowledge," conceived from the posture of "witness," the main quality of the essays being the "authenticity" that derives from "the daily contact and intellectual intimacy that the author had for many consecutive years with Brancusi."[13] V. G. Paleolog's discourse is here presented as being highly valuable because he works with "the intellectual tools and entire humanistic arsenal available to him in the first half of the twentieth century" and because he did not attempt to "distort this mirror of Brancusi's work by means of structuralist reflections or aesthetic informational analysis."[14] V. G. Paleolog argues that Brancusi is

---

9. Cited in Petre Gigea-Gorun, *V. G. Paleolog și Brâncuși – Un dialog etern* [V. G. Paleolog and Brancusi – An Eternal Conversation], Craiova, Scrisul românesc, 2003, p. 408.

10. *Idem*, p. 17.

11. Marin Sorescu, "Brâncuși s-a născut alaltăieri" [Brancusi Was Born the Day before Yesterday], *Informația Bucureștiului*, 06.05.1974.

12. From the letter that V. G. Paleolog sent in 1975 to Ștefan Voitec, deputy for Craiova and president of the Grand National Assembly, reproduced in Petre Gigea-Gorun, *op. cit.*, p. 48.

13. V. G. Paleolog, *Brâncuși-Brâncuși*, vol. I, Craiova, Scrisul Românesc, 1976, p. 5.

14. *Idem*, p. 6.

"a beginning and an ending," he is a "school, as they would say in the textbooks of Art: his achievement sums up what a number of generations of sculpture might have been able to produce in successive moils. His moil summarizes."[15] Brancusi is "a cosmogony" and his work is unique, universal and timeless. He allowed his "soul to plunge into the pre-animist depths of the human spirit and sub-intuitions of the individual"[16] (it was in these plunges that the chance synchronisation with the influence of African art on Western art took place). But it was not until the *Portrait of Princess X* that Brancusi "attained the New World of the Beautiful and became prophetic. A new, bizarre, unheard-of prophecy: he heralds the return to the golden age of the man of times past, of times past that are counted in thousands and thousands and thousands of years."[17] This prophecy was confirmed by the discovery of a Palaeolithic statuette in the Lespugue cave in 1922, a statuette which "looks like it came from the studio, from the hands, from the sensibility, from the mind of Brancusi."[18] V. G. Paleolog's exegesis continues in the same tone, connecting Brancusi's work with notions such as "reform of the spirit," "the primitive and generative sensibility of the Great Adam," "Truth and Life," the "fecund matrix of nature and the primitive stem of mankind."[19]

In keeping with this strain of primitivism, he introduces the idea of Brancusi's Dacian origins: "the name Brancusi is the only one that has been passed down to us in a letter by letter orthography on a funerary post from the Roman beginnings in Dacia. Not being included in Roman onomastics, the name can only be Dacian."[20] The idea can also be found in later essays, in which he speaks of the proto-folkloric elements present in Brancusi's work and draws a parallel between Brancusi's "aphorisms" and "delirious nonsense," which find their origin in the "pagan archaic world, when our Thracian-Getae ancestors practised sun worship."[21] He believes Brancusi came into contact with this proto-folklore, which was the "perquisite of human societies shielded from urban pollutions," in his native village of Hobița, "where the evolved spiritualism of Zagreus the Dacian combines with the apperception of things in themselves, an absolute expression of the living."[22] Speaking of the Monumental Ensemble at Târgu Jiu, V. G. Paleolog con-

---

15. V. G. Paleolog, *C. Brâncuși*, Craiova, Ramuri, 1938, p. 5.

16. *Idem*, p. 15.

17. *Idem*, p. 16.

18. *Idem*, p. 21.

19. *Idem*, pp. 23–24.

20. *Idem*, pp. 6–7.

21. V. G. Paleolog, *Procesul sculpturii moderne* [The Process of Modern Sculpture], Craiova, Ramuri, 1944, p. 140.

22. *Idem*, p. 142.

tradicts the general opinion of Brancusi's contemporaries, who, he says, regard him as a "poor, alienated Romanian soul." Paleolog is of the opinion that "Brancusi's art does not lend itself to cheap nationalism in questionable taste, as he seeks the sources of inspiration not in a facile exteriorisation of the Romanian conscience, but in its depths, in that as yet unidentified and unstudied proto-folklore, which we might call the 'geology' of our conscience."[23] In 1939 Paleolog wrote in French an essay entitled "Brancusi's Pagan Calendar," which "reflects oral information received from Constantin, which he knew from family tradition,"[24] and in which he claims that Brancusi, whenever he came back to Romania, "was interested in finding out about his ancestors', the Dacians and Getae, concept of the Zodiac," so that "from this ancient Illyrio-Thracian or Pelasgian concept" he might bring back to life, in the tradition of Sarmisegetuza, "the cosmogonic concept of the Plaza of Time," at whose centre would be erected "the Column of Endlessness, a gnomon of solar and intergalactic time."[25] This line of interpretation can also later be found in Mircea Eliade, who believed that Brancusi had "found the source of Romanian inspiration after his encounter with primitive and archaic artworks."[26] Eliade sees the *Endless Column* as "a Romanian folk motif: the Column of the Sky, which extends a mythological theme found as early as pre-history and which is quite widespread throughout the world. The Column of the Sky supports the firmament, in other words it is an *axis mundi*."[27]

In his 1938 publication, Paleolog also discusses the contemporary bibliography on Brancusi, who was perceived as an artist highly appreciated around the world, but who for his own country—"the country with a cardboard Arch of Triumph"— was "a pride in which enters almost completely the coyness of misunderstanding," his name being uttered by "the stewards of the Beautiful with the coyness of incomprehension."[28] If in Romania Brancusi was not understood, in France he was discriminated against, the explanation being "the strangeness of his art in comparison with French destinies, since through Brancusi sculpture has slipped from the golden hands of French genius."[29]

Although throughout his writings Paleolog argues for the "universality" of Brancusi, we often find references to the way in which he brings honour to Romania. Here is an example from the end of the 1938 text: "Through Brancusi,

---

23. *Idem*, p. 231.

24. V. G. Paleolog, *Brâncuşi-Brâncuşi*, p.143.

25. *Idem*, p. 144.

26. Mircea Eliade, „Brâncuşi şi mitologiile" [Brancusi and Mythologies] in *Mărturii despre Brâncuşi* [Testimonies about Brancusi], Târgu Jiu, Editura Fundaţiei "Constantin Brâncuşi", 1997, p. 14.

27. *Idem*, p. 21.

28. V. G. Paleolog, *C. Brâncuşi*, pp. 5–6.

29. *Idem*, Notiţă Bibliografică [Bibliographical Note], p. 27.

our country takes pride of place in the unfolding of this new idealism, in this new parade of human genius. (…) Brancusi is the purest Romanian glory that the individuality of our nation imposes on civilisation. Through Brancusi, civilisation becomes indebted for the first time to our dear country."[30] In *The Process of Modern Sculpture* he writes: "The entire major work of sculptor Brancusi will bear the holy, indelible seal of the nation to which it belonged," and it has its "roots embedded in the sacred loam whose substance is the 'leaven' of the people: in it leavened and grew the genius of Brancusi."[31] And in *The Youth of Brancusi*, he regards Brancusi as "first and peerless in the new history of the world's mind."[32]

PETRE PANDREA was a man of the left, a lawyer, writer and journalist. After taking a law degree in Bucharest, he was awarded a seven-year scholarship to Berlin, during which time he also worked as a press attaché in the Romanian Legation. Flirting with the idea of studying sculpture in his youth and a lifelong consumer of the arts, who "gave free rein to his passion,"[33] during a visit to Paris, the young doctoral student visited Brancusi's studio, introducing himself as an "Oltenian and European, with boldness, with love, with reverence, and with familial rights, earned thanks to their shared Oltenianism, over conversation and sociability in his entourage."[34] He visited him on a number of occasions between 1927 and 1939 in Paris and Bucharest. A fascinating character, as a lawyer in the 1930s he represented people and organisations that had fallen into official disgrace, which in 1948 led to his arrest and imprisonment for four years without trial. After his release, having been readmitted to the bar, he became the lawyer of the nuns of Vladimireşti and the monks of Sihastru, monasteries that had been abusively closed down, and this led to a further arrest and, this time, a conviction. He spent five years in the Aiud Prison, where, he confessed, he thought much about Brancusi, meditating "on the substance of being a lawyer and being a sculptor, clay models and human souls."[35] Immediately after his release in 1964, he began writing *Brancusi: Memories and Exegeses*. In the preface to the 2009 edition of the book, Ştefan Dimitriu writes: "choosing to write a monograph about Brancusi, Pandrea took advantage of the

---

30. *Idem*, p. 24.

31. V. G. Paleolog, *Procesul sculpturii moderne*, p. 227.

32. V. G. Paleolog, *Tinereţea lui Brâncuşi* [The Youth of Brancusi], Bucharest, Editura Tineretului, 1967, p. 210.

33. Petre Pandrea, *Brâncuşi: Amintiri şi exegeze* [Brancusi: Memories and Exegeses], Bucharest, Vremea, 2009, p. 17.

34. *Idem*, p. 19.

35. Petre Pandrea quoted in Ştefan Dimitriu, "Brâncuşi – Izvoare morale şi filosofice" [Brancusi – Moral and Philosophical Sources], introduction to Petre Pandrea, *Brâncuşi: Pravila de la Craiova* [Brancusi: The Codex of Craiova], Bucharest, Vremea, 2010, p. 9.

opportunity to cry out between the lines of the book his own sufferings and to define his own beliefs yet again, in a unique and desperate testament he was thereby able to hand down to posterity."[36] This was the only book that Pandrea published during the communist regime, and is in fact merely the first part of a 1,200-page typed trilogy that the author had prepared for the press. The other two parts were not published until after 2000, when the original manuscripts were discovered. Pandrea himself did not see the volume as a scholarly work, but rather as "memoirs, fragmentary and mosaic-like memories of a great man" whom he often visited, written with "the professional distortions of the jurist and the melancholy of the memoirist."[37] Pandrea is aware of "the controversy over Brancusi's aphorisms and sayings,"[38] but puts forward as an argument in favour of the authenticity of his recollections the fact that Peter Neagoe confirms, in his novel *The Saint of Montparnasse*, "the precision and exactness" of his collection of Brancusi's sayings.[39] He sees the sculptor as "an Oltenian and Romanian artist of world validity with universal themes, problems, aspirations and solutions," "anchored in the free peasant class of the Oltenian peasantry," which was a "progressive class, with revolutionary ferment." He believes that "without folklore, without fairy tales, without the free peasants, without the peasantry, without the 1907 uprising and without the older progressivism of Tudor [Vladimirescu], Iancu Jianu and Radu Șapcă, the sensitive soul of Brancusi cannot be understood," since "his aesthetics, philosophy and ethics are those of a free peasant pandour, who became an expatriate artistic proletarian."[40] In the same spirit, Pandrea speaks of Brancusi's disappointment at the end of his life, which was caused by his contemplation of "the agony of the West," where a "fatal pyramid" had been created: "down below the exhausted slaves and up above the pale flowers." In Pandrea's opinion, the sculptor, who was unable to assimilate with the West, "remained Balkan and proudly Carpathian."[41] Although he cites Brancusi in close relation with the ideology of the left, Pandrea was censored in the 1970s, and the other two parts of his text on the sculptor were not published until 2010. In the second volume of his trilogy, Pandrea presents Brancusi as an "Oltenian knower of the law," who "provided us with a shining example of modern art, with roots in the national soil and with the style of the ancient Codex of Craiova, written in legends, in fairy tales, in proverbs, in traditional art and in a specific style of life, with the judgement and prejudices

---

36. Ştefan Dimitriu in the introduction to Petre Pandrea, *Brâncuşi: Amintiri şi exegeze*, p. 6.

37. Pandrea, *op. cit.*, p. 17.

38. *Idem*, p. 210.

39. *Idem*, p. 155.

40. *Idem*, pp. 167–168.

41. *Idem*, pp.190–191.

of the free peasant class, with the ethics, aesthetics and vision of the centuries-old pandour,"[42] and in the third volume he "puts in their place all those who had denigrated (…) the genius, uniqueness and self-consciousness of Brancusi."[43] He contrasts the image of the uncultured peasant with that of the "universal teacher, the noble Wallachian bookman": "Brancusi was not an upturned library, but an assimilated library, through the pinnacles and sociological masterpieces of humanism."[44] He discusses the peril of "ideological" interpretations of Brancusi, giving the example of Jean Cassou who "sees in Brancusi rather a picturesque peasant," and prefers a "vulgarisation" of the artist, in the sense of "popularisation": "popularisation is excellent as long as it is not vulgarisation, that is, a question of good taste and common sense, easily solvable among well-meaning people of good faith."[45]

IONEL JIANU was one of the most important Brancusiologists of the diaspora. An essayist, translator, art critic and art historian, in the early 1940s he founded in Bucharest the Căminul Artei [Home of Art] gallery and publishing house, where he published his first monographs on Romanian painters, and in 1945 he founded *Lumină și culoare* [Light and Colour] magazine. Between 1951 and 1958 he was head of the visual arts section of the State Publishing House for Literature and Art, and in 1958 he was transferred to the Meridiane publishing house, where he remained until 1961. From 1954 until 1961, when he emigrated from Romania, settling in Paris, he was a teacher at the "Nicolae Grigorescu" Institute of Arts, in the Romanian Art History Department. In Paris, in 1962, he founded—"through great personal sacrifice, in order to promote the work of Brancusi in France and throughout the world"[46]—the Arted publishing house, where he published the following volumes: *Brancusi* (1963), *Introduction à la sculpture de Brancusi*, in collaboration with Constantin Noica (1976), *Témoignages sur Brancusi*, in collaboration with Petru Comarnescu and Mircea Eliade (1967). In the same year, the International Association of Art Critics awarded Jianu and Petru Comarnescu the Gold Medal for their contributions to knowledge of Brancusi's work.

Like in the case of V. G. Paleolog and Pandrea, the driving force of the exegesis was direct contact with Brancusi, which, according to Jianu's own account, first occurred when he was a student in Paris, although it was not until 1938, in Târgu

---

42. Petre Pandrea, *Brâncuși. Pravila de la Craiova*, p. 22.

43. Ştefan Dimitriu in the introduction to Petre Pandrea, *Brâncuși: Amicii și inamicii* [Brancusi: The Friends and the Foes], Bucharest, Vremea, 2010, p. 9.

44. Petre Pandrea, *Brâncuși: Amicii și inamicii*, pp. 298–299.

45. Petre Pandrea, *Brâncuși: Amintiri și exegeze*, p. 273.

46. Ioana Dinulescu, "Ionel Jianu, promotor al artei brâncușiene" [Ionel Jianu, Advocate of Brancusi's Art], *Ramuri*, 9/2008.

Jiu, that the initiatory encounter took place, in which Petru Comarnescu also participated: *"the whole night he told us the story of his life, his adventures, his struggle, his defeats, his successes, and it was an unforgettable evening, an evening in which he conquered and converted us both. We became not only unconditional admirers of Brancusi, but also promoters of his work in Romania and abroad."*[47] After emigrating to France, Jianu was affected by the condition of the expatriate who is forced to leave everything behind and take with him "only memories and hopes." Besides his books about Brancusi, in 1986 he also published *Romanian Artists in the West*, an encyclopaedic work in which "Romanian particularity is organically integrated into universality."[48] He confessed: *"I did not leave the homeland for good. I left the homeland with the thought of serving Romanian culture as I have served it for fifty-six years."*[49]

To return to Brancusi, the sculptor was to remain the central subject of Jianu's writings and channelled his desire to make a contribution to the promotion of Romanian culture. His first book about the sculptor was published in 1963. After trying in vain to find a French publisher interested in the book, "Jianu made the heroic decision to set up his own publishing house. Despite the worried advice of his friends and their scepticism, he set out, as he himself puts it, madly down the road: *But there has to be a speck of madness in everything you do when you want to do things that are extraordinary."*[50] We may note that in the discussion of Brancusiology, besides the theme of sacrifice, there now also occurs quixotic heroism, and the image of a Brancusi discriminated against by the French, previously suggested by V. G. Paleolog, also recurs. Jianu believes that the book played a major role in making the Romanian authorities reconsider their attitude to Brancusi's work: "The Romanian Embassy in Paris had asked for twelve copies to send to the homeland, to the Central Committee of the Romanian Communist Party, whereas the four copies the author himself sent to friends in the homeland, including Petru Comarnescu, never reached their recipients. The book and the plea Jianu makes therein, that Brancusi represents the Romanian peasant's way of thinking about the world, radically changed the destiny of the genius son of Hobița in the homeland. The Monumental Ensemble at Târgu Jiu (…) which had been left derelict, came to the attention of the Romanian authorities once more. As a result, it was restored and designed to serve as an international tourist centre (…). *This was my great satisfaction and my first vindication against those who had banished me from the homeland,"* confessed Ionel Jianu.[51]

---

47. Cited in Ioana Dinulescu, *ibidem*.

48. Mircea Handoca, "Cuvânt înainte" [Foreword] to Ionel Jianu, *Brâncuși*, Cluj, Dacia, 2003, p. 8.

49. Cited in Ioana Dinulescu, *op. cit.*

50. Ioana Dinulescu, *op. cit.*

51. *Ibidem*.

Jianu's view is placed in contrast with that of Sidney Geist, "an American writer who never met Brancusi, never had any contact with him, and who, as we shall see, has understood nothing of the work of Brancusi or its spiritual dimension." Thus takes shape the idea that "correct" interpretation of Brancusi can only be achieved by Romanians. Sidney Geist, Petru Comarnescu similarly writes,[52] "believes that in order to be a peasant you have to wear folk costume all the time. He does not realise that Romanian peasants bear no resemblance to American farmers. Romanian peasants have their own spirituality, their own traditions, their own artistic style, which Brancusi expressed with genius."[53]

In order to impose this reading of the peasant/archaic character understood as a state of mind, Jianu resorts to an interesting strategy: that of inviting recognised figures to contribute to the following publications dedicated to Brancusi. Hoping to have it presented in Bucharest at the International "Brancusi" Colloquium in 1967, he published with Mircea Eliade and Petru Comarnescu a collection of three essays, *Témoignages sur Brâncuşi*, which "were oriented towards an understanding of the question of the origins and meaning of Brancusi's work along the natural lines of his belonging to his own tradition."[54] Although the attitude intersects in places with the official rehabilitation of Brancusi in Romania, whereby the "imposing figure of Brancusi all of a sudden became a 'national genius' alongside Eminescu and Enescu (themselves previously ostracised)," it nonetheless did not fit with the "materialist and atheist background of the promoted ideology."[55] Jianu's position towards the official Romanian policy (as well as towards Sidney Geist's interpretation[56]) is also reflected in *Introduction à la sculpture de Brancusi*, written in collaboration with Constantin Noica and first published in 1976, through comments such as the following: "Brancusi indeed wholly ignores the class struggle and historical materialism."[57] After the publication of the text, Noica wrote to him: "The fact that you begin by bringing to light Brancusi's peasant matrix might seem 'patriotic' for an instant; but straight away the reader sees what a sacral and well-structured meaning the peasant perspective has in our country. (…) all of a sudden you provide, like Mircea Eliade, a deep spiritual meaning to peasant rusticity and you are able to set the 'bucolic' (I might have said the 'metaphysical') in opposition to all ideologies."[58] Jianu argues for a reading of Brancusi in the key of the spirituality of the Romanian

---

52. In a letter dated 11 July 1964.

53. Ionel Jianu, *Brâncuşi*, Bucharest, Meridiane, 2002, p. 9.

54. Nina Stănculescu, in the foreword to *Mărturii despre Brâncuşi*, p. 9.

55. *Idem*, p. 8.

56. In a footnote Jianu explodes Sidney Geist's claim that "an entire series of Brancusi's works reveals his socialist sympathies." Ionel Jianu, *Brâncuşi*, p. 11.

57. Jianu, *op. cit.,* p. 11.

58. Cited by Mircea Handoca in the foreword to Ionel Jianu, *Brâncuşi*, Cluj, Dacia, 2003, p. 8.

peasant, elevated to a universal dimension by contact with the Western cultural context: "It is undeniable that the work of a Picasso, of a Chagall or of a Brancusi might have been different if it had not had the opportunity of benefiting from the stimulating contact with the Paris School. This contact freed their latent forces. (…) Their genius flourished beneath the sky of Paris, but their roots remained deeply embedded in their native soil."[59] He regards Brancusi as "an old shepherd, a peasant, a demiurge from the old folk legends"[60] and speaks of how in the work of Brancusi are reflected communion with nature, the sense of the cosmos, the symbols of a peasant culture with deep roots in prehistory.

The end of the chapter "The Brancusi Mystery" is relevant to Jianu's interpretation: "This wise man had been a shepherd in the Carpathians, who had come to Paris to hew in stone his own vision of the world, bringing with him the spiritual dowry of his ancestors and through his achievements opening up a new chapter of the human adventure in search of the miracle of life."[61]

"As far as we are concerned, we are happy to have been among the first to begin to elucidate the Romanian elements in Brancusi,"[62] says PETRU COMARNESCU of himself. An essayist, journalist, translator, and art and literary critic (also, as has been recently discovered, a Securitate informer[63]), he is acknowledged for his "intuitions as a man of culture, a writer with multiple talents, who had the professional scope of an interdisciplinary researcher, attentive to everything around him, without neglecting either the whole or the detail."[64] He was among the organisers of the first symposium dedicated to Brancusi in 1967, and his research into the life and work of the sculptor stretched over more than three decades. Despite this, he did not manage to gather together all these materials into the monograph on Brancusi he planned, and his only work on the subject was published posthumously.

Comarnescu was the first Brancusiologist to talk about Brancusi in terms of mythologisation, with all its advantages and disadvantages. As he writes in the foreword to the volume: "Around the genius of Brancusi and the work he left a myth has

59. Ionel Jianu, "Tradiţie şi universalitate în arta lui Brâncuşi" [Tradition and Universality in Brancusi's Art] in *Mărturii despre Brâncuşi*, p. 59.

60. Ionel Jianu, *Brâncuşi*, Bucharest, Meridiane, 2002, p. 7.

61. Jonel Jianu, *Brâncuşi*, Cluj, Dacia, 2003, p. 26.

62. Petru Comarnescu, *Brâncuşi: mit şi metamorfoză în sculptura contemporană* [Brancusi: Myth and Metamorphosis in Contemporary Sculpture], Bucharest, Meridiane, 1972, p.139.

63. Lucian Boia recently published *Dosarele secrete ale agentului Anton: Petru Comarnescu în arhivele Securităţii* [The Secret Dossiers of Agent Anton: Petru Comarnescu in the Archives of Securitate], Bucharest, Humanitas, 2014.

64. Monica Grosu, "Petru Comarnescu şi literatura confesivă" [Pentru Comarnescu and the Literature of Confession], *Pro Saeculum,* 3/2009, p. 30.

been woven. (…) Brancusi has become a battlefield for international and Romanian criticism, around which a modern myth is being created, as an occasion for scholarly explanations."[65] Like Ionel Jianu, he talks about "the presence and role of Romanian folkloric elements and of forms of folk style in Brancusi's creative act,"[66] but also about "their interpretation from the perspective of a cultivated artist"[67] and about "his humanist aspirations in which folklore interweaves with universality, and the archaic with the neo-primitivism of a spirit belonging to the modern world."[68] In his essay "Universality and National Specificity" he too takes a stand against Sidney Geist and the tendency on the part of "foreign commentators who know too little about our folklore and folk art to be able to perceive the Romanian roots of Brancusian creation and its very spirit, which is so bound to a particular vision and Romanian wisdom."[69] In the chapter "Brancusi's 'Peasanthood'" he regards peasanthood as "more a metaphor than a reality," emphasising the correlations between peasant and universal culture: "Only a tree with so deep roots, growing in bountiful soil and full of sap, can bring forth so beautiful fruits."[70] Comarnescu interprets along the same lines even Brancusi's journey to Paris on foot as "something natural to the former shepherd from the pastures of Bistrița, (…) a kind of spiritual transhumance for the sake of art." He even views Brancusi's clothes and accessories within the framework of peasant/universal confluences: the correct clothes and rucksack of the international tourist are contrasted with the cane and the flute "on which Brancusi played during moments of suffering and yearning for the homeland."[71] Comarnescu always stresses the notion of a synthesis, of a "fruitful encounter (…) between the course of world art and that of Romanian art, thereby forming a larger and more powerful course."[72] As Ruxandra Demetrescu notes, Comarnescu was also responsible for the broadest and most ambitious attempt to decipher "Romanian specificity," which he published in 1930, and in which he was interested in identifying the traits of the Romanian soul: "an especial feeling for nature, the sense of measure and liveliness which naturally and ineluctably bind together in a harmonious and pure serenity of life."[73]

---

65. Comarnescu, *op. cit.*, p. 17.

66. Petru Comarnescu, "Confluenţe în creaţia lui Brâncuşi. Elemente de folclor şi stil popular în procesul înnoitor al sculpturii mondiale" [Confluences in Brancusi's Creation. Folklore and Traditional Style Elements in the World Sculpture's Renewal Process] in *Mărturii despre Brâncuşi*, p. 27.

67. *Idem*, p. 37.

68. *Idem*, p. 51.

69. Petru Comarnescu, *Brâncuşi, mit şi metamorfoză în sculptura contemporană*, p. 139 (originally published in 1966 in *Tribuna* magazine).

70. *Idem*, p. 145.

71. *Idem*, p. 147.

72. *Idem*, p. 155.

73. Petru Comarnescu, "Specificul naţional în cultură şi artă" [The National Specificity in Culture and

Throughout his life, Barbu Brezianu's main occupation was research into the work of Brancusi, which, as Sorana Georgescu-Gorjan says in an article, "he understood with the subtlety of a poet."[74] He is a "symbol of spiritual resistance in the turbulent times that marked the history of Romanians in the twentieth century,"[75] and is perceived as an "extraordinary Brancusian Sherlock Holmes, who records with the liveliest intelligence and the liveliest seriousness all the data referring to our Maestro," constantly engaged in "open warfare against the profiteers of murky situations and the grobian peddlers of artistic fictions."[76] Of the same generation as Micea Eliade, Emil Cioran, Eugène Ionesco, Mircea Vulcănescu and Constantin Noica, he studied law and from 1934 to 1949 worked as a lawyer, prosecutor and judge. In 1949 he was arrested and sent to the Cape Midia construction site on the Danube-Black Sea Canal. In 1953, George Oprescu gave him a position as a part-time researcher at the Romanian Academy's Institute of Art History, which is the circumstance in which he became an art critic. Besides his activity as a poet, prose writer and translator, he was to be recognised as the most important Romanian Brancusiologist. Beginning with his articles on the sculptor's artistic origins published in the press of the 1960s, his contribution totals more than one hundred studies and articles for the foreign and Romanian press. Brezianu took part in the organisation of the two Brancusi exhibitions at the National Museum of Art in Bucharest in 1956 and 1970, also editing the catalogue for the second of these, and in 1967 he was involved in organising the first International "Brancusi" Colloquium. Starting with 1968, when he was awarded the Order of Cultural Merit of the Socialist Republic of Romania for "outstanding work in the field of the visual arts," he received various prizes and honorary titles, including Citizen of Honour of Târgu Jiu (1999) and Man of the Year 2001 on the occasion of International Brancusi Year.

Brezianu published his main study on Brancusi in four editions: 1974, 1976 (revised and expanded, with translations into French and English), 1998 (further revised and expanded), and 2005 (in English). In the preface to the 1998 and 2005 editions, Sidney Geist says: "Mr. Brezianu's impeccable scholarship, and unparalleled knowledge of the sculptor's Romanian background combine to make his study a mine of pertinent information, and of penetrating insights."[77] Indeed, the

---

Art] quoted in Ruxandra Demetrescu, *(Dis)continuități. Fragmente de modernitate românească în prima jumătate a secolului al 20-lea* [(Dis)continuities. Fragments of Romanian Modernity in the First Half of the 20th Century], Bucharest, Simetria, 2010, p. 169.

74. Sorana Georgescu-Gorjan, „Barbu Brezianu – Tinerețe și prietenie fără de sfîrșit" [Barbu Brezianu – Endless Youth and Friendship]; <http://centrulBrâncuși.ro/2013/01/14/barbu-brezianu-tinerete-si-prietenie-fara-de-sfarsit/>.

75. <http://www.arhiva-brezianu.ro/biografie—m153>.

76. Marcel Mihailovici and Pavel Șușară quoted in Sorana Georgescu-Gorjan, *op. cit.*

77. Sidney Geist in the introduction to Barbu Brezianu, *Brancusi in Romania*, Bucharest, Allfa, 2005, p. 4.

study displays obsessive research, down to the tiniest details, of Brancusi's life and work, an obsession that may also be perceived in the way in which Brezianu collects and archives absolutely all the items of information he finds about the sculptor. This archive, which may now be consulted at the Barbu Brezianu Centre for Brancusian Studies of the "George Oprescu" Institute of Art History in Bucharest, represents a major source for researchers interested in the life and work of the sculptor. Through this "rigorous and refined historiographical approach, a major landmark in Romanian and foreign Brancusiology,"[78] Brezianu considers his research to represent "an attempt at as accurate and complete a reconstitution as possible of the history, fortunes and even of the spirit in which Constantin Brancusi's works, existing now or that have existed at any time in Romania—sculptures, drawings and handicraft—, have been created."[79] All these are meticulously inventoried in his catalogue raisonné, including the copies authorised by the artist or not, and are presented in detail: the artist's signature, the collections and exhibitions in which they were included, the bibliography, and so on. Besides this inventory of works, the author also presents the sculptor's family tree, a chronology of important events in the life of Brancusi and his works, and various documents connected to his life, including a list of the addresses where he lived. The author's aim is that the sum of these data should also show "the attachment of the artist to his own country" and the appreciation he enjoyed in Romania from his adolescence to the threshold of old age.[80] He deplores the times after 1938, when direct contact with Brancusi's sculpture was negatively affected.[81] After 1989, he was responsible for the introduction of the theory that Brancusi wished to donate the contents of his studio to Romania, but was officially turned down at two sessions of the Academy of the People's Republic of Romania in March 1951, which allegedly led to the artist renouncing his Romanian citizenship and confessing: *"With the traitors in Bucharest I have nothing to discuss. They have sold the Romanian people to the Russians. I prefer to stay and die in France."*[82] As early as the 1970s, in his effort to present Brancusi as an artist who integrates into the "great circuit of universal values" living folklore and an austere art which "for millennia has been practised in the old Geto-Thracian area,"[83] Brezianu sometimes takes a protochronist view, present-

---

78. <http://www.arhiva-brezianu.ro/biografie—m153>.

79. Brezianu, *op. cit.*, p. 7.

80. *Idem*, p. 11.

81. Barbu Brezianu, *Brâncuşi*, exhibition catalogue from the Museum of Art of the Romanian Socialist Republic, published by the State Committee for Culture and Art, 1970, p. 8.

82. Quoted from a written account by Dumitru Mazilu who received the information directly from the former ambassador of the People's Republic of Romania to Paris, to whom Brancusi made this remark during a visit viewed by Brezianu as a "tardy mission of reconciliation." Brezianu, *Brancusi in Romania*, p. 13.

83. Barbu Brezianu, *Brâncuşi*, exhibition catalogue, pp. 9–10.

ing the sculptor as an "absolute classic of sculpture," as a "forerunner of tactile sculpture (…) of architectural sculpture, of kinetic sculpture."[84]

NINA STĂNCULESCU, "the most sensitive, loving and subtle researcher of Brancusi's work,"[85] is a graduate of the Faculty of Literature and Philosophy and of the Theological Institute. She made her literary debut in 1954 with a children's story called "The Linnets' Nest," later reprinted in the collection *Gnats, Flowers and Lots of Children*. In 1964 she joined the Meridiane publishing house as an editor, and began to publish works of art criticism and history, many of them on the culture of the Far East. "The last survivor of an exceptional family of Brancusiologists that included Barbu Brezianu and Ion Pogorilovschi,"[86] she has dedicated a large part of her research to the figure of Brancusi, in individual works and also in anthologies and translations of books about the sculptor's life and work. This continuous devotion, according to the author, is the result of an encounter with Petru Comarnescu, who opened to her the "gates to the great titan,"[87] and was rewarded in 1987 with an Honorary Degree from Bucharest University, and in 2002 with the Brancusi Prize for Excellence, bestowed by Târgu Jiu Municipal Hall. Nina Stănculescu's "obsessive preoccupation with Brancusi" began in 1972, with the posthumous publication of Petru Comarnescu's *Myth and Metamorphosis in Contemporary Sculpture*, leading her to conclude her doctoral thesis on "The Concept of Nature in Modern Art" with an exegesis of Brancusi's work "as a powerful and obvious example of modern art once more rooting itself in nature, thereby expressing a deeply human and deeply Romanian signifier."[88]

Nina Stănculescu's next published work on Brancusi dates from 1976 and marked the centenary and the "Brancusi" Colloquium in Bucharest—*A Book from the Heart for Brancusi*. We can detect an emotional note in the very title, which might be interpreted through the filter of gender-related discussions: a solitary figure among the great mass of male Brancusiologists, Nina Stănculescu, "almost overwhelmed by the texts she has traversed,"[89] makes "a selection from the 'heart,'" content to gather "fleeting rays, a bundle of light, as large as his stature" in a "homage to him

---

84. *Idem*, pp. 12, 117.

85. Mioara Mincu, foreword to Nina Stănculescu, *Brâncuşi: Rugăciune pentru mileniul III* [Brancusi: Prayer for the Third Millenium], Bucharest, Carol Davila, 2001, p. 5.

86. Magdalena Popa Buluc, "Carte de inimă despre Brâncuşi, artistul care voia sa sculpteze lumina" [A Book from the Heart about Brancusi, the Artist Who Wanted to Sculpt the Light], *Cotidianul*, 16 October 2010.

87. Nina Stănculescu, *Carte de inimă pentru Brâncuşi* [A Book from the Heart for Brancusi], Bucharest, Albatros, 1976, p. 5.

88. Nina Stănculescu, *Brâncuşi*, Bucharest, Albatros, 1981, p. 159.

89. *Ibidem*.

whose heart overflowed in its striving and simple and tireless labour to draw closer, through his works, to the most secret core of our hearts."[90] The author confesses that, after the experience of editing the volume, "the presence of Brancusi and his work to her personally, far from concluding what it had to say, on the contrary continued to go deeper," giving birth in 1981 to a second book from the heart for Brancusi. The book is not "a fictionalised biography, nor a scholarly monograph, but rather a kind of 'spiritual journal,'" in which the author tries in vain to avoid "the effusions of an affection that she knows cannot be fully hidden,"[91] and finally she embraces this subjectivity. All the topics that Nina Stănculescu develops are here extremely idealised: the communion with nature exemplified in the life of the village of Hobiţa, "a village of pastors and shepherds, fleet of mind and wise, for centuries in brotherhood with the sky, the mountains, the waters, the earth and the roads, with dangers, with the beauty and the deep cogitation of these things";[92] the "urbanisation"[93] of Brancusi that began in Craiova and was completed in the "crucible"[94] of Paris, which, surprisingly, leads him to find himself once more in Romanian spirituality; the sufferings and cursed solitude of the genius which are interpreted as "wide-ranging communion with all that surrounds him, with all those who surround him, with the works of nature and of his own hands, with the entire universe, with himself";[95] the discipline and obsession of labour to be found in the recurring image "Brancusi hews" (despite all the difficulties he encounters); the artist's studio, the "forge," "ceases to be the hidden backdrop of his achievement, the backstage of the performance," and becomes "the authentic, lay temple of human existence," where "life, that is, creation, flows from every part, envelops you and blossoms."[96] Here we also encounter the author's fascination for oriental culture. She believes that it was Brancusi's obsession "to reshape the sculptural tradition according to the criteria of the Far East (of which he was not even aware) and of his ancestors inscribing in wood, in clay or wool their existence and continuance."[97] Finally, she explains the universality of Brancusi's art via a concept (close to what we might call today globalisation) connected to Romania's geopolitical context: "An exponent of liminal lands and a continuous connection between all roads, those of the migratory peoples, of merchants, of diplomatic and cultural exchanges between North and South, between the oriental East and the occidental West,

90. Nina Stănculescu, *Carte de inimă pentru Brâncuşi*, p. 5.
91. Nina Stănculescu, *Brâncuşi*, pp. 159–160.
92. *Idem*, p. 9.
93. *Idem*, p. 13.
94. *Idem*, p. 67.
95. *Idem*, p. 103.
96. *Idem*, pp. 98–104.
97. *Idem*, p. 90.

Brancusi achieved this communion of feeling and thought, according to the dimensions of a profoundly human response of his times to human fate."[98]

We may also note a certain amount of ideological opportunism in the arguments employed to contextualise Brancusi. In her pre-1989 publications, Nina Stănculescu tried to justify the value of Brancusi's work via the connection between the influence of folk art on the sculptor's work and the values of the "people," or the proletariat to be more precise, defined using a quotation from Karl Marx as "the most progressive, revolutionary, organised part of society, with demands of transformations that encompass the whole of humanity." She calls Brancusi the "exponent of the masses," mentioning that "it has been recorded that he had links with the socialist movement," and argues that "the tenacious work of Brancusi is thereby joined, literally, to the struggle waged at the social and political level by the leaders of the revolutionary movement of his time." She even quotes Anatoly Lunacharsky, who "was impressed by the art of Brancusi, intuiting primarily its high traditional strain," and who believed that his works in metal belonged to "neo-realist directions."[99]

The volumes she published after 1989, on the other hand, emphasise the Christian Orthodox dimension of the work of this "sublime craftsman in the tradition of his grandfather, who is said to have hewn an entire church with a hatchet"[100]—also known as "the great patriarch of Hobița"[101]—a dimension that draws on the guidance of Father Dumitru Stăniloaie, who supervised Stănculescu's degree dissertation at the Theological Institute. Some commentators believe that "she became accustomed to theological reflection thanks to inner reading of the works of the Craftsman from Hobița, in which she deciphered the Creation of the World, Love, Wisdom, the Theophanies..."[102] Brancusi's work is now presented as "evolving continuously towards the perfection of spiritual Beauty radiating the beneficial forces of a pure Joy of divine grace,"[103] and the town of Târgu Jiu as a space that has become sacred as a result of its vicinity with Tismana Monastery, which, according to the sayings of Metropolitan Serafim, "is a centre of spiritual radiation for the entire country."[104] Nina Stănculescu regards even the similarity between the Brancusian public monument in Târgu Jiu and the Dacian sanctuary at

---

98. *Idem*, p. 152.

99. The chapter "Idealul lui Homo Aestheticus" [The Ideal of Homo Aestheticus] in Nina Stănculescu, *Izvoare și cristalizări în opera lui Brâncuși*, pp. 62–80.

100. Nina Stănculescu, *Brâncuși: Frumos și har* [Brancusi: Beauty and Grace], Târgu Jiu, Editura Fundației "Constantin Brâncuși", 1997, p. 23.

101. Mioara Mincu, foreword to Nina Stănculescu, *Brâncuși: Rugăciune pentru mileniul III*, p. 5.

102. Virgil Cândea in "Scurtă introducere" [Short Introduction] to Nina Stănculescu, *Brâncuși: Rugăciune pentru mileniul III*, p. 8.

103. Nina Stănculescu, *Brâncuși: Rugăciune pentru mileniul III*, p. 9.

104. *Idem*, p. 128.

Sarmisegetuza as due to "the ancestral experience according to archetypes, Christianly decanted and organically fulfilling themselves in modernity," and she believes that the Târgu Jiu ensemble is "a focus of radiation and salvation from dissolution for an entire universe."[105] In her most recent publication, *The Brancusian Temple of Love*, Nina Stănculescu describes Brancusi as a representative of this "blessed space of Hesychastic beliefs that gradually and profoundly infiltrated the mentality and even the everyday life of people," who felt the need "to implant into mimetically anthropomorphic sculpture the vastness of the spaces of cosmic nature, at the same time renewing the lost connection with transcendence, with God, from ancient symbolic art, such as that of his ancestors" and who left behind him "a vast work, like a healing herb against the nihilism, confusion and divisions of our times."[106]

CONSTANTIN ZĂRNESCU is a writer and journalist, who, since 1972, has worked as an editor for the *Tribuna* cultural journal, a publication that has played an important role in the history of Brancusiology, publishing since 1964 almost weekly articles, memoirs, essays, studies and translations to do with Brancusi's life and work. In 1976 he edited *Homage to Brancusi*, and besides his work as an editor for the magazine, Zărnescu published between 1980 and 2007 five editions of *The Aphorisms and Texts of Brancusi*, as well as a number of books on the sculptor, the most recent of which is *The Code of Brancusi's Works*—whence I extracted the definition of Brancusiology that opens this chapter—which the author claims to be a "critical vision" on which he laboured for almost forty years.[107] In the preface to the first edition of the *Aphorisms*, Marin Sorescu says that although Zărnescu "is not a member of the caste of philosophers or art critics, the author possesses the organ of the 'idea,' the passion to unite with precision of taste" and presents him as the youngest Brancusiologist to "venture to deal with the creator of the *Sleeping Muse*, after his work was bound in leather boards as definitive and as buckled as the Bible by fanatical researchers such as V. G. Paleolog and Petre Pandrea, to mention only the Romanians, and only the Oltenians among the Romanians."[108] Proof of recognition of Zărnescu's contribution to decoding Brancusi's works came in 1997, when he was awarded the Prize of Gorj Prefecture for the sum of his Brancusiological activity.

Zărnescu constructs his theories around the motif of the eye, which he interprets in Brancusi's works as representing "the philosophical-mythological concept

---

105. *Idem*, p. 131.

106. Nina Stănculescu, *Templul brâncuşian al iubirii* [The Brancusian Temple of Love], Bucharest, Editura Online Virtual, 2011, pp. 4–10.

107. Constantin Zărnescu, *Codul operei lui Brâncuşi*, p. 10.

108. Marin Sorescu, preface to Constantin Zărnescu, *Aforismele şi textele lui Brâncuşi* [Brancusi's Aphorisms and Texts], Craiova, Scrisul Românesc, 1980, pp. 5–6.

of endless life through which the man, the artist, the Christian praises God's Great work."[109] The chapter on the "sole eye" of the *Kiss* is called "A Unique Revolution in the Long History of Art. *The Kiss*, the Mythological-Political Equality of Man and Woman" and proceeds from Sidney Geist's comment: "No kiss from any other historical period is in more intimate accord with contemporary feminist thought, for Brancusi's love embrace is in perfect equality."[110] The gaze of *Mademoiselle Pogany* is viewed as belonging simultaneously to a Byzantine figure and a real woman, seemingly subdued "before the patriarchal myth of masculinity." Zărnescu here refers to the Jocasta Complex and wonders whether Brancusi, "so knowledgeable in matters of the myth of femininity," thought of the same thing.[111] The rhomboid module of the *Endless Column* is viewed as originating in "the ancient Carpathian civilisation of wood," where it represents "the eye of the house" replacing even the "divine triangle" or the "sole eye of the Creator" on the frontispiece of Orthodox churches built by peasant craftsmen.[112]

The eye is conceived on the one hand in a mystic register, as a "magic corridor of the profound inner initiatory journeys," and on the other hand as a generator of the "civilisation of the image, of today's audio-visual."[113]

ION POGORILOVSCHI, essayist and philosopher of culture, graduated from the University of Iași with a Degree in Philosophy and went on to take a doctorate with a thesis on Brancusi's *Road of the Heroes' Souls*, first published in 1976, followed by an English translation in 1987 and republished in 2000 in an expanded Romanian edition. He confesses that even when he was an assistant lecturer in the Philosophy Department of Iași University working on his doctorate, "the art of Brancusi represented the space of redemptive retreat for his philosophical meditation, at the time harshly controlled at the social level," and "ten years later, when the 'doctor in philosophy' had become an unqualified labourer in a factory, in order to resist marginalisation, he began to review and expand his work dedicated to the Sculptor."[114] Pogorilovschi made a name for himself as a Brancusiologist and philosopher of culture, with a large part of his work being dedicated to Brancusi and to the Monumental Ensemble at Târgu Jiu in particular. At the "Constantin

---

109. Constantin Zărnescu, *Brâncuși și civilizația imaginii* [Brancusi and the Civilization of Image], Cluj, Dacia, 2001, p. 110.

110. *Idem*, pp. 12–14.

111. *Idem*, pp. 73–74.

112. *Idem*, pp. 107–108.

113. *Idem*, pp. 110–111.

114. Ion Pogorilovschi, *Brâncuși, apogeul imaginarului: Comentarea capodoperei de la Târgu Jiu* [Brancusi, the Apogee of the Imaginary: A Commentary on the Masterpiece from Târgu Jiu], Târgu Jiu, Editura Fundației "Constantin Brâncuși", 2000, p. 7.

Brancusi" Municipal Cultural Centre, he initiated and edited the *Brancusiana* series of books and was editor-in-chief of the *Brancusi* journal from 1995 to 2000. In the introduction to *Brancusi, the Apogee of the Imaginary*, Pogorilovschi confesses that the publication of the book in the *Brancusiana* collection, "from the sculptor's native hearth," is "felt by the author to be a felicitous consonance in space, a consonance that fulfils his entire exegetic project."[115] In the obituary published in the Târgu Jiu local press, he is presented as being among those who "toiled till the last moment of their lives at the court of the Last Gorj Emperor" and who "will be reunited in the heavens with the immortal Brancusi, having on earth enlightened mortals with their understanding of what the man from Hobița bequeathed us." From the same article we also find out that "Ion Pogorilovschi's greatest disappointment was and remains the failure to found in Târgu Jiu the World Institute of Constantin Brancusi Studies and Research," to which he planned to donate his entire library.[116] He also published works on the philosophy of culture, such as *The Archetype of Romanian Lyric Expression* and *The Eminescu Miracle. Three Generative Approaches*, and in his works on Brancusi he often drew parallels with the folk poem *Miorița* and the poetry of Eminescu. He adopts the term *necroeroticism* from George Călinescu's analyses of Eminescu's poetry and develops the idea of a connection between Brancusi's work, *Miorița* and, of course, the national sensibility: "After the older creation of *Miorița*—a masterpiece of Romanian literature—here is Brancusi's *Road* which, in the heart of a modern epoch, emphasises in a masterly way a thrilling recurrence: the same marvellous topos of artistic expression—the topos death/wedding. It certainly belongs to the indestructible nucleus of the Romanians' vision of the world."[117] He believes that the term *necroeroticism* is unjustifiably too seldom employed in Brancusiology and sees this as a "deficiency, a methodological shortcoming, since it is precisely the meaning of this term that optimally expresses the ideational and emotional superabundance of the Brancusian theme of *The Kiss*."[118] Extrapolating from the theme of the kiss, he interprets the *Boundary Stone* as a "sculptural personification of the two territories kindred by blood (Bessarabia and Northern Bukowina) closely embracing over and above the injustice of the world's history" and speaks of "the patriotism of Brancusian creation that leaves behind the templates of the doctrinaire and ideological bluster."[119] This theory is put for-

---

115. *Idem*, p. 8.

116. <http://stirile.rol.ro/De-ce-n-a-ajuns-la-Targu-Jiu-Colectia-Pogorilovschi—352423.html>.

117. Ion Pogorilovschi, *A Commentary on the Masterpiece of Brancusi: The Road of the Heroes' Souls*, Iași, Junimea, 1987, p. 281.

118. Ion Pogorilovschi, *Brâncuși: Geneza 1905-1907* [Brancusi: Genesis 1905–1907], Bucharest, Universalia, 2007, p. 289.

119. Ion Pogorilovschi, "'Bornă pentru provinciile românești' – un gînd pentru Basarabia și Bucovina de Nord" ['A Landmark for Romanian Provinces' – a Thought for Bessarabia and Northern

ward by Pogorilovschi in *Brancusiana and Brancusiada* (2000), a collection of articles published over the course of thirty years, in thirty different periodicals, and which in his eyes is "a kind of report on a lifetime's preoccupation: researches and meditation induced by the most illustrious avatar of the Romanian creative type in art."[120] In 2001 he was appointed to the national commission organising the commemorative events to mark the International Brancusi Year and held a scholarly conference at the Philosophy Institute, with the talks being published in the volume *Brancusi, Artist-Philosopher*. In 2002 he published a second collection of articles and essays dedicated to the sculptor, *The Last and the First*. In more recent volumes, such as *Brancusi: Sophrosyne or the Wisdom of the Earth* (2005) and *Brancusi: Genesis 1905-1907* (2007), he continued to "relate the sculptor's work, imaginary and self more closely to his native ethno-cultural space" and to "promote in Brancusiology the method of archetypal criticism as one that is par excellence suited to and evidentiary of the modernity of the Romanian creator."[121] Thus, although he recognises that he is primarily interested in the consonance of the Târgu Jiu Monumental Ensemble with the "symbolic patterns of thought peculiar to the Carpathian ambience or space" and with the "Romanian tradition in its most genuine and profound aspects," he believes that beyond the ethnic framework, Brancusi opens up to analysis "the comprehensive area of the invariants of universal symbolic thought," which is "unitary (in its diversity) with the whole of mankind."[122]

RADU VARIA is one of the most controversial Romanian Brancusiologists. An art critic and historian, Varia left the country at the beginning of the 1970s and settled in Paris and then New York. For the last twenty years, he has collaborated with various institutions in the international art and academic context, has organised exhibitions and has published texts about the work of Horia Damian. He regarded himself as a good friend of Salvador Dalí, who, according to Varia, asked him to join him in the conception of his museum in Figueras and who even dedicated a poem to him, *Oui! à la Roumanie. Pour Radu Varia*, which ends with the words: "And to be like him, and forever, I proclaim myself Salvador Dalí, Catholic, apostolic, Roman and Romanian published."[123]

<hr>

Bukowina], article from 1990 republished in Ion Pogorilovschi, *Brâncuşiana şi Brâncuşiada* [Brancusiana and Brancusiada], Bucharest, Eminescu, 2000, pp. 60–68.

120. Ion Pogorilovschi, introduction to *Brâncuşiana şi Brâncuşiada*, p. 5.

121. *Idem*, p. 6.

122. Ion Pogorilovschi, *A Commentary on the Masterpiece of Brâncuşi: The Road of the Heroes' Souls*, pp. 241–242.

123. "Magdalena Popa Buluc în dialog cu criticul Radu Varia, Doctor în Istoria artei şi civilizaţiei al Universităţii din Paris: 'În artă, ce nu e legat de spiritualitate nu valorează nimic'" [Magdalena Popa Buluc in conversation with art critic Radu Varia, PhD in the History of Art and Civilisation

In 1986, Rizzoli published Varia's book about Brancusi, the result of his constant interest in the sculptor's work, which was republished in French and Japanese in the following years. At the time, as Sidney Geist notes in a review, there were not many publications about Brancusi by Romanian authors that had been translated into English (apart from Barbu Brezianu's 1976 book, which had not, however, been widely available). Geist sees Brancusi as "a valid reason for national pride," giving this as the reason for the plethora of Romanian exegeses: "Anyone in Romania who has an opinion on anything has one on Brancusi." Geist, who recognised the value of Brezianu's research, regards Varia's book as "immediately recognisable as a glamorous product of the coffee-table genre, too extravagant in its images and design, while the text employs a literary style relentlessly overblown, numbingly flamboyant and cultural references too diverse: like other works on Brancusi, this one cannot deal with its subject without constantly invoking all the great names and texts in the history of thought, as though Brancusi's eminence were to be established by association: Balzac, the Bhagavad Gita, Blavatsky, Bloy, Buddha, the Cabala, Calvino, Coomaraswami, Dante. (...) In this book I see for the first time a poem by Huang-Chong-Ki."[124]

Varia presents Brancusi to the international public in a manner that is over-spectacular: "Constantin Brâncuşi, the greatest sculptor of modern times, was born in Romania. (...) These lands are a repository of ancient European civilizations, redolent with Celtic mythology, predisposing their people to a spontaneous vibrant awareness of archaic consciousness. (...) Whenever a genius succeeds in bringing the archaic values to life in a work that vivifies them, such a work becomes coeval with the origin of all things."[125]

Despite his rather dubious hypotheses as to Brancusi's connections with Milarepa, freemasonry in Craiova, alchemy, Celtic mythology and Egyptian culture, Varia is received as a specialist in Brancusiology and immediately after the changes of 1989 he organised an exhibition titled *Brancusi: Masterpieces from Romanian Museums* at the Gagossian Gallery in New York. The exhibition would have later been travelled at museums in Detroit, Baltimore and Washington, but the plans were halted as a result of public concern in Romania regarding the possibility that the works might not be returned to the country, which led Minister of Culture Andrei Pleşu to cancel all previous arrangements. The American press quoted Sidney

of the Paris University: 'In art, what does not relate to spirituality has no value'], *Cotidianul*, 16 December 2011; <http://www.cotidianul.ro/in-arta-ce-nu-e-legat-de-spiritualitate-nu-valoreaza-nimic-167159/>.

124. Sidney Geist, "Brancusi, Brancusi: A review of *Brancusi* by Radu Varia and *Brancusi* by Pontus Hultén, et al.," *The New Criterion*, Volume 6, January 1988, p. 60; <http://www.newcriterion.com/articles.cfm/Brâncuşi—Brâncuşi-5955>.

125. Radu Varia, *Brancusi*, New York, Rizzoli International Publications, 1986, p. 11.

Geist, who believed that this had to do with Brancusi's reception in Romania: "The more his reputation grew outside, the more they came to accept him politically in Romania. For that reason the debate over the itinerant sculptures found its way to the National Assembly, where senators made stirring speeches about the necessity of protecting their national patrimony."[126] This event was the first in a series of public scandals, which led to Radu Varia being perceived in Romania as having a personal financial interest in Brancusi, as being an enemy of Romania who wanted to sell Brancusi, literally and figuratively, to the foreigners.

In 1991, Radu Varia founded the "Constantin Brancusi" International Foundations in New York and Bucharest, which enjoyed the political support of the Iliescu regime in the initiative to restore the Monumental Ensemble in Târgu Jiu. Although Varia regarded the initiative as "the most important, most generous and most competent to have been taken by anybody since 1989 in the benefit of Romanian art, and the final, disastrous result is exactly commensurate with the stupidity, incompetence and dishonesty of those who hindered the finalisation of the project,"[127] the decision to dismantle the *Endless Column* made him a persona non grata locally, proof of which were protests and open letters from Târgu Jiu against the project. Gathered together at the "120th Anniversary of the Birth of Constantin Brancusi" National Symposium held in Târgu Jiu, local specialists argued that there was "a subtle patriotic connotation in the fact that Brancusi did not ask for foreign specialists to produce his Masterpiece in our spiritual space" and that this tacit connotation was about to be damaged through "the attempt to transform the operations to restore and conserve the Brancusian works in Târgu Jiu into a personal business" of Radu Varia.[128] In an account of the proceedings of the symposium, Zenovie Cârlugea talks about a "conspiracy of silence that reeks of a boycott and national betrayal," which gave rise to the protest against the "'Europeanists' who have forgotten the tradition and the already universalised values of Romanian culture."[129]

More recently, another project in which Radu Varia was involved, as the organiser of a permanent exhibition that would have presented his project to restore the

---

126. "Bucharest, Brancusi Brouhaha," *Artnews*, March 1991, reproduced in *Brancusi: Masterpieces from Romanian Museums*, catalogue published by Gagossian Gallery New York, 2011.

127. "Magdalena Popa Buluc în dialog cu criticul Radu Varia, Doctor în Istoria artei şi civilizaţiei al Universităţii din Paris: 'În artă, ce nu e legat de spiritualitate nu valorează nimic'", *Cotidianul*, 16 December 2011; <http://www.cotidianul.ro/in-arta-ce-nu-e-legat-de-spiritualitate-nu-valoreaza-nimic-167159/>.

128. Open letter to the Government of Romania, reproduced in *Brâncuşi, acum. Comunicări Ştiinţifice prezentate în cadrul Simpozionului "Brâncuşiana 96" organizat la Târgu Jiu* [Brancusi Now. Scholarly Presentations at the 'Brancusiana 96' Symposium Organised at Târgu Jiu], Târgu Jiu, Editura Fundaţiei "Constantin Brâncuşi", 1997, pp. 154–155.

129. Zenovie Cârlugea, "Simpozionul Naţional *Constantin Brâncuşi, 120 de ani de la naştere*" in *Idem*, p. 161.

Endless Column, involved the opening of a "Brancusi" Interpretation and Visitors Centre as a result of a partnership between the World Monuments Fund, the Romania Infinity Foundation/Ioana Banu Ertegün and Ahmet Ertegün and Târgu Jiu Municipality. The project was abandoned in 2011 as a result of pressure from the local community, which viewed it as "an unprecedented act of cultural terrorism that violates the most intimate wellsprings of the national cultural identity."[130]

Since the 1990s, Radu Varia has given lectures on Brancusi at the Romanian Academy and at various international universities and cultural institutions, and in 2011, he gave the Sir William Gillies Annual Lecture at the Royal Scottish Academy in Edinburgh, on the subject "Brancusi, A Great Spiritual Experience." On that occasion he was decorated with the Silver Medal of the Royal Scottish Academy, and in the same year, President of Romania Traian Băsescu awarded him the Romanian Order of Cultural Merit, for "Radu Varia's personal contribution to the enrichment of the Romanian and universal cultural heritage."

A writer, art critic and art historian, as well as a graduate of the Faculty of Orthodox Theology in Bucharest, CRISTIAN-ROBERT VELESCU currently teaches Art History at the National University of Arts in Bucharest. He is the author of a number of volumes on modernity and the historic avant-garde, and has a particular interest in the work of Constantin Brancusi. His doctoral thesis, which he defended at the Art Academy in Bucharest in 1991, *Iconological References in the Work of Constantin Brancusi*, was published two years later as *Brancusi the Initiate*, followed in the late 1990s by a further two works: *Brancusi Alchemist* and *The Concepts of Constantin Brancusi's Poetics*. In 2004, with Doina Lemny he edited *Undiscovered Brancusi. Notes and Romanian Correspondence*.

Unlike many fellow Brancusiologists, in these works Velescu does not speculate on Romanian spirituality in relation to universal spirituality. Besides the already established sources of Romanian folklore and oriental thought, he introduces a third, Platonism, exploring it in connection with initiatory, esoteric Pythagoreanism, Eleusianism and even alchemy. This theory, which is "rigorous, elegantly constructed and profoundly contributory in its hypotheses and conclusions,"[131] is based on the books in Brancusi's library, his presumed readings and his presumed exchanges of ideas on these subjects with certain cultural figures with whom he was in contact. In his third book, the author outlines "the more general coordinates of a Brancusian 'poetic,' one firmer and 'truer' than that which might be derived

---

130. Narcis Daju, "Opriţi asasinarea lui Brâncuşi!" [Stop the Assassination of Brancusi!], open letter, 18 February 2011; <http://www.gorjnews.ro/slider/opriti-asasinarea-lui-Brâncuşi-scrisoare-deschisa.html>.

131. Barbu Brezianu, foreword to Cristian-Robert Velescu, *Brâncuşi iniţiatul* [Brancusi the Initiate], Bucharest, Editis, 1994, p. 9.

from a mere reading of the 'aphorisms', which are often phantasmal and distorted through uncritical reading."[132] Although Velescu on numerous occasions underlines that he does not wish to portray Brancusi as an artist philosopher, but to present the Platonic philosophy as one of the many sources for his art, he nonetheless openly distances himself from those exegeses that emphasise the Romanian folkloric source, even dedicating a chapter of his *Concepts of Constantin Brancusi's Poetics* to the question "How much of a 'peasant' was Brancusi?" He interprets the biographical details of Brancusi's childhood, his attempts to run away from home to be more precise, as attempts to separate himself from the rural context: "the repeated escapes might be interpreted as a genuine and obviously premature renunciation of the peasant world and implicitly the folkloric universe that it is supposed still to have conserved at the end of the nineteenth century"[133] and concludes: "traditional art and folklore are not part of the meaningful substance of Brancusi's work."[134] Adopting the discourse of international critics such as Margit Rowell and Friedrich Teja Bach, who argue that only Romanian exegesis regards folklore as a principal source for Brancusi's work, Velescu is convinced that such a claim will not be accepted by the Romanian Brancusiologists who insist on "the 'folklorised' wellspring, which they are a priori and at all costs determined to discover, and which reveals itself to be the true fata morgana of Brancusiology."[135]

DOINA LEMNY is one of the most active researchers from the diaspora to have dedicated their careers to the study of Brancusi's work. She defended her doctoral thesis on Brancusi at the Sorbonne in 1997. Although she emigrated to Paris in the early 1990s, Lemny still regards herself as very close to Romania, as she declares in an interview: *"The fact that I live and work in Paris does not mean I have turned my back on Romania, on the contrary, I believe I have done the country a greater cultural service here than I would have done in Iași, where I began my career. And then again, my country, our country, is Europe. I cannot but quote Brancusi in this respect, who lived in a world without borders: 'My homeland, my family! It is the world that spins, the breath of the wind, the passing clouds, the water that flows, the fire that warms, the green grass—the dry grass, the soil, the snow.'"*[136]

---

132. Cristian-Robert Velescu, *Conceptele poeticii lui Constantin Brâncuși* [The Concepts of Constantin Brancusi's Poetics], Bucureşti, Univers enciclopedic, 1999, p. 6.

133. *Idem*, p. 177.

134. *Idem*, p. 181.

135. *Idem*, p. 184.

136. Silvia Vrînceanu Nichita, "Doina Lemny – O focşăneancă are grijă de 'moştenirea' Brâncuşi la Paris" [Doina Lemny – A Woman from Focşani Takes Care of Brancusi's 'Legacy' in Paris], interview in *Ziarul de Vrancea*, reproduced in <http://lapasprinvrancea.blogspot.ro/2011/04/doina-lemny-o-focsaneanca-are-grija-de.html>.

Since 1990, Lemny has worked at the Centre Georges Pompidou. She has been involved in the study of the Brancusi archive in the collection of this institution and in the third reconstruction of the sculptor's studio. As a result of this research, she edited *L'Atelier Brancusi, La Collection* (1997), the seven issues of *Les Carnets de l'Atelier Brancusi* (1998–2002), *La Dation Brancusi: dessins et archives* (2003) and *Brancusi* (2012). Besides publications for the Centre Georges Pompidou, she has also published other studies on the sculptor, including *Brancusi* (2005), *Brancusi au-delà de toutes les frontières* (2012) and, in collaboration with Cristian-Robert Velescu, one of the most important contributions to Romanian exegesis, *Undiscovered Brancusi. Notes and Romanian Correspondence* (2004).

She believes that "the mystery Brancusi cultivated lends charm to the figure and obliges the researcher to continue analysis of the work and to try to grasp its relationship with the creator,"[137] that "the life and the work are inseparable in his case"[138] and that despite the details about Brancusi's personality present in his studio notes, in his correspondence and in the testimonies of those who knew him, he remains a mysterious figure. In her view, Brancusi represents "a successful combination of the peasant from the Carpathians and the modern artist from Montparnasse,"[139] and his "atypical and impossible to classify" work will always preserve its "secret."[140] She sees him as an *homme du monde*, as he called himself many times, whose work "seems to have its origins in the art of the Cyclades, in the Romanian Neolithic, in more recent African art or in the Far East."[141]

This exegetical view that promotes an image of the universal artist leads Lemny to take a critical stance against the initiative to repatriate Brancusi's remains and against the reinvention of the Memorial House at Hobița. In an interview, she declares: "everything that is being bandied about now, 'our Brancusi,' the return of Brancusi's bones, are comedies that ought not to be taken seriously" and "to be buried in Montparnasse Cemetery is an honour." She urges that we concentrate on deciphering the universal meaning of the sculptor's work: "Brancusi remains a native of Gorj, he remains a Romanian, but he is universal and this is what everybody needs to understand."[142] In this respect, the events and commemorations she

---

137. *Ibidem.*

138. Doina Lemny, *Constantin Brancusi*, Paris, Oxus, 2005, p. 15.

139. Doina Lemny, *Brâncuşi, artistul care transgresează toate hotarele* [Brancusi, the Artist Who Transgresses All Borders], Bucharest, Noi Media Print, 2012, p. 6.

140. Doina Lemny, *Constantin Brancusi*, pp. 14, 15.

141. *Idem*, p. 12.

142. Doina Lemny quoted in Minodora Sucea, "Doina Lemny: 'Revenirea osemintelor lui Brâncuşi – o comedie...'" [Doina Lemny: 'The Return of Brancusi's Remains – a Comedy...'], *Gorjeanul*, 17 March 2013; <http://www.gorjeanul.ro/actualitate/doina-lemny-%E2%80%9Erevenirea-osemintelor-lui-Brâncuşi-%E2%80%93-o-comedie%E2%80%A6%E2%80%9D#.U3xmr9KSzj4>.

has initiated or in which she has participated have always combined national pathos with the universal: various celebratory evenings organised in partnership with the Romanian Cultural Institute in Paris in the 2000s, and more recently a documentary film[143] which combines a poetic vision with a pedagogic commentary, produced for a *Homage to Brancusi* exhibition at the European Parliament in Strasbourg. She was also involved in the procedure to have the Monumental Ensemble in Târgu Jiu declared a UNESCO World Heritage site.

As one of the few women Brancusiologists of Romanian nationality, we cannot but draw a parallel with Nina Stănculescu, remarking on the same type of relationship to Brancusi, which might be interpreted as "feminine." For example, she believes that the sculptor, "in his effort to attenuate the hardness of his materials, resorts to poetry and tenderness; he does not strike the marble or the wood: his gesture is that of a caress, whereby he imprints soul on them."[144] She is even interested in Brancusi's love life, mentioning that he was "adored by all the women who met him,"[145] and dedicating to the subject an entire chapter ("'Les femmes': muses, amies, amantes") of her 2005 work. Like any other genuine Brancusiologist, she declares that she has dedicated her entire life to her research, but her seriousness in this endeavour also combines with passion: *Without passion, to me research is barren, without interest, and becomes uninteresting for the reader too.*[146]

Discussing Doina Lemny's most recent work on Brancusi, Cristian-Robert Velescu remarks on a change of approach and a more obvious scholarly caution. He believes that the author "has imposed upon herself, obviously of her own free will, certain sacrifices. She has given up—probably not without a pang of regret—the substantial, juicy documentary information which in the Oxus monograph seemed to flow 'as from a wellspring' in favour of this more measured approach, which leaves generous 'space for evolution' to the most applied visual analysis."[147]

MATEI STÎRCEA-CRĂCIUN, a doctor of anthropology and history, is currently a researcher at the Romanian Academy's "Francisc Rainer" Institute of Anthropology.

---

143. *Ansamblul sculptural de la Târgu Jiu — Constantin Brâncuși* [The Sculptural Ensemble in Târgu Jiu – Constantin Brancusi], 2012, documentary film coordinated by Doina Lemny and produced at the initiative of Victor Boștinaru and Catherine Trautmann – MEP, with the support of Târgu Jiu City Hall and the *În premieră cu Carmen Avram* broadcast on Antena3 TV channel; <http:// victorbostinaru.ro/2012/07/ansamblul-sculptural-de-la-targu-jiu-constantin-Brâncuși/>.

144. Doina Lemny, *Constantin Brancusi*, p. 14.

145. *Idem*, p. 207.

146. Vrînceanu Nichita, *op. cit.*

147. Cristian-Robert Velescu, "Cartea de artă: Brâncuși, recitit dintr-o perspectiva românească și occidentală" [The Book of Art: Brancusi Re-Read from a Romanian and Western Perspective], *Romania literară*, No. 45/2012; <http://www.romlit.ro/brncui_recitit_dintr-o_perspectiv_romneasc_i_occidental>.

In 1992 he published his first monograph on Brancusi "with the feeling of having reached a threshold of analysis that cannot easily be crossed,"[148] and in 2010 the volume *Brancusi. Material Languages*, a study that "approaches the sculptor's work from a perspective specific not so much to art history or aesthetics as much as to symbolic anthropology."[149] He believes that Brancusian symbolism is simultaneously traditionalist and innovative—he calls it *hylesic* symbolism—and presents Brancusi's work as reconstructing "the phylogeny of the human spirit descending into history beyond myths as far as the unifying fulcrum of materials, a common denominator of all cultures of Earth."[150]

His analyses of Brancusi's sculptures contain ideas of bewildering divergence: analogies between the construction of the poetic image in Eminescu and the plastic image in Brancusi;[151] analogies between the *Maiastra* and the sculptor's Romanianness;[152] analogies between the sculptor's work and the revolution of knowledge brought about by Darwin's theory,[153] anti-discrimination discourse from the interwar period[154] and reconciliation of the Judaic and Christian "equation"[155] with the Arabic one.[156]

He concludes that "of all Brancusi's acts of daring, the greatest, in relation to our own time, remains that of having conceived modern art as an institution responsible for managing the dreams—the future—of contemporary civilisation at the level of the human species"[157] and he believes that "ethnocentric exegesis has frequently wagered on the singular, original facet of Romanian folklore as a source of inspiration for Brancusian creation," whereas Brancusi's peasanthood is per-

---

148. Matei Stîrcea-Crăciun, *Brâncuși: Limbajele materiei* [Brancusi: Material Languages], Bucharest, Anima, 2010, p. 19.

149. *Idem*, p. 16.

150. *Idem*, p. 338.

151. *Idem*, p. 71.

152. "It is the only work whose title, deliberately untranslatable, explicitly convokes Romanian mythology to participate in the project of Brancusian aesthetics. (...) Transposed in the major range of high art, the symbol of the enchanted bird dizzyingly rises from Romanian fairy tales only to swoop down into the consciousness of planetary modernity." *Idem*, p. 95.

153. *Idem*, p. 117.

154. "It is beyond any doubt that thanks to its abstract nature, Brancusian sculpture will have appeared to the artist's American friends as an art purged of segregation. (...) *The Prodigal Son* was conceived (...) as if deliberately in order to convey the pacifying image of hands stretched out to each other, ready to grasp, in affirmation of solidarity rediscovered. This is why, rather than orient the *Prodigal Son* towards the homeland, it was important that the work arrive over the ocean, in the melting pot of all ethnicities that is America." *Idem*, pp. 195-196.

155. *Idem*, p. 245.

156. *Idem*, p. 251.

157. *Idem*, pp. 338-339.

suasive "precisely because the artist uses it to proclaim himself a citizen of the world."[158]

As Andrei Pleşu remarks in a text of his, although Brancusian exegesis is vast, "there is nonetheless a disappointing discrepancy between the large number of commentaries and commentators and their real hermeneutic benefit, for what has been said can be condensed into a limited series of commonplaces: Brancusi and the primitive arts, Brancusi and the birth of modern sculpture, Brancusi and the triumph of handicraft, (...) Brancusi and Milarepa, Brancusi and the (Platonic) essences, Brancusi and the Romanian peasant."[159]

This chapter does not claim to exhaust the whole of this exegetical production, but rather sets out to outline the views of a number of the most influential Romanian Brancusiologists and their attempts to identify national elements in the work of Brancusi. According to the definition given by V. G. Paleolog, quoted by Constantin Zărnescu, the Brancusiologist is a "cultivated and informed person who is not only the chronicler of an artist, of an epoch, but also sacrifices himself for one—the one who was the tip of the column, who renewed the path, the road, in this respect none other than the unique case of the world-renowned sculptor Constantin Brancusi."[160] In the selection of the authors who were discussed in this chapter, it was not professional qualifications, but sacrifice and the fact of having dedicated their whole careers to the life and work of Brancusi that were the decisive factors. Zărnescu even believes it is an advantage for Brancusiologists not to have had an education in the history or theory of art, that they can be "people from various arts and trades who have professionalised themselves throughout their lives,"[161] thereby augmenting the complexity and diversity of the questions brought into discussion in order to elucidate "the titanism of the work and sacrifice of a great Romanian,"[162] with Brancusiology becoming a true interdisciplinary field. Continuing this idea, this is how Marin Sorescu summed it up in 1979: "*The Endless Column* is constantly washed by the rains, preserving, after every season, its brilliance and unfinishedness intact. Likewise, the Brancusian mystery, through being frequented, is merely freshened, without any corner being dented."[163]

---

158. *Idem*, p. 309.

159. Andrei Pleşu, "'Specificul naţional' la cîţiva comentatori români ai operei lui Brâncuşi" ['National Specificity' in Some Romanian Commentators of Brancusi's Oeuvre], text from 1975, reprinted in Andrei Pleşu, *Ochiul şi lucrurile* [The Eye and the Things], Bucharest, Meridiane, 1986, p. 56.

160. Constantin Zărnescu, *Codul operei lui Brâncuşi*, p. 5.

161. *Idem*, p. 5.

162. *Idem*, p. 10

163. Marin Sorescu, preface to Constantin Zărnescu, *Aforismele şi textele lui Brâncuşi* [Brancusi's Aphorisms and Texts], Craiova, Scrisul Românesc, 1980, pp. 5–6.

PART 4

Popular Appropriation

In the 1980s, many contemporary theorists of the phenomenon believed appropriation to be synonymous with a strategy that was in essence critical towards consumer culture. More recently, however, a series of arguments have been made that demonstrate yet again the two-directional appropriations between the art world and consumer culture, which encourages us to view the phenomenon from a new angle and to consider the possibility that the whole of contemporary culture is based on appropriation in one way or another. In this respect, we might set out from the questions put forward by Sven Lütticken: "If the culture industry is based to a significant degree on the appropriation of material from art and various subcultures, as well as from different historical epochs and cultures, why should appropriation as an artistic strategy have a special status?"[1] He observes that while "the current art world freely indulges in Situationist chic (…) which uses and perverts Barthes and Broodthaers by assuming its appropriations are automatically critical,"[2] in a consumer culture there is constant appropriation of elements from the artistic context without any claim to a critical dimension.

Discussing authors' rights and their economic and deontological justification, Michael Spence reminds us of the complexity of the situation:[3] on the one hand the theorists of postmodernism claim that nobody can lay claim to copyright in a culture of the quotation and pastiche, and on the other hand ethical obligations are invoked seriously enough to be mentioned in the Universal Declaration of Human Rights.[4] Of interest to this research is the argument from harm done to a creator by the unauthorized use of his work, included in contemporary copyright regulations and usually made up of two distinct parts: on the one hand it is considered that "the unauthorized user causes harm to the creator of work simply by the use of the work" and on the other hand the creator of the work does a would-be user no wrong by preventing unauthorized use.[5] Michael Spence explains such arguments and their weak points: the author might be harmed if, through unauthorised use, her/his work is altered in such a way that she/he will no longer be able to use it in

<hr>

1. Sven Lütticken, "The Feathers of the Eagle," *New Left Review*, 36, Nov.–Dec. 2005, p. 109.

2. *Idem*, p. 118.

3. He finds no real justification for the current copyright regulations, believing along with many other left-wing intellectuals that the history of such regulations is in fact a history of disputes between three interest groups: authors, producers/mediators (publishers, galleries, estates, presses, etc.) and institutional users (libraries, universities, etc.). Michael Spence, "Justifying Copyright" in Daniel McClean, Karsten Schubert (eds.), *Dear Images. Art, Copyright and Culture*, London, Ridinghouse/ICA, 2002, p. 402.

4. Article 27(2) of the Universal Declaration of Human Rights: "Everyone has the right to the protection of the moral and material interests resulting from any scientific, literary or artistic production of which he is the author."; <http://www.un.org/en/documents/udhr/index. shtml#a27>.

5. Spence, *op. cit.*, p. 393.

the sense in which it was created. Spence admits that this argument is based on the contested claim that the meaning of the work can change through use and gives the following situation as an example: "Imagine that a visual artist creates a particular image to promote affirmative action on the grounds of race. If that image is appropriated by a neo-Nazi group, it may no longer have value for the artist. Even without their altering of the actual image, its use by the neo-Nazi group may change its meaning, may render it liable to be read differently by an anticipated audience."[6]

Applying this argument to the case of Brancusi, we might say that his appropriation by various public discourses in Romania, whether nationalist or not, endangers in the first place the artist's image as an individual producer of subjectivity (subjectivity in his case being also the result of contact with the international artistic context in which he was active) and in the second place his image as an "universal artist," with the risk thereby arising of an "incorrect" reception of his work at the international level and his "ghettoization" in the enclave of a "minor" culture, such as the Romanian one.

To return to the argument justifying copyright regulations, its second part is based on the idea that "the creator of the work does a would-be user no harm in excluding her/him from its use." But Spence contests this reasoning, arguing that when a work becomes an important part of the social/cultural life of a community, "it may be that exclusion from the use of the work does a would-be user a real harm." The use of the work may be necessary if it has come to represent within the community "a range of meanings for which no adequate alternative means of expression exist." Under such circumstances, the work might be used "either to contest or to invoke the range of meanings for which it is a cipher," while "excluding the would-be users from the work in all such situations is effectively to silence them."[7] Thus, the community would suffer if it were prevented from using the work in question in its own discursive production or construction of its own identity.

If we look at Brancusi from this perspective, it is obvious that in the last century in Romania his image served various strategies of identity construction in relation to the West, and in the present it has become an important part of the national social and cultural life. This fact, according to Michael Spence's reasoning, would give twenty-first-century Romanians the right to continue using the image of Brancusi to invoke a range of meanings which I discuss at greater length in the chapter "Brancusi and Romania," meanings that also appear very obvious in the comments made in the visitors' books from the Brancusi Studio in Paris.[8]

---

6. *Idem*, p. 394.

7. *Idem*, pp. 394–395.

8. In an interview, Doina Lemny declares the following: *"Romanians come to the Brancusi Studio as if on a pilgrimage to a temple. The staff that supervise the studio often convey to me moving accounts. Every year,*

To lend nuance to the discussion of copyright as viewed on the boundary between collective heritage,[9] national ideology and international legislation (always presented as neutral, but in reality masking the financial interests of the capitalist system), we should look at the figure of Che Guevara, one of Cuba's main icons, who has been the object of state worship since his death in 1967. Ariana Hernandez-Reguant analyses copyright caught between socialist and capitalist ideology, the "creative" potential of areas that develop at the junction between the nation state and transnational capitalism. She argues that "the culture industries, under neoliberal capitalism, were refashioned as copyright industries and moved to the forefront of globalization processes" and, adopting Jacques Attali's argument,[10] notes the fact that unexpectedly for the current global economic system the state may still be the ultimate copyright owner (at least, as it relates to patents and copyrights).[11]

On the other hand, to return to Michael Spence's argument, we may argue that "the control over the meaning of expressive works may even be seen as entailed in the right to free speech."[12] Thus, we may bring back into discussion the institution of the museum itself, understood in the tradition of Foucault to be an example of "instances of state power as it is embodied in the built environment" or as an illustration of heterotopia "as a space of difference."[13] The museum is an example of heterotopia not only because it juxtaposes different objects and different historical periods in the same space, but also, above all, because it operates with deeper differences, differences between objects and concepts, differences specific to the act of interpretation. Thus, interpretation arises as a relationship between things

---

I receive a copy of the visitor's book: almost seventy per cent of the impressions are from compatriots, who reveal their joy at being able to see this exceptional ensemble." Silvia Vrînceanu Nichita, "Doina Lemny – o focşăneancă are grijă de 'moştenirea' Brâncuşi la Paris," *Ziarul de Vrancea*, 7 April 2011; <http://lapasprinvrancea.blogspot.ro/2011/ 04/doina-lemny-o-focsaneanca-are-grija-de.html>.

9. See *Korda versus Lintas and Rex* (2000), in which the author of the famous photographic portrait of Che Guevara won his case against the British advertising agency that had used the portrait in a Smirnoff vodka campaign, although the latter invoked the argument that the image was clearly part of the universal public domain and had been used intensively in other international campaigns, including the design of a Swatch product in 1995.

10. Jaques Attali, *Noise: The Political Economy of Music,* Manchester, Manchester University Press, 1985.

11. Intellectual property ultimately ends up owned by the state. But before this happens—a period of fifty to seventy-five years after the author's death—copyright is usually owned by corporations or private estates. Ariana Hernandez-Reguant, "Copyrighting Che: Art and Authorship under Cuban Late Socialism" in Jonathan Xavier Inda, Renato Rosaldo (eds.), *The Anthropology of Globalization. A Reader*, Malden, Blackwell Publishing, 2008, pp. 259, 263.

12. Spence, *op. cit.*, p. 395.

13. Michel Foucault, "Des Espaces Autres," lecture given in 1967 and first published in *Architecture, Mouvement, Continuité*, no. 5, October 1984, pp. 46–49.

and the words used to describe them, and this relationship always gives way to a gap between the two, which can be productive to a greater or lesser degree.

To return to Brancusi and his appropriation outside the art world's system of representation, as I also discussed in the chapter "Brancusi and Romania," his international legitimation is the real reason behind his becoming a flag for various communities in Romania, to the same extent for nationalist communities such as Dacologists or Orthodox fundamentalists or for transnational communities such as yoga practitioners and freemasons.

Among the most interesting Romanian public discourses in which extremely creative conceptual aberrations have occurred is Dacology, the pseudo-science that claims that the origins of the Romanian people are purely Dacian and negates the effects of Roman colonisation. It is well known that founding myths are essential to any community, thereby easily becoming politicised depending on the values and identity projects of the period in which national history is reconstructed. On the territory of Romania there has been a very clear dynamic: in periods open to the West, Roman origins have been emphasised, and in those dominated by a nationalist discourse, Dacian origins. The Latinist movement, which developed in opposition to Ottoman/Austro-Hungarian rule and to the vicinity to the Slavs was predominant up until the nineteenth century, when it was refined by the national-romantic ideology. The end of the nineteenth century, which brought political maturity and professionalization of historiography, archaeology and linguistics, succeeded in bringing about a convenient consensus as to joint Dacian and Roman origins: the Romanians now benefited from association with the great achievements of Roman civilisation, but also the historic right to their territory. At the beginning of the twentieth century, *Prehistoric Dacia* by Nicolae Densușianu, "an erudite fantast" as Lucian Boia calls him, put forward a theory according to which the Carpathian-Danubian region was the cradle of mankind, where all the nations, languages and civilisations of the world were born. This theory, which is closer to fiction than to science, and which, in Dan Alexe's view, shows "proto-Nazi stridencies in its obsessive emphasis on the biological, on race and ethnicity,"[14] was to be adopted by numerous nationalist discourses in Romania, including the nationalist communism of the 1980s and the contemporary Dacia Revival movement, which sprang up within the Romanian diaspora in the United States.

In local art criticism there is an established strain that seeks to find Brancusi's sources not in folklore, but "in the structure of a *pre-Romanian local background*, understood to be the source and foundation of the authentic national spirit."[15] Andrei

---

14. Dan Alexe, *Dacopatia și alte rătăciri românești* [Dacopathy and Other Romanian Aberrations], Bucharest, Humanitas, 2015, p. 6.
15. Andrei Pleşu, "'Specificul Naţional' la cîţiva comentatori români ai operei lui Brâncuşi" in *Ochiul și lucrurile*, Bucharest, Meridiane, 1986, p. 60.

Pleşu argues that Dacian civilisation is the first to which most commentators spontaneously appeal, beginning in the interwar period and continuing with various famous Brancusiologists such as V. G. Paleolog down to the present.[16] Such theories were recently adopted by Napoleon Săvescu,[17] the founder of the International Dacia Revival Society in New York, and recycled as part of the activities of this organisation dedicated to the "True History of the Dacian People."[18] Thus, the thirteenth International Congress of Dacology held in Târgu Jiu in 2012 was dedicated to Constantin Brancusi. In issue eighty of *Dacia Magazin*, which published the papers read at the congress, made possible with the support of the Târgu Jiu Town Hall, Gorj County Prefecture, the "Constantin Brancusi" University, the Alliance of Romanian Business Owners Confederations, and the Elvira Godeanu Theatre, Napoleon Săvescu speaks of the connection between the Dacians and Brancusi: "Among the major objectives of the Dacia Revival Society, the place of honour has been and continues to be held by the constant promotion of exceptional values, created over the course of time by our compatriots. This is the explanation as to why this year we have dedicated the proceedings of the congress to the greatest sculptor of the Romanian nation, who became one of the greatest modern sculptors in the world, Constantin Brancusi, whose esteem for our Dacian ancestors he expressed adamantly" and whose sculptures were "inspired by the ancient and imperishable artworks of our Dacian ancestors."[19]

From a report on the congress,[20] we find out that Napoleon Săvescu officially opened the proceedings "in the presence of more than two hundred people from numerous counties and another six countries." The opening speech was followed by a "theatrical recital," as an introduction to the section "Traco-Geto-Dacian Motifs in the Sculpture of Constantin Brancusi," and by the "musical strains of the anthem *Brancusi the Immortal*," to lyrics by Napoleon Săvescu and Mariana Terra: "From his beloved homeland / To France he made his way / He with his chisel carved / The reunited Dacia / The whole world admires / The Dacian from the Carpathians / Who changed modern / Sculpture from the Dacians. / Magical bird / Airman's licence / In New York you find it / On every aviator. / A destiny that the god

---

16. A subject developed at greater length in the chapter on Brancusiology.

17. Napoleon Săvescu is a physician who emigrated from Romania in the Ceauşescu period and settled in New York, the president and founder of Dacia Revival International Society Inc. and The Romanian Medical Society of New York. His manifesto "Noi nu sîntem urmaşii Romei" [We Are Not the Descendants of Rome] is part of the RECONQUISTA programme initiated by Artur Silvestri (a figure associated with protochronism in the 1970s and 1980s).

18. <http://www.dacia.org/daciarevival/dacia-revival>.

19. Napoleon Săvescu, editorial in *Dacia Magazin*, No. 80, August 2012, p. 1; <http://www.dacia.org/daciarevival/dacia-magazin-2012/391>.

20. <http://www.dacia.org/daciarevival/brancusi-2012>.

Zalmoxis gave him / And now he amazes the world / The unequalled Brancusi. / Scorching is the stone / He sculpted / The kiss of immortality / On the Gate resurrected / With the chisel and hammer / He the iron awakened, / The Endless Column / Made the Dacians immortal."

Another interesting appropriation of Brancusi outside the representational system of the art world has come about in the intellectual production of the Romanian Orthodox Church. In the abovementioned text on the national specificity of Brancusian exegesis, Andrei Pleşu also looks at its Christian strain, speaking of Petru Comarnescu, who "interprets the artist's reservations towards Michelangelo's 'beef steak' as deriving from the 'old peasant coyness towards the body,' encouraged at the ethical level by Christian morality and at the aesthetic level by Byzantine iconoclasm."[21] He believes that in fact Brancusi's religiosity was rather "diffuse, wavering between pre-Christian animism and Far Eastern esotericism"[22] and explains the genealogy of the oriental interpretation as follows: "The theme of the sculptor's Indian sources has often been touched upon, but more often than not in an amateur way: they invoke Brancusi's readings of Milarepa, his plans for the temple of Indore, the throwaway remarks with which the artist was in the histrionic habit of entertaining his visitors."[23] This esoteric strain of Brancusian exegesis has been recycled as part of initiatives that popularise yogic theories and practices in Romania, ranging from the controversial MISA group, which in 2009 published *Aphorisms and Thoughts of the Romanian Artist Genius and Yogi Constantin Brancusi*, selected by Gregorian Bivolaru, to Sahaja Yoga Romania, which in 2001, to mark the Brancusi Year, produced *Brancusi about Brancusi*.[24] A text first published on the MISA [The Movement for Spiritual Integration into the Absolute] website presents Brancusi as a sculptor of genius who practised yoga and who "is part of the national treasure and successfully represents us abroad," his sculptures being exhibited in museums throughout the world and his name being universally honoured: "His entire life, Brancusi adhered to a perseverant spiritual practice. His spiritual guide was the great Tibetan yogi Milarepa, who guided him on the astral plane. But above all else, his work itself stands as a testimony to his yogic practice. Esoteric knowledge, such as the use of the golden section, synthesised in his works of genius, unequivocally demonstrates the fact that Brancusi was an initiate."[25] This material has been taken up by various webpages, including the MISA Yogis' blog and the Dacica Association, a non-profit organisation from Timişoara whose aim is to promote Romanian/ Geto-Dacian cultural, medical, traditional spiritual val-

---

21. Pleşu, *op. cit.*, p. 62.

22. *Idem*, pp. 62–63.

23. *Idem*, p. 75.

24. <http://www.sahajayoga.ro/index.php/Actualitate/SAHAJA-YOGA-ROMANIA.html>.

25. <http://yogaesoteric.net/content.aspx?lang=RO&item=4952>.

ues, which are viewed as being in close connection with oriental values. We may observe how in this context, in a way that was anticipated by Mircea Eliade in his scholarly texts, the Dacian reclamation of Brancusi encounters the yogic one. Moreover, another paradox should also be mentioned: Brancusi is laid claim to by the MISA yogic community—which is obsessed with "unmasking Masonry" and the "conspiracy of the global dictatorship/satanic cabal of the Illuminati group"[26] and by the community of Romanian freemasons in equal measure.

Thus, the arguments put forward by Radu Varia and used to a certain extent by Cristian-Robert Velescu, after corroborating Varia's information with that provided by Friedrich Teja Bach in his work on Brancusi, are adopted from the art critic in the ideological discourse of the Romanian masonic community.[27] Radu Varia talks about the possibility that in 1894 Brancusi was initiated into the *Frères de Craiova* and presents the city of Craiova as an outpost of Vienna and the crafts guilds (long since having become secret societies), which disguised their presence in Craiova, either within the artisanal enterprises, or among teachers invited to teach at the Trade School[28] where Brancusi himself studied. He interprets the sculptor's journey to Paris as being initiatory, making use of the photograph that shows Brancusi as a journeyman (*Wandergeselle*) holding a cane. In the same spirit, Cristian-Robert Velescu discusses a number of other arguments "in favour of the fact that Brancusi could have been a repository of esoteric concepts and teachings."[29] He re-reads a passage from Matila C. Ghyka's *Le Nombre d'Or*, which makes the connection between corporative rituals and those of the Pythagorean brotherhood and freemasonry, thereby confirming Radu Varia's hypothesis. These theories have been adopted in various extreme discourses that can be found on the Internet merely by searching for the name Brancusi. The following is a prime example: "What did Brancusi know about the reptilians/extra-terrestrials/fallen angels/demons/vampires? Answer: a lot. It is no longer any secret that Brancusi was a big mason illuminatus, as it was only through initiation that he managed to become famous. His works express nothing other than the secrets of the masons, such as the Table of SILENCE, with twelve chairs, the Column of the INFINITE, with thirty-three pyramids, the Gate of the KISS (the man-demon fusion—stargate), and many more…"[30] Such conspir-

---

26. <http://misa-yoga.blogspot.com/search/label/Masonerie>; <http://www.yogaesoteric.net/content.aspx?lang=RO&item=3480>.

27. Cristian-Robert Velescu, he chapter "Phaidruntes, sau 'Cel care face să străluească statuile'" [Phaidruntes, or 'The One Who Makes Statues Shine'] in *Brâncuşi Iniţiatul* [Brancusi the Initiate], Bucharest, Editis, 1993, pp. 117–127.

28. Radu Varia, *Brancusi*, New York, Rizzoli International Publications, 1986, p. 33.

29. Velescu, *op. cit.*, pp. 117–127.

30. "Domnişoara Pogany a lui Brâncuşi – o fiinţă extraterestră?" [Brancusi's Mademoiselle Pogany

acy theories aside, Brancusi is also laid claim to in the official discourse of Romanian Freemasonry, from articles in the masonic journal, which has been published since 2009 under the auspices of the Masonic Press Agency,[31] to presentations of the artist on the webpages of various lodges: the National Grand Lodge of Romania/ Comparative Ritualistic and Masonic Research Lodge,[32] the Regular Grand Lodge of Romania I/R:L: Phoenix,[33] and the Athenaeum Respectable Lodge/Ancient Scottish Rite and Accepted Lodge.[34] In a videotaped interview,[35] Tudorel Nițulescu, the Grand Master of the National Grand Lodge of Romania, claims that Brancusi was born a mason, and the Athenaeum Lodge, in a text titled "Brancusi's descendants are prepared to do great deeds," presents in detail the activities of the village lodge of Hobița, founded by Tănasie Lolescu, who never missed an opportunity to recount the attempt to demolish the *Endless Column* in the 1950s.[36]

One of the most extravagant Brancusian exegeses is based on the very name of the village where Brancusi was born, Hobița, and puts forward in the purest protochronist style a theory according to which "American poet Ezra Pound, after visiting Brancusi's studio in Paris, then wrote an essay about the magical space he discovered during his visits. It is almost impossible for a man of letters from the English Academy, such as J. R. R. Tolkien, not to have read Ezra Pound's article and it is highly plausible that writer J. R. R. Tolkien, prior to his later fame, will also have visited, in the capacity of an 'illustrious anonym,' Brancusi's studio in Paris, where the Oltenian sculptor was rearranging space, reinventing reality. A New Reality of sculptural discourse, where the world of the hobbit might also have lain hidden. Then, the legitimate question may be put: Is there any connection between the words *hobbit* and *Hobița*?"[37]

– An Extraterrestrial Being?], article published under the pseudonym Came, in February 2013; <http://www.cocoon.ro/?p=491>.

31. <http://jurnalmasonic.blogspot.ro/2013/02/constantin-brancusi-137-de-ani-de-la.html>.

32. <http://masonerie.com/simpozionul-constantin-brancusi-6004/>.

33. <http://www.mlnar.ro/brancusi-omul-universal>.

34. <http://www.rlathenaeum.com/aparitii-in-presa/untitledpost>.

35. Interview taken by Narcis Daju in 2010; <https://www.youtube.com/watch?v=WOcM9isxJZo>; <http://www.gorjnews.ro/povara-brancusi/masonii-se-impauneaza-ca-brancusi-le-e-frate-dar-nu-misca-un-deget-pentru-el.html>.

36. Videotaped testimony of Tănasie Lolescu; <https://www.youtube.com/watch?v=QGlGrsJLQ8s>; <https://www.youtube.com/watch?v=k_4CxUx9UOY>; <http://adevarul.ro/locale/targu-jiu/povestea-tanasie-lolescu-venerabilul-lojei-masonice-satesti-hobita-1_527b913cc7b855ff56ca3edf/index.html>.

37. "Arme ideologice" [Ideological Weapons], text published by Titus Octavian Filipas on *Blogul ideologic* [The Ideological Blog]; <http://blogideologic.wordpress.com/tag/o-poveste-cu-un-hobbit/>.

To return to the reclamation of Brancusi along Orthodox lines, two texts have been published by clerics of the Romanian Orthodox Church. Setting out from interpretations of this kind in the specialist literature (Paleolog, Pandrea), the first text, by Calinic Argatu,[38] re-contextualises a number of the sculptor's aphorisms, speculating on "his very rich biographical contacts with the services of the Church, with Church music and chant" and reading them from the perspective of "the asceticism of Christian Orthodox morals." The author takes a critical stance towards the claims of the yogic community and states that he has never been convinced that the "Brancusian greeting *Peace and Joy*—these elements being the two Christian keystones—originate in Tibet and the poems of Milarepa."[39] He believes that "many of Brancusi's principles seem to have been drawn from an Orthodox catechism" and that "he was not only an apostle of peace and joy, but also a moralist" in the tradition of "peasant morality, which is a Christian Orthodox morality and is distinct from the protestant concept of ethics."[40] He also sees Brancusi in the role of "a therapist, a doctor of souls" and comments on the "indictment which, in the bundle of maxims and observations recorded by Pandrea,[41] brings against the derogations of Western morality."[42] A few years later, drawing greatly on Calinic Argatu, Daniel Patriarch of the Romanian Orthodox Church published, in 2007, *Brancusi: Christian Orthodox Sculptor*, in which he highlights the "presence of Christian Orthodox spirituality" in the life and work of Constantin Brancusi, "that faithful and wise son of the Romanian Orthodox Church, who made known worldwide the unimagined valences of the Romanian soul."[43] The text is in fact a restructured and augmented version of the lecture "Sculpted Matter: An Epiphany of the Creator's Light. Orthodox Spirituality in the Work of Brancusi," which the Patriarch gave in

---

38. Calinic Argatu is a Romanian Orthodox cleric, Archbishop of Argeş and Muscel. He was an elected deputy in the parliament of 1990–92, for the Argeş National Salvation Front. He has been a member of the Union of Romanian Writers since 2006. In 2007 he was unmasked as a Securitate collaborator.

39. Calinic Argatu, *"Pace şi bucurie" cu Brâncuşi: argumente pentru o dimensiune creştină* ['Peace and Joy' with Brancusi: Arguments for a Christian Dimension], Cluj, Dacia, 2001, pp. 5, 6.

40. *Idem*, pp. 18, 19.

41. The following are examples recorded by Petre Pandrea and commented by Calinic Argatu: "The modern tragedy has its sources in erotic disorders, in the fear of what tomorrow will bring and in the ubiquity of alcohol consumption"; "Existentialist fear is the fear of the lack of daily bread"; "Exercise contemplated without the experience of the muscles, ephemeral cinema and excess reading without careful study seem to me to be the three cancers of modern civilisation"; "Malthusianism is applied through abortions and cheap contraceptives. It is the cancer of the West." Petre Pandrea, *Brâncuşi: Amintiri şi exegeze*, Bucharest, Meridiane, 1976, pp. 262–265.

42. Calinic Argatu, *op. cit.*, p.18.

43. Daniel, Patriarch of the Romanian Orthodox Church, *Brâncuşi: Sculptor creştin ortodox* [Brancusi: Christian Orthodox Sculptor], Iaşi, Editura Trinitas, 2007, pp. 6, 7.

2006 at the "George Enescu" University of Arts in Iaşi, when he was awarded the title of Doctor Honoris Causa. According to the Patriarch, "the faith and spiritual life of artist Constantin Brancusi are not borne out by an intellectual, systematic, academic theology, but by an implicit, worshipful or liturgical theology, which is hymnographic and iconic in expression, which awakens in the believer not only intellectual reflection on existence, but also a Christian spiritual outlook on life," and "many of Brancusi's works bear in them light from the inner light of the icons, of the hymns and of the Orthodox liturgical prayers."[44] The Patriarch of the Romanian Orthodox Church concludes the book as follows: "Now, on the fiftieth anniversary of the great Christian Orthodox artist Constantin Brancusi's passage to things eternal, we pray to Christ the Lord, Who is the 'Light of the World,' the 'Path, the Truth and the Life,' that he rest with the righteous, in the light and joy of the Kingdom of Heaven, the soul of His servant, he who multiplied the talents he received from the Good Lord and gave through his art to many people the light and joy to experience more intensely and more wisely the great gift and miracle of life on earth and in heaven."[45]

A phenomenon which manages to combine in a surprising way the most heterogeneous range of claims to Brancusi is that generated by writer Laurian Stănchescu, the initiator of the campaign to repatriate the artist's remains. From his own account it seems that he has been interested in the subject for forty years, but his first public action, the *Culture March*, did not occur until the autumn of 2010 when he set out on foot from the Romanian Athenaeum in Bucharest, arriving in Sarmizegetusa Regia ten days later, with the aim of drawing attention to the state of Romanian culture. It was during the march that the idea of repatriating Brancusi's remains took shape, an idea which he has propounded ever since, in countless manifestations and public events, which have finally persuaded various authorities to support the initiative. Public commemorations of Brancusi are nothing new, they have a rich history. As Irina Cărăbaş argues in a study on the topic, such commemorations, which began in the post-Stalinist period, have perpetuated a "cultic" format, which we also find in the present-day actions organised by Stănchescu. This format democratically included contributions from art professionals and simple admirers of the sculptor, academic lectures as well as poetry recitals and musical interludes, and these were always followed by articles in the press and printed homages, which enjoyed a nationwide audience. The first commemoration of this kind was organised in 1967 and contributed to the birth of the Brancusi cult, which continued to grow and to be refined up until 1976, when the Brancusi Centenary provided a new opportunity for the materialisation of the rituals previously performed. Finally, Irina Cărăbaş argues that the role of such commemora-

44. *Idem*, pp. 45, 47.
45. *Idem*, p. 52.

tions was important "in infusing the collective memory with the image of an idealized artist whose name became a floating signifier, able to adapt not only to the context that created it but even to outlive it."[46]

The commemorations have continued in the same style through the post-communist period, but with an important added element: Orthodox Christianity. For example, in 2006 at least two of the commemorations to mark the fiftieth anniversary of Brancusi's death were held in Montparnasse Cemetery. One of them began as a pilgrimage from Târgu Jiu organised by Brancusiologist Ştefan Stăiculescu: "a pious collective journey" to the sculptor's grave and studio, to which Ştefan Stăiculescu invited relatives of Brancusi from Hobiţa, writers, journalists, priests, teachers and students from Târgu Jiu and Craiova. In front of around two hundred people, the parish priest of the Romanian Orthodox Church in Paris officiated a religious service, after which *Kolyva* prepared at a hotel by "a number of ladies from the Gorj society" was served, while Stăiculescu handed out Brancusi flags, medallions and posters.[47] For the second commemoration in Montparnasse Cemetery—at which the metropolitans of Oltenia and of the Romanian Orthodox Metropolia of Western and Southern Europe officiated a *Te Deum* for the immortality of Brancusi and at which were present Romania's UNESCO representative, French officials, diplomats, Brancusiologists and students—the Cultural League for the Unity of Romanians All Over the World[48] produced a jubilee medal and a commemorative plaque.[49] The president of the League, Victor Crăciun,[50] is also a passionate Brancusiologist, who has published various books about the artist,[51] and who more recently organised the *Rodin,*

---

46. Irina Cărăbaş, "Commemoration without Shores. Celebrating Brancusi in post-Stalinist Romania" in Irina Cărăbaş, Olivia Niţiş (eds.), *After Brancusi*, Bucharest, Unarte, 2014, p. 71.

47. Information taken from Constantin Zărnescu, "Cum a fost comemorat sculptorul în Franţa (Brâncuşi – 50)" [The Sculptor's Commemoration in France (Brancusi – 50)] in *Codul operei lui Brâncuşi* [The Code of Brancusi's Work], Cluj, Dacia, 2007, pp. 249-253.

48. This league reclaims Brancusi in the nationalist discourse that militates for unification with Bessarabia and the recreation of the Greater Romania: "The Cultural League for the Unity of Romanians All Over the World, interested in the idea of the recognition of Romanianness and the preservation of the Romanian language and culture, struck a Brancusi jubilee medal, which on the obverse had an image of the great Romanian sculptor and on the face a reproduction of his 1945 work *Boundary Stone*. Obviously, in Brancusi's conception, this is the Boundary Stone of Union. The League hopes to be able to obtain permission to make a copy and to erect it in Romania."; <http://stirile.rol.ro/print/jubileu—-brancusi-nemuritorul-38721.html>.

49. Information taken from "Jubileu – Brâncuşi, nemuritorul" [Jubilee – Brancusi the Immortal]; <http://stirile.rol.ro/print/jubileu—-brancusi-nemuritorul-38721.html>.

50. Victor Crăciun, who presents himself as "a man of culture and a patriot, a tireless fighter for the recreation of a unified Romania," is a literary historian born in Chişinău, who since 1990 has been President of the Cultural League for the Unity of Romanians All Over the World.

51. More recently, *Măiestrele şi Brâncuşi* [Măiestrele and Brancusi], Bucharest, Semne, 2010, and *Portretul-Autoportret Brâncuşi* [The Self-portrait/Portrait Brancusi], Bucharest, Semne, 2011, both published

Brancusi, Modigliani and Botarro exhibition, which opened on Romania's National Day in 2013. The exhibition was realised in partnership with the Romania-Luxembourg Business Forum, under the patronage of the Romanian Embassy to Luxembourg.[52]

To return to the commemorative initiatives of the Brancusiologists, after the various unrealised projects that V. G. Paleolog proposed to take place in Craiova, which I discussed in the previous chapter, the most extravagant unrealised project was that planned in 1965 by his son, Tretie Paleolog, the founder of the Circle of Brancusi Studies. The activities he proposed for a planned Brancusi Festival in 1966 included moving the artist's remains from Paris to Târgu Jiu and reinterring them under the *Second Table of Remembrance*: "The solemn event will take place on the final day of the Festival. Absolutely all the country's sculptors will be invited to attend, along with one sculptor from every country in Europe and one from the United States."[53] This idea, which Tretie Paleolog abandoned until 1974, when he came up with a different project—*Restoration of the Trilogy dedicated to Heroism by Brancusi in Târgu Jiu*—was revived in the post-communist period as the ultimate goal of writer Laurian Stănchescu.

In the study from 1999, Katherine Verdery discusses "postsocialist necrophilia," observing that this attachment to corpses is very much in line with politics in periods of major changes, such as the post-communist period, and gives as examples numerous cases of political burials and re-interments. She talks about the political life of famous dead bodies, from the ecclesiastical tradition of relics to the secular one of cultural saints or politicians, examining the political symbolism of the connections between the manipulation of corpses and the wider national and international contexts of such manipulations.

Verdery believes that "politics is not restricted to the actions of political leaders but can be engaged in by anyone, although such actors often seek to present their goals as in some sense public ones."[54] Such too is the case of Laurian Stănchescu, the initiator of the campaign to repatriate Brancusi's remains, who besides the fact of presenting this as a public action also manages to present it as being in the national interest, thereby attracting the political support of state and local institutions and even that of the Romanian Orthodox Church and the Romanian Academy.

From Verdery's perspective on politics, understood as "a realm of continual struggles over meanings, or signification," analysis of the implications of the repatria-

---

under the aegis of the Cultural League for the Unity of Romanians All Over the World, the second of which was even reviewed in *Gîndacul de colorado – Ziarul românilor de pretutindeni* [The Potato Beetle – The Newspaper of Romanians from All Over the World]; <http://www.gandaculdecolorado.com/arhiva/3520-sculptorita-milita-petrascu-noi-contributii>.

52. For further details of the exhibition and opening, see: <http://luxemburg.mae.ro/local-news/601> and <https://www.youtube.com/watch?v=WYoBx2wSYqk>.

53. Union of Artists Archive, File 26/1958, p. 9 (209).

54. Katherine Verdery, *The Political Lives of Dead Bodies: Reburial and Postsocialist Change*, New York, Columbia University Press, 1999, p. 23.

tion of Brancusi's remains is a good opportunity to discuss the cultural dimension, in the anthropological sense, of postsocialist politics and the political element, "both as strategies and maneuvering and also as activity occurring within cultural systems."[55]

Instead of treating nationalism in a traditional way, as a matter of territorial boundaries, state building, competition for resources, Verdery believes that it might also be viewed from the perspective of ancestor worship and the circulation of cultural "values." Setting out from post-structuralist theories of language and floating signifiers, she argues that a dead body has no meaning in itself, but rather is invested with meaning through culturally established relations with death and through the different ways in which the importance of a dead person is interpreted: "Their complexity makes it fairly easy to discern different sets of emphasis, extract different stories, and thus rewrite history. Dead bodies have another great advantage as symbols: they don't talk much on their own (though they did once). Words can be put in their mouths—often quite ambiguous words—or their own actual words can be ambiguated by quoting them out of context. It is thus easier to rewrite history with dead people than with other kinds of symbols that are speechless."[56]

The case of Brancusi perfectly illustrates this theory, with the initiative to repatriate his remains being based on a few words that the artist is supposed to have imparted on his death bed to the Bishop of the Romanian Church in Paris: *I die with my soul un-reconciled because I cannot give up the ghost in my own country and I will rot in foreign soil, far from the person dearest to me, my mother.*"[57]

According to Verdery, dead bodies have properties that make them particularly powerful political symbols, thereby becoming excellent means to accumulate an element essential for political transformations: symbolic capital. They can even be viewed as a "a site of political profit."[58] Thus, from 2011 to 2013, in the attempt to capitalise politically on the initiative to repatriate Brancusi's remains, many Romanian politicians, from the government and from local administrations, publicly associated their names with the campaign, from the mayors of Peştişani and Târgu Jiu and various deputies and senators to the Minister of Culture, the Prime Minister and the Patriarch of Romania.

The commemorations and events organised by Laurian Stănchescu since 2011 have managed to combine elements so heterogeneous that the reordering of

---

55. *Idem*, p. 25.

56. *Idem*, p. 29.

57. For the timeline of this action, presented from the perspective of Laurian Stănchescu, see *IDEEA. Manual de cultură universală*, Constantin Brancusi anniversary issue, no. 2/February 2013.

58. Verdery, *op. cit.*, p. 33.

"meaningful worlds that are simultaneously conceptual, political, and economic,"[59] of which Verdery speaks, become highly transparent. He may be viewed as a director who succeeds in mobilising various important social actors, putting on "spectaculars," so much so that the mass media become fascinated in the phenomenon, while every appearance in the press contributes yet further to its propagation. Beginning with the human chain in front of the Romanian Athenaeum (February 2011) and continuing with the vigil and almsgiving organised at the Hobiţa Memorial House at the beginning of the first Brancusi March[60] (May 2011) and the musical, cinematic and poetic interludes presented during commemorations of the artist's birth such as those at the Scala Cinema (February 2013) and the Floreasca Club (February 2014), each such event recruits prominent cultural and political figures. But the spectacle also unfolds at other levels in relation to the political: on the one hand the level of street protests such as the hunger strike in front of the government building (April 2012) and on the other hand the bureaucratic level of signature gathering, demands, petitions and political alliances. The following are two examples of the kind of discourse that brings to the stage the relationship between Brancusi and Romania, between art and politics.

Excerpt from the Open Letter that Laurian Stănchescu sent to President of Romania Traian Băsescu in 2011:

Give an order, Mr President, for the Romanian semantron to sound throughout the land for Brancusi, for the Romanian flag to be flown and for the national anthem to be sung! I am convinced that the whole of Romania will obey this order and all Romanians will place their hands over their hearts for Brancusi, because the Romanian heart is the tomb in which nothing ever perishes! Give the order Mr President, for the rebirth of Romanian culture and history, give the order for the rebirth of Romania, give the order for the country's salvation through culture! It is the only order that Romanians will obey and fulfil.

Excerpt from the Political Declaration of the Parliamentary Group of the Liberal-Democratic Party signed by PD-L Senator Ion Ruşeţ and presented to the Senate of Romania in 2011:

---

59. *Idem*, p. 49.

60. The action came to a premature end in Budapest, due to a lack of funds, as Stănchescu recounts:
"In Hungary we ran out of money for the journey, and so the march that ought to have continued as far as France had to be interrupted and I had to return to the homeland. (...) For the march, which lasted two months, I received 7,900 lei from Mr. George Becali, I borrowed a part of the money from Professor Minodora Stănculescu, and the rest I took from my savings."

Constantin Brancusi's last wish, to be buried in Hobița, has become my wish and I hope it will become yours. Romanian politics will thereby be elevated to the cultural-spiritual dimension of our people. We shall do this with honour, dignity and the faith that we shall succeed in bringing home the Romanian spirits that have enriched the cultural treasury of the world, in this way placing Romania on the axis of the major cultures. Colleagues, it is in our power to restore to Romania the brilliance lent by history and culture, to make it a happy nation, this being possible only if we too, the political class, promote and protect the national culture and make it a means and a mode of life. This will mean an unprecedented spiritual explosion in Romania, a national rebirth and a starting point towards a new Romania, at which the other nations will gaze full of admiration.

At another level still, Laurian Stănchescu's initiative also manages to intersect with high culture. Although the elite has frequently disassociated itself from his actions, The Romanian Academy has supported him since 2011 through an official letter offering him unreserved support. In 2012 the Romanian Academy invited him to give a lecture as part of the "Constantin Brancusi: New Documentary Reference Points" series of commemorative presentations, and in 2013 President of the Romanian Academy himself, Ionel Haiduc, appeared on stage at the Scala Cinema commemoration. The case of Laurian Stănchescu proves yet again that culture—elitist or popular—and politics/economics often collaborate in constructive harmony when it comes to "national cultural treasures." Katherine Verdery observes in the contemporary context "a worldwide concern with cultural property rights" which are invoked in actions to repatriate cultural treasures, be they objects of value or the remains of famous figures, and believes that the repatriation of dead bodies in the postsocialist period "refurbish national identities by 'nationalising' symbolic capital that had entered global circuits, thus affirming the individuality of East European nation states" in relation to the European Union.[61] Not at all surprisingly, the author cites Brancusi as one of these national treasures: "Where the repatriates are world-famous, they may bring world respect, countering the arrogance of foreigners inclined to say, for instance, 'Who would have thought that Romania, of all places, could produce cultural geniuses like Ionesco, Enescu, Eliade and Brancusi!'" Regardless of where the impetus for repatriations comes from "they draw wider notice and enhance the nation's global image. It is as if repatriating these cultural treasures and giving them proper burial localises part of the symbolic capital that they contain."[62]

---

61. Verdery, *op. cit.*, p. 49.

62. *Ibidem.*

In parallel with the instrumentalisation of Brancusi in the national discourse, he has also been claimed by very marginal discourses that advance various theories regarding: "the Târgu Jiu Monumental Ensemble which functions as a microwave emitter, in which the *Table of Silence* may be likened to an electron emissions source, where the *Chairs Alley* may be conceived as an electronic particle accelerator tube, the *Gate of the Kiss* as a modulator, with the Church playing the role of a powerful amplifier and the *Endless Column* an antenna with wave resonance guides";[63] "the relationship between the 'geometric archetype' and the energetic field";[64] the "telluric electric current and the pyramid effect of the components of the *Endless Column*."[65] Another theory refers to "Hollywood's aliens who always have something in common: they all look like Brancusi's *Mademoiselle Pogany*,"[66] as lawyer Gheorghe Piperea claims, suggesting that the Romanian State could take the Hollywood studios to court for breach of copyright.[67] Another speculation[68] speaks of the "precise map" hidden in the *Gate of the Kiss*, which supposedly points to "the place where Brancusi believed the most precious treasure of the Dacians was hidden, one more valuable than any quantity of gold": "The Brancusi code is really astounding; it seems that the artist genius wished at all cost to make Romania the centre of the world, the cradle of a very ancient or the most ancient religion, the seed of an entire civilisation—all these things born of the inestimable ancestral vestiges, existing or supposed to exist in the area between the Carpathians and the Danube, treasures perhaps only mythological, perhaps even real... There is also a continuation of such hypotheses, which present on the one hand arguments supporting a possible theory of a collaboration between Brancusi and

---

63. Lidia Bîrsan, Vasile Stratulat, *Lacrima Brâncuşi: Ansamblul de la Târgu Jiu. Simbolism şi Ezoterism* [The Brancusi Tear: The Ensemble at Târgu Jiu. Simbolism and Esotericism], Bucharest, Kogaion, 1994. The authors also put forward theories about the *Endless Column* as a huge lingam, a symbol of the spirit of fertility, about the Kundalini energy that circulates through the Monumental Ensemble, and about its healing and therapeutic properties.

64. Jeana Morărescu, "Relaţia dintre 'arhetipul geometric' şi câmpul energetic corespunzător" [The Relationship between the 'Geometric Archetype' and the Corresponding Energy Field] in *Brâncuşi, acum. Comunicări ştiinţifice prezentate în cadrul Simpozionului "Brâncuşiana 96" organizat la Târgu Jiu* [Brancusi Now. Scholarly Presentations at the 'Brancusiana 96' Symposium Organised at Târgu Jiu], Târgu Jiu, Editura Fundaţiei "Constantin Brâncuşi", 1997, pp. 67–72.

65. "Coloana Infinitului din Târgu Jiu emite energie" [The Endless Column from Târgu Jiu Emits Energy], anonymous material published in *Memoria. Revista gîndirii arestate*, 1–2/2012, p. 19–21.

66. George Piperea, "Al cui e chipul de extraterestru?" [Whose Is the Face of the Extraterrestrial?]; <http://www.juridice.ro/162314/al-cui-e-chipul-de-extraterestru.html>.

67. "România poate da în judecată Hollywood-ul pentru extratereştrii copiaţi după Brâncuşi" [Romania Can Sue Hollywood for the Extraterrestrials Copied from Brancusi]; <http://www.realitatea.net/pogany-extraterestri_864303.html>.

68. Pavel Floresco, *Brâncuşi – Enigma: Taina lumii şi secretul vieţii* [Brancusi – The Enigma: The Mystery of the World and the Secret of Life], Bucharest, Virtual, 2013.

Henri Coandă—once fellow apprentices in the studio of Auguste Rodin—in the search for the recipe of immortality or the philosopher's stone and, on the other hand, for reference points of the Dacian sanctuary, regarded as the oldest divine temple of all times. It seems that according to a Brancusi sculpture with a complementary meaning on the map, the Ialomicioara Cave houses, in an inaccessible grotto, priceless ancestral relics. A second cave that might contain the elixir of life and other inestimable treasures is Scărişoara."[69] Gyorgy Tozser also speaks of a "Brancusi code," based on the divine proportion,[70] expressing the belief that "if Dan Brown had known him, he would have written the Brancusi Code, not the Da Vinci Code."[71]

From a left-wing perspective, which views copyright as closely connected to capitalist ideology, the problematic relationship between elite culture and the culture/copyright industry has reached the stage in which it requires a re-evaluation, because while contemporary consumers are celebrated as "happy hackers," the copyright industry is in fact becoming more and more fundamentalist.[72] The critical dimension of cultural production based on the appropriation of elements or languages specific to consumer culture will always be overshadowed by the suspicion that it is in fact merely a reaffirmation of capitalist ideology. Nor is the Appropriation Art movement now regarded as being critical towards consumer culture, although according to Sven Lütticken it is not surprising that the theorists and critics connected with *October*[73] magazine idealised in the 1980s artists associated with the movement and presented them as mythologists à la Barthes in opposition to Andy Warhol, who was viewed as "a rather dubious figure, an overly commercial has-been."[74] We might also remark upon the way in which reciprocal appropriation is perceived in the left-wing intellectual sphere: ten years later, in 1990, the same magazine, *October*, reacted to the announcement that MOMA was

---

69. Pavel Floresco quoted in Alin Ion, "Codul secret lăsat de Brâncuşi în Poarta Sărutului – opera ascunde detalii despre locul comorilor nepreţuite ale dacilor – ipoteza controversată a unui cercetător" [The Secret Code Left by Brancusi in the Gate of Kiss – the Work Hides Details about the Site of the Priceless Treasures of the Dacians – the Controversial Hypothesis of a Researcher], *Adevărul*, 10 August 2015; <http://m.adevarul.ro/locale/targu-jiu/codul-secret-lasat-brancusi-poarta-sarutului-opera-ascunde-detalii-despre-locul-comorilor-nepretuite-dacilor-ipoteza-controversata-unui-cercetator-1_55c77589f5eaafab2c648e31/index.html>.

70. Gyorgy Tozser, *Clubul inorogilor* [The Club of Unicorns], Oradea, Durans, 2001.

71. Gyorgy Tozser quoted in Carmen Cosman, "Codul lui Brâncuşi, mai spectaculos decît Codul lui Da Vinci" [The Brancusi Code Is More Spectacular than the Da Vinci Code], 14 December 2011; <http://citynews.ro/eveniment-15/codul-lui-brancusi-mai-spectaculos-decat-codul-lui-da-vinci-210746>.

72. Lütticken, *op. cit.*, p. 125.

73. The exception is Benjamin Buchloh.

74. Lütticken, *op. cit.*, p. 123.

preparing an exhibition titled *High and Low: Modern Art and Popular Culture*—in which
it was detected an intention on the part of the museum to present the high/low
relationship employing the classic model of sublimation[75]—and organised a symposium to discuss "other ways of modelling[76] the relationship between high art and
mass culture, ways which differ from and oppose the sublimation model," arguing for the possibility of perceiving mass culture as a specific historical phenomenon that cannot be assimilated into the discourse of art history without ignoring
its own historical specificity. In this context, there is a reconsideration of the inter-
face between art and consumer culture, which is jettisoned in favour of a discussion in which "the field of popular culture is projected as the only proper site of
avant-garde activity or of resistance."[77] This is obviously an atypical perspective and
one that does not find favour with the greater part of the art world, precisely because
it has the potential to erase the boundaries between elites and consumers of popular culture and to reconnect art with the social sphere in a non-hierarchical relationship.

To return to Brancusi, he was and continues to be appropriated and embraced
by popular culture, at the individual level, and serves, without discriminating as to
social class, both the rhetoric of national ideals and consumer culture, advertising images, interior and product design, and fashion. He has even come to represent the concept of "virility" in the Romanian popular imagination, which reminds
us of the words of Marcel Janco in *Contimporanul*: "Only a sinewy and sensual people could have given the world Brancusi."[78]

Recycling of Brancusi, which over the years has fascinated artists including Vlad
Nancă and Mircea Cantor, makes us think of Benjamin Buchloh once again, who
talks about the transformation of aesthetic practice into advertising, the "process
of transformation from practice to object, from object to sign, from use value to

---

75. According to this model, the function of art is to transform/sublimate common experience, elevating
it from the banal to the extraordinary, and it is the artist of genius who achieves this.

76. These potential alternative models identified by Rosalind Krauss are influenced by the theorists
of the Frankfurt School, particularly Theodor Adorno and Walter Benjamin, Jean Baudrillard (the
simulation model), Roland Barthes (the desublimatory model), the theorists of the Birmingham
School and Michel de Certeau (the re-appropriation model). Rosalind Krauss, in the introduction
to *High/Low. A Special Issue, October*, 56, Spring 1991, p. 4.

77. Krauss, *op. cit.*, pp. 3–5.

78. Ruxandra Demetrescu observes that Romanian art criticism of the interwar period even
developed "a topos of the virile artist." Marcel Janco quoted in Ruxandra Demetrescu, "Modernitate, tradiție, avangardă. Repere în literatura artistică românească 1908–1946" [Modernity,
Tradition, Avant-Garde. Landmarks in the Romanian Artistic Literature 1908–1946] in *(Dis)con-
tinuități. Fragmente de modernitate românească în prima jumătate a secolului al 20-lea* [(Dis)continuities.
Fragments of Romanian Modernity in the First Half of the 20th Century], Bucharest, Simetria,
2010, p. 196.

exchange value, from exchange value to sign exchange value (...) from aesthetic practice to advertising."[79]

As may be observed, the history of attempts to appropriate Brancusi in the Romanian context began even during the artist's lifetime and has developed spectacularly, whether we are talking about government strategies, commercial campaigns, or individual initiatives. In this research my aim has not been to function according to the paradigm of cultural elites upset by the fact that the image of Brancusi has escaped beyond the boundaries of the art world, or to discover the extent to which such multiple processes of interpretation/recycling unfold in opposition to the artist's original intentions. Rather, I have been interested in observing and commenting on the phenomenon as it arises from gaps in the system of interpretation, personally receiving it as one that is extremely productive, at the boundary between high art and the social sphere.

---

79. Benjamin H.D. Buchloh in Maria Gilissen, Benjamin H.D. Buchloh (eds.), *Section Publicité du Musée d'Art Moderne et des 'Aigles/Marcel Broodthaers*, catalogue published by Marian Goodman Gallery New York, 1995, p. 97.

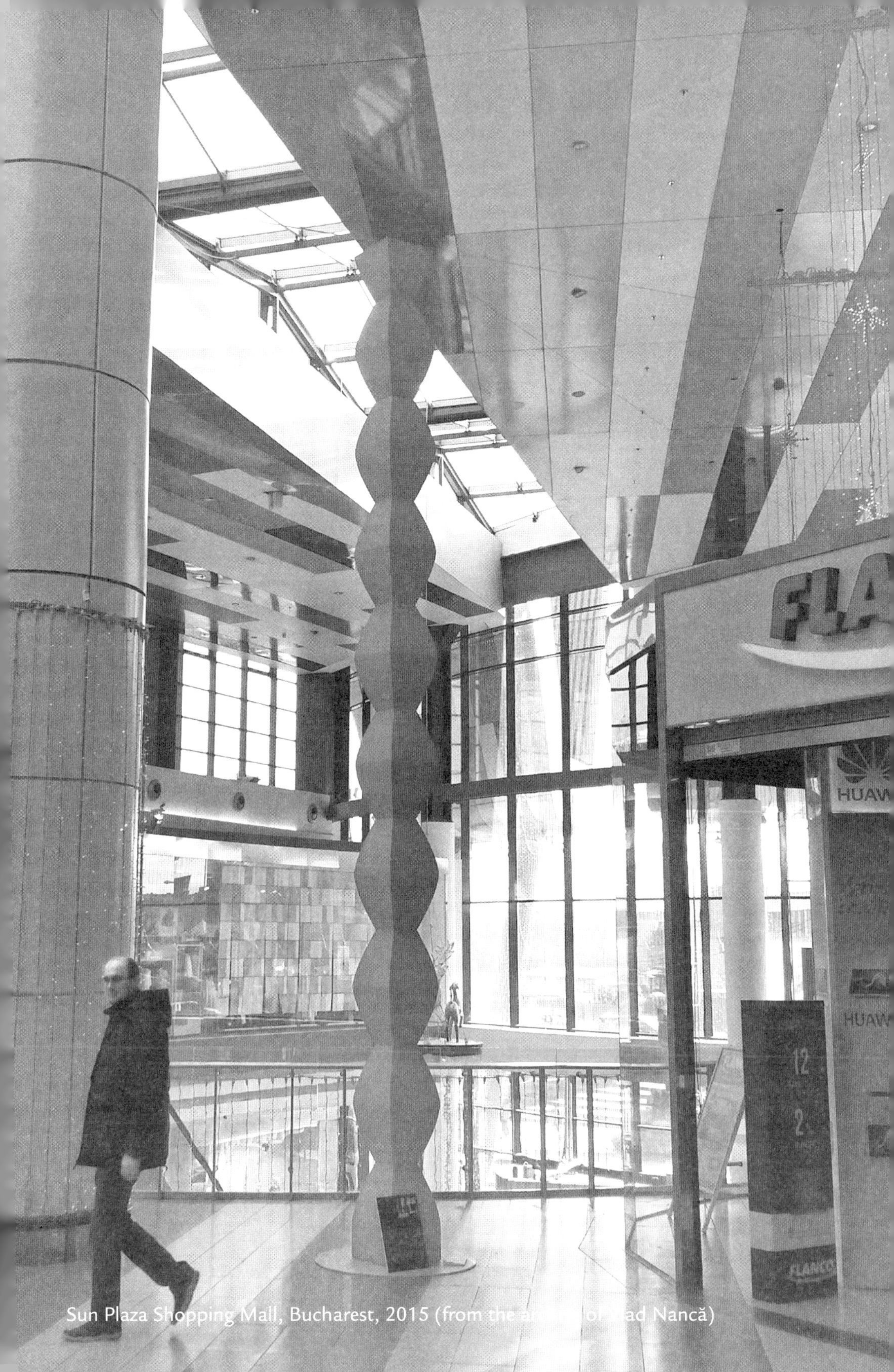

Sun Plaza Shopping Mall, Bucharest, 2015 (from the archive of Vlad Nancă)

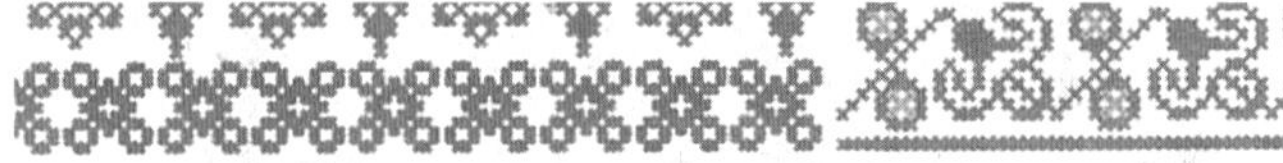

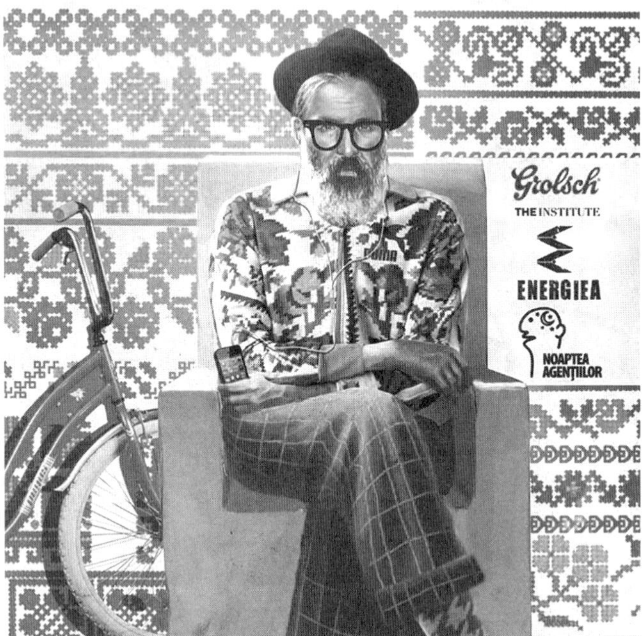

[What Does the Romanian Creative Look Like?]
Promotional campaign by Grolsch & *The Institute*, 2013

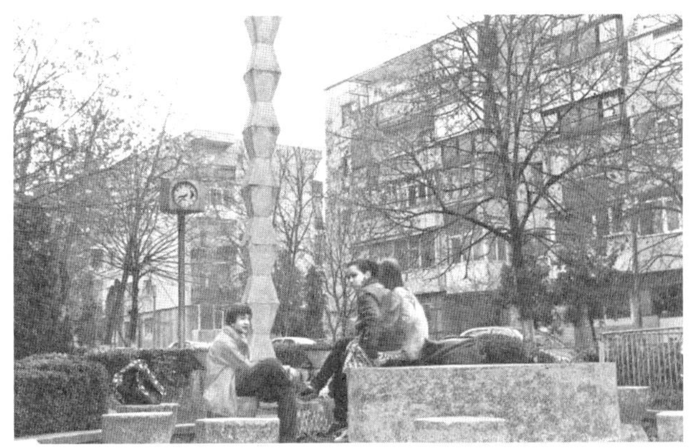

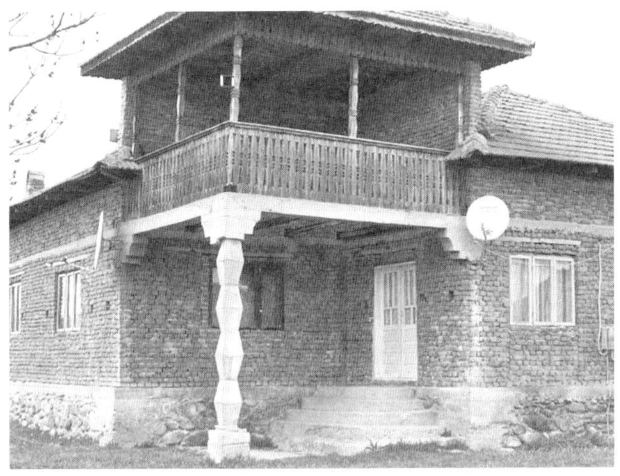

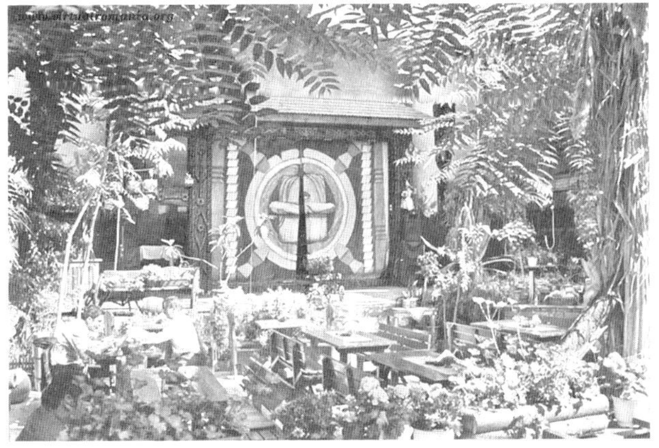

Usages of Brancusi in vernacular architecture and design
pre- and post-1989

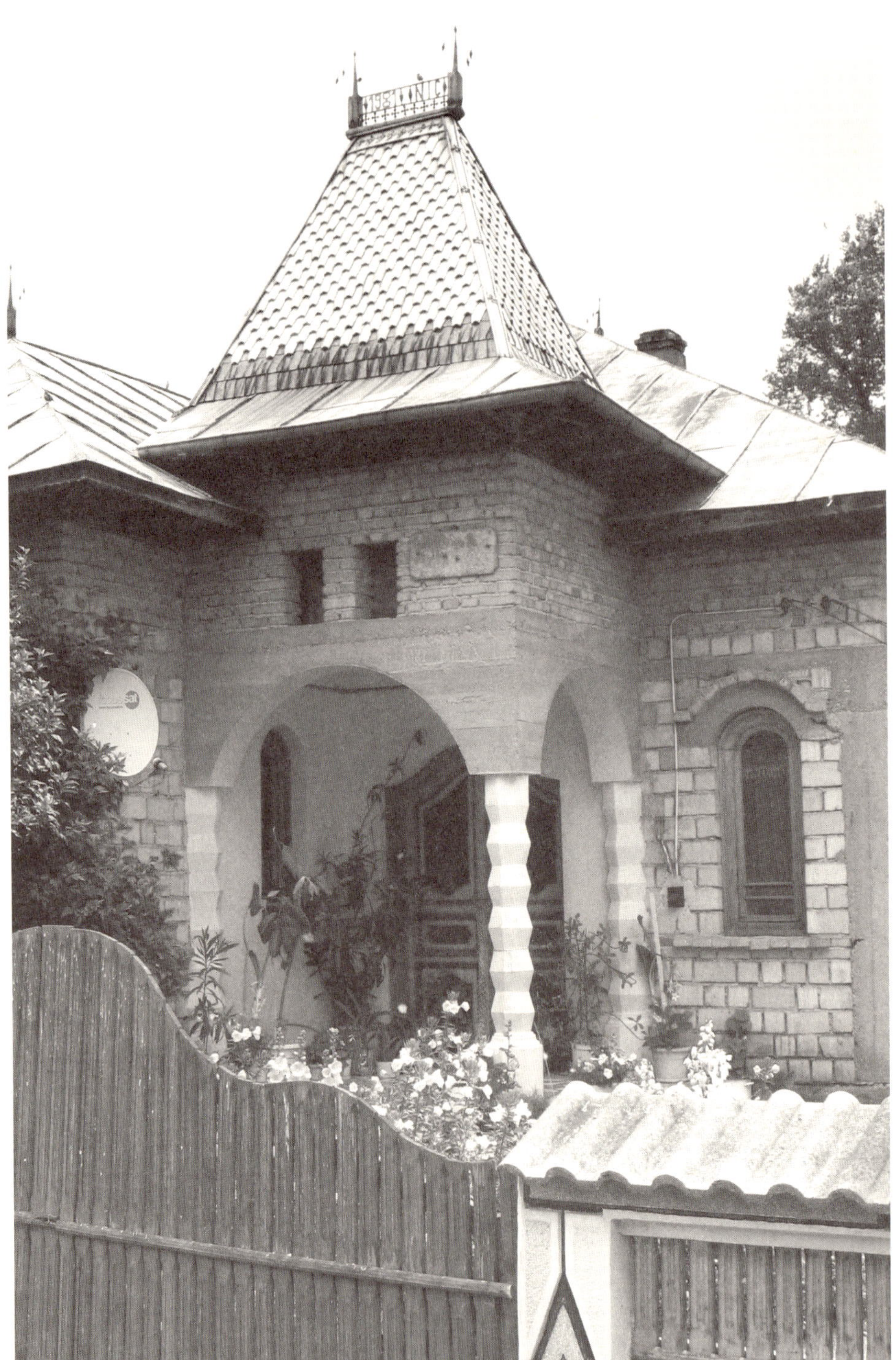

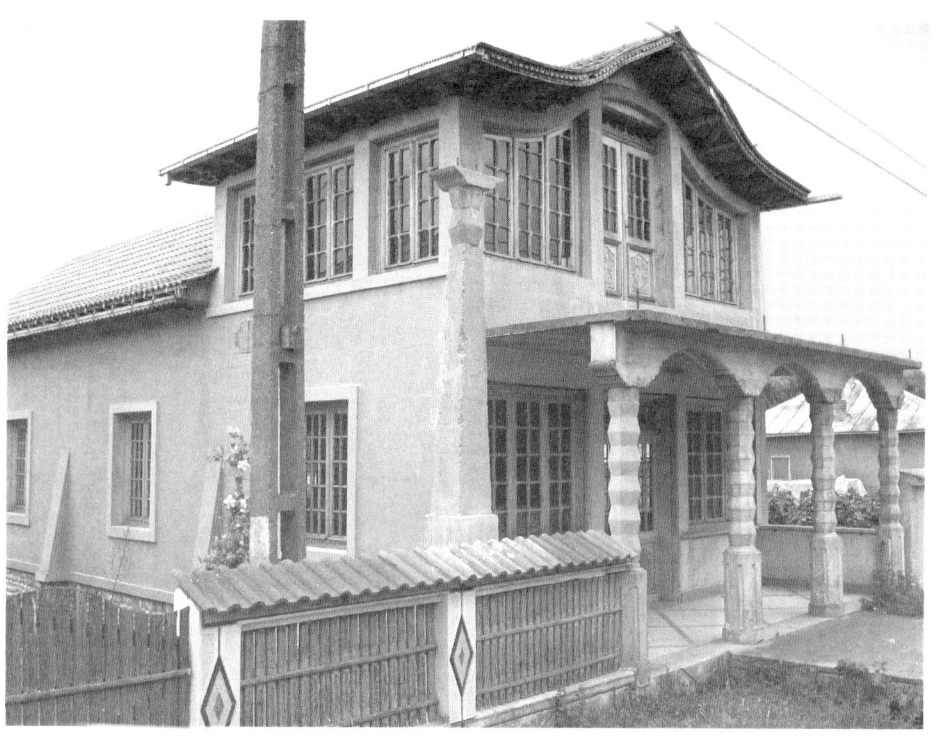

Usages of Brancusi in vernacular architecture and design post-1989
(from the archive of Mirela Duculescu)

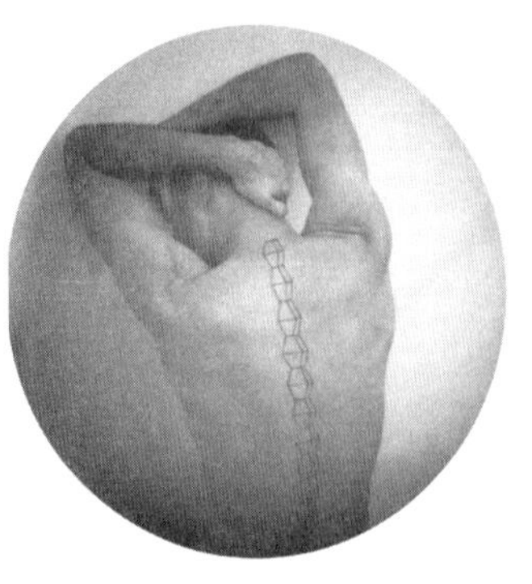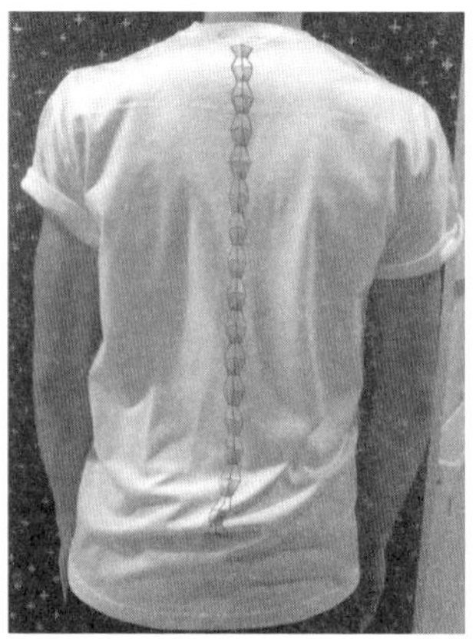

Photograph by Ștefan Cosma / Idelier T-shirt, 2012

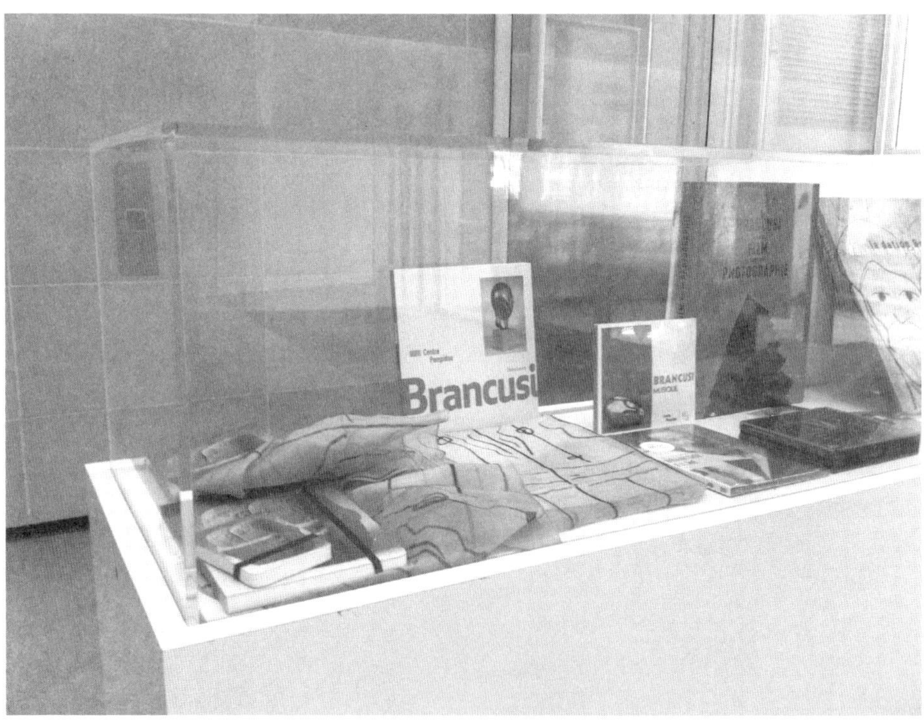

Vitrine in the foyer of the Brancusi Studio/MNAM, Paris, 2013

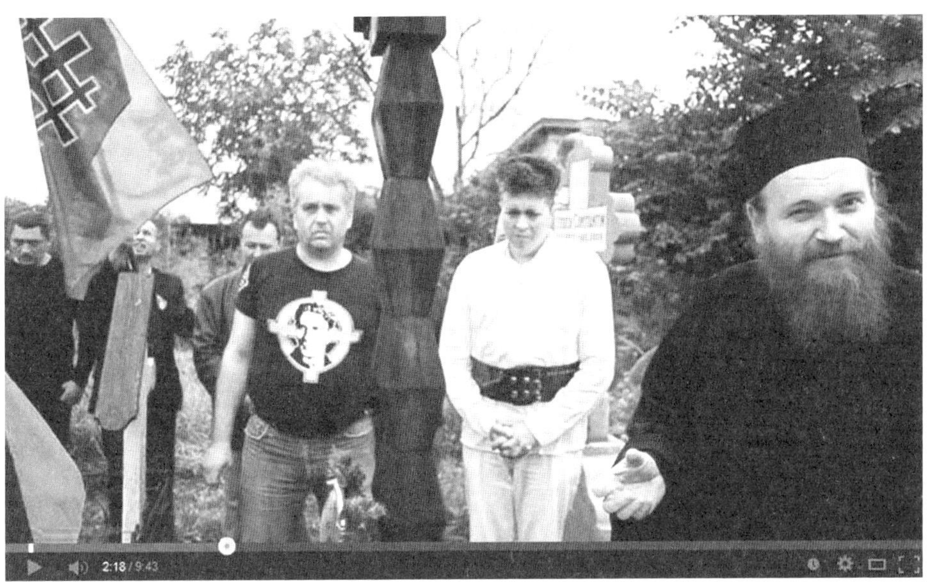

Aniversary of the far-right legionnaire movement, Ciolpani Cemetery, 2014

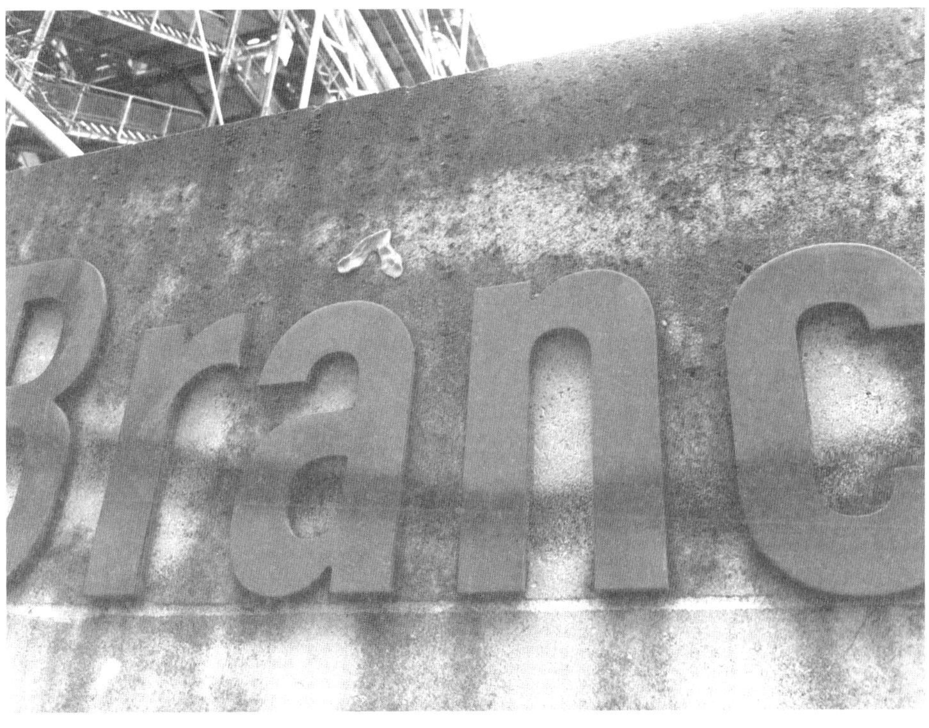

Chewing gum circumflex stuck to the façade of the Brancusi Studio/MNAM, Paris, 2013

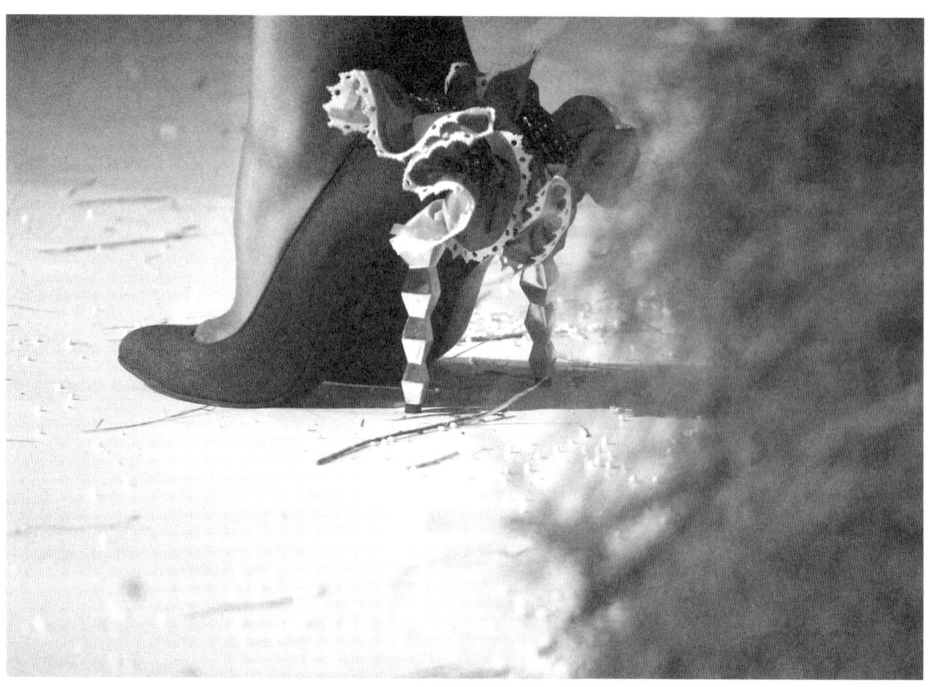

Shoes by designer Mihaela Glăvan produced as part of the 100%RO project, 2011

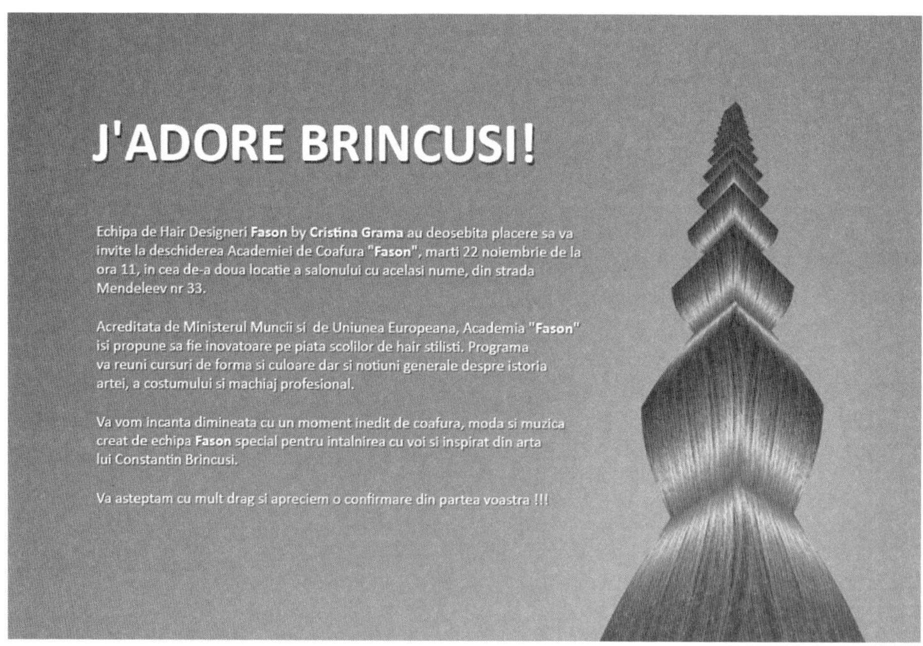

Invitation to the opening of Fason Hair Styling Academy, Bucharest, 2011

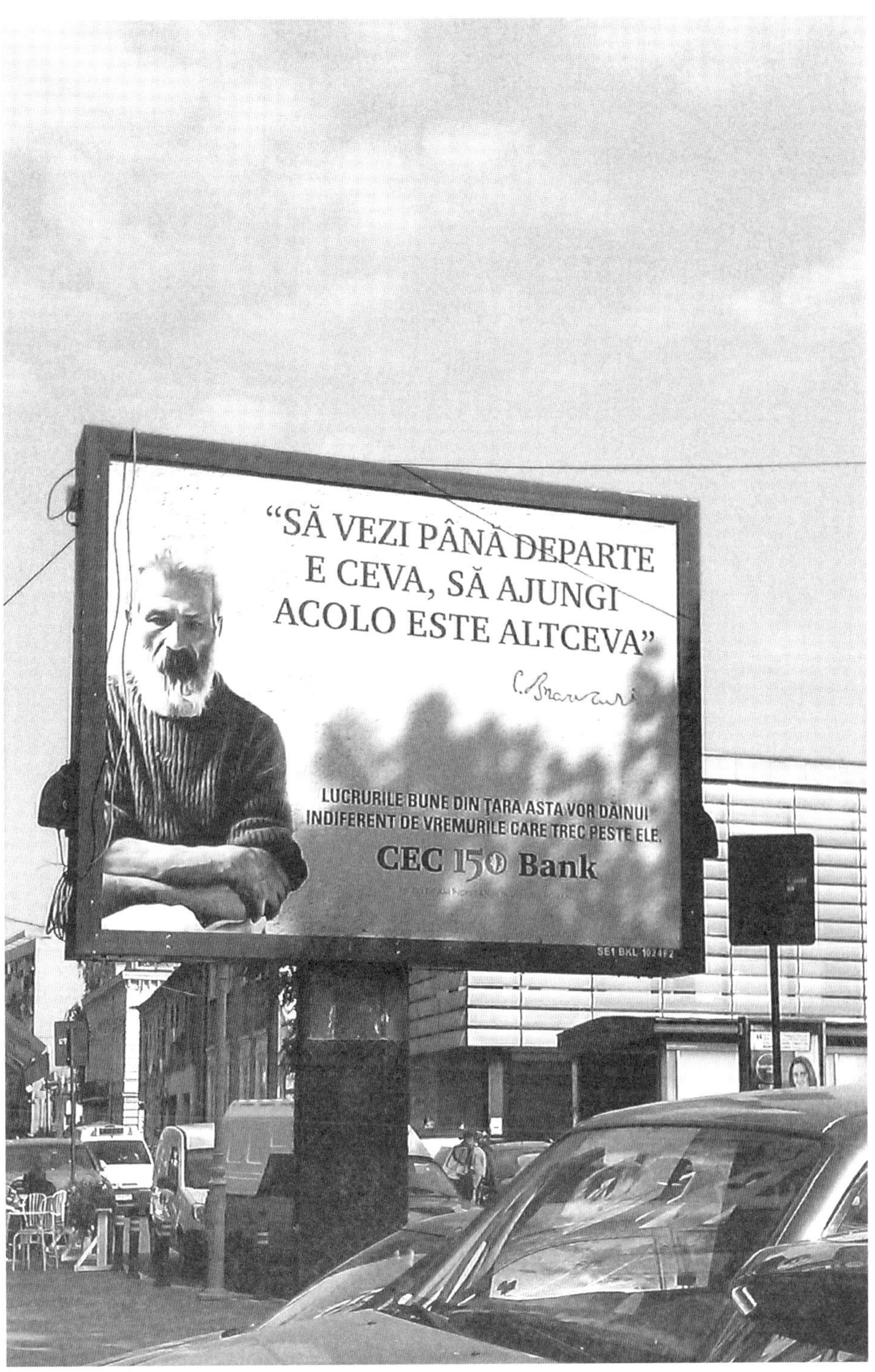

[The good things in this country will last regardless of the passing of time.] CEC Bank advertising campaign, 2014 (from the archive of Aurora Király)

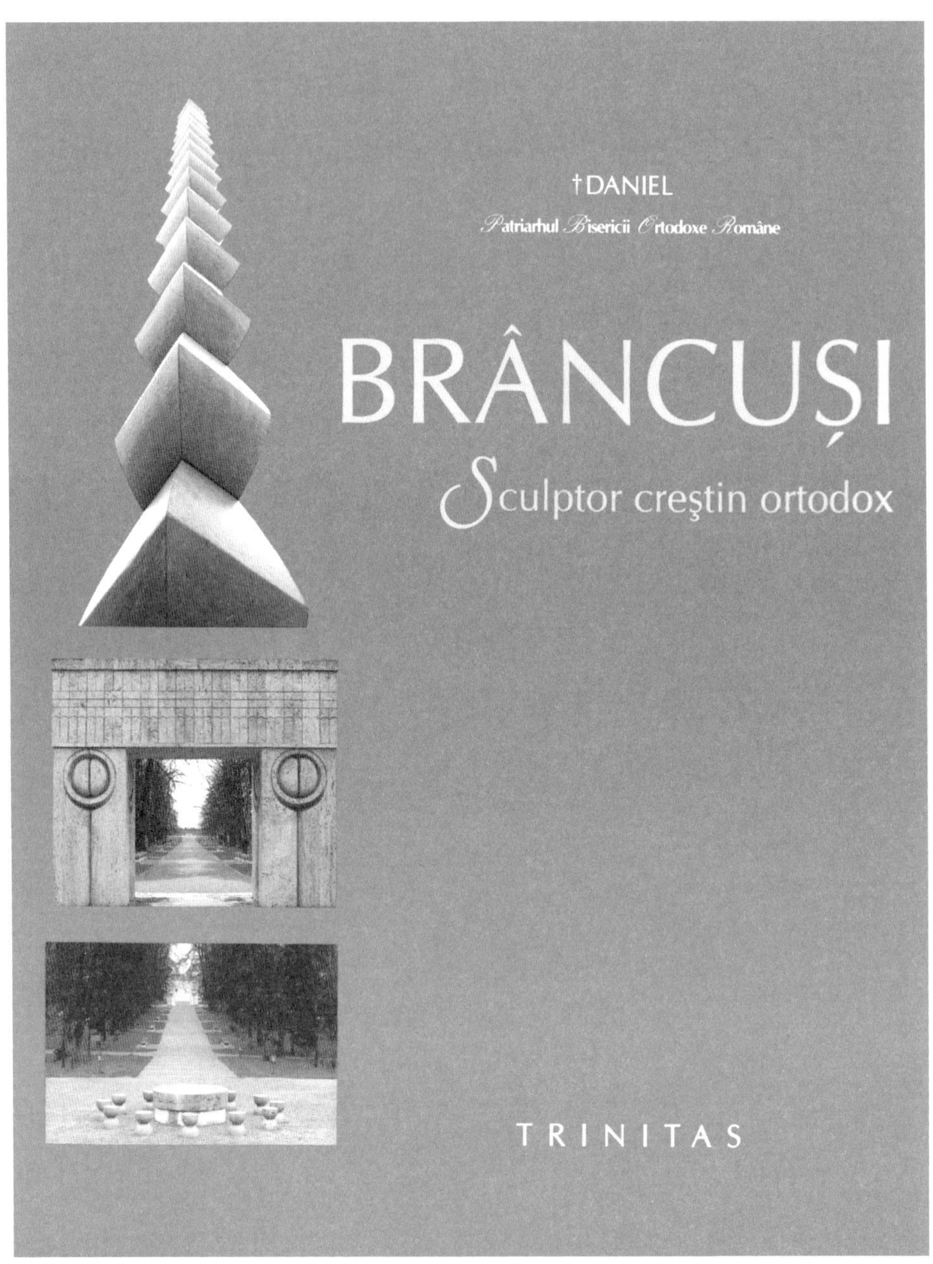

Brancusi: Christian Orthodox Sculptor, volume published by Daniel, Patriarch of the Romanian Orthodox Church, 2008

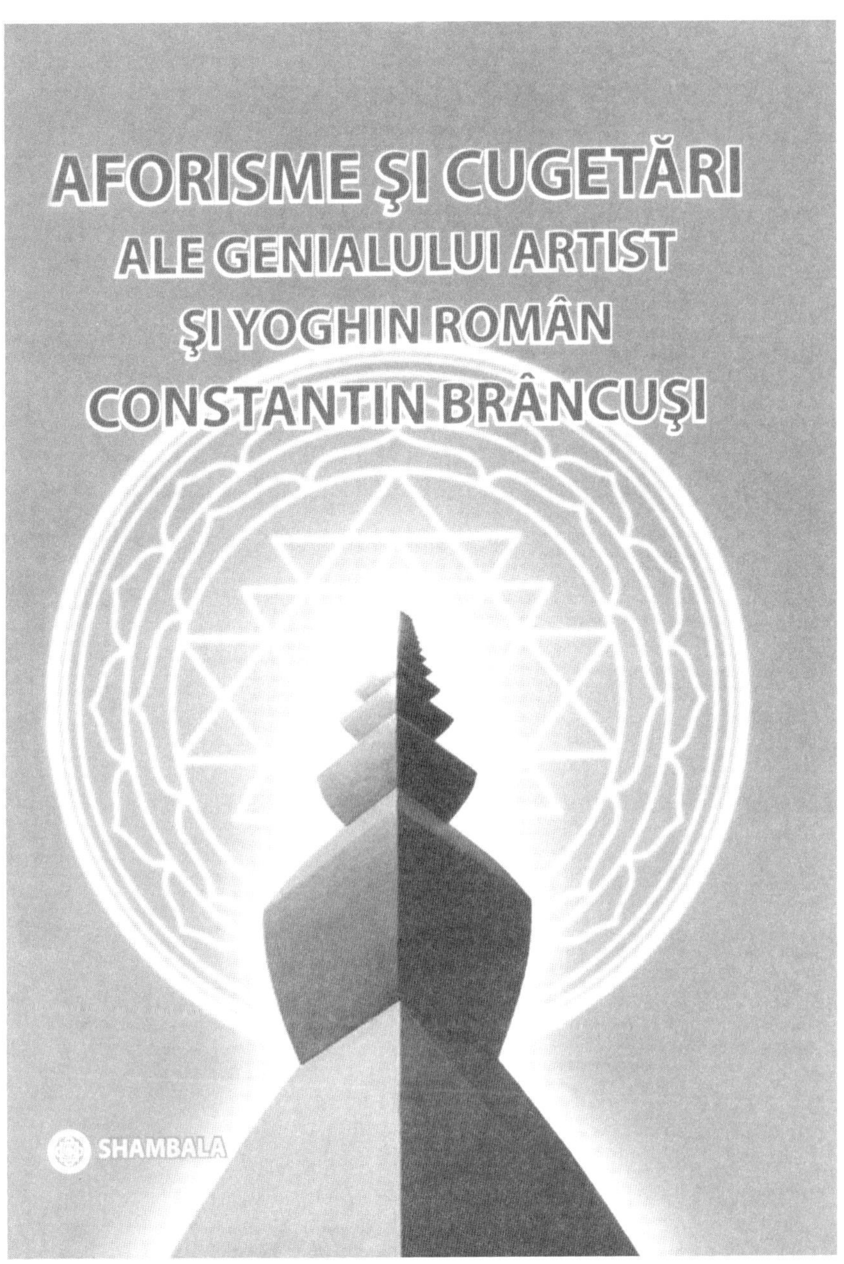

Aphorisms and Thoughts of the Romanian Artist Genius and Yogi Constantin Brancusi, volume edited by Gregorian Bivolaru, founder of the controversial Movement for Spiritual Integration into the Absolute (MISA), 2009

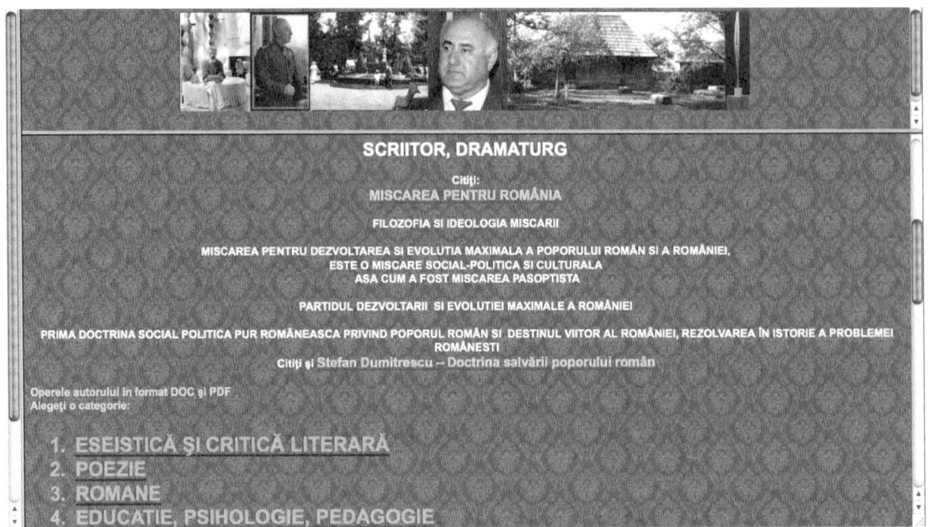

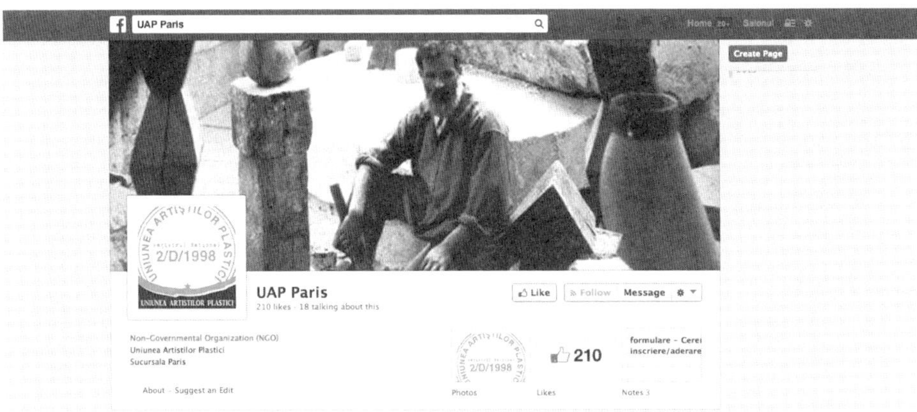

Usages of Brancusi on the Internet
Web page of the Movement for Romania, where the image of Brancusi appears alongside those of Marshal Ion Antonescu and the author of the movement's ideological texts / Facebook page of the Romanian Union of Artists, Paris Branch

Constantin Brancusi
April 24, 2013

"Eu sunt un prince paysan" Constantin Brancusi

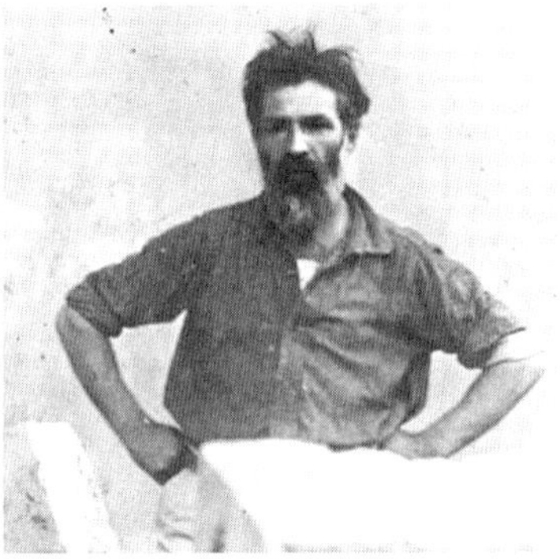

Like · Comment · Share 144 6 90

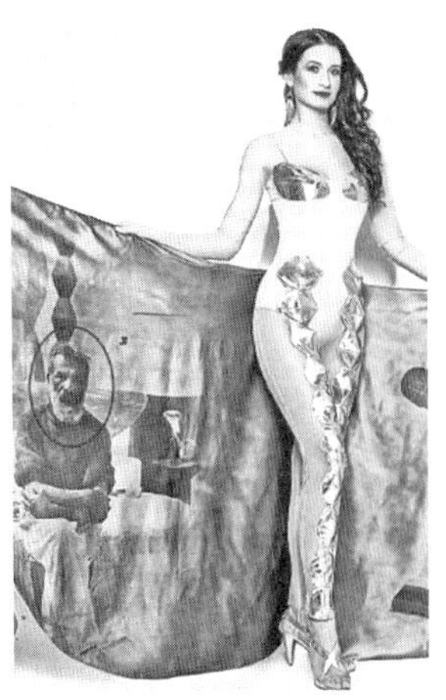
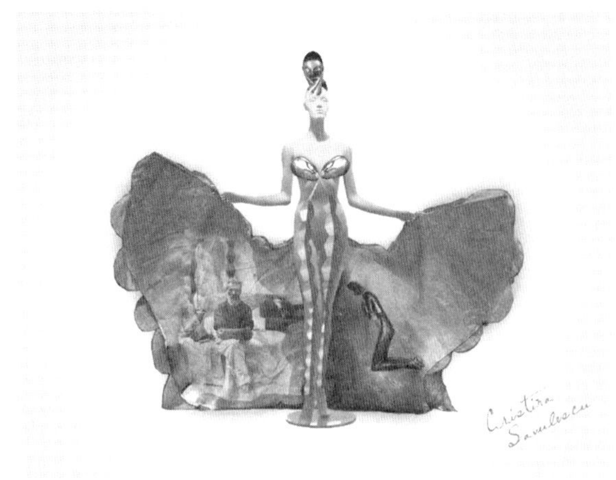

Costume for Miss Romania by designer Cristina Săvulescu, 2012

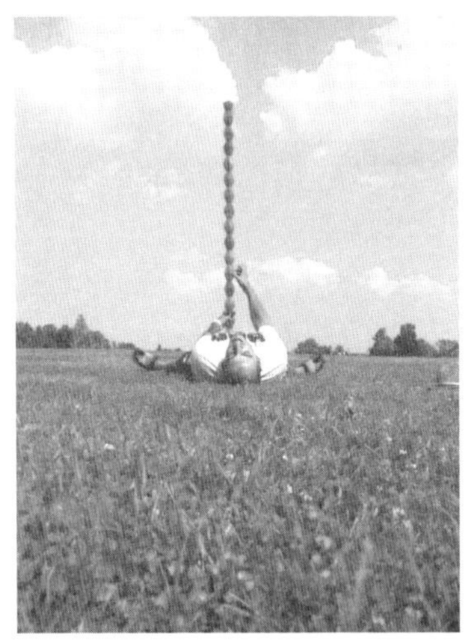

Pop singer CRBL at Târgu Jiu, 2012

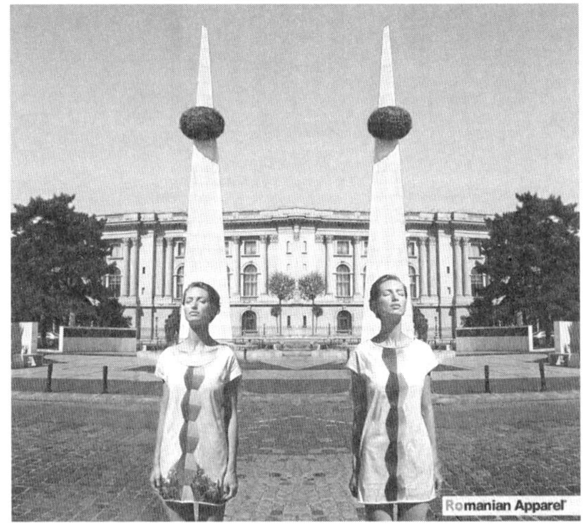

Dress by designer Lana, Romanian Apparel collection, 2011

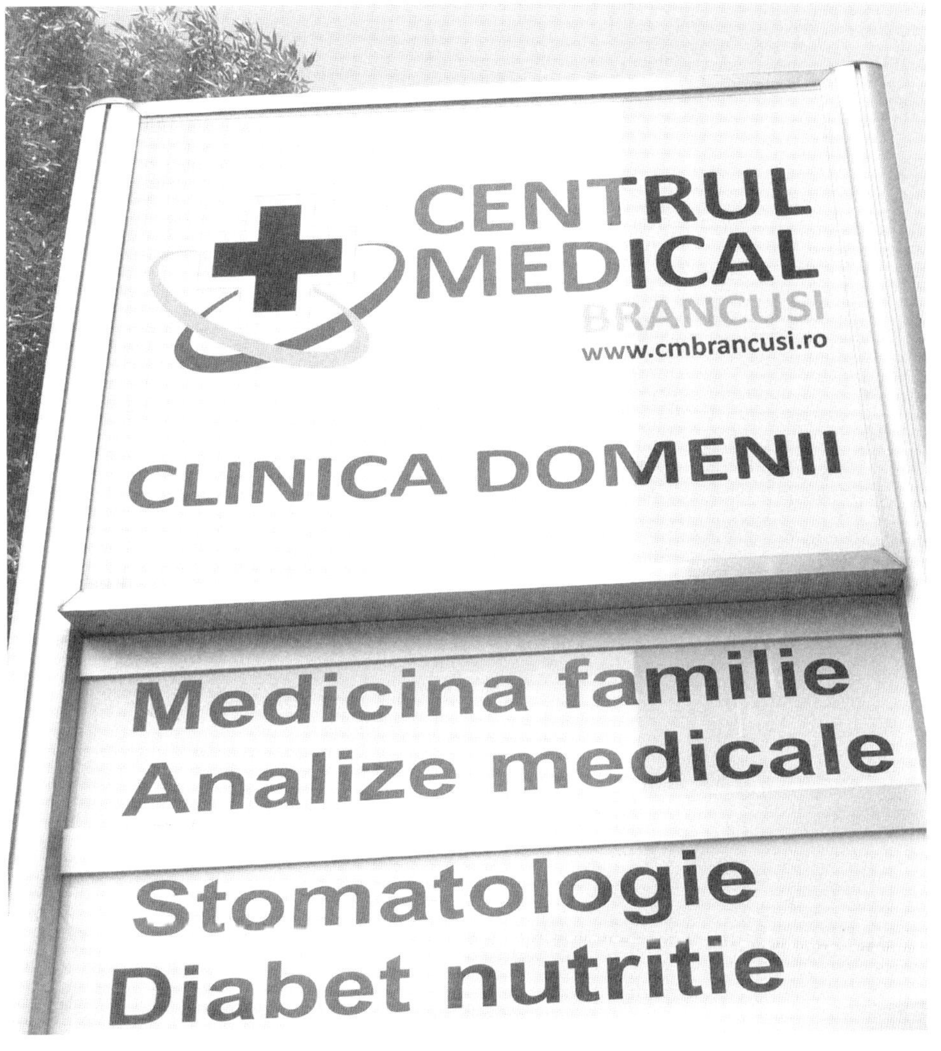

Brancusi private clinic, Bucharest, 2014

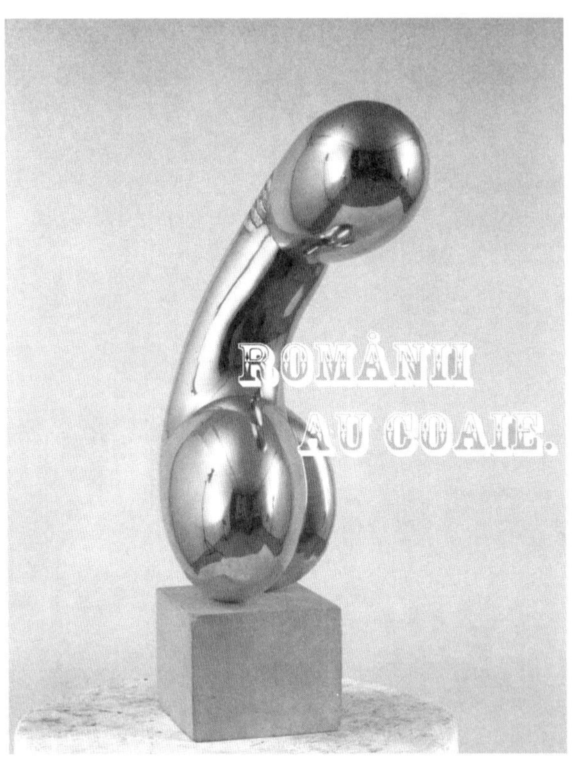

[Romanians Have Balls.] Found image

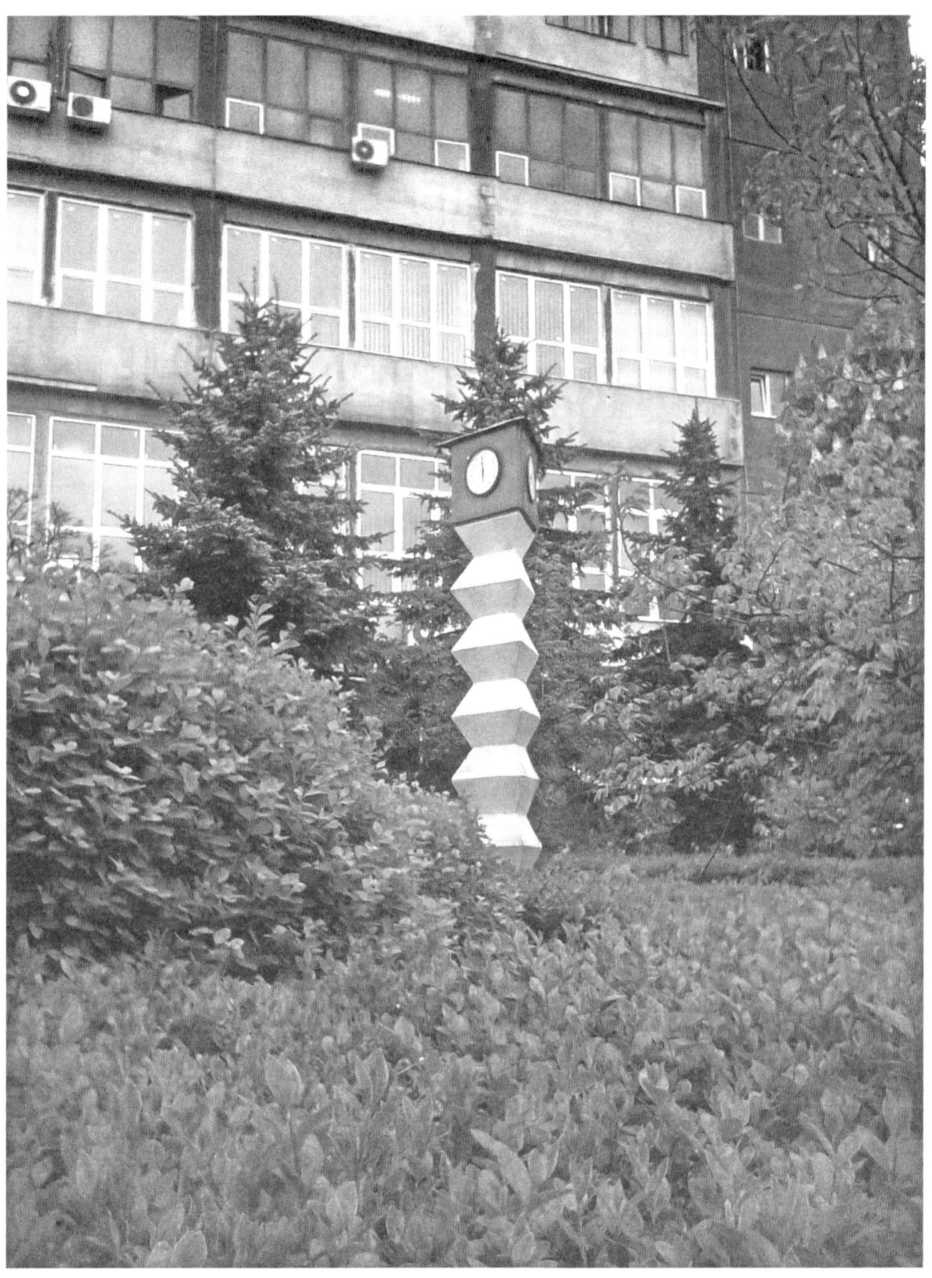

Usages of Brancusi in vernacular architecture and design post-1989
(from the archive of Vlad Nancă)

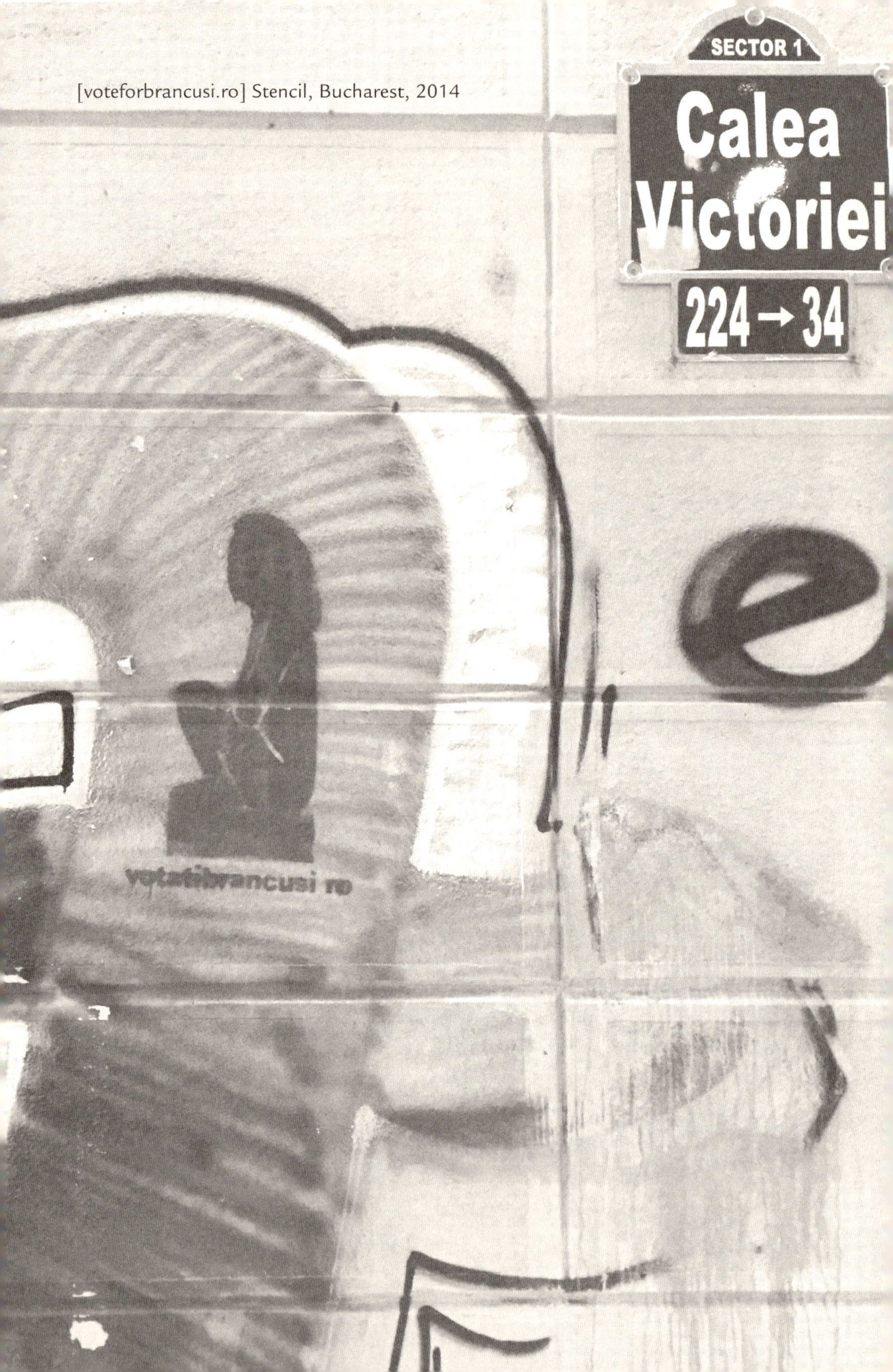

[voteforbrancusi.ro] Stencil, Bucharest, 2014

PART 5

Brancusi as a Character,
between Reality and Fiction

In attempting to outline a complex image of the process of mythologising Constantin Brancusi, we cannot overlook the literary texts that take the famous sculptor as a central character. In a text about Brancusi, Pontus Hulten argues that the sculptor's life story has become too fictionalised, thereby running the risk of affecting his work. Although he talks of "the banality of the points of view that distort the subject, with what is complex and magnificent becoming simple and ordinary,"[1] a discussion of such points of view can be extremely relevant to understanding the strategies whereby what is simple and ordinary can be idealised and turned into legend. Theorists like Ernst Kris and Otto Kurz observe "a recurrence of certain preconceptions about artists in all their biographies," which have common roots "that can be traced back to the beginnings of historiography."[2] The two authors identify certain anecdotes that can be found in numerous artistic biographies—a literary genre that emerges in Ancient Greece and comes to maturity during the Renaissance, when the figure of the artist becomes socially important—and have been perpetuated to the present. Thus, fictionalised moments connected to the birth and childhood of the artist, his first contact with art, the artist's calling to art (usually an extraordinary occurrence), his innate and precocious talent, his tenacity in confronting adverse circumstances all combine with historical details, giving rise to the myth of the artist.

Before commenting on Brancusi as a character, as he appears in the four plays and two novels I shall examine below, it is interesting also to discuss the way in which the image of Brancusi *the man* took shape, since the fictional character is constructed either as a result of a direct relationship between the authors and Brancusi or setting out from the image that popular culture has recycled from the various testimonies of those who knew him personally, combined with the aphorisms and texts attributed to Brancusi. But direct contact with Brancusi does not automatically generate a mirror image, just as his photographic self-portraits are not mere snapshots, but carefully staged images. As Anna Chave emphasises, we should take account of "Brancusi's long-running exercise in masquerade," which should be viewed "as an attempt to inhabit, to remake, and to challenge certain social stereotypes,"[3] and of the context of the Parisian bohemia, which cultivated exotic experiences and in which the sculptor wished to find a place. Chave argues that it suited Brancusi in the end "to assume a role many had long reserved for

---

1. Pontus Hulten, Natalia Dumitresco, Alexandre Istrati, *Brancusi*, Paris, Flammarion, 1986, p. 43.

2. Ernst Kris, Otto Kurz, *Legend, Myth, and Magic in the Image of the Artist*, New Haven, Yale University Press, 1979, p. 3.

3. Anna Chave, "Brancusi's Masquerade: Social Standing, Self-Image, and Photographic Im/posture" in *Brancusi: Masterpieces from Romanian Museums*, catalogue published by Gagossian Gallery New York, 2011.

him: the part of a simple yet sage soul whose life never changed, but instead—like his art—somehow transcended time."[4]

Highly important to this discussion of Brancusi as a character is the volume *The Undiscovered Brancusi: Notes and Romanian Correspondence*, published after Centre Pompidou received an archive, which up until 2001 had remained in the possession of the artist's heirs, containing drawings, notes and correspondence. Before this publication, much of the information about Brancusi and his artistic creed had been indirect, drawn from the accounts and texts of those who knew him and often adapted in such a way as to make it impossible to know the original source. In this way, the image of Brancusi that took shape over the course of time was one of contrasts: wise and ludic, simple and mysterious, taciturn and hospitable, ascetic and gourmand, peasant and philosopher, "shaman and showman,"[5] *"prince-paysan."*[6]

A number of Romanian authors who had direct contact with Brancusi wrote about him in their memoirs or published biographies that were fictionalised to a greater or lesser degree. In 1967, V. G. Paleolog, whom Petru Comarnescu regarded as "an Oltenian Creangă, with the knowledge of an economist, sociologist and philosopher," published *The Youth of Brancusi*, in which he drew upon "the wealth of confessions and memories that the artist shared with him," and in which are interwoven the "deeds of his life and interpretations of lofty significance, with a profound human echo." Here, Brancusi appears "splendidly bodied forth as a man, as an artist, as an emissary of tradition and modernity, of Romanian and universal culture."[7] Also part of the Oltenian strain, Petre Pandrea published in 1976 the first episode in a series dedicated to the sculptor, *Brancusi: Memories and Exegeses*. The author himself says that it is a volume made up of "fragmentary and mosaic-like memories of a great man" whom he often visited, written with "the professional distortions of the jurist and the melancholy of the memoirist," who "comments on ideas and events recorded with approximate fidelity" from the position of the "court clerk of a famous trial conducted in the tribunal of visual arts and contemporary philosophy."[8] In regard to *The Saint of Montparnasse*, "a novel written with love for Brancusi and his art," Peter Neagoe relied, according to his own account, "on living documentary material which to a large extent 'darkened' his possibili-

---

4. *Ibidem.*

5. Reginald Pollack, "Shaman and Showman. An Intimate Portrait of the Legendary Romanian Sculptor Constantin Brancusi, by the Artist Who Was His Next-Door Neighbour in Paris," *Art and Antiques*, 05/1988, p. 95.

6. Petre Pandrea, *Brâncuşi: Pravila de la Craiova*, Bucharest, Vremea, 2010, p. 64.

7. Petru Comarnescu, foreword to V. G. Paleolog, V.G. Paleolog, *Tineretea lui Brâncuşi*, Bucharest, Editura Tineretului, 1967, pp. 9–12.

8. Petre Pandrea, *Brâncuşi: Amintiri şi exegeze*, Bucharest, Meridiane, 1976, pp. 5, 10, 69.

ties of turning Brancusi's life into literature."[9] Petre Pandrea believes that, between a biography and a novel, "with well-developed inventiveness and narrative," "Peter Neagoe's memoirs show credibility and lifelikeness," with "the conversation of Brancusi being conveyed with fidelity to the point of notary-like authenticity."[10]

Although in all the materials there is talk about the extraordinary memory of the respective authors—Paleolog's is "fantastic,"[11] Neagoe's is "phenomenal and similar to that of Nicolae Iorga"[12]—or, in Pandrea's case, about the methods "of the stenographer, of the court clerk, of the jurist at a public trial" whereby he recorded "fragments and allocutions characteristic of the sculptor with the oral genius of the prophet, the saint, the hero, Aesopus, Păcală, Nasreddin Hodja, or *Salonlöwe*,"[13] it is impossible to regard these texts as objective, given the authors' respect, love, admiration and obsession when it comes to Brancusi. But as Irina Cărăbaş also remarks in a text that analyses the image of Brancusi's studio as presented in the novels *The Interview* and *The Saint of Montparnasse*, "what is interesting in the literature that makes art its subject is ultimately not so much its documentary value as its capacity to put forward images, myths and stereotypes of the artist and the art, and thereby to create a parallel history of art."[14]

As far as the texts and aphorisms attributed to Brancusi are concerned, they ought to be viewed with the same scepticism. From the ideas expressed by the artist in conversations in his studio to the mythologised form thereof we find today, there were countless versions transmitted via different channels. The aphorisms were first published in the catalogue of an exhibition of the sculptor's work at the Brummer Gallery in 1926 (in English), whereafter they were reproduced in other catalogues, magazines and publications about Brancusi, including Petre Pandrea's *Brancusi: Memories and Exegeses*, "collected by the author from living speech or from catalogues"[15] and by Constantin Zărnescu in *Brancusi's Aphorisms and Texts*, published in 1980 and now in its sixth edition. Zărnescu makes use of various sources—visitors to the studio who collected and published aphorisms in various publications and also documents that cannot be verified: "letters, the confessions made by some Brancusiologists—V. G. Paleolog, Carola Giedion-Welcker, Milița Petrașcu et al.—to the author."[16] More recently, another two (trilingual) publications have appeared:

---

9. Ioan A. Popa, preface to Peter Neagoe, *Sfântul din Montparnasse*, Cluj, Dacia, 1977, pp. 5, 12.

10. Pandrea, *op. cit.*, p. 77.

11. Petru Comarnescu, foreword to V.G. Paleolog, *Tinerețea lui Brâncuși*, p. 5.

12. Petre Pandrea, *Brâncuși: Amintiri și exegeze*, p. 78.

13. *Idem*, p. 77.

14. Irina Cărăbaş, "Literary Representations of Brancusi's Studio," *Rev. Roum. Hist. Art*, Beaux-Arts Series, Tome XLIX, Bucharest, 2012, p. 126.

15. *Idem*, p. 258.

16. Constantin Zărnescu, *Aforismele și textele lui Brâncuși*, Craiova, Scrisul Românesc, 1980, p. 238.

Brancusi: Carver in the Spirit by Ștefan Stăiculescu and *Thus Spoke Brancusi* by Sorana Georgescu-Gorjan. Since 1926, the number of aphorisms has grown from the thirteen originals to 120 in the "Codex of Brancusi" compiled by Petre Pandrea, 254 in Zărnescu's volume, 274 in Ștefan Stăiculescu's volume, and 550 in Sorana Georgescu-Gorjan's volume.

To return to *The Undiscovered Brancusi*, the publication highlights the inaccuracy of writings attributed to Brancusi, the literary adaptations carried out by the authors of collections, and problematic translations. In the volume, the manuscripts were published in the original version (including the original spelling and syntax) and classified according to content (since they could not be dated).

Although the existence of pages that contain the best-known aphorisms, transcribed with careful spelling and handwriting, some of them even titled "Aphorisms," seems to prove Brancusi's intention to publish them—he was of "the conviction that he was in possession of a treasure, feeling he was invested with the mission to pass it down to future generations not only via his art"—Doina Lemny wonders whether the publication of the volume is not "an impiety towards the memory of Brancusi, who was so discreet and reserved."[17] If it is an impiety, it would appear to be a welcome one. Lemny believes on the one hand that the volume provides "the Romanian public with the opportunity to get even closer to the artist who in the depths of his soul always remained Romanian" and, on the other, that no matter how many documents might come to light "the creator and his work continue to be enveloped in the same shadows of mystery, which confer on the man nobility, and on the work an inexhaustible profundity and inestimable value."[18]

The Interview by Ilarie Voronca

Ilarie Voronca was one of the most interesting authors of the Romanian avant-garde. He began his career in the cenacle of Eugen Lovinescu and later become one of the main proponents of modernist trends connected to Futurism, Dadaism and in particular Constructivism. After aligning himself with *Contimporanul* magazine's "Manifesto to the Activist Youth," in 1924 he published the single issue of *75 HP* magazine with Victor Brauner and Stephan Roll and contributed to manifestos published by other avant-garde magazines such as *Punct* and *Integral*. Published in *unu* magazine, his contributions began to show the influence of Surrealism, which became stronger after Voronca settled in Paris in 1933 and began to write in French. He gave up manifestos, essays and poems, and started to write poetic prose and fantastic stories.

---

17. Doina Lemny, Cristian-Robert Velescu (eds.), *Brâncuși inedit: Însemnări și corespondență românească*, Bucharest, Humanitas, 2004, pp. 21, 41.

18. *Idem*, pp. 21, 42.

The Interview may be regarded as an oneiric prose poem, as Ion Pop suggests in his preface to the 1989 translation, albeit constructed using real-life references to Brancusi and his work, whom the author knew personally. The relationship between the two is presented as "quite close," since Brancusi agreed to illustrate with a number of drawings the poems in the volume *Plants and Animals* from 1929.[19] In the introduction to the volume, Barbu Brezianu talks of "the ascendancy which the sculptor exerted over the writer," who "openly affirmed his devotion" to Brancusi and believed that "he was 'blessed' to count himself among his closest friends."[20]

The Interview is an account of initiation into the mysteries of creation that the author, under a false identity, experiences during a visit to the studio of the "sculptor of the mountains." This adventure, which begins with a search for sensational details that might provide the subject for a newspaper article and ends with a meditation on war and death, takes place in a strange world between reality, dream and nightmare. The story provides what Ion Pop calls "the symbolic equivalent of the complex laboratory of modern art, conceived as a domain of absolute availability of the spirit, of demiurgic free play, whereby what might be considered as given nature is destructed and recomposed according to the creator's will."[21] We recognise the theatrical scenery of the studio in the Impasse Ronsin, Brancusi's qualities as a "visionary curator"[22] who composes with great attention the installations made up of different works from his studio and "the spectacle carefully directed by the sculptor, an integral part of which was the unveiling of the sculptures covered by pieces of canvas."[23]

In Voronca's text, the figure of the Creator is constructed as a hybrid of God and Brancusi—"an avuncular figure with a smiling face," "harsh hands with short fingers like a surgeon's," "with a voice full of goodness," who speaks of the creation of the world in terms of a process of artistic creation: "I have carved mountains," "I wished to associate my art with the knowledge of the gardener as much as the instinct of animals and plants," "in my builder's hands this world was nothing but a preliminary model." From the outset, the Creator appears to us as a character weighed down by frustrations: on the one hand he is dissatisfied that people have come to value the creation more highly than the creator: "Vast forms did I carve in the clouds, did I hew in the wind, until one fine day, casting a glance at

---

19. Barbu Brezianu, introduction to Ilarie Voronca, *Interviul. Unsprezece povestiri* [The Interview. Eleven Stories], Bucharest, Cartea Românească, 1989, p. 15.

20. *Idem*, pp. 22–23.

21. Ion Pop, "Reîntîlnire cu Ilarie Voronca" [Meeting Ilarie Voronca Again] in Ilarie Voronca, *Interviul. Unsprezece povestiri*, p. 16.

22. Pollack, *op. cit.*

23. Robert Payne, "Constantin Brâncuși," *World Review*, 3 October 1949.

this old work, I noticed the great success it enjoyed. All had forgotten me, all fought fiercely to possess the work." The other motive for frustration is connected to the fact that people have focussed their attention on only one of his works—namely *the world*, which He made in six days, ignoring "the other works that have remained unknown": "Can anybody imagine that all the resources of my talent were exhausted in a single work? (...) They contemplate only my sculptures made from clay, from fire, from water and from air." Although the Creator "unleashed the terrible storms against this work" and "shattered the statues into fragments," the people "clung to their material visions, refusing to turn their gaze to the creations dear to him." We may therefore speculate that the *other works* are none other than the sculptural work of Constantin Brancusi, here presented as occupying the highest rung on the ladder of universal values and which can be revealed only to the chosen, to the initiated, to those prepared to contemplate. An obvious similarity may be observed between what the Creator confesses—"only for my own joy and that of the initiates who from time to time come to seek me do I labour on my secret work"—and one of the famous aphorisms of Brancusi, in which he talks about the same initiation through contemplation: "Contemplate my works until you will see them. Those close to God have seen them."[24]

Throughout this initiatory journey into the imaginary, the Creator appears misunderstood, solitary and discouraged, "depressed and preoccupied with the fate of mankind," continuing his "fantastical labour, without pause and without ever being satisfied" in his search for the joy, peace and equilibrium which, according to another of Brancusi's aphorisms, can only be gained through renunciation.[25] The spiritual asceticism that drives the Creator is abruptly counterbalanced in Voronca's "Afterword," where he remembers "the steaks with garlic sauce that were one of the specialities of sculptor B., the partial or complete model of the creator" and "the memorable feasts in the company of the noble and ingenious old man." If there is any shadow of a doubt as to the source of inspiration for the character of the Creator, it is dispelled by the author himself: the features and gestures of the Creator "belong to celebrated sculptor B., a peasant from a country on the Danube."[26]

---

24. Constantin Zărnescu, *Aforismele și textele lui Brâncuși*, p. 100.

25. "Art's mission is to create *joy*; and it is possible to create artistically only in equilibrium and in spiritual peace... And peace is obtained through renunciation. *La paix et la joie; la joie et la paix! Voila!...*" Constantin Zărnescu, *Aforismele și textele lui Brâncuși*, p. 114.

26. All the quotations in this chapter, unless otherwise stated, are from Ilarie Voronca, *Interviul. Unsprezece povestiri*, Bucharest, Cartea Românească, 1989.

After he studied art in Bucharest, where he was a fellow student with Brancusi, Peter Neagoe emigrated to America, returning to Europe after the First World War and settling in Paris, where he abandoned his career as an artist and instead became a writer, integrating into the community of expatriate American intellectuals. In Paris he met Brancusi once again and made him the central character of his novel *The Saint of Montparnasse*, posthumously published in 1965. Neagoe "dedicated his work to the Romanian peasant,"[27] with the volumes he published in his lifetime taking as their subject the realities of the Transylvanian countryside. Believing that Brancusi "achieved the level of the universal because he is an authentic Romanian" and that "his art has a limpidity that only a man of the soil, a genius of the people, the people itself can achieve,"[28] Neagoe decided to dedicate a book to him, with his fascination for the Romanian peasant finding its fulfilment in this homage to the sculptor. The friendship between the two was "without clouds and without storms" and lasted until the sculptor's death. Petre Pandrea regarded the novel as "a funerary monument erected by a friend in honour of the friend from his youth, the friend of a lifetime."[29] Presented in the preface as "the yield of a sentimental and artistic impulse," written with "sincerity and great devotion," "with love for Brancusi and his art,"[30] the novel is a fictionalised biography of the sculptor (although the author places the emphasis on the accuracy of the details, the book often being read as a scholarly work). The narrative traces the chronology of Brancusi's life, with an emphasis on the period he spent in Paris. Besides a number of details not in keeping with the reality, detected by various Brancusiologists, the fictional additions mainly relate to Brancusi's spiritual, sentimental and love life. A fictional character, Mihai Romanov, is also added, appearing at crucial moments in the sculptor's life and witnessing his death.

Brancusi is presented as a mischievous and unruly child, who breaks social rules but is in constant communion with nature. As a child he finds his vocation while making "mud pies" in his father's pottery workshop. He cultivates this vocation through harsh discipline and is prepared to pursue it despite discouragement from his family, who regard art as a waste of time, a game ("Not even a ploughman looks at the field he has sown more happily than Constantin looks at a stone"). Brancusi regards carving as "work, although nobody agreed with him," and dreams of "becoming free and carving as much as he liked"; he dreams of "escaping and being

---

27. Ioan A. Popa, preface to Peter Neagoe, *Sfântul din Montparnasse*, p. 6.

28. Peter Neagoe quoted by Ioan A. Popa in *op. cit.*, p. 7.

29. Petre Pandrea, *Brâncuși: Amintiri și exegeze*, p. 74.

30. Popa, *op. cit.*, pp. 6, 12.

free." The sculptor's yearning for freedom, likened to that of "the shepherd who, under the vast sky, plays on his whistle notes springing from the depths of his soul," is present throughout the novel, and is presented as the reason why he never marries or has children. "The desire to sculpt flooded his entire being—he had to give shape to the figments of his imagination." The years of his artistic training in Romania do not play an important part in the novel, although it is here that the sculptor's anti-academic attitude takes shape, which is later sublimated in the famous Rodin episode. "Perseverant and hardy, endowed with a peasant's strength of labour," he manages to survive his "pilgrimage" and arrives in the "holy city," where he becomes preoccupied with "finding a path whereby to transcend his own self, to blend slowly into the universe." In his searches he comes to spend "three nights a week at the National Library," where he discovers oriental culture ("in the silence of the library, the thoughts that tormented him exploded like firecrackers"). In this way there takes shape the image of a saint, not in the Christian Orthodox manner, but rather in the Buddhist mould, with the Brancusi character explaining his working process as follows: "Man can reach perfection in an infinitesimal moment of harmony. Meditation prepares me for art. This is the secret: in creation a moment of preparation is necessary." Brancusi is presented as a true yogi: his programme of meditation begins with "exercises whose aim is to allow the mind to control certain parts of the body" and continues with "practice of the art of concentration, in order to erase the barrier between spirit and matter." He thus comes to rely more on "intuition than on judgement," with intuition being "complemented and sharpened by meditation and discipline." Neagoe presents in detail the Hatha Yoga techniques followed by Brancusi. Through the discipline of the Oriental ascetics he comes to liberate his self, sometimes helped by "moderate doses of drugs," which make him imagine himself to be "an Indian sadhu in search of the truth, an explorer trying to discover the astonishing snatches of a world little accessible to the consciousness." Thus, "contemplation leads to the crystallisation of the form sought," and his genius is guided by his guardian spirit, Milarepa, who "leads him to the realisation of the work" and shows him the way whereby he will revolutionise modern sculpture. In Neagoe's novel Brancusi is a character of contrasts. Here, for example, Modigliani addresses him, while trying to portray him: "You are as cunning as a fox; but you cannot act like a fox because you are a humane peasant. Nor can you appear in the guise of a scientist, although you are as absent. You are an excellent cook. I have never tasted a steak better than the one you cook. But how can I paint you as a cook? I know that you do not eat for days in order to attain a revelation. But nor are you a saint, since your eyes light up when you see girls. You are too complex." The presentation of Brancusi's love life occupies a large part of the novel, with the women in his life playing the "role of highlighting the man's deeply human side, his integrity of character, his sincerity and the profundity of his feelings,"[31] although in the end these female characters represent merely a temptation which Brancusi manages to resist so that he can dedicate himself wholly to his sculpture and his spiritual life. Brancusi, presented as a virile man on whose face can be read "self-confidence and manliness," is initiated into the secrets of sex by Rada, a girl from his village, "whose body he kneads like a piece of clay" during the long winter nights. In Bucharest he meets Livia, the daughter of his teacher, whom he saves from depression with his "strong arms" and "his lips that brought oblivion," but who in the end makes him realise that "love is like a piece of bread. You eat it when you are hungry; then you put it aside in order to create." In Paris he is torn between Marthe, whom he regards as of inferior intellect and exploits to keep house and to pose for him, consoling himself that "she had greater need of him [than he had of her]" and accepting "her devotion without regarding it as a debasement," and Elaine, a rich, "perverse and carnal" American, with whom he embarks on a stormy relationship based on physical attraction, which is consummated in "long hours of passion." In this relationship, Brancusi appears as a "thoroughbred animal" in whom "the manliness of the mountain peasant was fully at home," but who cannot adapt to the superficiality of Elaine's lifestyle and tries without success to convert her to Buddhism. In the end he loses both women and is overwhelmed by a feeling of loneliness: "Elaine was unable to offer his spiritual peace, and Marthe was not capable of encouraging him." After the disappointment caused by Elaine, who remains "heartless and vulgar," Brancusi transforms himself from a "slave of her passions" into the "full master of his six chakras" and begins to live a life of abstinence, in the belief that "the bodily appetites are the root of all evils" and that "you cannot attain perfection by sinning." He thus becomes one of those ascetics who "fully enjoy the presence of the seminal fluid, which make their bodies radiate energy," he henceforth dedicates himself "body and soul" to his art and "lives a simple life and remains pure in spirit, even if he has to isolate himself in order to do so. Recognition and success no longer mean anything to him. He becomes the 'priest' who transforms the profane into the sacred." In his studio, the "visitors felt that they were in close proximity to a saint. He had the gift of healing people's pains, and radiated goodness."

During the course of the novel, in the tradition of a Brancusi of contrasts, Peter Neagoe portrays a character who is simultaneously "a scion of the Dacian ancestors," a Romanian peasant, "the grandfather of us all," a "merry Father Christmas," and above all a Tibetan ascetic, perhaps even "the reincarnation of Milarepa."[32]

---

31. *Idem*, p. 11.

32. All the quotations in this chapter, unless otherwise stated, are from Peter Neagoe, *Sfântul din Montparnasse*, Cluj, Dacia, 1977.

"For universal culture, the mosaic of the Romania brand has two names in capital letters: Eliade and Brancusi. Mircea Eliade is a guru of the history of religions, Constantin Brancusi a revolutionary genius of modern sculpture."[33] This is how an article from 2006 begins, published in "the year of grace that has been named 'Brancusi Year,' as well as 'Eliade Year,' thanks to the practice of marking round numbers: 130 years from the birth of Brancusi, 20 years from the death of Eliade."[34] There was an attempt to exploit this felicitous alignment of two Romanian stars in the international firmament in 2011, when there was a plan to organise a *Brancusi* commemorative performance, which would have included excerpts from Eliade's play combined with aphorisms of Brancusi, conceived by director Alice Barb as part of a project initiated by writer Laurian Stănchescu and which would have been presented at Romanian Cultural Institutes and at Romanian embassies on the Bucharest-Paris route. The project was not realised due to a lack of funds.

The conjunction of the two figures first occurred in 1967, when Eliade published his essay "Brancusi and Mythologies," at the invitation of Ionel Jianu, in *Testimonies about Brancusi*. The volume insisted "on the profoundly modern and personal ways in which Brancusi was able to draw spiritual sap from his ancestral roots" and oriented "the understanding of the problematic of origins and the significance of Brancusi's art along the natural track of his belonging to his own tradition, thereby responding to subjective, erroneous interpretations made from ignorance or bad faith that have arisen in time."[35] Eliade begins his essay as follows: "I was recently re-reading the file of the heated controversy surrounding Brancusi: has he remained a 'peasant from the Carpathians,' although he lived for half a century in Paris, at the very centre of all modern innovations and artistic revolutions? Or, on the contrary, as American critic Sidney Geist believes, has Brancusi become what he is thanks to the influences of the Paris School and the discovery of exotic arts, particularly African sculpture and masks?"[36] Throughout his essay, he argues that Brancusi went back to the universal archaic sources and managed to "rediscover the presence-in-the-world of a Neolithic peasant," his works being "solidary with the universe of Romanian plastic forms and folk mythology," but "only after he understood the importance of modern art did he also rediscover the riches of his own peasant tradition, whose artistic potential he also divined."[37]

---

33. Maria Nițu, "Brâncuşi omagiat de Eliade" [Brancusi Paid Homage by Eliade], *Pro Saeculum*, 3/2006, p. 29.

34. *Ibidem*.

35. Nina Stănculescu, foreword to *Mărturii despre Brâncuşi*, Târgu Jiu, Editura Fundaţiei "Constantin Brâncuşi", 1997, p. 9, 10.

36. Mircea Eliade, "Brâncuşi şi mitologiile" [Brancusi and Mythologies] in *Mărturii despre Brâncuşi*, p. 13.

37. *Idem*, pp. 19–17.

Already in this essay, Eliade was interested in the *Endless Column*, in which he saw "a Romanian folk motif that is an extension of a mythological theme found as early as pre-history: the Column of the Sky that holds up the firmament."[38] Based on this interest Eliade wrote a three-act play in 1970: *The Endless Column*. The play is set in Târgu Jiu, in different periods of time: 1937, when Brancusi began work on the Column; 1938, before its inauguration; and 1957, when the sculptor passed away. None of the characters apart from Brancusi is named and, according to Eliade's directions, "no matter what the style of the production, the Column must dominate the set." The Brancusi character is constructed as a respected Master from the very first scene, when the inhabitants of the town, in a panic because children have been climbing the Column never to return, humbly arrive to beg him to shorten it: "Master, be not wroth, for I beg you as a God!" This first line of the Commissar is extremely revealing of the relationship between Brancusi and all the other characters, who have complete faith in him ("He must know what he is doing, because he is a great craftsman"). At first he seems absorbed in his work, tortured by the arduous process of creation, and regards the children's disappearance as an interesting detail ("If it is a spell, if it draws them like a magnet, then know that it is well"), and imparts to the townsfolk the secret of the Column: it will have no end, it will soar above the heavens, and if the heavens have not existed hitherto, he will create them, like God ("If I erect the Column as I know how, as I have lately learned how to do so, then the Heavens too will begin to exist!"). In the end, he shows mercy and reluctantly agrees to incline the Column as long as he works on it, thereby saving the children from death. After Brancusi reveals his humane qualities and interest in the good of the community, the character of the Girl appears for the first time,[39] as a mirror of the artist's thoughts, always steering the conversation towards the connection between the Column and the monument in India. She also brings out Brancusi's qualities as a teacher ("Girl: To whom else might I have gone, Master? Who else could have taught me? Brancusi: But I, what can I teach you? Girl: Whatever you want, Master. Dance, for example, or wisdom. The Wisdom of the Earth"). As a character she emphasises the power relationship between Brancusi and the rest of the world (Girl: "This is why all love you; they love you because you teach them"), shifting it to the area of gender issues when she falls to her knees and implores the Master to take her to Paris, offering to be his maid ("You will not be sorry. I will do everything: clean your house, dust your studio, cook for you...").

In the second act Brancusi does not appear on stage very much. On the other hand, the reception of the Column in various social circles is presented: people

---

38. *Idem*, p. 21.

39. Maria Niţu puts forward the idea that the *Girl* character was inspired by Florence, one of the daughters of collector Agnes Meyer, a "special friend" of Brancusi. Maria Niţu, "Brâncuşi omagiat de Eliade", p. 31.

of culture in Târgu Jiu rejoice because the inauguration of the Column will put them at the "centre of the world's attention" and the town will become "a spiritual centre belonging to the entire world"; realising that the Column "is a unique masterpiece" that "does honour to an entire nation," the people of Bucharest, aware that the capital of a "small" nation does not count on the international stage, suffer because it was not erected in Bucharest; in circles where culture is not at a premium, there is talk of the waste of money and the "sacred steel" that could have been used to defend the country's borders in the form of bullets and cannons; the King, who "never tires of looking at it," would have liked to have it at one of his palaces, and the Patriarch wishes "to convince Master Brancusi to erect the Column at Curtea de Argeş" that it might become "a symbol of the history of the nation and of the Church"; foreign people of culture would like to move it to one of the West's cultural centres, to Paris or New York, that it might enjoy greater visibility. "It may be guessed that Brancusi was very sincerely amused by what was happening around him," as he believes that although "all the places (Paris and New York and Târgu Jiu) were important if you know what to do with them (and by means of them)," the Column was made for his native land.

The final act presents an aged, ill, weary, exhausted Brancusi—although his genius remains intact—who has come to view the Column once more, hoping that it will make him feel better. In the conversation with the Girl, he remembers another scene in which a group of young people visited him in his Paris studio as if he were a guru who might "enlighten" them and give them the "key." This final lesson is connected to the Monument in India, which he did not make precisely because, after "understanding Buddha" for the first time, he realises that "the absolute cannot be represented in any form, nor even suggested." This is Eliade's spiritual explanation of why, after the Târgu Jiu Monumental Ensemble, Brancusi merely recycled older themes and works. The explanation he gave in the essay of 1967 is different and connected with folkloric tradition: "the continual repetition of the same motif (…) is characteristic of folk and ethnographic arts in particular, where exemplary models demand endless repetition and 'imitation' for reasons that have nothing to do with an artist's 'lack of imagination' or 'personality.'"[40] At the end of the play, after his genius is vindicated, Brancusi ascends to the heavens against a backdrop of Indian music. He slowly begins to climb the column, with his "head held erect," and disappears into the light. The music abruptly stops.[41]

---

40. Mircea Eliade, "Brâncuşi şi mitologiile," p. 21.

41. All the quotations in this chapter, unless otherwise stated, are from Mircea Eliade, *Coloana nesfârşită* [The Endless Column], 1970, manuscript in the collection of the Museum of Romanian Literature, Bucharest.

Ştefan Dumitrescu is a writer and the spokesman of the Bucharest Bureau of Futurology. In 1992 he won a competition that allowed him to write a sequel to Marin Preda's novel *Delirium*, organised by *Expres Magazin* (run by Ion Cristoiu) and Marin Preda's family, and was put forward for the Nobel Prize for Literature by the "Romanian Aid" Cultural Society, the Union of Romanian Writers from Moldova and the Canadian Association of Romanian Writers, as well as a number of individual cultural figures.[42] As the chief ideologue of the Bucharest Bureau of Futurology, he came up with the "Doctrine for the Salvation of Romanian People and the Renaissance of Romania or the Burebista Doctrine," "The Psychology and Pedagogy of the Romanian People," "The Decebal Doctrine," "The Movement for Romania, or the Project of the Party of Maximal Development and Evolution of Romania," works "that help the Romanian people to know and understand itself better, to know its history, to know the causes that have made the Romanian people have the unhappy, horrible destiny it has had (…) and to discover how to become a dignified people, a powerful, disciplined, rich and happy people, which is no longer lied to, robbed, manipulated and trampled by all. A people that will not disappear."[43] In another of his works, Ştefan Dumitrescu claims that the salvation of the nation can be achieved only through its values and geniuses, and this is where he intersects with the subject of Brancusi: "The Dacian-Romanian people did not disappear after the Dacian-Roman wars of 100–106, nor did it disappear after 1,900 years of being trampled by so many invaders, but alas, it might disappear now, in the most shameful and painful manner, assimilated by the Gypsy people, destroyed by the great masked War waged very cleverly and subtly against us from outside the country, whose Victim we have been for twenty years!! Faced with this very grave situation, that of the disappearance of the Romanian people in the next decade or decades, we the Bucharest Bureau of Futurology have formulated the Theory of the Salvation of the Romanian People, when it finds itself in peril, in the situation of disappearing, by means of its greatest values and characters, by its best sons, by the true patriots of this nation. By its Geniuses!"[44] In keeping with this patriotic fervour, in 2007 Ştefan Dumitrescu dedicated to Brancusi a play in three parts. With this theatrical essay, "the author without doubt adds yet anoth-

---

42. Ştefan Dumitrescu quoted in Laurenţiu Ungureanu, "Ce-i mai uneşte pe români?" [What Still Unites the Romanians?], *Adevărul Weekend*, 26 July 2012.

43. Ştefan Dumitrescu, *Mişcarea pentru România* [The Movement for Romania], 2008, p. 29; <http://stefandumitrescu.sapte.ro/> (note the first page of the website, where the image of Brancusi appears alongside those of Marshal Ion Antonescu and the author).

44. Ştefan Dumitrescu, *Doctrina Salvării Poporului Român* [The Doctrine for the Salvation of the Romanian People], Editura Online Semănătorul, 2011, p. 8.

er pearl to his labours as a writer, the crowning work of his fruitful toils hitherto. The essay might be regarded as a true doctoral thesis. A roundel carved in stone, that ancient stone that the sculptor takes 'from its universal place in which it has rested for billions of years' in order to lend it the shape of his imagination."[45]

The play is set in the sculptor's studio. Brancusi is now aged and "his thoughts and ideas, his inner voice, will be heard in the auditorium through a speaker or many speakers, giving the impression that the artist's voice, which will be faint (husky, as if coming from another world) and sad, comes from somewhere far away. From everywhere at once, from the whole universe." Throughout the text, the author's stage directions for the sound are very precise: the waves of the sea, the sad, desolate cries of seagulls, church bells, songs of grieving, a dog howling for the dead, the sad call of an alphorn, etc. In the first act, Brancusi philosophises aloud about the condition and power of the genius, about his relationship with God, about the matter/spirit binary, about the differences between an artist, a philosopher and a poet. He is aware of the destiny of the Genius, who, "when he attains an awareness of his value, of his gigantic power in the world, begins to be visited by the reckless and diabolical thought of surpassing God," but his elevation above Nature and God will be "beautiful, full of purity" and will be "nothing other than the loftiest appreciation of them." But even so, he cannot risk usurping God and is forced to sacrifice himself for the good of humanity and destroy his work in order to save the world from doom: "his beard blows in the wind, his eyes gleam wildly, sweat runs down his face, he runs and grabs a hammer and breaks some of the works in the height of madness." Speaking of sacrifice he draws an analogy with the fate of the Romanian people, which he views as similar to Argeș Monastery. All that the nation had built was undermined when the foreign "vandals" came: "this cathedral which is the Romanian nation and people demands too great a sacrifice, which we shall never be able to make, and what we shall build by day will collapse by night." Brancusi realises that he has in fact gone beyond genius ("Genius means clear-sightedness and aspiration. Genius is a dreadful thunderbolt that illumines and burns. But I am a pastor, a shepherd from the mountains of Oltenia who walks with a lamp in his hand… I have gone beyond genius") and speaks of the "sight" of the being that goes beyond genius, which "comes from the fatherland, from the homeland and from the soil of the nation," from "the soil soaked with the soul and the blood of the ancestors" ("Lord, when the plough turns the Romanian soil, it ploughs the dense soul that has been laid down by each dead man and has been compacted like the earth by the porch of a house. The Romanian peasant when he eats his bread, he eats soul. And in the beginning there was as much soul as gurgles through me like wind through a whistle"). Later,

---

45. Ioan Miclău, "Brâncuși (eseu teatrologic)" [Brancusi (An Essay in Theatre Theory)], *Revista de artă și cultură Iosif Vulcan din Australia;* <www.revistaiosifvulcan.wordpress.com>.

Brancusi wonders whether genius might be a disease as bad as "the disease of love" or "the disease of woman" and begins to converse with an immaterial and melancholic Mademoiselle Pogany about the role of the woman, whom he sees as a "womb of the world" from which men drink for the sake of their well-being. Woman senses genius and gives birth to genius, she claims to serve and worship the gifted man, and Mademoiselle Pogany is attracted to Brancusi like "a moth that came from the pitch darkness and burned its wings on the flame of his candle." From Mademoiselle Pogany, Brancusi's thoughts turn to his mother and "howling in pain" he asks himself: "Why do we die? I have fought against death… With art and my genius!" but consoles himself with the idea that his mother must be happy because she has done her duty as few other humans have done: she gave "a son who carried the torch of the world farther on its way, who did so much for mankind, for its benefit…" He continues to talk to her, meditating on the loneliness to which geniuses are condemned and the sacrifices he had to make on the altar of art ("Ever since I went out into the world I have been a soldier that does battle in the wilderness, far away, against the unseen and the unheard. Mother, I left everything behind, pleasures, everything, to be solitary, lucid, powerful, there, before the infinite and the unknown. Just as a soldier on the battlefield, in range of the enemy's gun, I stood for decades alone, my chest bared to the infinite. It was hard, Mother, very hard, harder than I can relate. How to describe something that cannot be captured in words? It was as if I were flayed alive and left in a strong wind blowing from the universe, from the unknown… and it is cold. And the sensation stings, but it is happiness! What sharp, howling happiness my life has been, Mother!").

In the final scene, Brancusi appears on his deathbed, at the moment of judgement, when the Voice of the Lord scolds him for having forgotten his duties as a man so that he might give everything to his genius, for not having left descendants, for having abandoned his mother and his homeland. Reconciled and with a feeling of having done his duty, he gives arguments that demolish all these accusations, believing that at the end of his life he ought to be rewarded, rather than admonished, and finally the Voice ends up agreeing with him: Brancusi has sacrificed himself in order to "toil in the deserts of creation and the spirit," he did not abandon his homeland, but "brought it into the world and poured it into the Universe."[46]

---

46. All the quotations in this chapter, unless otherwise stated, are from Ştefan Dumitrescu, *Brâncuşi*, Biblioteca Online Citatepedia, 2007.

Valeriu Butulescu is a writer and an engineer with a doctorate in technical sciences. In January 1990 he founded the *Semnal* weekly, the first privately owned publication in the Jiu Valley, and *Papagalul*, a magazine of political humour. Valeriu Butulescu has been involved in politics since the early 1990s, he was the spokesman of the National Coal Company during the period of the last Mineriads, and more recently he has announced his intention to stand for election as Mayor of Petroșani for the National Liberal Party. In 2011 he was awarded Petroșani Town Hall's Excelsior Prize for promoting the municipality's cultural image abroad, and in 2012 the Sibiu Branch of the Romanian Union of Writers Prize for Excellence. He has made a name for himself thanks to his aphorisms, which, alongside his pride in being an Oltenian, are probably at the bottom of his interest in Brancusi. In 2009 he published the one-act play *The Golden Bird (The Infinite Brancusi)*, which, like Ștefan Dumitrescu's play, focuses on the last moments of Brancusi's life. Here, however, Brancusi appears as a grouchy old man who can no longer walk ("a bust resting on a wheeled plinth"); he is mentally unstable, quickly moving from a good to a bad mood, from outbursts of anger to sadness. He is cared for by a couple (Natalia and Alex), who venerate him and are totally dedicated to him: they collect nettles from the edge of the railway tracks for him; they pose on their knees kissing, at the authoritarian command of the sculptor, who wishes to sculpt "an ascendant kiss." Convinced of the sculptor's importance, throughout the play they piously write down his words, which to them are like "golden sentences." They regard him as a tree, which, unlike Rodin, does not cast shade, but radiates light, as "a titan of modern art." But as Brancusi says, "sometimes even titans weep, they weep titanic tears": in his final moments he is overwhelmed by homesickness and confesses that Târgu Jiu "was and will remain the centre of [his] world"; that the Bistrița river taught him "the patience to polish," and it was in the field at its edge that he organized his "first solo exhibition, with all the sheep attending the opening"; that the voice of Maria Tănase, "the Lady of our people's music," fills his soul with joy. Besides the relationship with his heirs, we find two scenes to do with the Cold War dynamic: one in which we see the sculptor's relationship with Romania under "the red terror" and another, which is dedicated to his relationship with America. In the fourth scene, a character named Mihai appears, a lawyer and "fighter for national liberation" who comes to Brancusi's studio full of enthusiasm bearing the news that "the Americans are going to rid us of the communists," asking that the sculptor sign a protest against the Kremlin, in which "intellectuals in exile demand that the Soviets immediately leave Romania." Although Alex believes that "Brancusi has done more for the country than any political party," he introduces the lawyer with whom Brancusi begins a conversation in which he confesses that he does not like the communists ("they are villains… more hateful than the legionnaires"), but that he is apolitical, the same as all art should be ("my ideology is the sublime reduced to the essential. I am a member of the party of sensitive men"). Likewise, he does not dramatise the reception of his art in 1950s Romania. When he hears that sheep graze around the *Endless Column*, he is glad, saying: "my country is the most beautiful sheepfold in the world" and when he hears that the authorities wanted to topple the Column with a tractor, he considers it merely a rumour, saying that "the Column's plinth is the whole of Oltenia." When he is alone, Brancusi recognises that in Romania the "times are sombre," but this does not prevent him from dreaming of returning home ("The Romanian Academy has pronounced: it has no need of my cockerels! No matter! What they need are the bourgeoisie's golden cockerels [coins]... Comrade Călinescu claims that I, Constantin Brancusi, am not a creator, because I do not express myself 'through essential means'... Perhaps I am to blame here! I should have extended a helping hand to the new rulers... I would have got into the Bolsheviks' good books... Even now I could sculpt a woman from a collective farm milking a cow 'through essential means'... Princess X as a sower, the caryatid of people's power! No, no! I have created sculptures for the blind! But never for the stupid! The greatest artists of my country pull at the yoke... Jalea carves brawny miners, brave steel workers... Ressu's work is full of tractors! Oh, Lord! I am afraid to go back to my nest... Sombre times for an enchanted bird..."). At the opposite extreme, he is invited by two American emissaries to erect in Chicago the tallest Column in the world: 400 metres[47] of stainless steel. At first he seems enthusiastic about the idea, but in the end he turns down the large sum of money offered by the Americans (the Column could even have been built from "wads of dollars"), patriotically deciding that "the one in Gorj will remain the tallest." Although rejected by his own country, his soul still remains there. At the end of the play, there is a doubling of the artist in *Brancusi the Immortal:* "the lucky Oltenian, born with a star on his brow" who "wanders the world, leaps from museum to museum, from biennale to biennale," and *Costache the Man*, who prepares his death in detail: he invites Archbishop Teofil to give his final blessing, imparts food, drink and a sculpture to the two American visitors, gives them candles to light for the soul "of the departed," prepares his chisel so that he might "sculpt even in the other world" to make "Heaven more beautiful." Finally, this Heaven proves to be his native village of Hobiţa, whither he sets off joyfully (after the Golden Bird has endowed him with miraculous powers) to help his nephews build their house. Dressed in peasant garb, armed with a shepherd's cane and Oltenian shoulder bags, he makes a spectacular exit, while

---

47. From the letters of lawyer and collector Barnet Hodes quoted by Natalia Dumitresco and Alexandre Istrati it appears that in reality Brancusi proposed a height of 61m, 91.5m or 122m. Pontus Hulten, Natalia Dumitresco, Alexandre Istrati, *Brancusi*, Paris, Flammarion, 1986, p. 263.

in the background Maria Tănase's song "Tri-hu-ri-hu-ri-hu" sounds heart-rend-ingly, transforming into an Oltenian folk dirge.[48]

Compared with the other versions of Brancusi's old age and death examined hitherto, Valeriu Butulescu's version is perhaps the closest to the reality, although it is to a large extent idealised also. From the accounts of Natalia Dumitresco and Alexandre Istrati, it would seem that Brancusi suffered depressive moods in which he brooded obsessively on a "universal cataclysm," and he had prostate gland prob-lems and a skin eczema that caused him more irritation than pain. In his final years, he moved around only with difficulty, his belly swelled, and he spent much of his time on the couch in his studio. A few days before his death, he began to talk Romanian to everybody, even to the French doctors who visited him every day, "as if he were returning to the sources of his childhood." A puncture was made and the liquid was drained from his swollen abdomen. He was prescribed an intravenous drip for nourishment. He began to lose contact with reality, and the last words he uttered before he lapsed into a state of coma were *"Haide, bă, haide, bă"* [Come on, hey, come on, hey]. After another day of unconsciousness alternating with spasms, he died during the night. "His face was serene, as if expressing what he had stated so many times: I am not afraid, I am ready to depart."[49]

BRANCUSI VERSUS THE U.S.A. BY TATIANA NICULESCU BRAN

Tatiana Niculescu Bran is a writer and journalist. She worked for the BBC World Service until 2008. In 2014–2015 she was a spokesperson for the newly elected pres-ident of Romania, Klaus Johannis. In 2006, she published her first non-fiction novel, *Confession at Tanacu*, followed shortly thereafter by *The Book of Judges*. At the initiative of Andrei Șerban, she adapted them for the stage in a play that premiered in New York in 2007, and later accepted director Cristian Mungiu's proposal to adapt her books for a film titled *Beyond the Hills*, which won the prize for best screenplay at the Cannes Film Festival in 2012. In 2010 she published her play *Brancusi versus the U.S.A.*, which was received as an act of courage, in conditions in which "to write about Brancusi as if he was a human being and not a chapter in a book is riskier than writing about exorcisms performed on novice nuns. To have the courage to break the statue into pieces and free the man sequestered within."[50] Brancusi is here

---

48. All the quotations in this chapter, unless otherwise stated, are from Valeriu Butulescu, *Pasărea de aur (Infinitul Brâncuși)* [The Golden Bird (The Infinite Brancusi)], Biblioteca Online Citatepedia, 2009.

49. Natalia Dumitresco and Alexandre Istrati in Pontus Hulten, Natalia Dumitresco, Alexandre Istrati, *Brancusi*, p. 265.

50. Lia Bugnar, "Apropie-te, nu mușc, sînt doar un sculptor de geniu!" [Come Closer, I Will Not Bite, I Am Only a Sculptor of Genius!], 2010; <http://editura.liternet.ro/carte/272/Tatiana-Niculescu-Bran/Brâncuși-contra-SUA.html>.

viewed through the eyes of his illegitimate son, who, filled with resentment and hatred, is nonetheless driven by the need to understand his father. He therefore visits the Memorial House at Hobiţa, where he has two encounters: the first is initiatory, with "a man gaunt from fasting, shaven-headed, his skin green, seated in a lotus position"—Milarepa, who helps John to be reincarnated in the person of his father (in an attempt to transform his hatred of him into love); the second with the authorities of the 1980s communist regime. The son of Brancusi is not a fictional character: John Moore is also mentioned in "the first complete biography"[51] of Brancusi, published by Alexandru Buican in 2006, while in 2011 the Romanian press published a sensational article with the title "*Libertatea* Has Found Constantin Brancusi's Secret Son" stating: "Fifty-four years after the death of his famous father, John Moore lives as discreetly as ever in France. (…) Deliberately concealed in anonymity from the very beginning, John Moore, a Frenchman of seventy-seven, is the best example of the fact that Brancusi, our great artist, remains as surprising as ever even after his death."[52] Doina Lemny is of the opinion that the relationship between Brancusi and Vera Moore does not appear in the older biographies because he was very discreet in his liaison with her; it was not until after the letters between them emerged (from John Moore's archive and from *Dation 2001*) that the relationship came to be known, a relationship which in 1934 produced a son, whom Brancusi did not recognise (nothing could change the artist's decision to preserve his freedom and not to be caught up in family life).[53] The character in the play, John Morgan, is full of resentment, which is made clear in his description of Brancusi: "He cared only about his birds . . . about flight . . . stone and marble and (…) he was not interested in having a child! Did he know how we lived during the war? (…) Did he ever care?"

---

51. This is how *Brâncuşi. O biografie* [Brancusi. A Biography] is presented by its author, Alexandru Buican, a Romanian jurist who lives in the United States (and who has recently published a biography of Vlad Dracula). He explains in the introduction that the work of Brancusi was a revelation to him very early in life. Of the opinion that "the work is best explained through biographical events" and believing that "revelation is not the same thing as understanding," he begins the research for this volume in order to understand "in what exactly the truth of the work resides." Although the contradiction between *erudite* and *artistic* biography seems to him a "false problem," he believes that his book falls into the *artistic* category, but without "descending into the domain of disgusting *fictionalised lives*" (as Peter Neagoe does, whose book he does not even use "for orientation, let alone documentation"). The biography is based on "passionate but by no means easy detective work" over the course of five years' research into the vast body of memoirs left by American authors who knew Brancusi, works to be found in the New York Public Library. Seeing Brancusi as a "great exile" (and identifying with him), Buican believes that the results of the "toil" he expended on the book will be "the re-annexation to Romania of one of its most splendid and prematurely exiled territories: sculptor Constantin Brancusi." Alexandru Buican, foreword to *Brâncuşi. O biografie*, Bucharest, Artemis, 2006, pp. 7–12.

52. *Libertatea*, 14 February 2011.

53. Doina Lemny, *Constantin Brancusi*, Paris, Oxus, 2005, pp. 222–223.

In the second scene John is teleported back into the past and "gradually becomes Brancusi, under the pressure of those around him and of the circumstances." A Brancusi "in long johns, barefoot, bare-chested," practising yoga with Tibetan music in the background. Although he believes that "profound and repeated meditation can lead to ecstasy," he does not give up absinthe and hashish parties in the company of "celebrities" such as Modigliani, Steichen, Duchamp, Ezra Pound and Gertrude Whitney, which end in orgies, in "thrashing bodies that embrace without knowing who is who." After he plays an Oltenian dirge on the whistle and roasts a hen, Brancusi "dances like a savage, shod in wooden clogs. He is not drunk; he is happy. He dances till he falls to the floor in exhaustion." During such an outburst, he meets and makes advances to pianist Vera (later John's mother), like a true charmer, reciting his famous aphorisms to her, now "looking her in the eye," now "slightly dizzy, shy." In his relationships with women, he shows tenderness, but he can very easily become wrathful, furious, swearing and hitting those who annoy him, even succumbing to mental instability in a scene in which he has a fit of hysteria because the light does not fall well on the works Duchamp has arranged in an exhibition: "he clutches his head, runs madly from one exhibit to another," he kicks everybody out, and finally bursts into tears, because "his maidens are violated by shadows." The beginning of the play is obviously based on *The Saint of Montparnasse* and the aphorisms attributed to the artist, while the second part, concerning the New York trial, is inspired by minutes translated by Petru Comarnescu. The trial, brought at the initiative of Duchamp, who believed that they ought to take advantage of the incident to create publicity in the press for the exhibition that was about to open, is re-contextualised at the end of the play, when the communist authorities boast about Brancusi, "the man who fought the American state and won, just as the socialist order will win" the Cold War. While Eliade dedicates a scene to the reception of the *Endless Column* at the time of its inauguration, Tatiana Niculescu Bran constructs the final scene of her play as a comment on Brancusi's reception during the communist regime. This is how the Securitate agent answers John when he refers to Brancusi as the father of modern art: "That is a bourgeois interpretation! Brancusi was a patriot who made our country famous abroad! The son of a peasant! And from Paris he came home to make the *Endless Column* in Târgu Jiu!" This discourse is not very different from the present discourse, apart from the fact that the post-1989 discourse has reclaimed this "bourgeois interpretation" in an increasingly aggressive protochronist drive.[54]

It is interesting that although the author presents a more human Brancusi, he is not humanised enough to be of interest to the younger generation of directors.

---

54. All the quotations in this chapter, unless otherwise stated, are from Tatiana Niculescu Bran, *Brâncuşi contra SUA* [Brancusi versus the U.S.A.], Editura Online LiterNet, 2010.

Because of excessive exposure to the image of Brancusi as national hero, many artists have ended up developing an aversion towards the subject, regarding it as "elitist,"[55] with the only possible attitude towards it being complete contestation. Such is the case of the performance *The Kiss Gate*, produced by Brynjar Bandlien and Manuel Pelmuş in collaboration with Ştefan Tiron in 2008 at the National Dance Centre Bucharest, where Brancusi's *Kiss* becomes "the cultural, historical and political frame for [their] need to address certain private, political and social urgent issues."[56] The show was part of the *Crooked Days* programme organised by Brynjar Bandlien, a programme that investigated in a performative way normality in the cultural context of the present. In these conditions, Brancusi appears as a representative of the norm, of authority, of the elites and of the patriarchy, towards which the artists take a critical stance. They invited Brancusiologist Matei Stîrcea-Crăciun to give a lecture about Brancusi, during which the two performers moved towards each other very slowly until they made contact, embraced, and kissed. Regarding "re-enactment as interrogating history and politics of representation,"[57] they laid out the performance space according to the structure of the Monumental Ensemble in Târgu Jiu, in such a way that the audience occupied the place of the *Table of Silence* and Matei Stîrcea-Crăciun that of the *Endless Column*, while the two performers became the *Gate of the Kiss*. In the current Romanian cultural context, in which national heroes such as Brancusi are almost sanctified while contemporary culture is deprived of the least financial support, the more radical voices on the art scene believe that "to be crooked even a little bit, to deviate, to jump out of line, to alter, to diverge from the line laid down before you is fundamentally beautiful, moral and the only viable way of doing politics and of looking history straight in the eyes."[58] This is the attitude of our generation towards the Romanian cultural policies of the present, as expressed by Cosmin Costinaş in the *Crooked Manifesto*: "Because Brancusi is not national culture and national value (...), because both he and we have been exiled, because both he and we have been rejected, because neither he nor we work to represent our country, we are not messen-

---

55. *"I talked about the play to an extremely talented director regarded as a rebel by the critics and even audiences. He was looking for a play to put on at the time. I told him: 'Do this play about Brancusi, it's completely crazy and doesn't have anything to do with what we imagine about him.' He told me that he didn't want to do an elitist play. Isn't it the height of irony that a man who was the incarnation of simplicity and whose work stunned the whole world for its simplicity and essentiality, isn't it comic,' I said, 'that he should be categorised as an <elitist subject>?' The director was exactly the type in whose face Brancusi would have exhaled a reek of onion and bacon lard and told to fuck off."* Lia Bugnar, "Apropie-te, nu muşc, sînt doar un sculptor de geniu!".

56. Brynjar Bandlien and Manuel Pelmuş, "The Kiss Gate" in *Cursul Zilelor Strîmbe* [Crooked Days Textbook], The National Dance Centre Bucharest, 2008, p. 23.

57. *Ibidem.*

58. Cosmin Costinaş, "Manifestul strîmb" in *Cursul Zilelor Strîmbe*, p. 325.

gers, diplomats, heralds or tourist agents, we are not Romanian presences abroad who will cleanse your thick-skinned faces of the shame of those we enslaved and exterminated, neither he nor we will promote you or make beautiful objects for you."[59]

59. *Idem*, p. 326.

2009 → 2015

Selected Works

Moștenirea lui Brâncuși

Proiect pentru Pavilionul României
la Bienala de la Veneția

Motto:

"Nu trebuie respectate sculpturile mele. Trebuie să le iubești și să ai dorința să te joci cu ele..." C.B.

"Lumea poate fi salvată prin artă. Artistul face, în fond, jucării pentru oameni mari; el este ca și viermele de mătase." C.B.

Argument / Text motivațional

A venit vremea să așezăm Moștenirea lui Brâncuși la locul ei de cinste, iar Pavilionul Național al României la Bienala de la Veneția constituie cadrul perfect pentru acest lucru. Moștenirea lui Constantin Brâncuși prezintă un model de ecosistem cultural complex, care trebuie să fie stimulat și ocrotit odată ce a fost transplantat *in situ*. Ne propunem să respectăm diversitatea și rolul Moștenirii lui Brâncuși și să o valorificăm într-un context mai amplu. Am hotărît că este singurul fel prin care putem răspunde într-un mod neechivoc la provocările și crizele actuale. În prezent există avertismente care confirmă direct ceea ce bănuiam de ceva vreme. Deja am fost avertizați că "promovarea non-valorilor trebuie să înceteze" (Dan Puric). Există o reacție adversă față de adevăratele valori din partea celor care ar trebui să susțină și să promoveze aceste valori autentice. Am reușit să identificăm efectul nociv al unor blesteme istorice și culturale. Este vorba de blestemul nerecunoașterii acestor valori de către străini, blestemul furtului anumitor reușite și descoperiri locale, care este direct legat de blestemul elitelor trădătoare. Cunoaștem foarte bine momentul cînd țara, aservită unor doctrine înșelătoare, a refuzat Moștenirea lui Brâncuși. Am asistat la dezamăgirea exprimată de publicul larg, de toți cei care nu o dată l-au susținut pe Constantin Brâncuși în topuri instituite de străini (cazul Saatchi Art). Nu în ultimul rînd, după discuții avute cu specialiști și pasionați în domeniu, trebuie să ținem cont și de reconsiderarea unor poziții personale cu privire la opera și Moștenirea lui Brâncuși.

Vom transforma Pavilionul României într-un loc de cult viu dedicat lui Constantin Brâncuși, cadrul Bienalei de la Veneția permițînd conjuncția dintre un spațiu de reprezentare națională și artistul erou național.

Zilnic, comunicări avînd ca temă Moștenirea lui Brâncuși vor fi prezentate de persoane desemnate anume, la ore prestabilite, de la un pupitru special amenajat în interiorul Pavilionului. Sesiunea de comunicări este deschisă specialiștilor și nespecialiștilor, cu participare națională și internațională (open call). Orice document scris trebuie să fie însoțit de o un "obiect martor", o materializare a argumentului prezentat în textul scris. Pe parcursul celor șase luni, comunicările vor fi tipărite și citite publicului prezent. Mai departe, toate textele însoțite de materialul lor vizual ajutător vor fi incluse în nucleul de lucrări situat în centrul Pavilionului. Comunicările vor oferi specialiștilor și nespecialiștilor ocazia de a prezenta și dezbate teorii cu privire la Moștenirea lui Constantin Brâncuși.

Simetric, pe celaltă latură a Pavilionului vom înălța un altar dedicat Moștenirii lui Brâncuși. Altarul va fi încununat de o piesă centrală (o replică) din creația lui Constantin Brâncuși încadrată de doi agenți de pază special angajați. Acest altar va fi altarul popular al publicului și admiratorilor marelui Brâncuși din toată lumea. Altarul va funcționa ca un suport pentru ofrande aduse spontan de vizitatori, delegații românești și personalități marcante ale lumii culturale. Acesta este un piedestal conceput ca suport fizic pentru coroane de flori și semne de adeziune și apreciere personală față de Constantin Brâncuși. Încurajînd direct aceste manifestări, vom asigura o creștere organică cu participare liberă pe tot parcursul bienalei. Acest altar oferă oricui ocazia să poată aduce *in situ* un prinos viu marelui artist.

În spațiul verde din fața Pavilionului vom organiza o tabără de sculptură deschisă prin concurs sculptorilor români. Este o tabără de creație avînd că model tabăra internațională de sculptură de la Târgu Jiu. Cîte doi sculptori selectați în fiecare lună (12 în total) vor lucra pe toată durata bienalei. Sculptorii și procesul lor artistic de creație vor constitui un punct de interes pentru vizitatorii bienalei. Ei vor demonstra publicului, la fața locului, că Moștenirea lui Brâncuși este vie în România. Odată realizate, sculpturile vor fi expuse în Pavilion, iar în final toate sculpturile din miniparcul sculptural vor fi donate unor instituții publice: institute culturale, ambasade, companii românești cu sediul în străinătate, spitale, școli și licee.

Am invitat un grup de tineri artiști să propună o serie de lucrări care vor declanșa dialogul cu Moștenirea lui Brâncuși și procesul de stratificare progresivă din Pavilion, urmînd ca în următoarele șase luni să se adauge restul de sculpturi. Toți cei invitați fie au lucrat în trecut cu Moștenirea lui Brâncuși, fie au arătat un interes viu în această direcție.

(....)

The Legacy of Brancusi

Project for the Romanian Pavilion
at the Venice Biennale

Motto:

"My sculptures do not require respect. You should love them and want to play with them…" C.B.

"The world can be saved through art. Ultimately, the artist makes toys for grown-ups; he is like a silkworm." C.B.

Argument / Motivational text

The time has come to place the Legacy of Brancusi in its place of honour, and the Romanian National Pavilion at the Venice Biennale is the perfect setting in which to do so. The Legacy of Constantin Brancusi is the model of a complex cultural ecosystem, which needs to be stimulated and protected once transplanted in situ. We intend to respect the diversity and the role of the Legacy of Brancusi and to capitalise on it in a broader context. We decided that this is the only way in which we can respond in an unequivocal way to the challenges and crises of the present. There are warnings that directly confirm what we have suspected for some time. We have already been warned that: "the promotion of non-values must cease." (Dan Puric) There is an adverse reaction to genuine values on the part of those who ought to be supporting and promoting authentic values. We have managed to identify the deleterious effect of some historical and cultural curses. We are talking about the curse of foreigners' ignorance of these values, the curse of the theft of certain local successes and discoveries, which is directly connected to the curse of the traitorous elites. We are well aware of the moment when the nation, servile to deceptive doctrines, rejected the Legacy of Brancusi. We witnessed the disappointment expressed by the wider public, by all those who on no few occasions supported Constantin Brancusi in the top tens set up by foreigners (such as Saatchi Art). Last but not least, we should take into account the reconsideration of personal positions regarding the work and Legacy of Brancusi, following discussions with experts and enthusiasts in the field.

We will transform the Romanian Pavilion into a place of living worship dedicated to Constantin Brancusi, with the setting of the Venice Biennale allowing the conjunction between a space of national representation and the artist as national hero.

Every day, a series of talks on the subject of the Legacy of Brancusi will be given by specially designated persons at pre-established hours from a special pulpit set up inside the Pavilion. The sessions are open to experts and non-experts alike, from both Romania and abroad (open call). Every written document must be accompanied by a "witness object," a materialisation of the argument presented in the written text. Over the course of six months, the talks will be printed and read to the public present. Further, all the texts and visual accompanying materials will be included in the nucleus of the works situated in the centre of the Pavilion. The talks will provide experts and non-experts with the opportunity to present and debate theories regarding the Legacy of Constantin Brancusi.

Symmetrically, on the other side of the Pavilion, we will install an altar to the Legacy of Brancusi. The altar will be crowned with a central piece (a replica) of a work by Constantin Brancusi, flanked by two specially hired security guards. The altar will be the people's altar, an altar for the public and admirers of Brancusi from all over the world. The altar will serve as a support for the offerings spontaneously brought by visitors, Romanian delegates and leading figures from the world of culture. It will be a pedestal designed as a physical support for wreaths and tokens of personal loyalty and appreciation towards Constantin Brancusi. By directly encouraging such manifestations, we will ensure organic growth with free participation throughout the biennale. The altar will offer anybody at all the opportunity to pay in situ tribute to the great artist.

In the green space in front of the Pavilion we will organise a sculpture camp, open to Romanian sculptors via a competition. It will be modelled on the international Targu Jiu sculpture camp. A pair of sculptors selected every month (twelve in total) will work for the entire duration of the biennale. The sculptors and their process of artistic creation will provide a point of interest to visitors to the biennale. They will demonstrate to the public, on the spot, that the Legacy of Brancusi is alive in Romania. Once completed, the sculptures will be exhibited in the Pavilion, and at the end, all the sculptures from the mini sculpture park will be donated to public institutions: cultural institutes, embassies, Romanian companies with offices abroad, hospitals, schools, and lycées.

We have invited a group of young artists to propose a series of works that will stimulate dialogue with the Legacy of Brancusi and the process of progressive stratification in the Pavilion, with the sculptures to be added over the next six months. All the invitees either have worked with the Legacy of Brancusi in the past or have shown a lively interest in this direction.

(...)

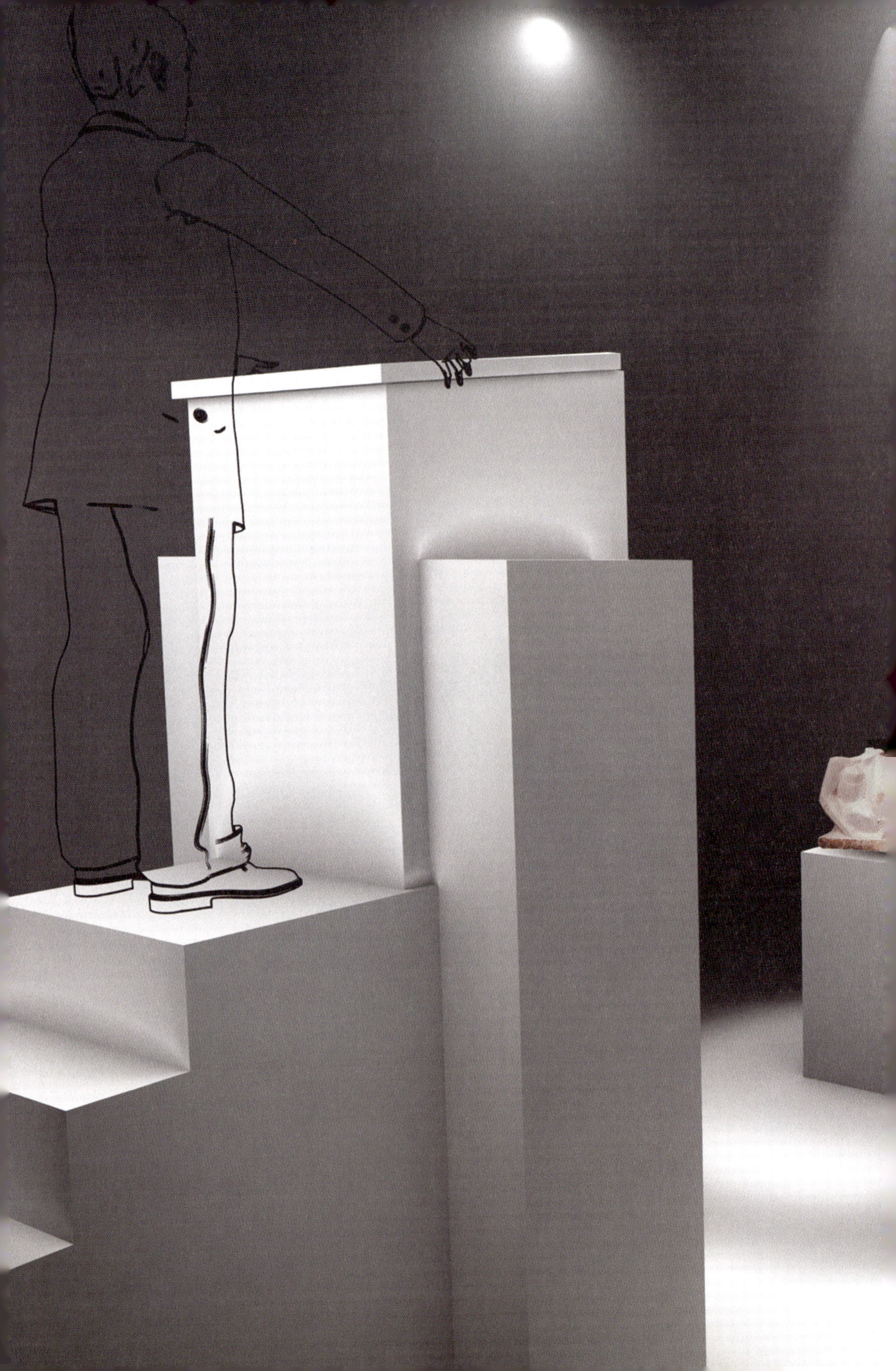

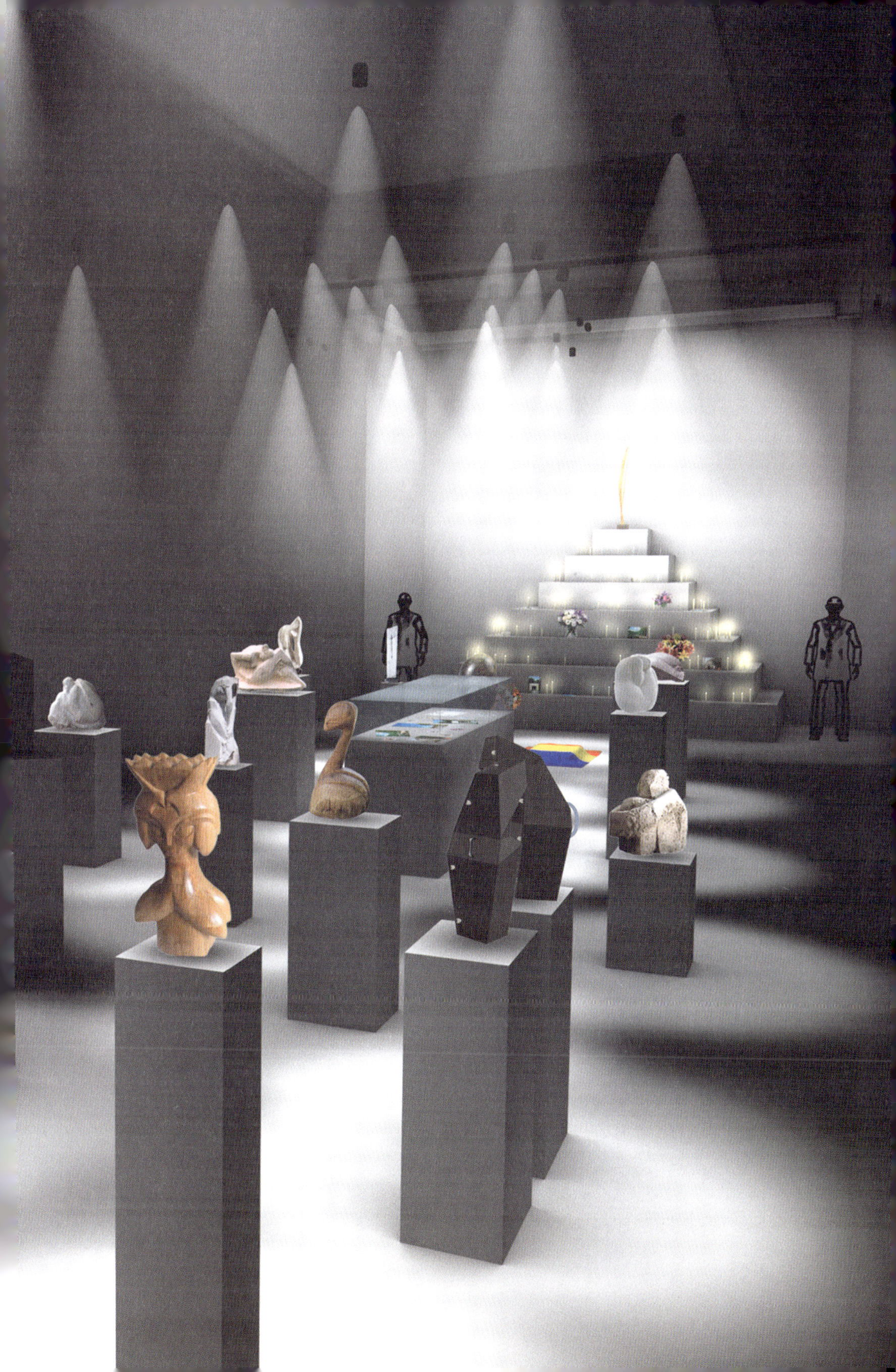

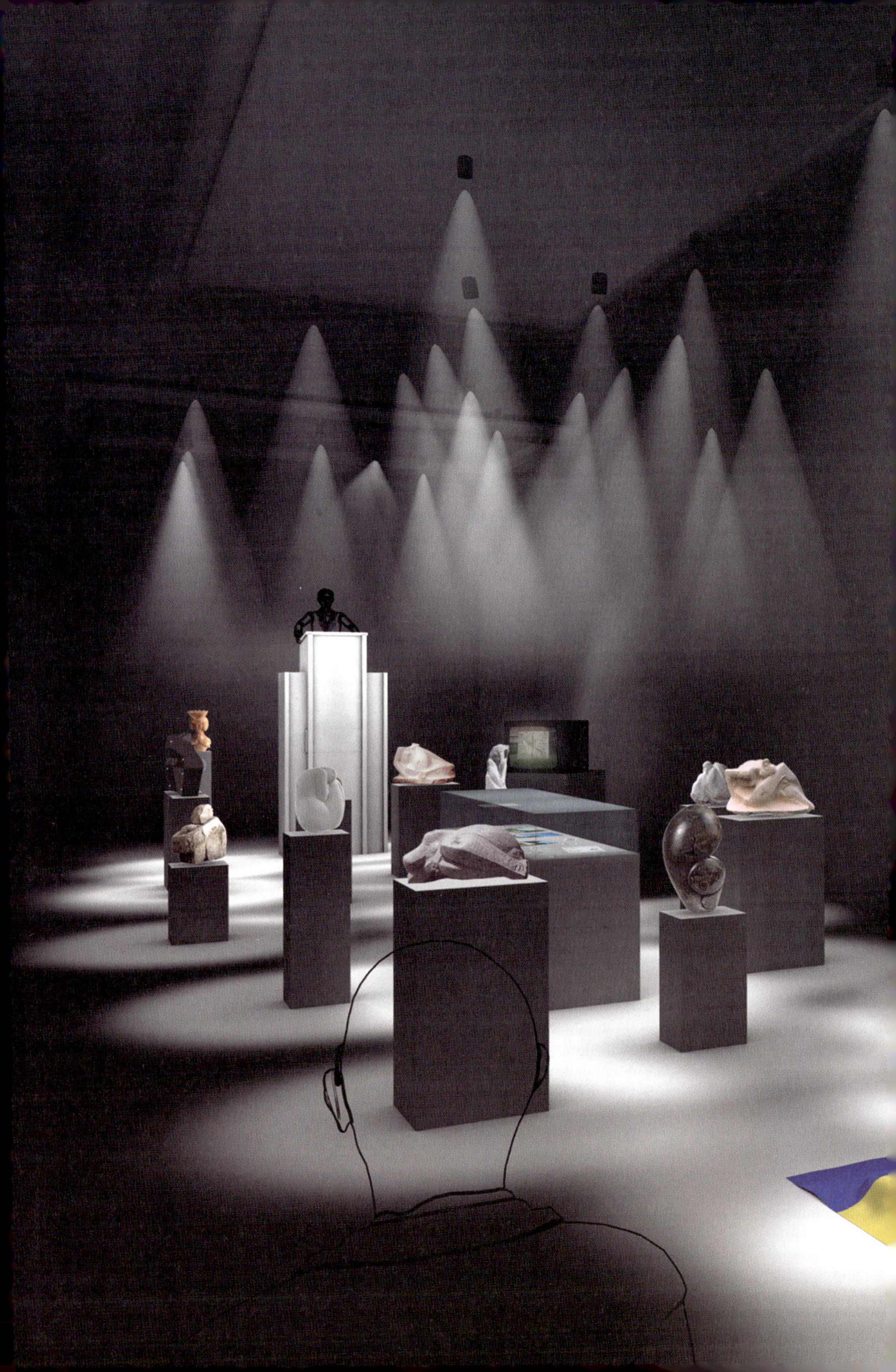

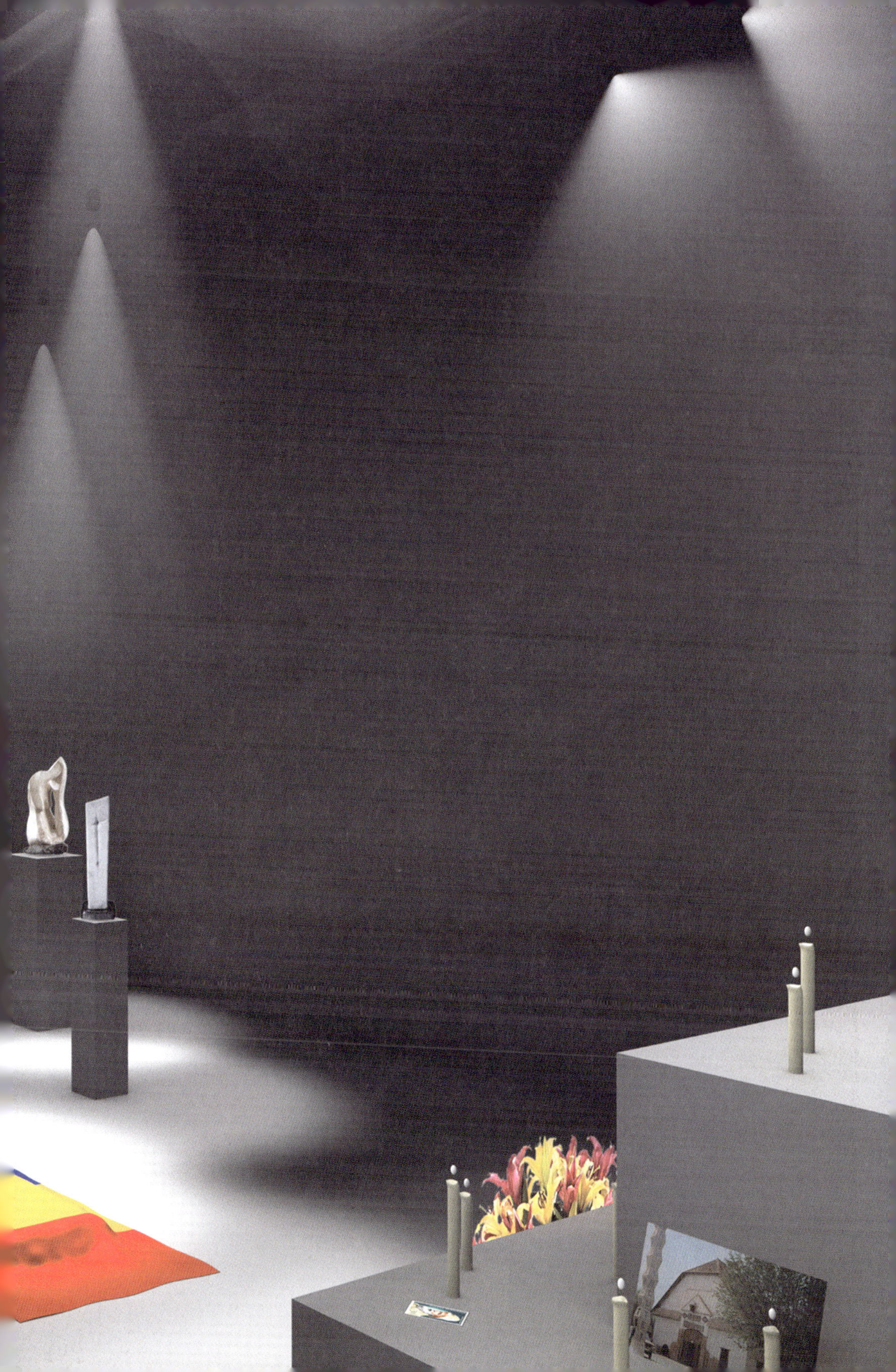

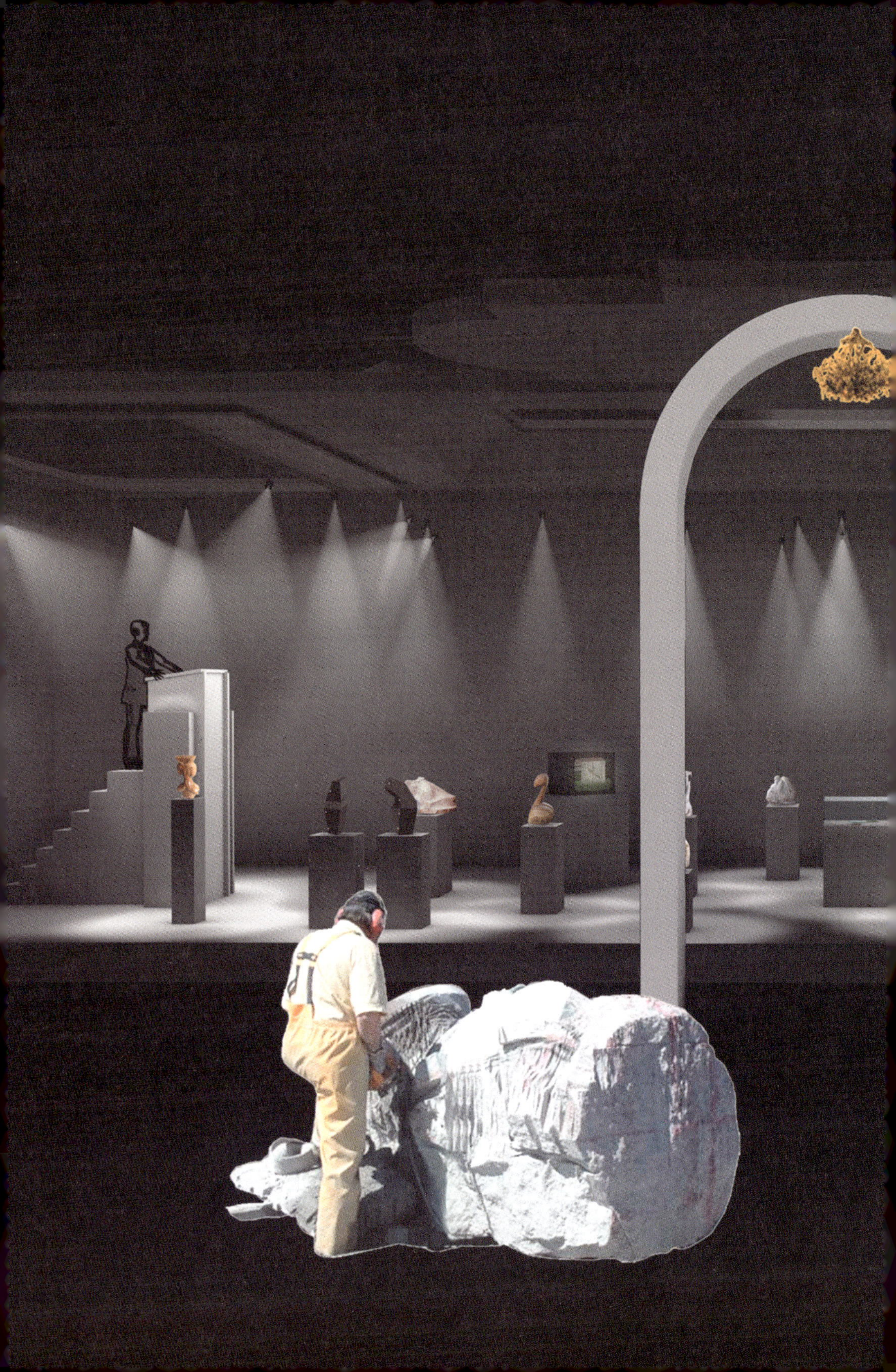

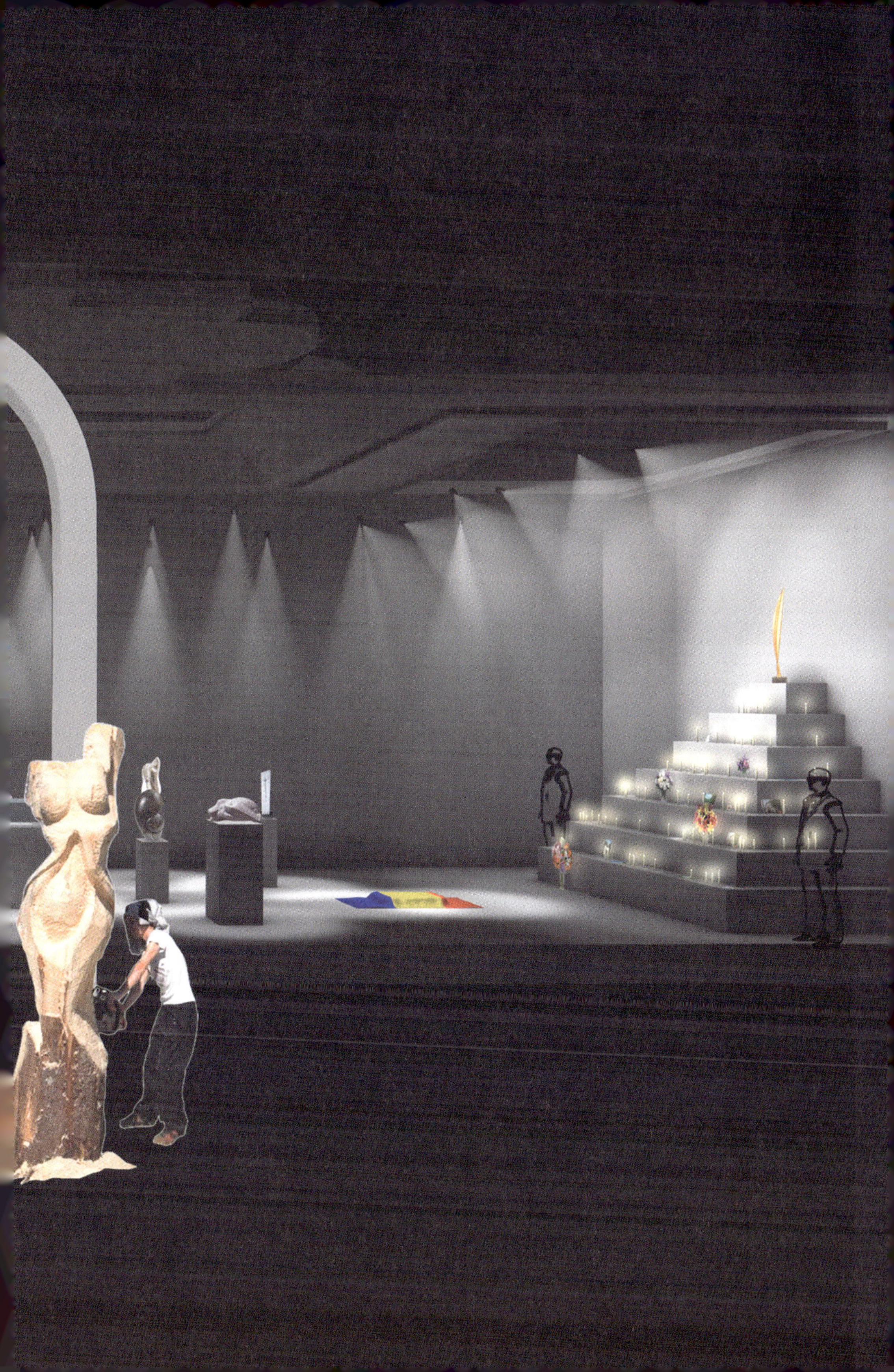

ROMANIA

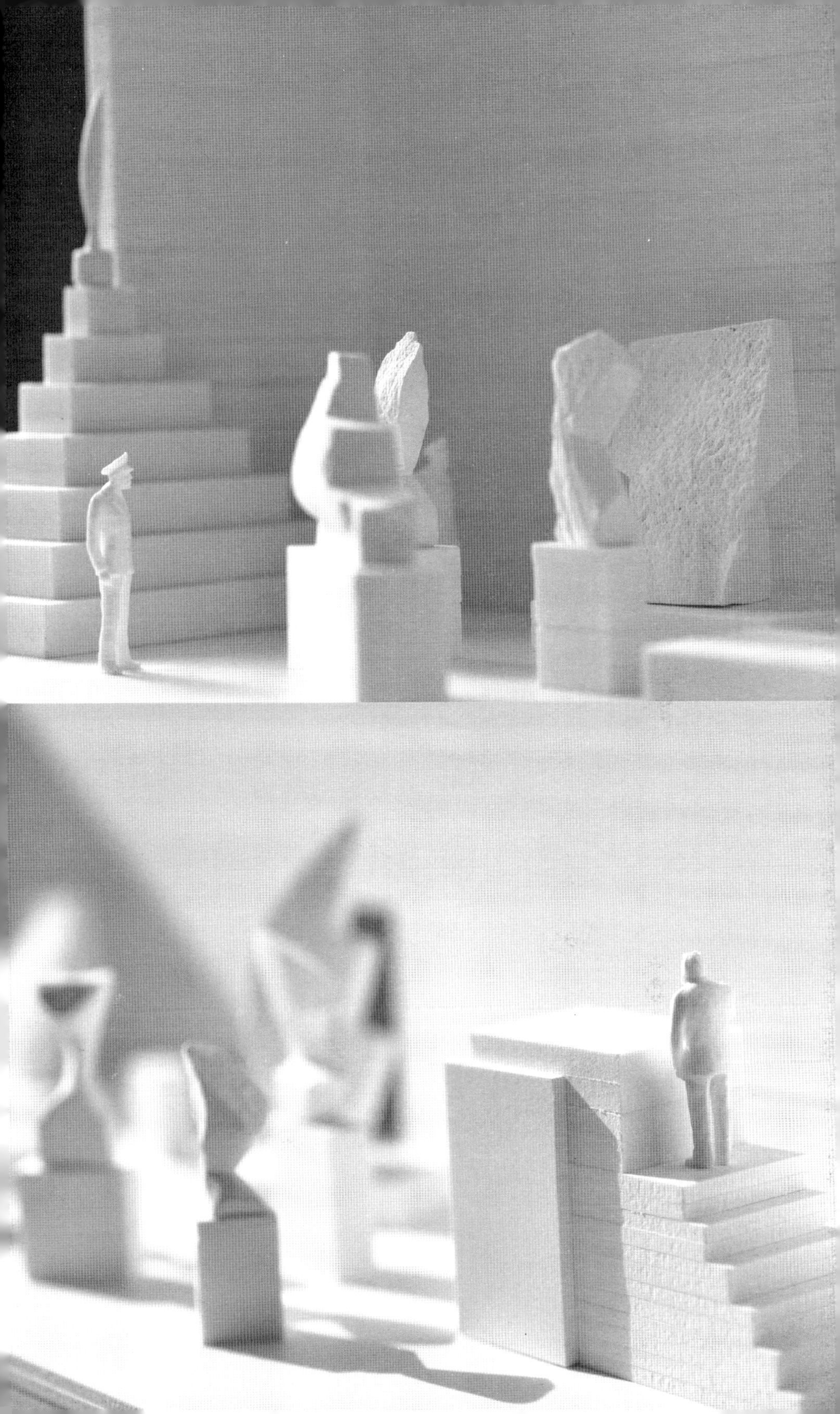

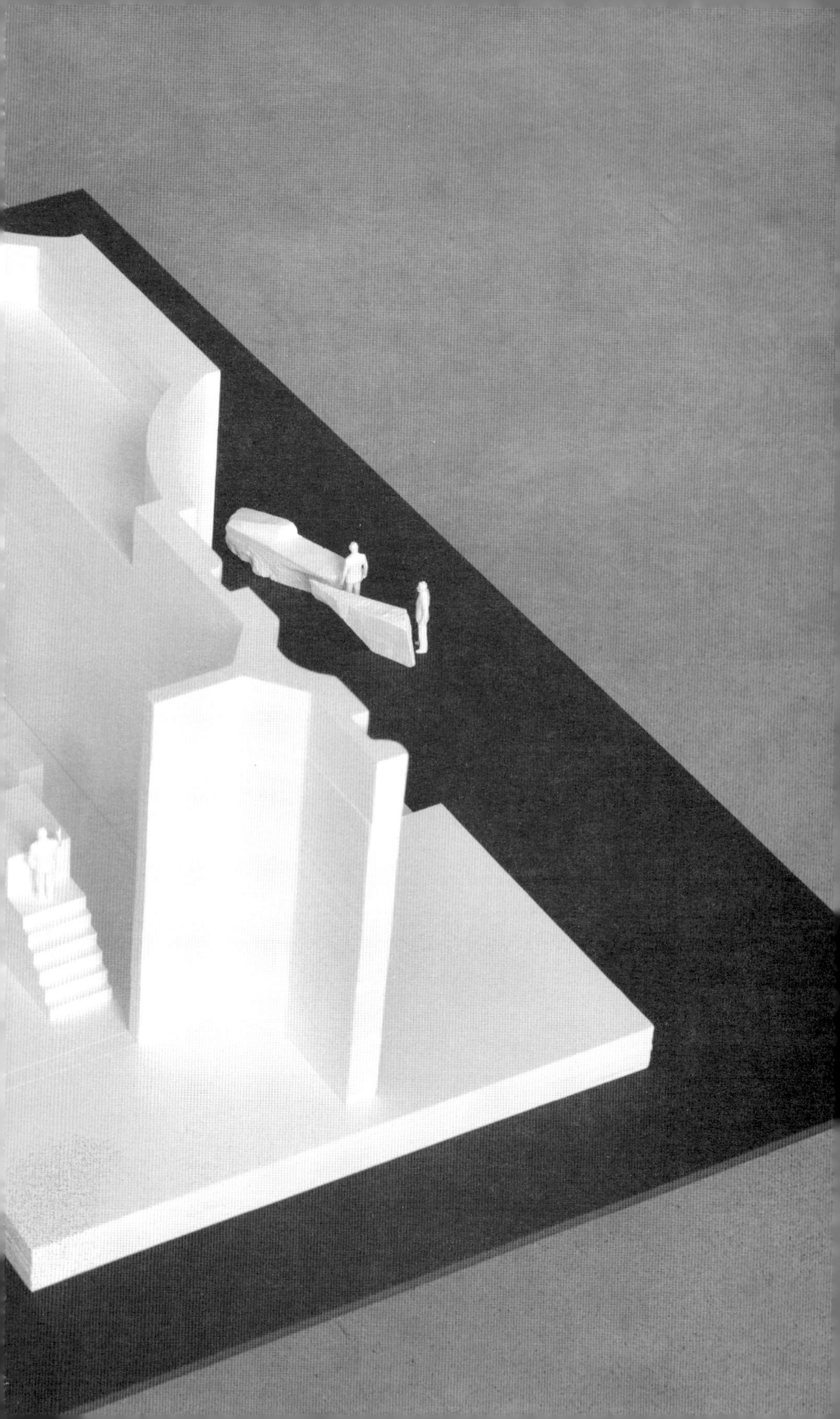

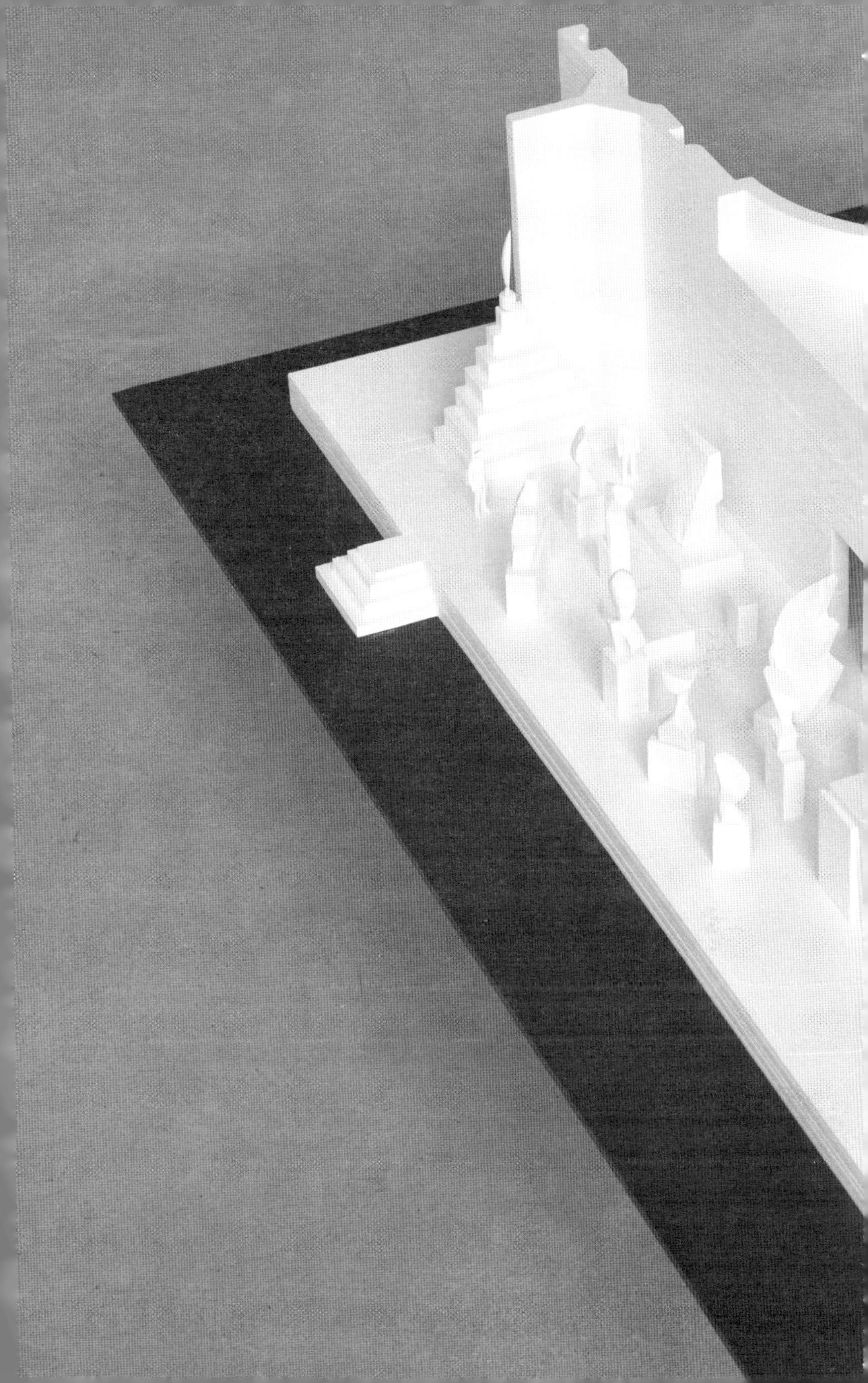

Moștenirea lui Brâncuși, 2009/2015

Proiect nerealizat pentru Pavilionul României la Bienala de la Veneția
în colaborare cu Ștefan Tiron
Text / simulări 3D / machetă 1:50, 80 x 50 x 20 cm (foto: Marius Poput)

În 2009, Alexandra Croitoru și Ștefan Tiron au aplicat la concursul organizat de Ministerul Culturii, Cultelor și Patrimoniului Național pentru Pavilionul României la Bienala de la Veneția cu un proiect artistic colaborativ, performativ și procesual, care urmărea să pună în discuție moștenirea culturală a lui Constantin Brâncuși, precum și "naționalizarea" ei. Proiectul s-a născut ca o reacție la "canonizarea" lui Brâncuși în contextul românesc și a împins la extrem un anumit tip de atitudine, de limbaj și de ritualuri omagiale specifice acestui cult.

Lucrarea conținea *in nuce* majoritatea temelor dezvoltate ulterior de cercetarea artistică a Alexandrei Croitoru. Configurația sa includea un pupitru/amvon pentru comunicări științifice deschise prin open call atît specialiștilor în brâncușiologie, cît și și pasionaților amatori; simetric, pe latura opusă a Pavilionului era planificat un altar dedicat moștenirii lui Brâncuși, un altar popular al publicului și admiratorilor lui Brâncuși din întreaga lume; în spațiul verde din fața Pavilionului era prevăzută o tabără de sculptură deschisă prin concurs sculptorilor români, avînd ca model tabăra internațională de sculptură de la Târgu Jiu; o serie de lucrări ale unor tineri artiști care au declanșat dialogul cu moștenirea lui Brâncuși completau proiectul.

Pavilionul României la Bienala de la Veneția este locul ideal pentru chestionarea cultului artistului devenit erou național. Istoria prezenței lui Brâncuși la Bienala de la Veneția reprezintă ea însăși o micro-istorie a receptării operei sale în România. Participările sale postume au oglindit politicile culturale autohtone: dacă expunerea sa discretă din 1960 releva locul său marginal în arta românească, cea din 1982 îl monumentalizează concomitent cu naționalizarea sa, iar invocarea numelui său în 1995 servește legitimării internaționale a producției sculpturale românești din acea vreme.[1]

Moștenirea lui Brâncuși se înscrie în traditia acestor invocări, reprezentînd însă o critică adusă acestui tip de instrumentalizare ideologică a artistului. Aparenta glorificare a figurii postume a sculptorului este subvertită prin juxtapunerea și exhibarea contradicțiilor produse de funcția-autor Brâncuși, atît în interiorul cît și în afara cîmpului artei. Circulînd sub forma unei utopii necesare, proiectul reclamă sarcina constantă și niciodată epuizată a denaturalizării mitologiei naționaliste constituite în jurul figurii lui Brâncuși în sfera publică din România.

---

1 Daria Ghiu, "In the name of Brâncuși: Complexes, Projections, and Historical Symptoms", *Kunsttexte.de*, http://edoc.hu-berlin.de/kunsttexte/2014-3/ghiu-daria-6/PDF/ghiu.pdf.

The Legacy of Brancusi, 2009/2015

Unrealised project for the Romanian Pavilion at the Venice Biennale
in collaboration with Stefan Tiron
Text / 3D simulations / scale model 1:50, 80 x 50 x 20 cm (photo: Marius Poput)

In 2009, Alexandra Croitoru and Stefan Tiron entered the competition organised by the Ministry of Culture, Religious Affairs and National Heritage for the Romanian Pavilion at the Venice Biennale, submitting a collaborative, performative and processual art project, which aimed to interrogate the cultural legacy of Constantin Brancusi and its "nationalisation." The project arose as a reaction to the "canonisation" of Brancusi in the Romanian context and pushed to the limit a certain type of attitude, language and ritualistic homage specific to such worship.

The work contained *in nuce* most of the topics subsequently explored in the research carried out by Alexandra Croitoru. Its configuration included a lectern/pulpit for academic papers solicited via an open call to specialists in Brancusiology, as well as enthusiastic amateurs; symmetrical to it, at the opposite side of the Pavilion, an altar to the legacy of Brancusi was planned, for the public and admirers of Brancusi from all over the world; in the green space in front of the Pavilion, there would have been a sculpture camp open to Romanian sculptors and modelled on the Targu Jiu international sculpture camp; a series of works by young artists engaged in a dialogue with the legacy of Brancusi completed the project.

The Romanian Pavilion at the Venice Biennale is the ideal place to question the cult of the artist as national hero. The very history of Brancusi's presence at the Venice Biennale represents a micro-history of the reception of his work in Romania. His posthumous inclusion in the biennale mirrored native cultural policies: whereas the discreet exhibition of his work in 1960 revealed his marginal place in Romanian art, the 1982 exhibition monumentalised the artist while at the same time nationalising him, and the invocation of his name in 1995 served to legitimise internationally Romanian sculptural production at that time.[1] *The Legacy of Brancusi* falls within the tradition of such invocations, but represents a critique of this type of ideological manipulation of the artist. The apparent posthumous glorification of the sculptor is subverted through the juxtaposition and exposure of the contradictions arising from the Brancusi author-function, both inside and outside the art world. Circulating in the form of a necessary utopia, the project reclaims the constant and inexhaustible task of denaturalising the nationalist mythology constructed around the figure of Brancusi within the public sphere in Romania.

---

1 Daria Ghiu, "In the name of Brancuși: Complexes, Projections, and Historical Symptoms", *Kunsttexte.de*, http://edoc.hu-berlin.de/kunsttexte/2014-3/ghiu-daria-6/PDF/ghiu.pdf.

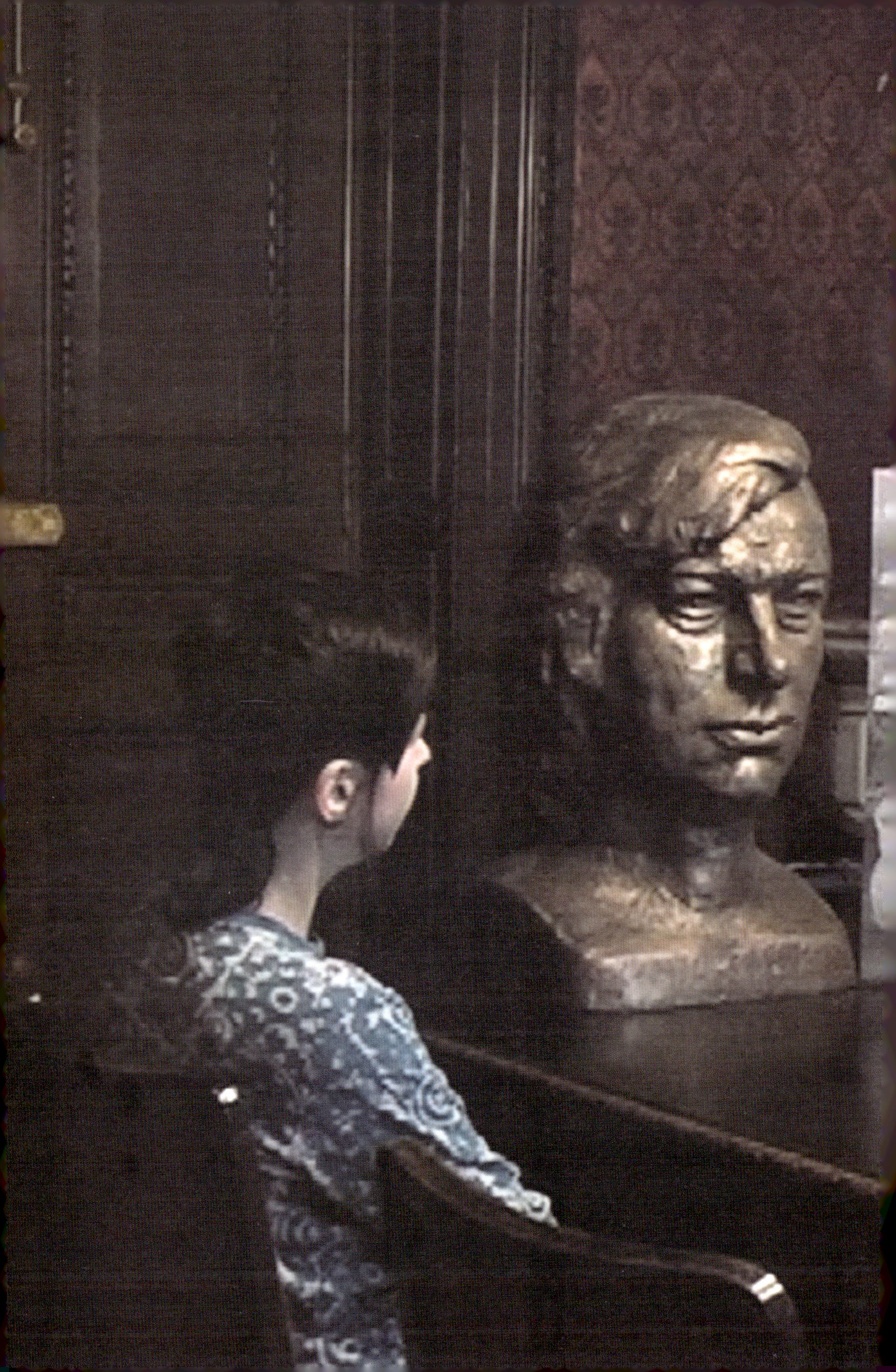

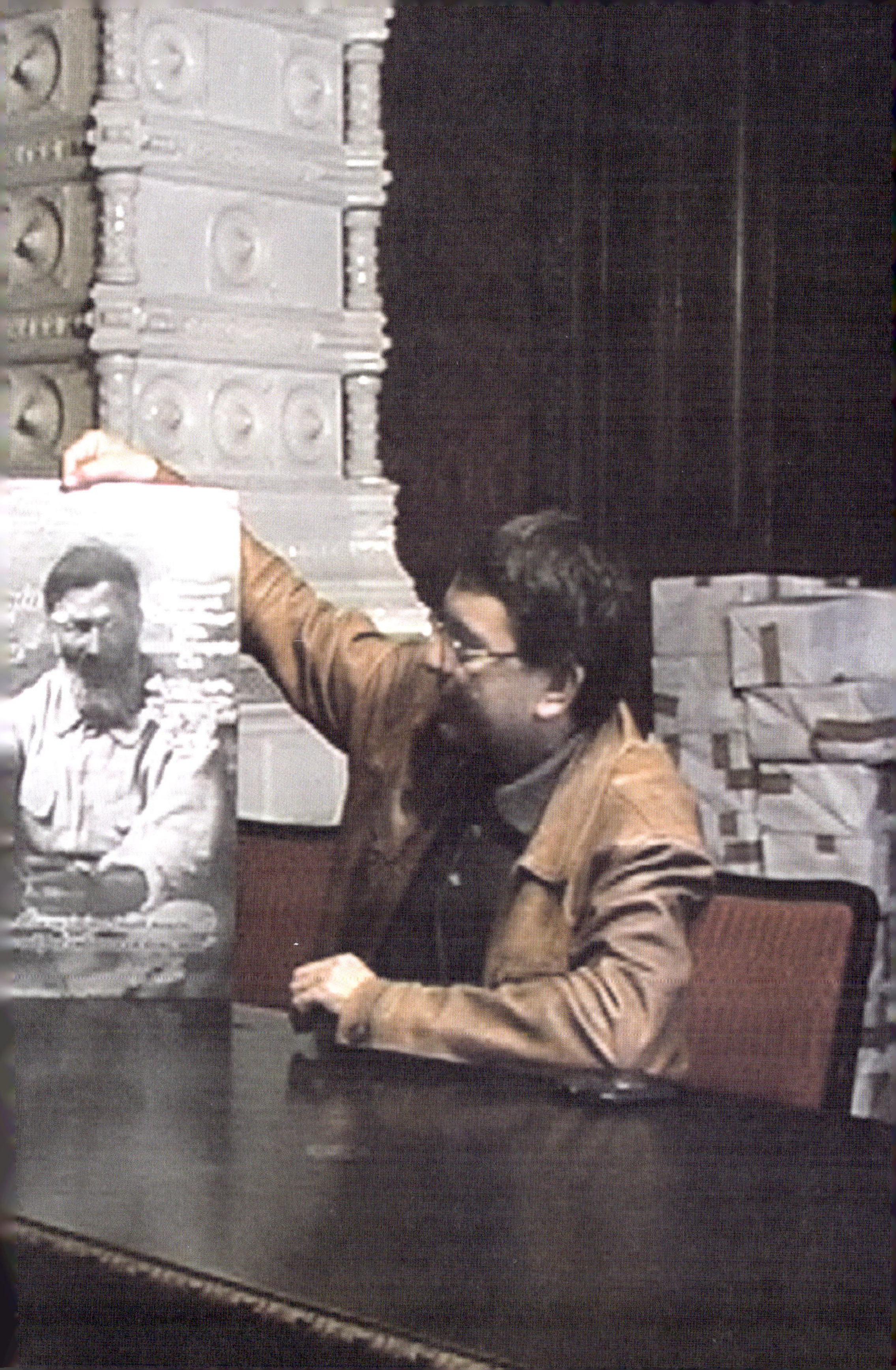

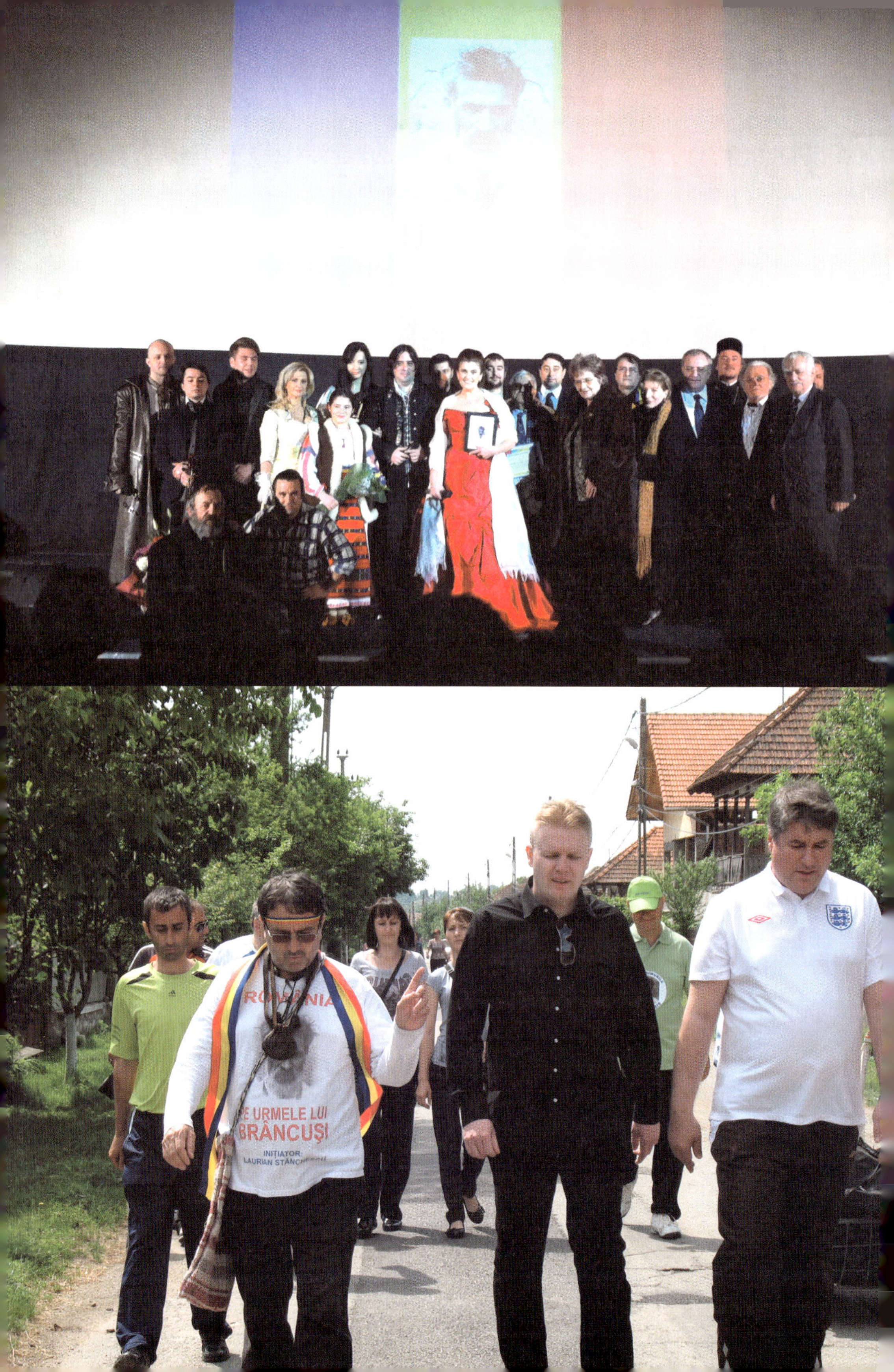

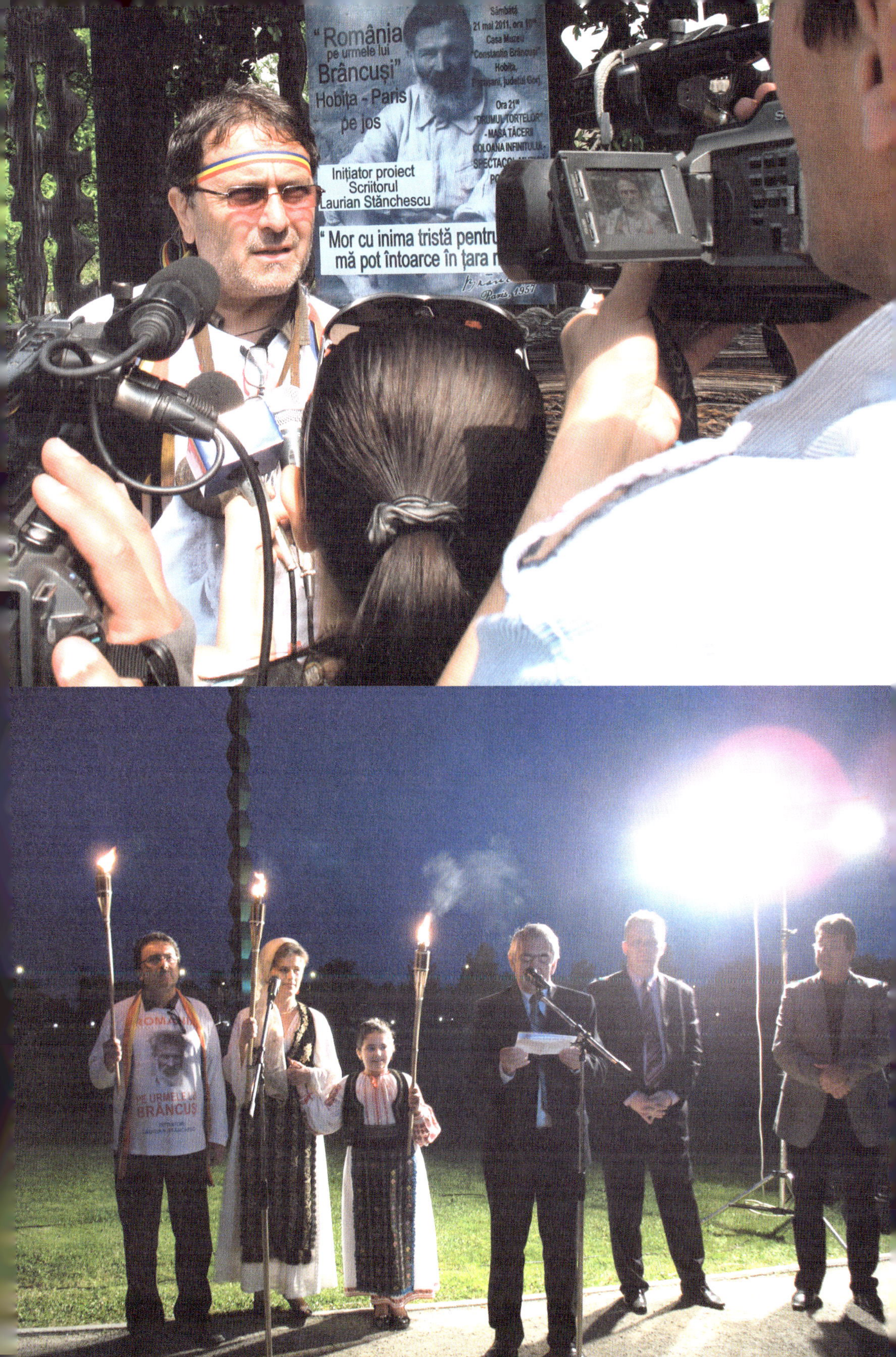
"România
pe urmele lui
Brâncuși"
Hobița - Paris
pe jos
Inițiator proiect
Scriitorul
Laurian Stănchescu
" Mor cu inima tristă pentru
mă pot întoarce în țara m

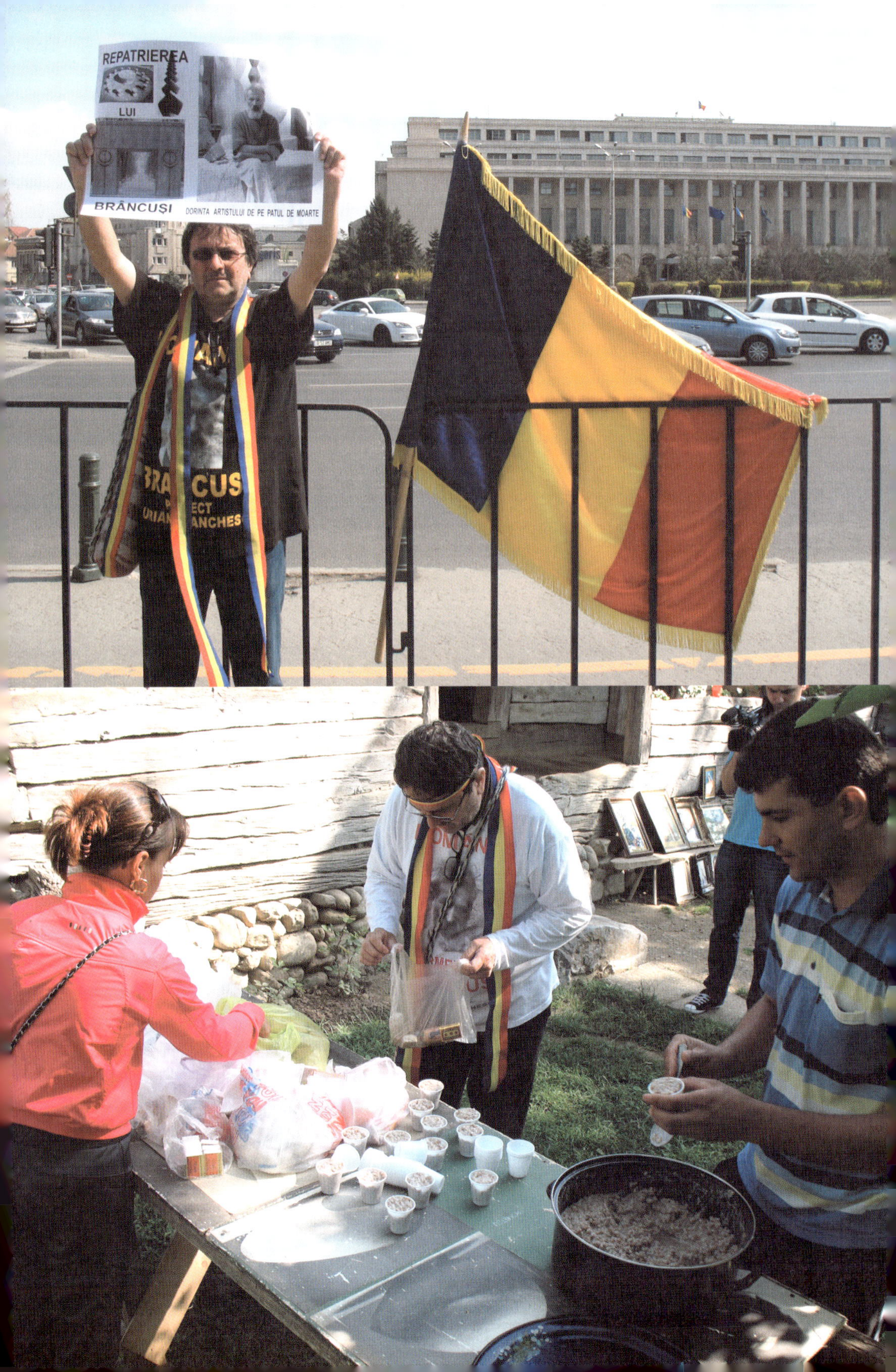

REPATRIEREA
LUI
BRÂNCUȘI   DORINTA ARTISTULUI DE PE PATUL DE MOARTE
BRÂNCUȘ

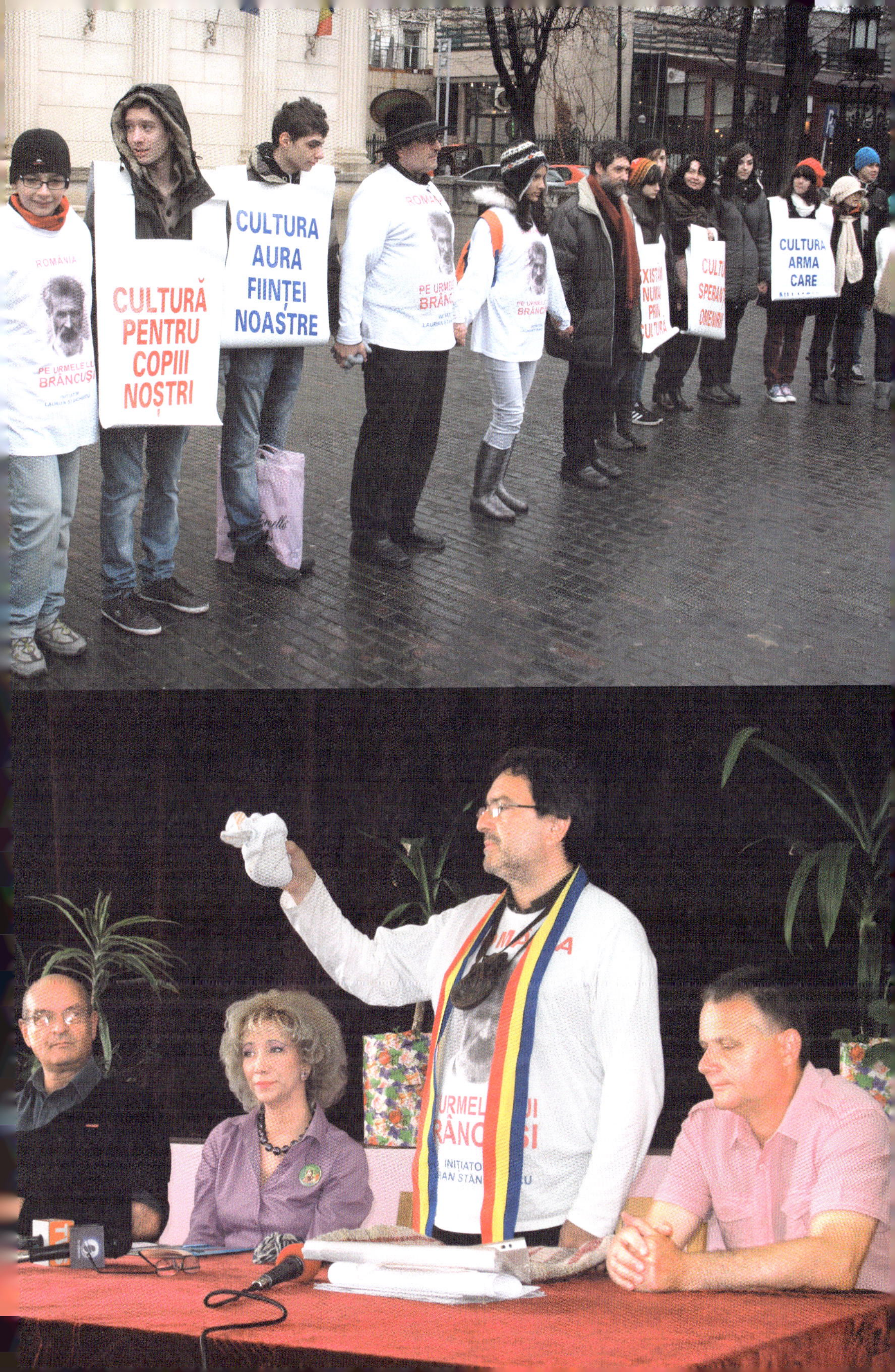
ROMANIA
PE URMELE LUI
BRÂNCUȘI
CULTURĂ
PENTRU
COPIII
NOȘTRI
CULTURA
AURA
FIINTEI
NOASTRE
CULTURA
ARMA
CARE

Timp de doi ani, Alexandra Croitoru a documentat demersurile publice făcute de scriitorul Laurian Stănchescu în vederea repatrierii osemintelor lui Constantin Brâncuși, transformînd problematica culturală tipic modernistă a exilului într-o dramă necropolitică asumată personal. Rolul de patriot militant, figura sa mesianică și relativa simpatie de care s-a bucurat în rîndul unor politicieni și chiar intelectuali sînt simptomatice pentru derapajele ideologice și criza identitară cu care se confruntă societatea românească de după 1989. Aceste manifestări cu caracter ritualic perpetuează clivajul dintre Est și Vest și exacerbează o atitudine reactivă față de Occident, exprimată prin glorificarea unor fantasme identitare și ficționalizarea istoriei. În documentația realizată de Croitoru cu instrumentele specifice jurnalismului utilizat estetic, subiectivitatea auctorială este prezentă minimal. Opțiunea retragerii discrete în spatele obiectivului, consemnînd fapte, gesturi și situații nespectaculoase, însă exemplare la nivel conceptual, poate sugera, la prima vedere, adeziunea artistei la proiectele pe care le consemnează. Cu toate acestea, asemeni celorlalte intervenții artistice ale Alexandrei Croitoru, care mizează pe exacerbarea elementelor naționaliste latente, absența comentariului artistic și aparenta identificare cu situația și personajele pe care le manipulează discret servesc la denaturalizarea mitului brâncușian prin expunerea consecventă a mecanismelor construcției sale simbolice și sociale.

Alexandra Croitoru în conversație cu Laurian Stănchescu
Uniunea Scriitorilor, București, 2011

Aniversarea a 137 de ani de la nașterea lui Brâncuși
Spectacol omagial la Cinema Scala
București, 2013

Marșul cultural Hobița – Târgu Jiu, 2011

Lansarea proiectului *România pe urmele lui Brâncuși: Hobița – Paris pe jos*
Hobița, 2011

Spectacol omagial la finalul *Marșului cultural Masa tăcerii – Coloana fără sfîrșit*
Târgu Jiu, 2011

Repatrierea lui Brâncuși
Protest în fața clădirii Guvernului
București, 2012

Pomană organizată la Casa memorială a lui Constantin Brâncuși
Hobița, 2011

Aniversarea a 135 de ani de la nașterea lui Brâncuși
Lanț uman în fața Ateneului Român
București, 2011

Prezentare la Colegiul Național "Constantin Brâncuși"
Craiova, 2011

←—— **Laurian Stănchescu, 2011 – 2013**

Proiect documentar [Documentary project]

For two years, Alexandra Croitoru documented the public actions undertaken by writer Laurian Stanchescu to repatriate Constantin Brancusi's remains. Stanchescu transformed the typically modernist cultural problematic of exile into a personal necro-political drama. His role as militant patriot, the messianic figure he cut, and the relative sympathy he enjoyed among some politicians and even intellectuals were symptomatic of the ideological aberrations and crisis of national identity with which Romanian society was confronted post-1989. Such ritualistic manifestations perpetuated the divide between East and West and exacerbated a reactionary attitude towards the West, expressed via the glorification of phantasms of national identity and the fictionalisation of history.

In the research Croitoru carried out, employing the tools specific to journalism, authorial subjectivism is minimal. The option to withdraw discreetly behind the camera lens, recording events, acts and situations that were unspectacular but exemplary at the conceptual level, might at first sight suggest an adherence on the part of the artist to the projects she was recording. But despite this, the same as in Alexandra Croitoru's other artistic interventions, which wager on exacerbating latent nationalistic elements, the absence of artistic commentary and her apparent identification with the situation and characters she discreetly manipulates serve to denaturalise the Brancusi myth through systematic exposure of the mechanisms of its symbolic and social construction.

Alexandra Croitoru in conversation with Laurian Stanchescu
Romanian Writers Association, Bucharest, 2011

The 137th anniversary of Brancusi's birth
Memorial performance held at Scala Cinema
Bucharest, 2013

The Hobita – Targu Jiu Culture March, 2011

Launching of the project *Romania in Brancusi's footsteps: A walk from Hobita to Paris*
Hobita, 2011

Memorial performance at the end of *The Table of Silence – Endless Column Culture March*
Targu Jiu, 2011

Repatriate Constantin Brancusi!
Protest in front of Government House
Bucharest, 201

Almsgiving at the Constantin Brancusi
Memorial House
Hobita, 2011

The 135th anniversary of Brancusi's birth
Human chain in front of Romanian Athenaeum
Bucharest, 2011

Public lecture held at "Constantin Brancusi"
National College
Craiova, 2011

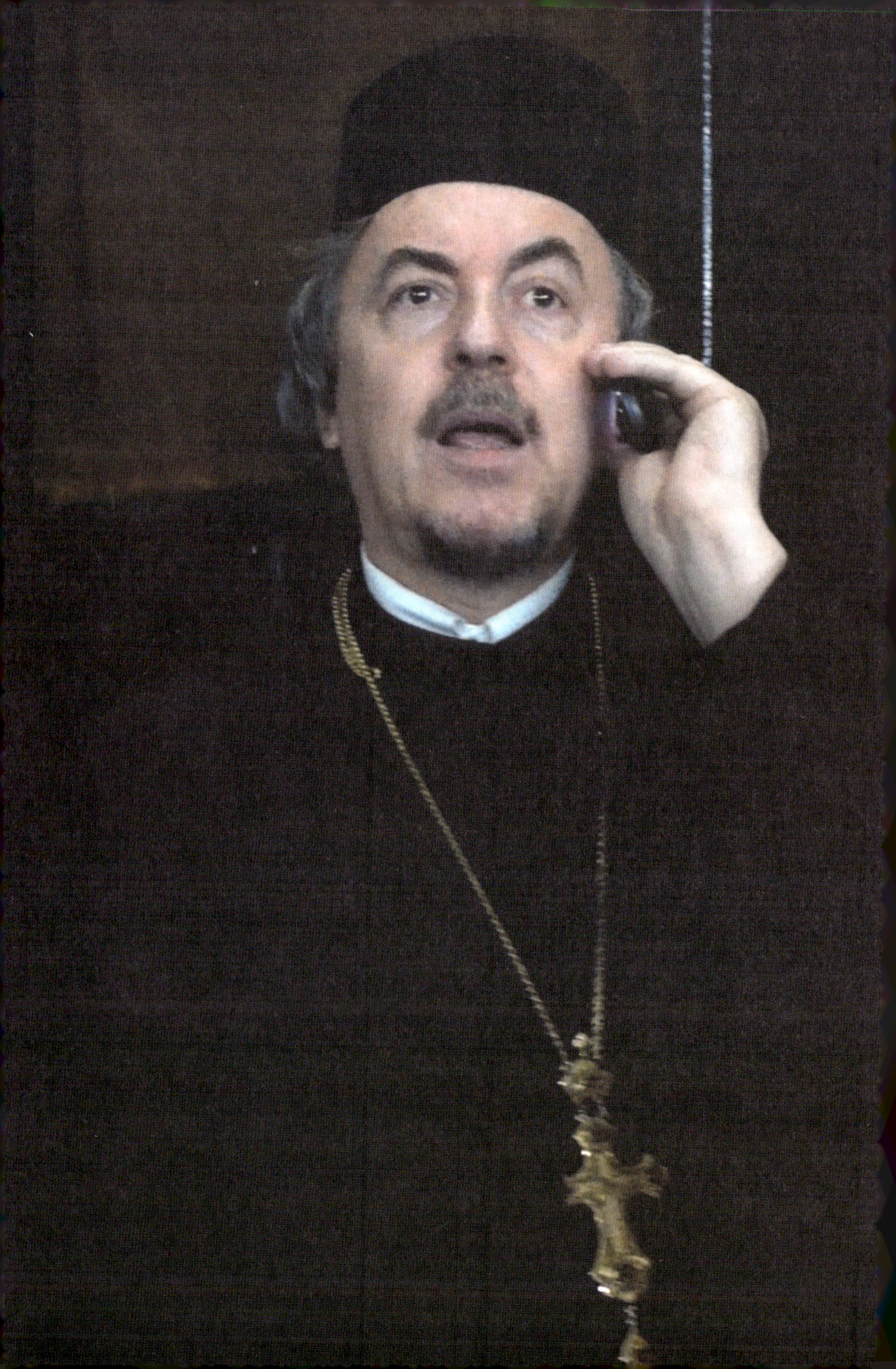

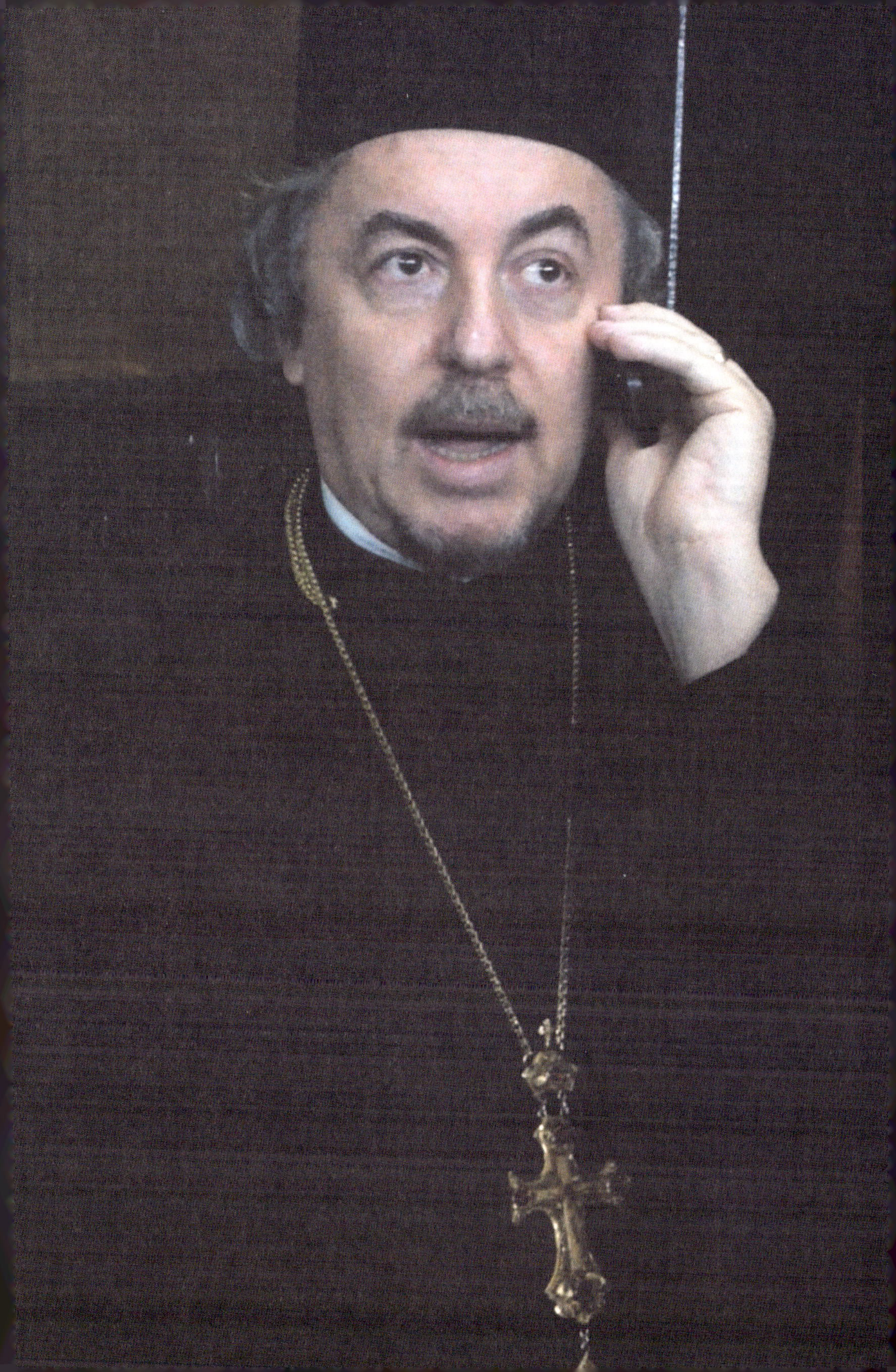

Lapidară și ironică, lucrarea a fost realizată cu ocazia spectacolului omagial organizat de Laurian Stănchescu pentru a celebra 137 de ani de la nașterea lui Brâncuși. Evenimentul reunește pe scenă planul cultural cu cel politic, beneficiind de prezența reprezentanților unor instituții cum sînt Academia Română, Guvernul României și Biserica Ortodoxă Română. Artista a decis să transforme unul dintre momentele de culise într-un video de sine stătător pentru a pune accentul, într-un mod ironic, pe derapajele care apar în interpretarea vieții și operei lui Brâncuși. Înregistrarea surpinde discursul unui reprezentant al Bisericii Ortodoxe în timpul unei conversații telefonice. Cu acest prilej, preotul subliniază caracterul creștin ortodox al ansamblului monumental de la Târgu Jiu și îl numește pe Brâncuși "un om al bisericii sale", care a realizat "o sinteză între Orient și Occident".

Asemeni unui simptom socio-cultural, preotul întruchipează un complex discursiv constituit din interpretări în cheie mistic-religioasă ale unor elemente disparate proprii vieții și operelor lui Brâncuși. Simplele operații de selecție și încadrare a unei situații de culise, caracteristice jurnalismului de investigație, acționează subversiv, producînd un efect de înstrăinare privitorului. Prin decontextualizarea situației de comunicare operată de Croitoru, care elimină din cadrul strîns orice informații adiacente cu privire la motivația și caracterul real sau imaginar, privat sau public ale acestui monolog, locutorul își diminuează forța persuasivă, iar discursul său își pierde credibilitatea. Totodată, înregistrarea deconspiră amploarea politicilor instituționale active în interpretarea postumă a operei lui Brâncuși, relevînd interferențele dintre apropierea sa naționalistă și cea creștin-ortodoxă.

←——— Fără titlu, 2013 [Untitled, 2013]

Video, 49''

Lapidary and ironic, the piece was filmed on the occasion of the spectacular event organised by Laurian Stanchescu to mark the 137th anniversary of Brancusi's birth. The event brought the cultural and the political spheres to the stage, enjoying the participation of representatives of institutions that included the Romanian Academy, the Romanian Government, and the Romanian Orthodox Church. The artist decided to transform a behind-the-scenes moment into a video work, as a way of ironically emphasising the aberrations that arise in the interpretation of the life and work of Brancusi. The recording captures the discourse of a representative of the Orthodox Church during a telephone conversation. The priest stresses the Orthodox Christian nature of the monumental ensemble at Targu Jiu and calls Brancusi "a man of his Church," who achieved "a synthesis between East and West."
In what may be likened to a socio-cultural symptom, the priest embodies a discursive complex made up of mystical-religious interpretations of disparate elements of Brancusi's life and work. Characteristic of investigative journalism, the mere operation of selecting and framing a behind-the-scene situation is subversive, exerting an effect of estrangement on the viewer. Croitoru de-contextualises the situation of communication, eliminating from the frame any adjacent information regarding motivation and the real or imaginary, private or public, nature of the monologue. The persuasiveness of the speaker is thereby diminished and his discourse loses credibility. At the same time, the recording exposes the sheer scale of the institutional policies at work in the posthumous interpretation of Brancusi's work, revealing crosscurrents between its nationalist and Orthodox Christian appropriation.

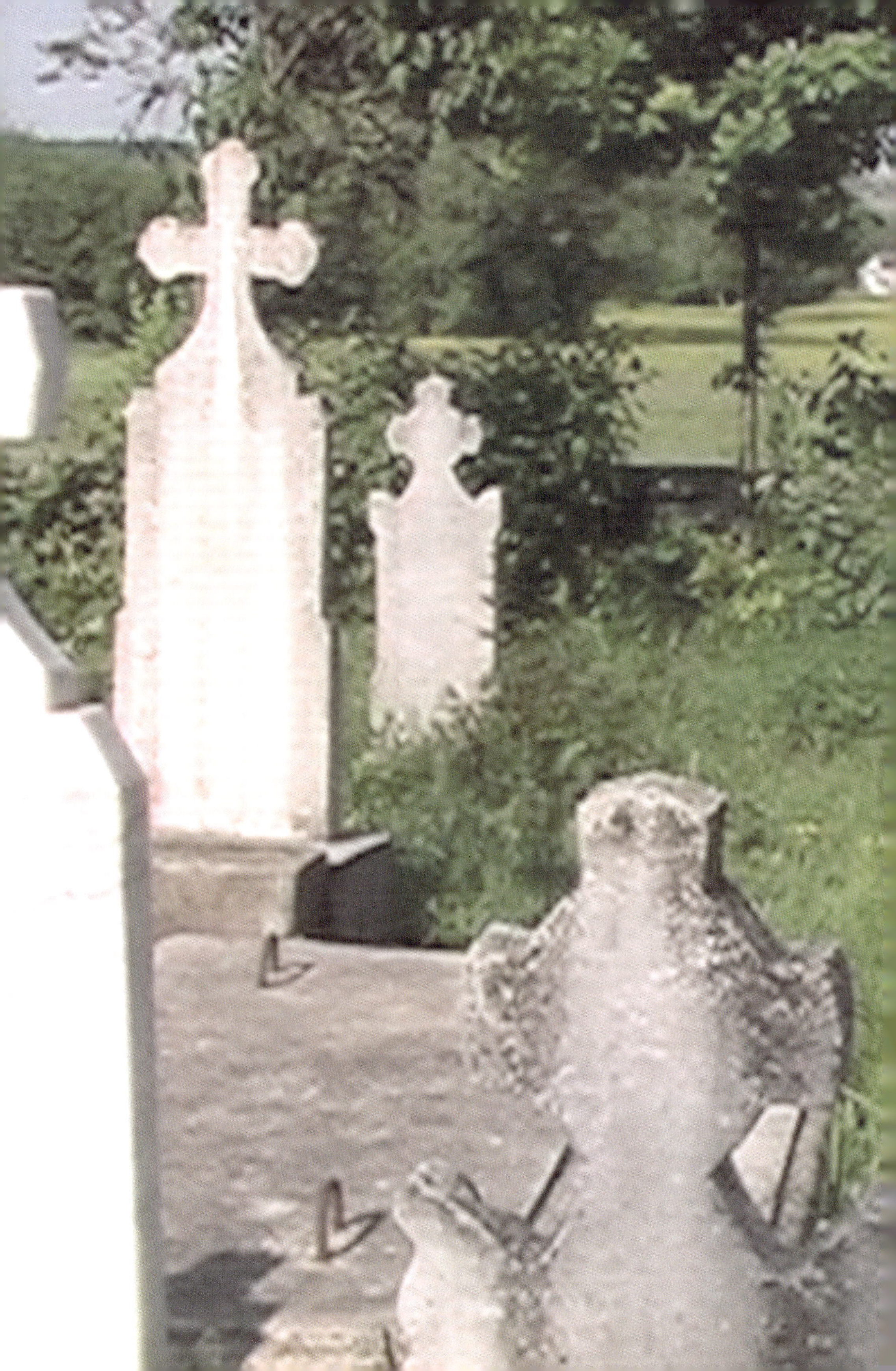

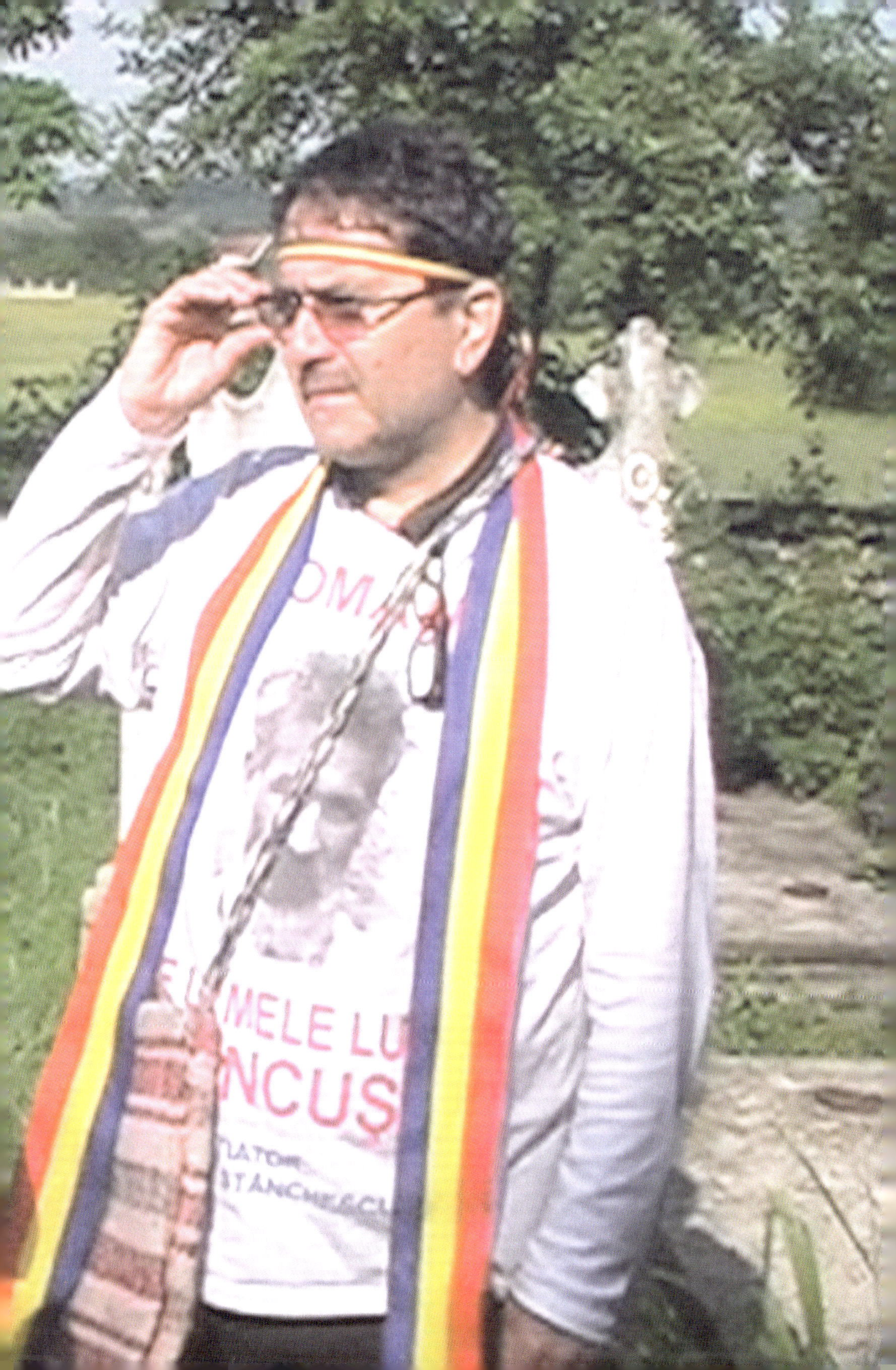
ROMÂN
MELE LU
NCUŞI

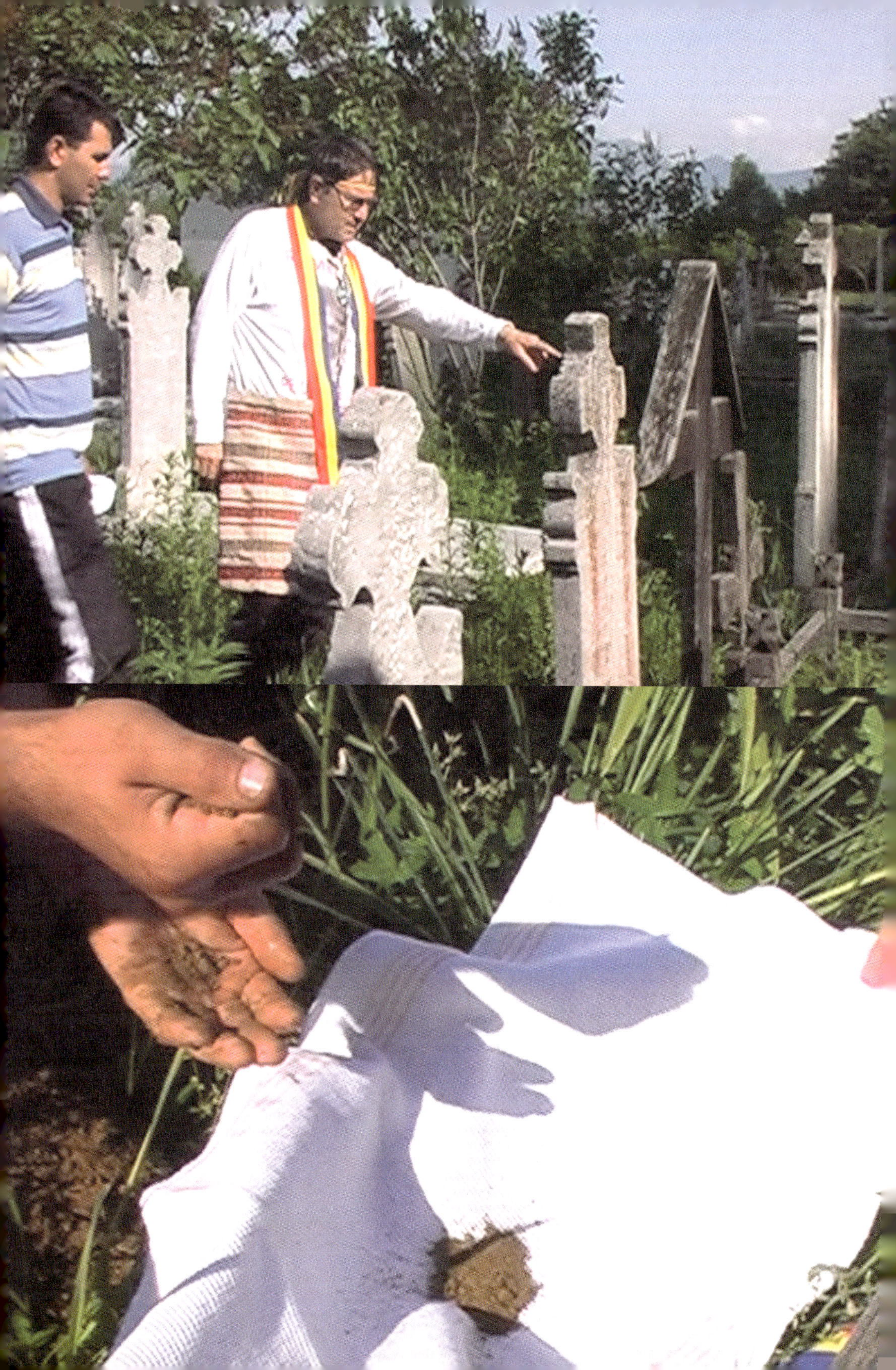

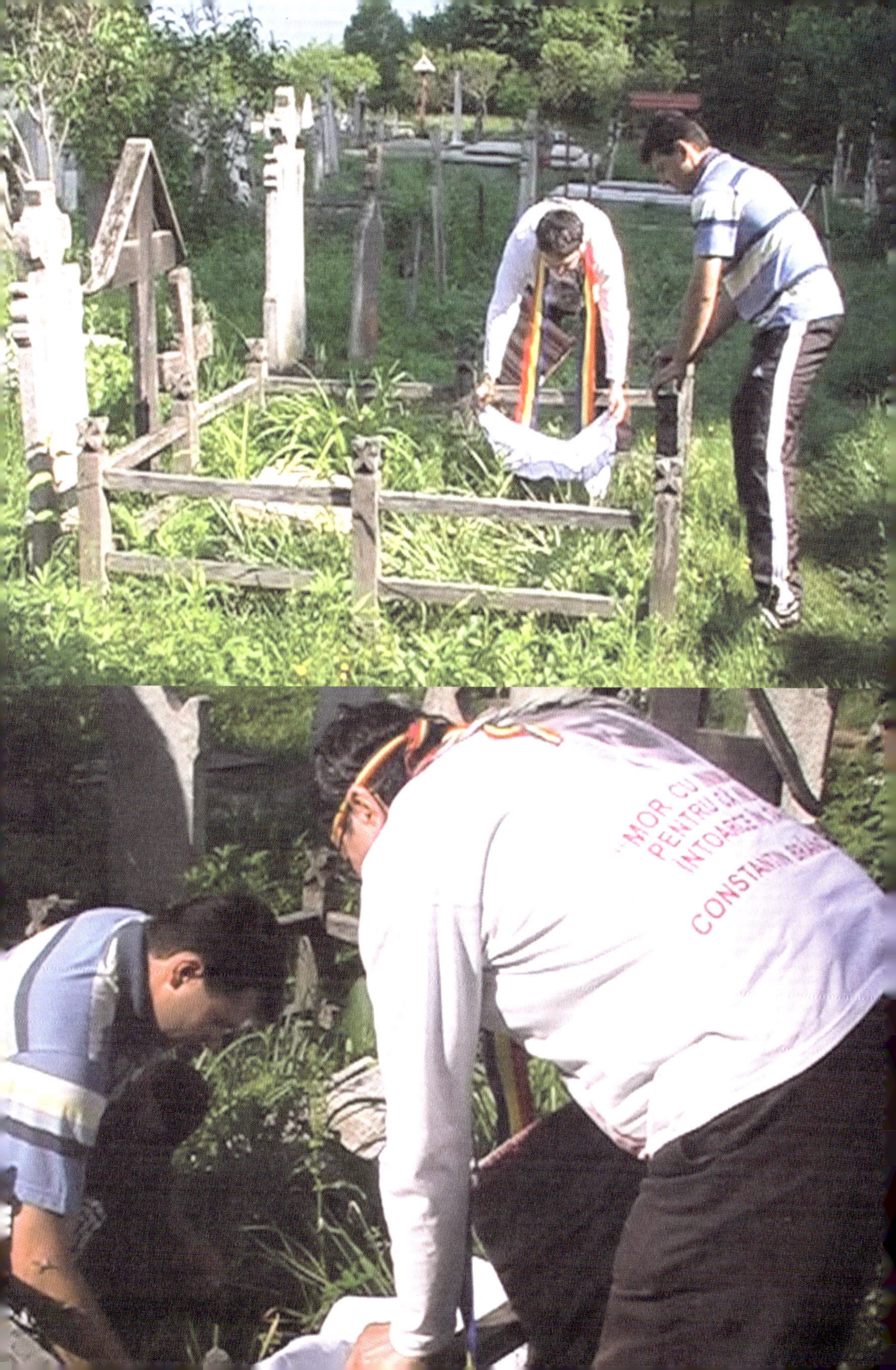
MOR CU
PENTRU
INTOARCE
CONSTANTA

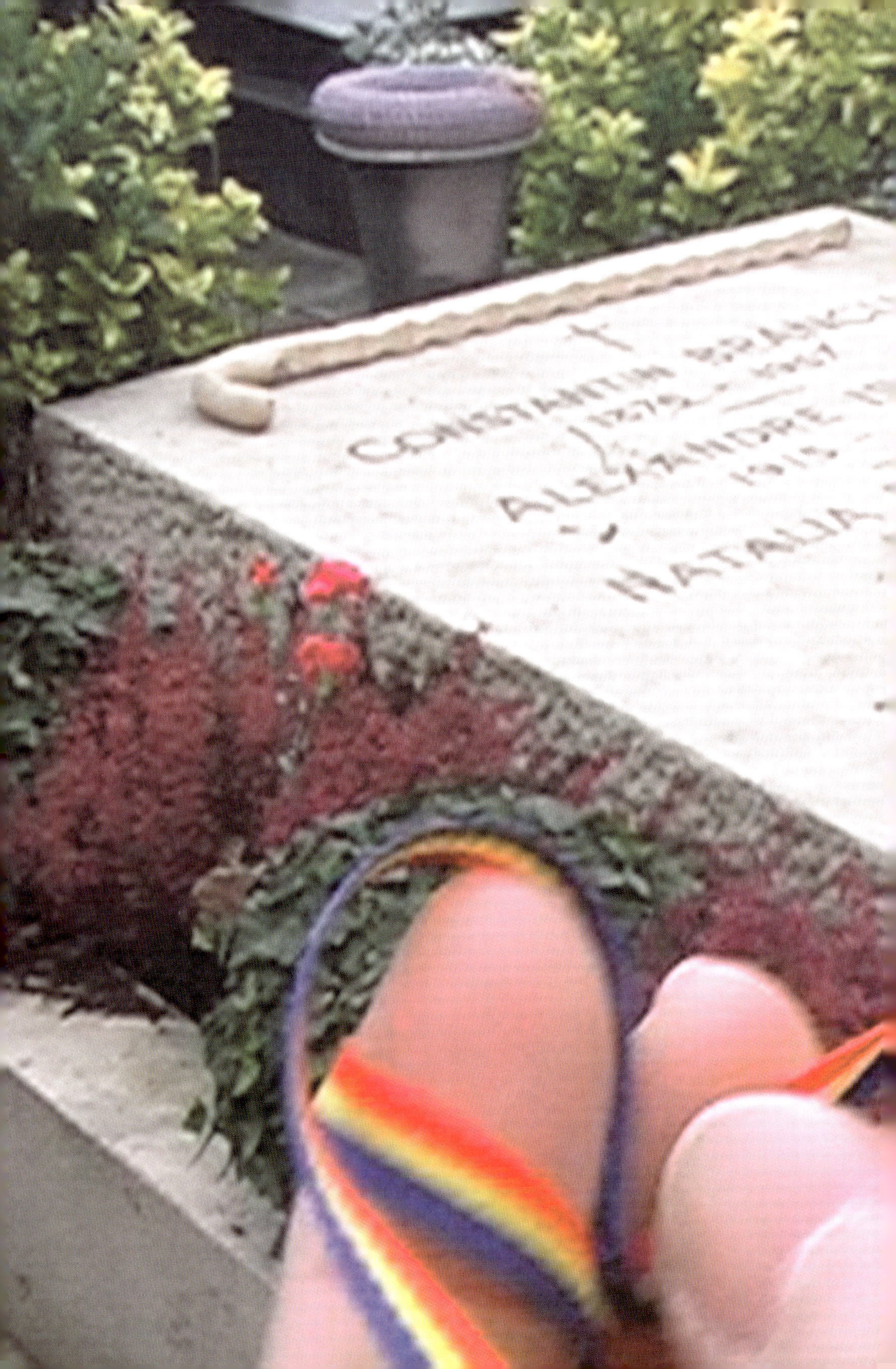

CONSTANTIN BRANCUSI
1876 — 1957
ALEXANDRE ISTRATI
1915
NATALIA

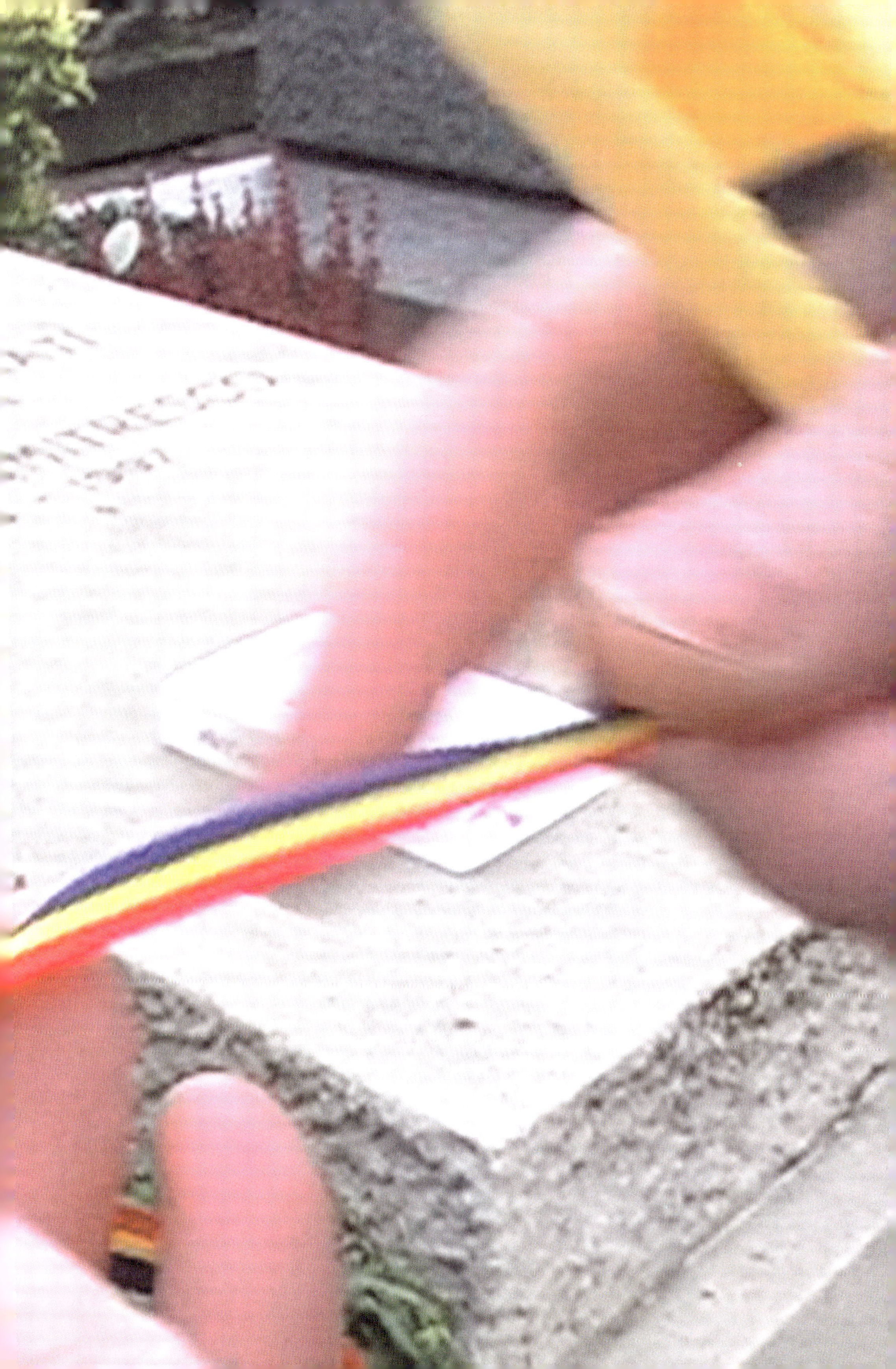

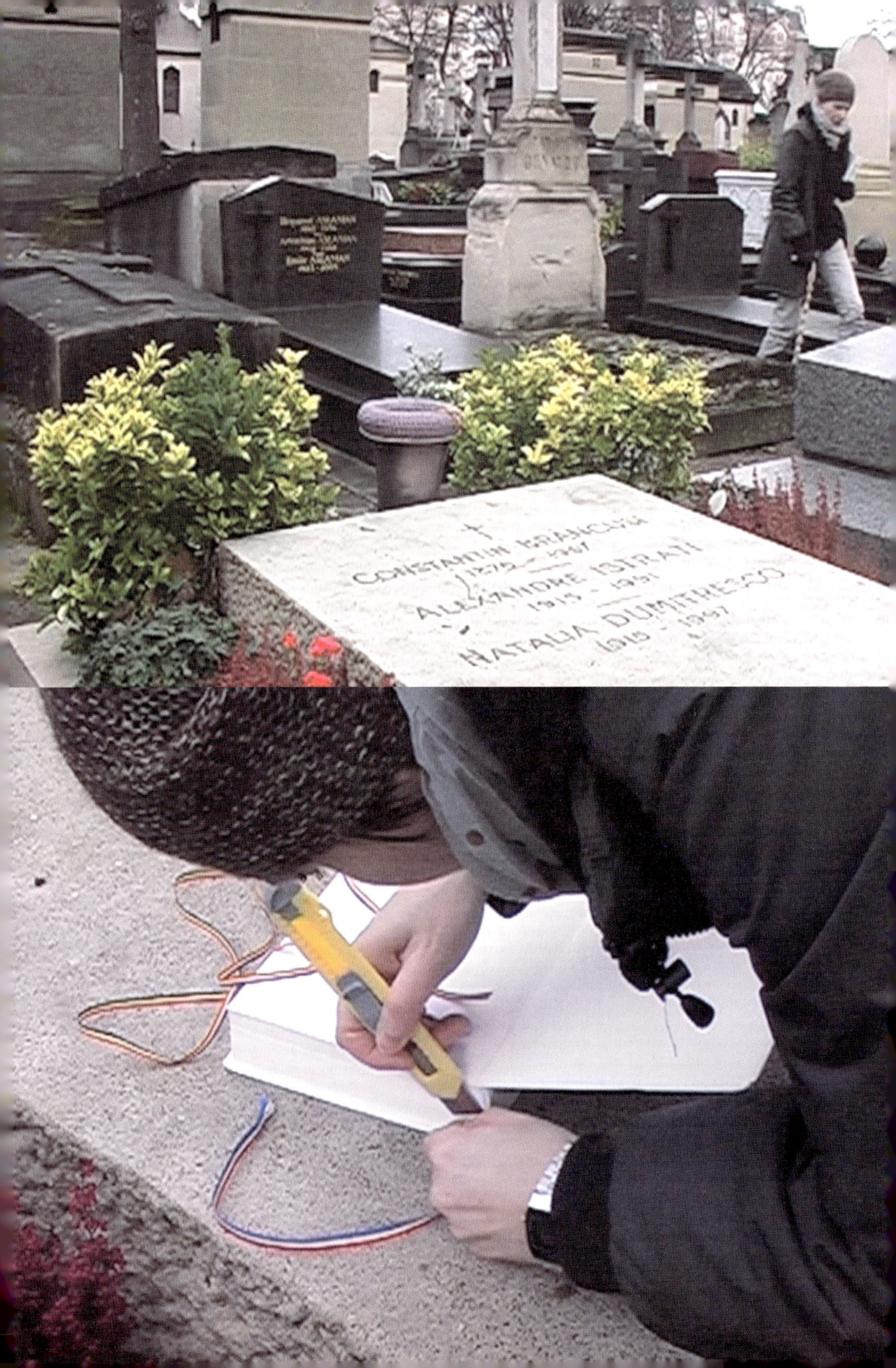

CONSTANTIN BRANCUSI
1876 — 1957
ALEXANDRE ISTRATI
1915 — 1991
NATALIA DUMITRESCO
1915 — 1997

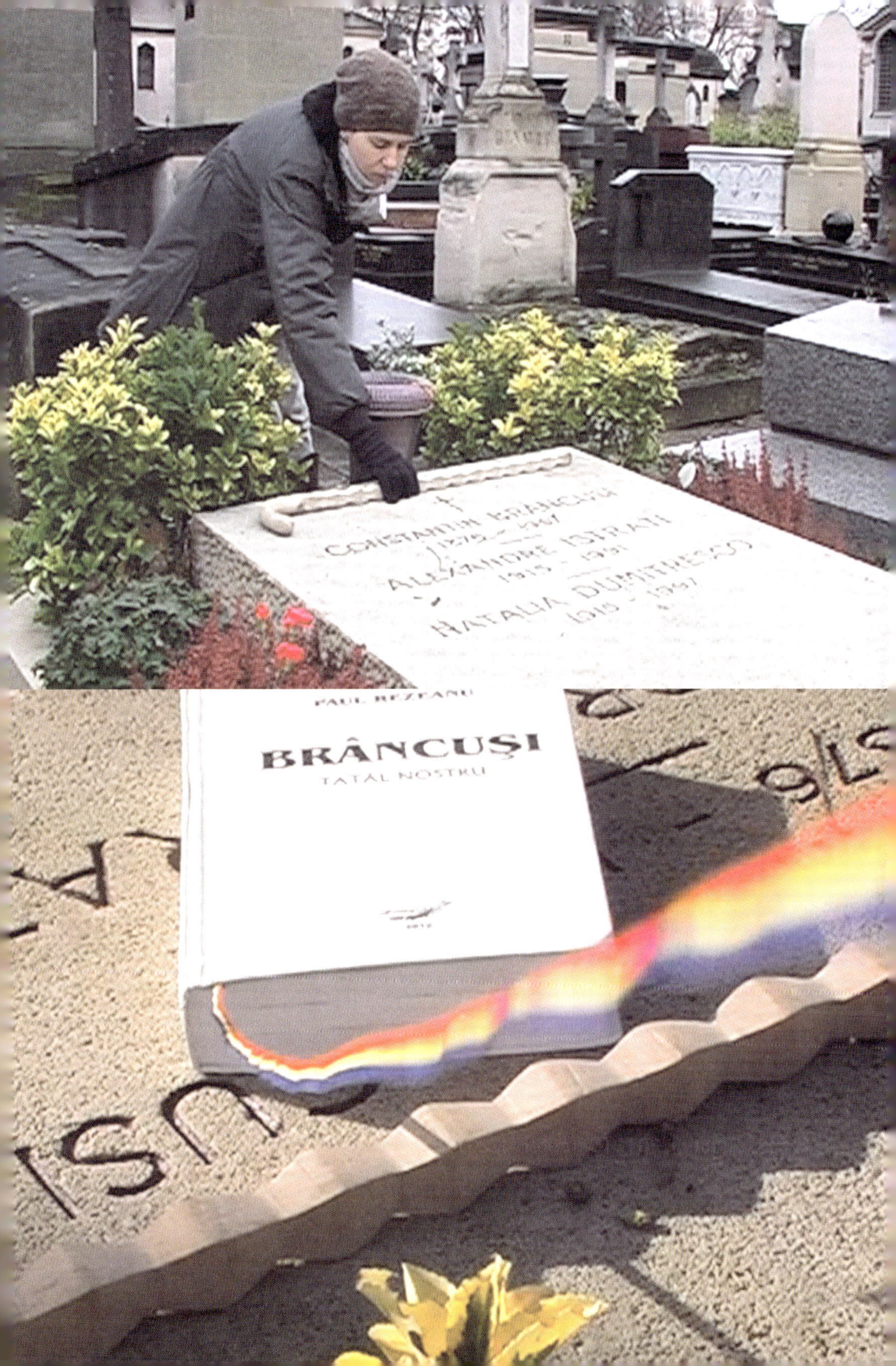
PAUL REZEANU
BRÂNCUȘI
TATĂL NOSTRU

Lucrările video din seria *Cimitir* au ca punct de plecare demersul solitar al lui Laurian Stănchescu de a transporta pămînt de la mormîntul mamei lui Constantin Brâncuși la locul de veci al artistului, cimitirul Montparnasse din Paris. De fapt, subiectul lor real îl constituie apologia "românității".

Cimitir I înregistrează momentul în care Laurian Stănchescu ia o mostră de pămînt de pe mormîntul părinților lui Brâncuși din cimitirul din Hobița, satul natal al sculptorului. Retorica înstrăinării legitimează mitul exilului involuntar în "străinătate", iar figura maternă (absentă) la care se face aluzie semnifică, prin metonimie, patria-mamă. Îndoctrinarea naționalistă a lui Laurian Stănchescu este evidențiată de vestimentația sa ostentativă, iar gestul, pretins solemn, devine în mod involuntar comic. Inexistența oricărui comentariu în această înregistrare sugerează, cu o discretă ironie, o estetică de inspirație factografică, potrivit căreia faptele brute sînt suficiente pentru a exprima cadrele ideologice care le oferă inteligibilitate.

Abordarea realistă este contrapunctată de o ulterioară prelungire ficțională a situației reale documentate. Filmată de această dată în Montparnasse, lucrarea *Cimitir II* poate fi privită drept o replică performativă la acțiunile inițiate de Stănchescu, menită să contracareze, prin îngroșarea caricaturală a gesturilor pios-comemorative cu aspect redemptiv, ideologia naționalistă care alimentează aceste atitudini. Intrînd în cimitirul parizian cu gesturi reverențioase, Alexandra Croitoru așază pe mormîntul lui Brâncuși, în chip de ofrandă, un obiect sculptural atipic – un baston comisionat sculptorului Napoleon Tiron. Obiectul, care ilustrează reciclarea motivelor brâncușiene în cultura populară, este acompaniat de o carte al cărei titlu – *Brâncuși. Tatăl Nostru* – prezentat în gros-plan exprimă fără echivoc statutul deopotrivă demiurgic și patriarhal oferit lui Brâncuși în România. Întregul ritual imaginat de artistă întreține echivocul între cultul strămoșilor, cel al eroilor și cel al sfinților, care se suprapun în cazul lui Brâncuși.

Prin recontextualizare, filiația artistică la care cel mai probabil face aluzie titlul cărții utilizate în lucrarea video devine, pe nesimțite, una națională. Cu gesturi atente, artista desface semnul de carte existent în culorile steagului Franței și îl înlocuiește cu unul care poartă tricolorul românesc. Semnificația gestului revizionist este evidentă. Violența vizualizată o întărește pe cea textuală, mai puțin sesizabilă, aflată pe coperta cărții. Prin intermediul unui gros-plan care întinde acest tricolor în afara cadrului, în mod simbolic, pînă în patrie, afirmarea hiperbolică a identității naționale răstălmăcește, aparent involuntar, coloana infinitului inscripționată pe bastonul-ofrandă.

←——— Cimitir I, 2011 [Cemetery I, 2011]

Video, 5'50''

←——— Cimitir II, 2014 [Cemetery II, 2014]

Video, 3'05''

The video works in the *Cemetery* series take as their starting point the one-man efforts of Laurian Stanchescu to transport soil from the grave of Brancusi's mother to the artist's resting place in the Montparnasse Cemetery in Paris. In fact, their real subject is an apologia for "Romanianness."

Cemetery I records the moment when Laurian Stanchescu takes a soil sample from the grave of Brancusi's parents in the graveyard at Hobita, the artist's native village. The rhetoric of estrangement legitimises the myth of involuntary exile to "foreign parts," and the (absent) maternal figure to which it alludes signifies, by metonymy, the motherland. Laurian Stanchescu's nationalist indoctrination is highlighted by his ostentatious garb, and his act, intended to be solemn, unwittingly becomes comical. The absence of any commentary in the recording suggests, with discreet irony, an aesthetic of factographic inspiration, according to which the raw facts are sufficient to express the ideological frameworks that lend them intelligibility.

The realist approach is in counterpoint with a subsequent fictional extension of the documented real situation. Filmed in the Montparnasse Cemetery, *Cemetery II* can be viewed as a performance in response to Stanchescu's endeavours, aimed at counteracting, by means of an exaggerated caricature of redemptive, piously commemorative gestures, the nationalist ideology that nurtures such attitudes. Entering the Parisian cemetery with reverent body language, Alexandra Croitoru places on Brancusi's grave, by way of an offering, an atypical sculptural object: a walking stick commissioned from sculptor Napoleon Tiron. The object, which illustrates the recycling of Brancusi motifs in popular culture, is accompanied by a book whose title *Brancusi. Our Father* shown in close-up, unequivocally expresses the simultaneously demiurgic and patriarchal status bestowed on Brancusi in Romania. The entire ritual imagined by the artist maintains the equivocalness between the cults of ancestors, of national heroes, and of saints that overlap in the worship of Brancusi.

Through re-contextualisation, the artistic filiation, to which the title of the book featured in the video work probably alludes, imperceptibly becomes a national filiation. With careful gestures, the artist undoes the existing bookmark, in the colours of the French flag, and replaces it with one emblazoned with the Romanian tricolour. The significance of the revisionist gesture is obvious. The visualised violence reinforces the less perceptible textual violence to be found on the book's cover. By means of a close-up that symbolically extends the tricolour outside the frame and as far as the motherland, the hyperbolic affirmation of national identity distorts, seemingly without intending to, the endless column carved on the walking stick offering.

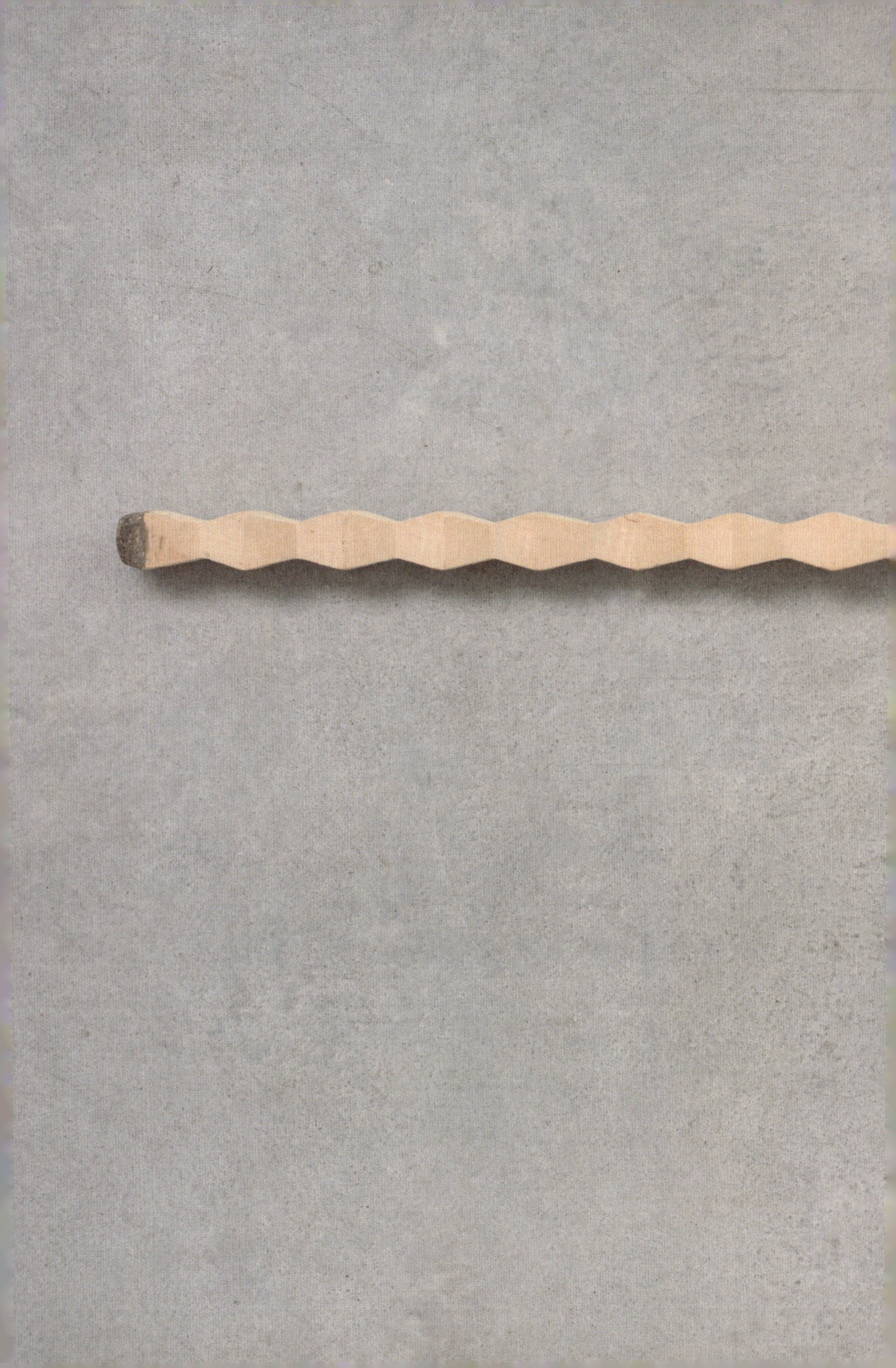

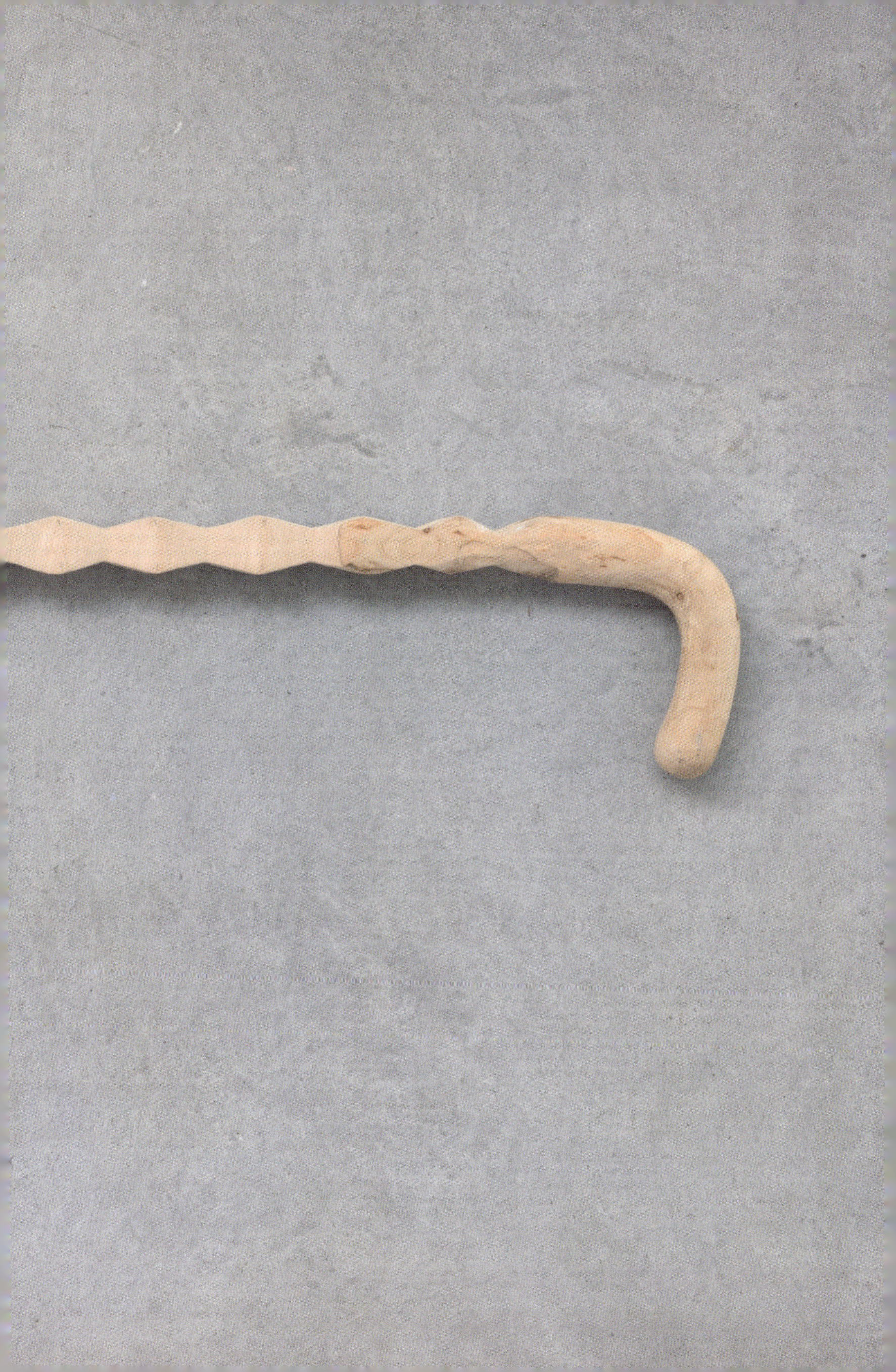

Materializată printr-un baston sculptat cu motivul coloanei infinitului, lucrarea constituie o sculptură conceptuală ce ironizează fetișizarea operelor lui Brâncuși. Atît titlul cît și obiectul evocă, la prima vedere, gramatica vizuală specifică sculpturii minimaliste, reconfigurată însă la dimensiuni artizanale și utilitare. La o privire mai atentă, înfățișarea sa îl recomandă drept un absurd *ready-made* reciproc, o sculptură monumentală transformată prin redimensionare în obiect utilitar. Însă procesul său de producție îl prezintă drept un *ready-made* asistat, un obiect utilitar ridicat la rangul de operă de artă printr-o intervenție manuală specifică artei înalte – mai precis, sculpturii. Astfel, acest obiect-fetiș sintetizează mai multe contradicții care se întîlnesc în destinul postum al operei lui Constantin Brâncuși. El combină arta pop cu meșteșugurile populare și cu cea elitistă și invocă etno-naționalismul aplicat în arhitectura urbană românească a anilor '80. Totodată, bastonul evocă arsenalul de mărunțișuri-kitsch asociate numelui Brâncuși ca brand comercial și vîndute la Centrul Georges Pompidou sau la Casa memorială din satul Hobița.

Asocierea dintre opera de artă și marfă realizată prin intermediul numelui artistului ca brand cultural, precum și asocierea dintre branding-ul artistic și cel de țară nu este, în acest context, întîmplătoare. Atît industria culturii, cît și discursul naționalist din România s-au folosit de Brâncuși în repetate ocazii, reciclîndu-i operele ca imagini lipsite de o semnificație intrinsecă, în maniera unor semnificanți flotanți. Obiectul a fost realizat la sugestia Alexandrei Croitoru de Napoleon Tiron, sculptor ce a făcut parte din generația prezentată în 1995 la Pavilionul României de la Bienala de la Veneția în expoziția *L' eredità di Brancusi in Romania*. Printr-un un simbol al celui considerat "vîrful sculpturii românești", tradiția sculpturală este astfel reciclată într-un obiect folosit pentru a chestiona finalmente tot acest eșafodaj în care valorile artistice și cele naționale se împletesc și dau naștere obsesiei brâncușiene.

←—— Baston, 2013

Obiect comisionat sculptorului Napoleon Tiron
83 cm (foto: Marius Poput)

Taking the form of a walking stick carved with the motif of the endless column, the work is a conceptual sculpture that ironises the fetishisation of Brancusi's works. At first sight, both the title and the object evoke the visual grammar specific to the minimal sculpture, albeit resized to handcrafted and utilitarian dimensions. On closer inspection, however, its appearance recommends it as an absurd reciprocal ready-made, a monumental sculpture transformed through resizing into a useful item. But its process of production equally presents it as an assisted ready-made, a utilitarian object elevated to the rank of artwork through the manual intervention specific to high art, sculpture, to be precise. Thus, this object/fetish synthesises a number of contradictions that can be encountered in the posthumous destiny of Constantin Brancusi's work. It combines pop art with folk craft and elitist art, and it invokes the ethno-nationalism that was present in Romanian urban architecture of the 1980's. At the same time, the walking stick evokes the arsenal of kitsch trinkets associated with the name of Brancusi as a commercial brand, which are on sale at the Georges Pompidou Centre and the Memorial House in the village of Hobita.

The association of artwork and merchandise via the artist's name as cultural brand, as well as the association between artistic and country branding, is not accidental in this context. Both the culture industry and the nationalist discourse in Romania have made use of Brancusi on repeated occasions, recycling his works as images devoid of intrinsic meaning, in the manner of floating signifiers. The object was fashioned by sculptor Napoleon Tiron at the suggestion of Alexandra Croitoru. Tiron is a member of the generation presented in the Romanian Pavilion at the Venice Biennale in 1995, as part of the *L' eredità di Brancusi in Romania* exhibition. Through a symbol of the man regarded as "the pinnacle of Romanian sculpture," the sculptural tradition is thereby recycled in an object ultimately employed to question the entire edifice in which national and artistic values interpenetrate and give birth to the Brancusi obsession.

Walking Stick, 2013

Object commissioned from sculptor Napoleon Tiron
83 cm (photo: Marius Poput)

~~*Romanian, awake!*~~

~~*Romanian, awake from deadly slumber /*~~
Man, awake / Set off down the good path /

~~*The scourge of inauspicious barbarian tyrannies /*~~
Vanquish the idleness and sloth that stay you /

~~*And now or never to a bright horizon clamber /*~~
Like an eagle you soar toward spheres serene /

~~*That shall to shame put all your enemies!*~~
Praise the gift of the world / Forget yourself!

Deşteaptă-te, Române!

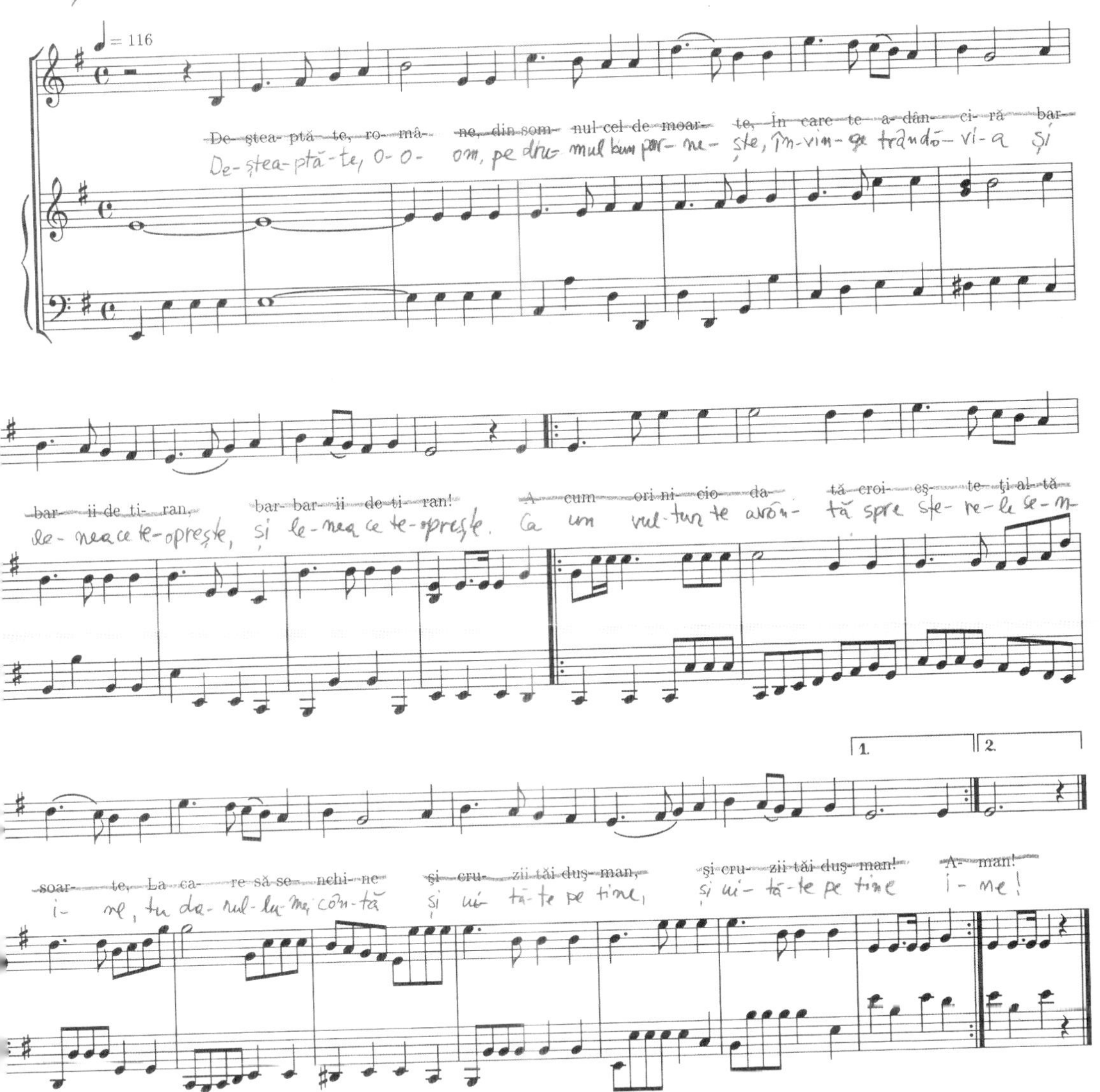

Constînd într-o piesă audio de natură conceptuală, lucrarea continuă interesul Alexandrei Croitoru pentru pentru aforismele brâncușiene văzute ca "pastile de înțelepciune" transmise noilor generații de artiști români, precum și, în sens mai larg, pentru mecanismele și procesele culturale care contribuie la solidificarea tradiției și la conservarea autorității sale atît în mediul artistic propriu-zis, cît și în afara sa.

Prin transformarea aforismului în imn național, interpretat de o soprană, intervenția artistică intersectează zona evenimentelor și a serbărilor populare naționaliste organizate, printre alții, de scriitorul Laurian Stănchescu. Finalul evenimentului care a celebrat 137 de ani de la nașterea lui Brâncuși la Cinema Scala din București, în cadrul căruia soprana Felicia Filip și trupa de muzică pop K1 au interpretat în cheie solemnă imnul României, a reprezentat o sursă de inspirație pentru această lucrare, ce poate fi citită în registre multiple.

Lupta pentru configurarea unei identități naționale este suprapusă motivului masculin al "revoluției artistice" atribuit lui Brâncuși, sublininiindu-se consubstanțialitatea dintre cele două procese de reconstrucție a imaginarului colectiv în cadrul discursului naționalist de dată recentă din Romania. Piesa muzicală rezultată a fost expusă sub forma unei intervenții audio în expoziția curatoriată de Bojana Pejić la Muzeul Național de Artă Contemporană din București în 2013 și care era intitulată *Good Girls: Memory Desire Power* – prima expoziție de grup de mari dimensiuni ce tematiza feminismul și feminitatea organizată în Romania. În acest context expozițional, lucrarea se dorea citită și ca un comentariu asupra patriarhatului ce domină contextul artistic autohton, în care se reciclează la nesfîrșit modelul modernist al geniului masculin, precum și virtuțile sale specifice. Nu în ultimul rînd, elogiul muncii artistice exprimat de aforism, ce poate servi instrumentalizării precarității acestui tip de muncă în cadrul capitalismului avansat prin legitimarea culturală a autoexploatării, este hiperbolizat și, implicit, ironizat.

⟵——— Imn (Deșteaptă-te om / Pe drumul bun pornește / Învinge trîndăvia și lenea ce te oprește / Tu ca vulturul te-avîntă spre sferele senine / Darul lumei cîntă / Uită-te pe tine!), 2013

Adaptare muzicală a aforismului lui Constantin Brâncuși pe notele Imnului Național al României, 55''

Consisting of a conceptual sound piece, the work is a continuation of Alexandra Croitoru's interest in Brancusi's aphorisms viewed as "gems of wisdom" passed down to new generations of Romanian artists, and, in the broader sense, in the cultural mechanisms and processes that contribute to reinforcing the tradition and conserving its authority both within the art world and outside it.

By transforming the aphorism into the national anthem, sung by a soprano, the artistic intervention intersects with the area of the nationalist popular events organised by writer Laurian Stanchescu among others. The finale of the event celebrating the 137th anniversary of Brancusi's birth, held at the Scala Cinema in Bucharest, as part of which soprano Felicia Filip and pop group K1 solemnly intoned the Romanian national anthem, was the source of inspiration for this work, which can be read in multiple keys. The struggle to shape a national identity is superposed upon the masculine motif of the "artistic revolution" attributed to Brancusi, underlining the consubstantiality of the two processes of reconstructing the collective imaginary as part of the recent nationalistic discourse in Romania. The resulting musical piece was exhibited in the form of an audio intervention in the exhibition curated by Bojana Pejić at Bucharest's National Museum of Contemporary Art in 2013, with the title *Good Girls: Memory Desire Power*—the first large-scale group exhibition on the theme of feminism and femininity to be held in Romania. In the context of the exhibition, the work was also intended to be read as a commentary on the patriarchy that is still dominant in the art world in Romania, in which the modernist model of the male genius and his particular virtues is endlessly recycled. Last but not least, the laudation of artistic labour expressed in the aphorism, which might serve to instrumentalise the precarity of this type of labour within the framework of late capitalism through cultural legitimisation of self-exploitation, is rendered hyperbolical and, implicitly, ironical.

Anthem (Man, awake / Set off down the good path / Vanquish the idleness and sloth that stay you / Like an eagle you soar toward spheres serene / Praise the gift of the world / Forget yourself!), 2013

Musical adaptation of Constantin Brancusi's aphorism set to the score of the Romanian National Anthem, 55''

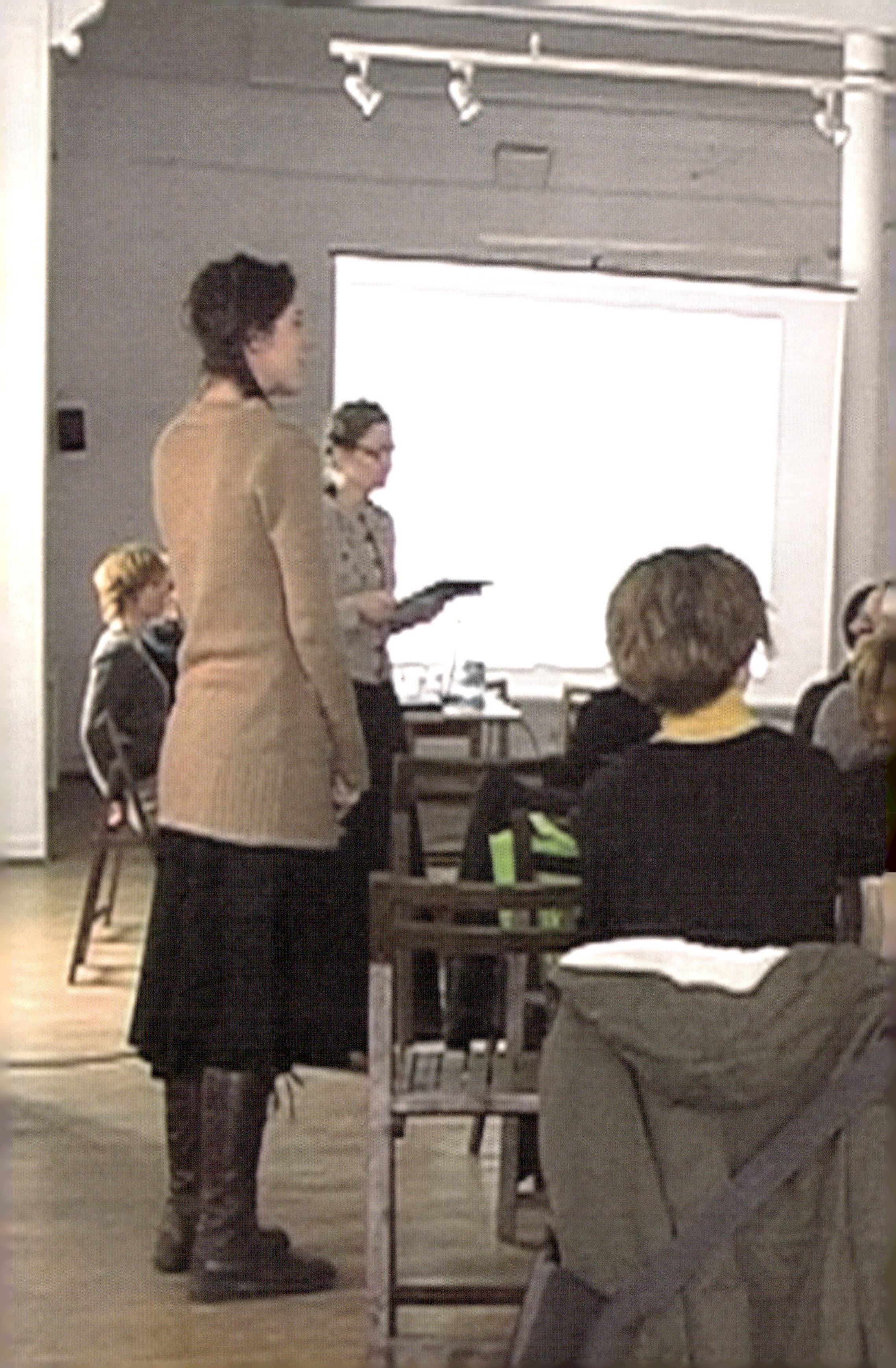

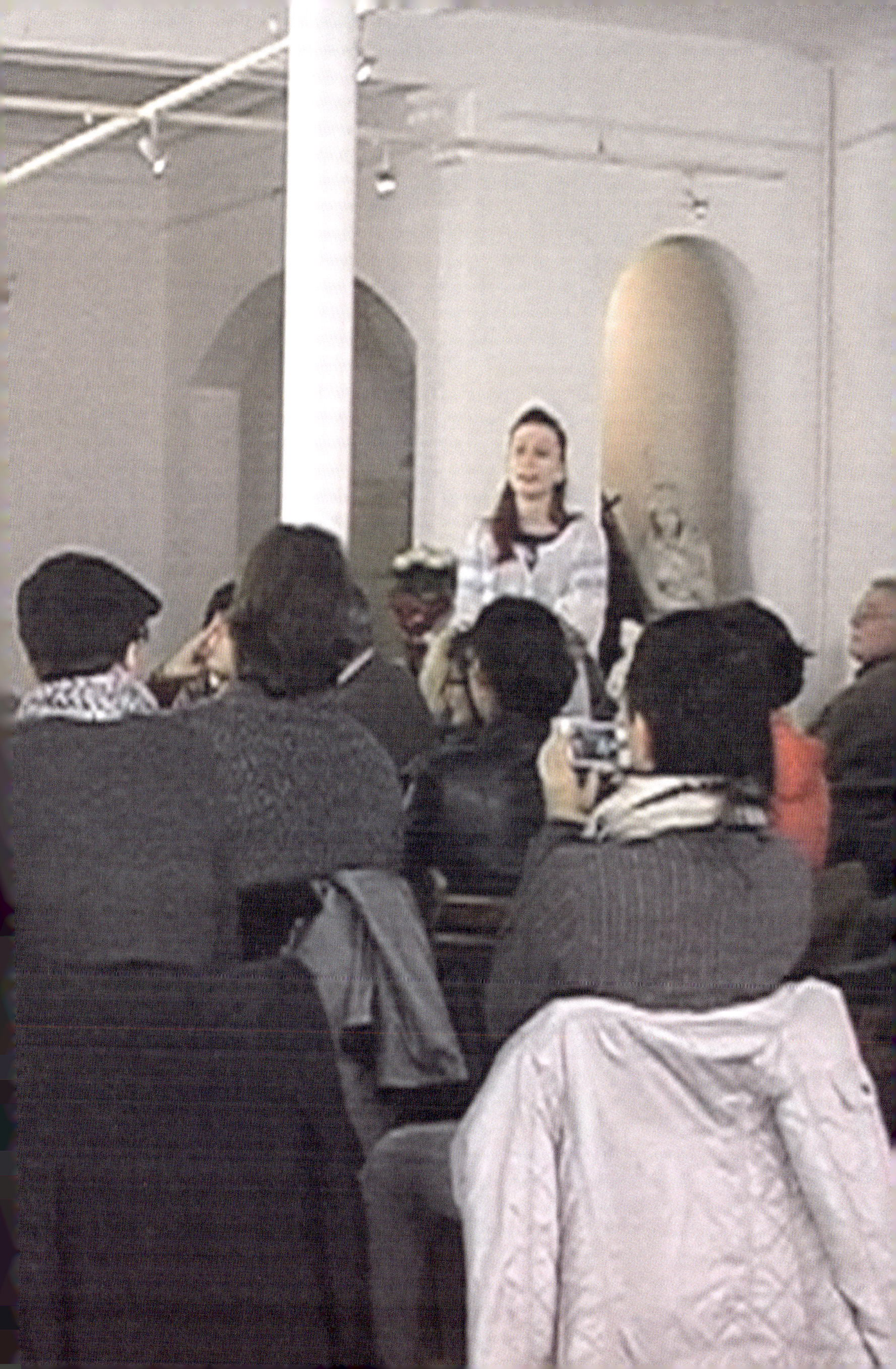

ION CARAION   MASA TĂCERII

Ed. Vinuler

Brâncuși

Geo Bogza
ROMÂNIA

S-a născut la Hobița în 1876.

Tăind piatra și lemnul cu mîinile lui de țăran din Gorj, el a deschis artei și spiritului omenesc poarta unui nou univers.

El este mai mult decît un sculptor, este un profet.

Tăind piatra și lemnul cu mîinile lui de țăran din Gorj, el a impus materiei fluiditatea spiritului.

El este mai mult decît un profet, este un artist de geniu.

Tăind piatra și lemnul cu liniștea sufletească și înțelepciunea unui lung șir de strămoși, el a mers direct la esențe, la expresivitatea formelor primordiale, la sîmburii vieții și ai cosmosului.

El este mai mult decît un artist de geniu, este un vizionar.

Tăind piatra şi lemnul cu miinile lui de ţăran din Gorj, el a descătuşat din miezul materiei zborul unic al pasării măiastre.

El este mai mult decît un sculptor, este un profet.

Tăind piatra şi lemnul cu mîinile lui de ţăran din Gorj, el a descătuşat din miezul materiei coloana fără sfîrşit, geometrie şi ritm al infinitului.

El este mai mult decît un profet, este un artist de geniu.

Tăind piatra şi lemnul cu mîinile lui de ţăran din Gorj, cutezător intotdeauna şi niciodată încercat de eroare, el a îmbogăţit muzeele lumii şi cerul ce se bolteşte deasupra pămîntului cu opere ce prevestesc filozofia şi arta viitorului.

El este mai mult decît un artist de geniu, este un vizionar.

Tăind piatra şi lemnul cu mîinile lui de ţăran din Gorj, el a impus materiei fluiditatea spiritului, a descătuşat din miezul ei fierbinte pasărea măiastră şi coloana fără sfîrşit, a deschis artei şi spiritului omenesc poarta unui nou univers.

El este mai mult decît un sculptor, mai mult decît un artist de geniu. Este un demiurg.

S-a născut la Hobiţa în 1876 şi nu va muri niciodată.

afirmarea idealurilor poporului român, de înfăptuire a unirii principatelor, cucerire a independenței de stat a României și propășire a culturii noastre naționale. Alături de Nicolae Titulescu, Dr. I. Cantacuzino, George Enescu, I. Levaditti, Traian Vuia, Constantin Parhon și Mihai Ralea în această Societate a studenților români a activat și Constantin Brâncuși.

În zilele premergătoare lui august 1944 în care cei șaizeci de militanți comuniști români — despre care scrie guvernului de la București Traian Vuia — cădeau în lupta poporului francez, a poporului român și a tuturor forțelor progresiste din lume împotriva fascismului, Constantin Brâncuși avea aproape 70 de ani.

Zborul spre înălțimi nu se oprise însă.

În semn de protest împotriva ocupației naziste, el a refuzat să părăsească în acești ani atelierul său din Impasse Ronsin, numărul 11, în care vorbea puțin, lucra mult și în care transportase gloria Montparnassului artistic cu cîteva străzi mai departe de locul în care a trăit fostul său maestru, Rodin. În anii ocupației Constantin Brâncuși nu a participat la nici o expoziție organizată în Franța. Mai mult, în toată această perioadă el n-a încetat să ia poziție — de cîte ori s-a ivit prilejul — împotriva trupelor cotropitoare, fasciste.

La fel ca și el s-au manifestat cunoscuta scriitoare Elena Văcărescu, marea actriță Maria Ventura, societară a Comediei Franceze — care a refuzat să apară în toată această perioadă pe scena teatrelor franceze care o consacraseră —, actorul I. Yonnel, societar și el al Comediei Franceze, dirijorul Stan Golestan, virtuosul Dinu Lipatti și nu numai el.

Colegi de ucenicie în atelierul lui Rodin, — dintre toți prietenii români ai zborurilor înalte —, au fost numai C. Brâncuși și H. Coandă.

Nevoia de înălțime, în primul rînd morală, nu a ocolit însă nici unul din spiritele luminate pe care România le-a dăruit culturii universale.

De aceea spuneam, la începutul acestor rînduri, că drumurile către frumusețe ale românilor — chiar atunci cînd această frumusețe s-a împlinit în altă parte decît între hotarele țării — au pornit, întotdeauna, fără nici o excepție, de pe pămîntul acesta avîntat spre înălțimi prin însăși structura sa geologică.

STÎLP

Tăcerea nu-i doar după moarte.
Fără cuvinte zboară dorul iubirii,
fără cuvinte își vorbesc prietenii,
tăcute sînt marile iubiri
și durerile sfîșietoare.

Aici e liniște și toate-ți vorbesc
de un bărbat a cărui Pasăre
zboară prin lume. El, stîlp fără sfîrșit
al acestui neam românesc.

VASILE GRUNEA

Brancusi

- Geo Bogza

He was born in Hobita in 1876.
Cutting stone and wood with his Gorj-region peasant's hands, for art
and the human spirit he opened the gate to a new universe.
He is more than a sculptor; he is a prophet.
Cutting stone and wood with his Gorj-region peasant's hands, he
stamped on matter the fluidity of the spirit.
He is more than a prophet; he is an artist of genius.
Cutting stone and wood with spiritual tranquillity and the wisdom
of a long line of ancestors, he went straight to the essences, to the
expressiveness of primordial forms, to the kernels of life and the
cosmos.
He is more than an artist of genius; he is a visionary.
Cutting stone and wood with his Gorj-region peasant's hands, he
unchained from the core of matter the unique flight of the bird of
paradise.
He is more than a sculptor; he is a prophet.
Cutting stone and wood with his Gorj-region peasant's hands, from
the core of matter he unchained the endless column, geometry and
infinity's rhythm.
He is more than a prophet; he is an artist of genius.
Cutting stone and wood with his Gorj-region peasant's hands, ever
intrepid and never belaboured by errors, he enriched the world's
museums and the sky that arches above the earth with works that
foretell the philosophy and the art of the future.
He is more than an artist of genius; he is a visionary.
Cutting stone and wood with his Gorj-region peasant's hands, he
stamped on matter the fluidity of the spirit, he unchained from its
boiling core the bird of paradise and the endless column, for art and
the human spirit he opened the gate to a new universe.
He is more than a sculptor, more than an artist of genius. He is a
demiurge.
He was born in Hobita in 1876 and he will never die.

Column

Vasile Grunea

Silence is not only after death.
Wordless flies the yearning for love,
wordless converse the friends,
silent are the great loves
and harrowing the pains.

Here is peace and all things speak to you
of a man whose Bird
flies through the world. He, endless column
of this Romanian nation.

„Cununa de aur" acordată în 1982 poetului Nichita Stănescu

Comitetul Festivalului Internațional „Serile de poezie de la Struga" (Macedonia, R.S.F. Iugoslavia) a acordat „Cununa de aur" pe anul 1982 poetului român Nichita Stănescu. După cum se știe Festivalul „Serile de poezie de la Struga" acordă în fiecare an „Cununa de aur" unor cunoscuți poeți din diferite țări ale lumii. „Cununa de aur" a revenit în edițiile sale precedente unor poeți ca W.H. Auden, E. Montale, Neruda, Guillevic, Leopold Sedar Sengor, A. Lundkvist, Rafael Alberti, etc. După cum a subliniat Jovan Strezovski, directorul comitetului acestui Festival, anul acesta alegerea s-a oprit asupra poeziei românești dat fiind faptul că la ora actuală „poezia română ocupă un loc bine meritat în lume" și, în special, asupra lu[i] Nichita Stănescu ca unul din c[ei] mai străluciți reprezentanți [ai] lirismului actual. În cadrul fe[s]tivității care a avut loc la Un[i]unea Scriitorilor au mai vorb[it] despre importanța acestui pr[e]miu D.R. Popescu, președinte[le] Uniunii Scriitorilor, Jovan K[o]teski, președintele Comitetul[ui] Festivalului internațional „Seri[le] de la Struga", Gheorghe Tom[o]zei și Constantin Chiriță. În c[u]vîntul său, poetul sărbătorit, N[i]chita Stănescu a consider[at] „Cununa de aur" drept „o rec[u]noaștere a calității poeziei r[o]mânești și un noroc persona[l]. Premiul va fi înminat poetul[ui] la Struga, în cadrul ediției ca[re] va avea loc între 26—31 augu[st].

T. Ș.

De la Ministerul Educației și Învățămîntului

Ministerul Educației și Învățămîntului informează că în anul universitar 1982—1983 va funcționa, la Facultatea de istorie și filologie a Universității din București, o secție fără frecvență pentru specializarea filozofie-istorie.

Înscrierile la concursul de admitere pentru această secție vor avea loc în perioada 21—25 iunie 1982, la secretariatul Fa[c]ultății de istorie și filozofi[e] Bulevardul Republicii nr. 13.

Condițiile de înscriere și cele prevăzute pentru profil[ul] filozofie, în broșura privind a[d]miterea în învățămîntul sup[e]rior, ediția 1981, și în revis[ta] „Forum" nr. 4/1982. Se pot î[n]scrie absolvenți ai liceului [cu] diplomă de bacalaureat încadra[ți] în muncă pe baza recomandă[rii] organizației de partid sau [de] tineret din care fac parte.

IN ATENȚIA CITITORILOR

In aceste zile, oficiile și agențiile P.T.T.R., factorii poștali,

Coloana infinitului

N-a fost de cind lumea dar pare de-atunci,
A fost condamnată, a fost arestată,
Rideau că ar fi o grămadă de stînci,
Au tras cu tractoare de ea să o scoată.

Ce poate-nsemna decit drumul în sus ?
Sfirșit nu-și găsește și milă nu știe,
Coloana e omul cel fără apus
Și duh pe-un nalt parapet de sicrie.

La marginea firii punind temelii,
La ora cînd cerul intreg e-o cunună,
In vorba „a fi" ea, coloana, e-un „i",
Punctată de soare, punctată de lună.

Priviți-ne-n ea dacă vreți să ne știți,
Poporul acesta coloană arată,
Mereu zbuciumați, totdeauna uniți
Și n-avem de gînd să murim niciodață.

Trudind totdeauna cinstit și modest,
Lăsăm infinitul distantelor astre,
Dar, citeodată, in semn de protest,
Il facem in țară, cu miinile noastre.

Și ca să se știe că sintem și noi,
Că nu stăm aici, pe pămint, cu chirie,
In pauza dintre-nfloriri și altoi
Ieșim la vreun munte și-l facem vecie.

Adrian Păunescu

8 VI 82

A început recoltatul orzului

pe atunci). Rememorînd principalele episoade ale luptelor desfășurate cu 22 ani în urmă în acel loc, evocînd faptele de eroism ale Ecaterinei Teodoroiu și ale altor luptători gorjeni, vorbitorul a încheiat reproducînd frumoasele cuvinte ce stau scrise pentru posteritate pe placa comemorativă de la pod: „Aici, bătrînii, femeile, cercetașii și copiii Gorjului au oprit năvala vrășmașe, apărîndu-și cu vitejie căminurile".

Deplasîndu-se, în continuare, pe digul Jiului, mulțimea a făcut un scurt popas la *Masa tăcerii*. Aici nu s-au mai rostit cuvîntări. În tăcerea clipelor, gîndurile celor prezenți parcă se îndreptau spre trecut, spre zbuciumata istorie a unui popor care și-a păstrat pămîntul, limba și cultura cu o dîrzenie și vitejie care-i fac cinste. În liniștea deplină, numai undele învolburate ale Jiului se auzeau parcă povestind celor prezenți și vestind lumii despre o pagină glorioasă scrisă cu ani în urmă în acest colț de țară, ca-n atîtea altele ale României.

Cortegiul s-a îndreptat apoi spre mausoleul Ecaterinei Teodoroiu. Acolo aștepta în întîmpinare purtînd în mîini o lumînare aprinsă și o tavă cu cele necesare, după tradiție, în asemenea ocazii, mama eroinei, doda Lena din Vădeni — cum îi spuneau localnicii. În cuvinte de o rară sensibilitate a fost înfățișat portretul neînfricatei luptătoare, cea care a rămas drept pildă de sacrificiu pentru binele poporului său, figură luminoasă în galeria eroilor neamului nostru.

Se încheia aici o manifestație de cea mai înaltă trăire sufletească. Deși a plouat mai tot timpul, lumea adunată a participat la momentele ceremoniei cu o încordată atenție și cu cel mai profund respect pentru tot ce s-a făcut întru cinstirea eroilor și mai ales pentru gestul marelui Brâncuși de a fi așezat pe pămîntul Gorjului și a fi ridicat în conștiința poporului și a lumii trei dintre cele mai reprezentative creații ale sale.

Întîlnirea cu *Brâncuși omul* și cu opera sa avea să rămînă pentru noi elevii Școlii normale ca și pentru toți cei care au fost martori la festivitatea din 27 octombrie 1938, drept unul dintre cele mai emoționante evenimente din viața noastră. Deși abia descifram atunci cîte ceva din intimitatea operei marelui artist, trăiam totuși sentimentul că ne aflăm în fața unei *realizări neobișnuite*.

În anii de mai tîrziu, aveam să înțelegem mai bine cît de măreață ne-a fost șansa de-a fi fost martori unui asemenea eveniment.

OMAGIU

Constantin Brâncuși n-a murit,
Constantin Brâncuși trăiește
l-am văzut șezînd gînditor la o masă
la care toți sorbeau tăcerea
și o simțeau în oase și în sînge
cum îi inundă vie,
l-am văzut lîngă o poartă
oltenească cu doi tineri ce se sărutau

contopind în sărutul lor cast și cald
toată dragostea lumii,
urcînd l-am întîlnit pe o coloană
a recunoștinței sau a aspirației
în susul sus, spre cer
sau poate
dincolo de cer.

MIRCEA M. POP

The Column of the Infinite   - Adrian Paunescu

It seems primordial and is immortal,
They condemned it, placed it under arrest,
As at a heap of rubble they did chortle,
To topple it with tractors they did their best.

What can it mean but eternal ascent?
The ruthless soaring column never ends,
It is mankind, whose light is never spent,
The human spirit that coffin transcends.

At Being's edge its base it edifies,
The sky above a wreath around it knots,
In the verb "is" the column is the "i",
On which the sun and moon both place their dots.

If you desire to know us, then behold
This nation that the column does reveal:
United in our fight since times of old,
Upon us death will never set its seal.

In labour ever humble, ever honest,
The infinite we leave to the stars in space.
But oft betimes we make our protest,
Fashioning it in our ancestral place.

And to let it be known that we are here—
No rent-paying short-term tenants are we—
Between the sowing and the reaping year,
We climb a mountain into eternity.

Homage   - Mircea M. Pop

Constantin Brancusi is not dead,
Constantin Brancusi is alive
I saw him sitting pensive at a table
at which all imbibed the silence
and felt it in their bones and blood
flooding them, alive,
I saw him by an Oltenian
gate with a young couple that kissed
merging in their warm, chaste kiss
all the love of the world,
ascending I found him atop a column
of gratitude and aspiration
in the highest heights, heavenward
or perhaps
beyond the heavens.

Lucrarea pornește de la lirica dedicată artistului descoperită în dosarul 57 – *Poezii brâncușiene* – al Arhivei Barbu Brezianu la care Alexandra Croitoru a avut acces pe parcursul colaborării cu Institutul de Istoria artei "G. Oprescu" al Academiei Române, în cadrul proiectului de cercetare *"Sfîntul din Montparnasse" de la document la mit. O sută de ani de exegeză brâncușiană*. Acest dosar, ce conține contribuții poetice din anii '60, '70 și '80 care au fost publicate în reviste precum *Amfiteatru*, *Ateneu*, *Ramuri*, *Tribuna*, *România literară*, *Confluențe*, este completat de poeziile apărute în antologia *Masa tăcerii* alcătuită de Ion Caraion în 1970, precum și în alte publicații omagiale. Aceste poeme prelungesc și evocă angajamentul ideologic al creațiilor literare dedicate Partidului Comunist care au alimentat cultul personalității lui Nicolae Ceaușescu. Ele dezvoltă tema artistului de geniu și motivul universalității culturii populare românești, ambele prezente deja în ficțiunile dramatice sau nuvelistice dedicate lui Brâncuși. Proiectul, de natură performativă, s-a materializat prin organizarea unui moment poetic, asumat cu seriozitate de un grup de actrițe, în cadrul conferinței internaționale organizate în octombrie 2013 de Institutul de Istoria artei "G. Oprescu" al Academiei Române în colaborare cu UNArte București. Supraidentificarea cu situațiile și discursul oficial pe care intenționează a-l submina, expunînd, prin reducere la absurd, lipsa de fundament a eșafodajului ideologic ce susține acest discurs, devine principala strategie critică a artistei. Această identificare excesivă devine o formulă retorică predilectă în dialogul său critic cu asumpțiile și convingerile ideologice pe care le cercetează. Intervenția, care a testat în acest context disponibilitatea istoricilor de artă români de a se desprinde de imaginarul politic al autorității și de automatismele retorice care perpetuează ideologia naționalistă, a fost inspirată de momentele poetice prezente în diverse manifestări omagiale dedicate lui Brâncuși. Un exemplu în acest sens este și evenimentul organizat în 2012 de Sorana Georgescu Gorjan la Centrul pentru activități recreative și inovare ocupațională al Primăriei Sectorului 2 din București, care se încheia cu cîteva versuri recitate de actrița Doina Ghițescu.

⟵ Omagiu, 2013

Performance în cadrul conferinței internaționale *After Brancuși*, 8'30''

The work sets out from poems dedicated to the artist discovered in File 57—
Brancusian Poems —of the Barbu Brezianu Archive, to which Alexandra Croitoru had
access during her collaboration with the Romanian Academy's G. Oprescu Institute
of Art History, as part of a research project titled *"The Saint of Montparnasse" from
Document to Myth. A Century of Constantin Brancusi Exegesis*. The file, which
contains poems from the 1960's, 70's and 80's, published in *Amfiteatru*, *Ateneu*,
Ramuri, *Tribuna*, *România Literară*, and *Confluențe* magazines, is supplemented
with poems published in Ion Caraion's *Table of Silence* anthology (1970) and other
volumes of homage. Such poems extend and evoke the ideological engagement of
literary works dedicated to the Communist Party, which fed the Ceaușescu personality
cult. They develop the theme of the artist of genius and the motif of the universality
of Romanian folk culture, already laid out in plays and novels taking Brancusi as their
subject.

The project took the form of a poetic interlude, performed with the utmost seriousness
by a group of actresses, during the international conference organised by the
Romanian Academy's G. Oprescu Institute of Art History in partnership with UNArte
Bucharest in October 2013. The artist's main critical strategy becomes
over-identification with the official situations and discourse she intends to undermine,
exposing, by means of a *reductio ad absurdum*, the lack of any solid foundation to
the ideological edifice on which the discourse is based. This excessive identification
becomes the rhetorical formula of predilection in her critical dialogue with the
ideological assumptions and convictions she is researching.

The intervention, which, in that context, tested how prepared Romanian art
historians were to distance themselves from the political imaginary of authority and
the rhetorical tics that perpetuate nationalist ideology, was inspired by the poetic
interludes to be found in various manifestations paying homage to Brancusi. One such
example was the event organised by Sorana Georgescu Gorjan in 2012 at the Centre
for Recreational Activities and Occupational Innovation of the City Hall of Bucharest
Sector 2, which closed with a poetic recitation by actress Doina Ghițescu.

Homage, 2013

Performance in the frame of the *After Brancusi* international conference, 8'30''

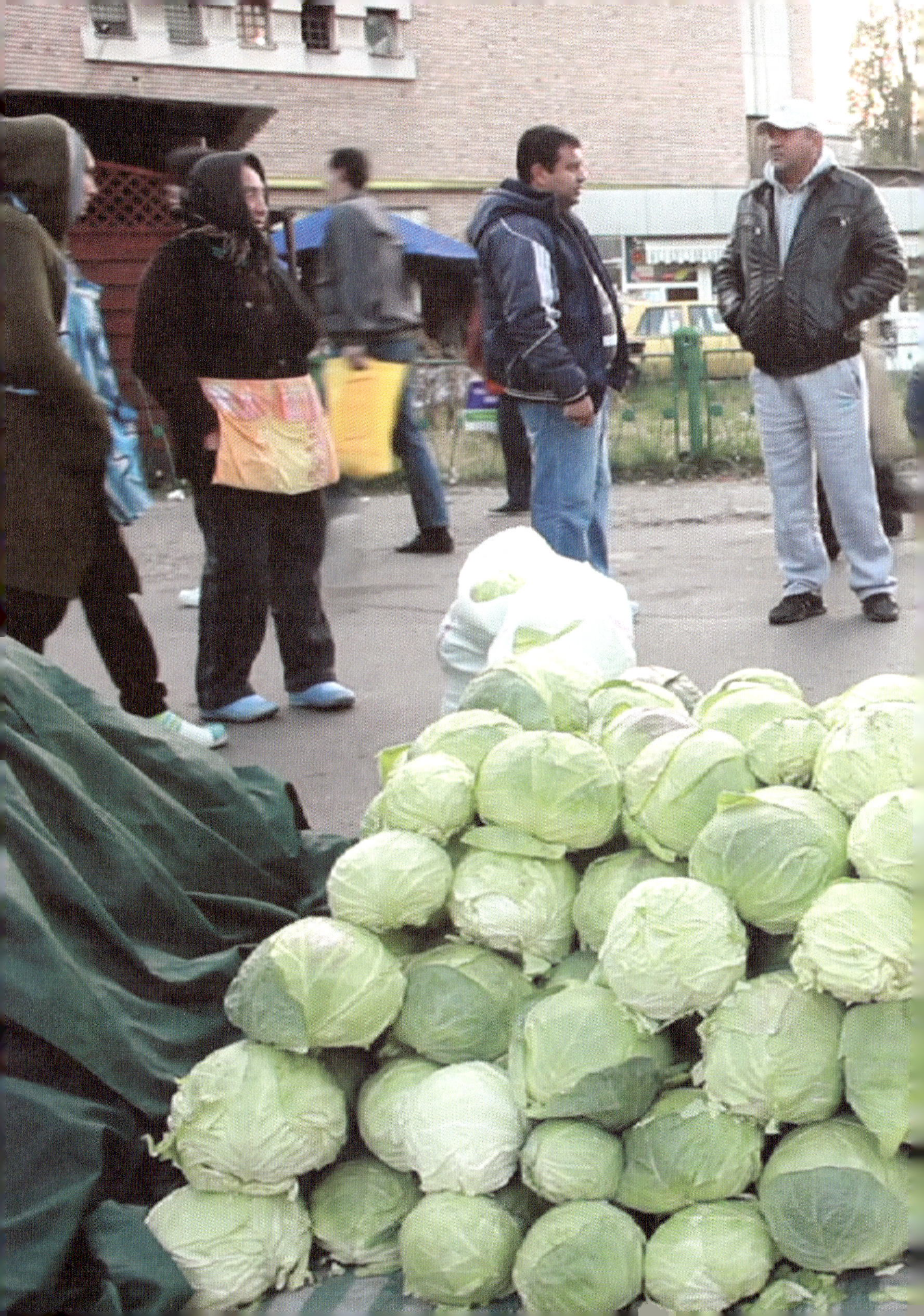

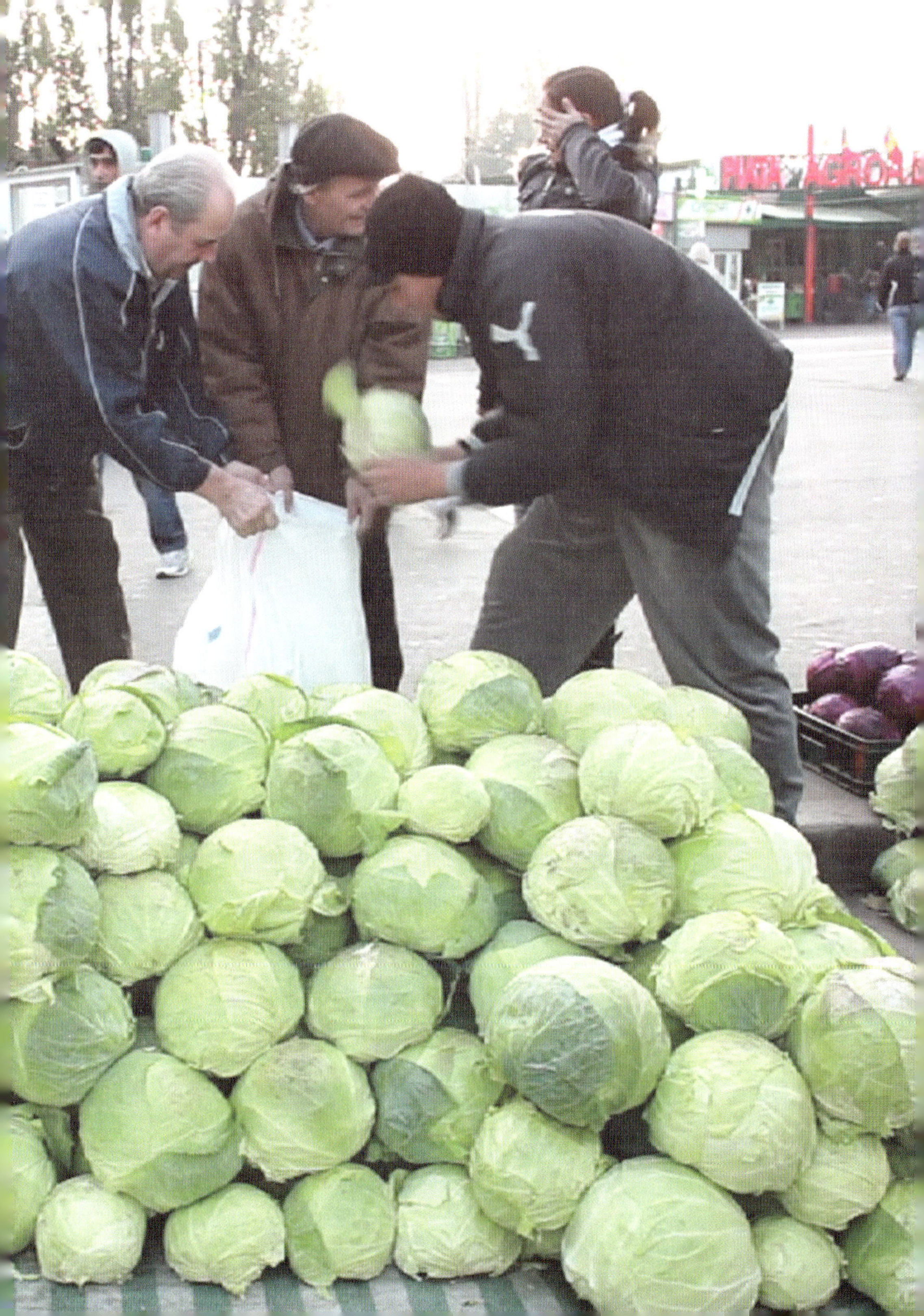

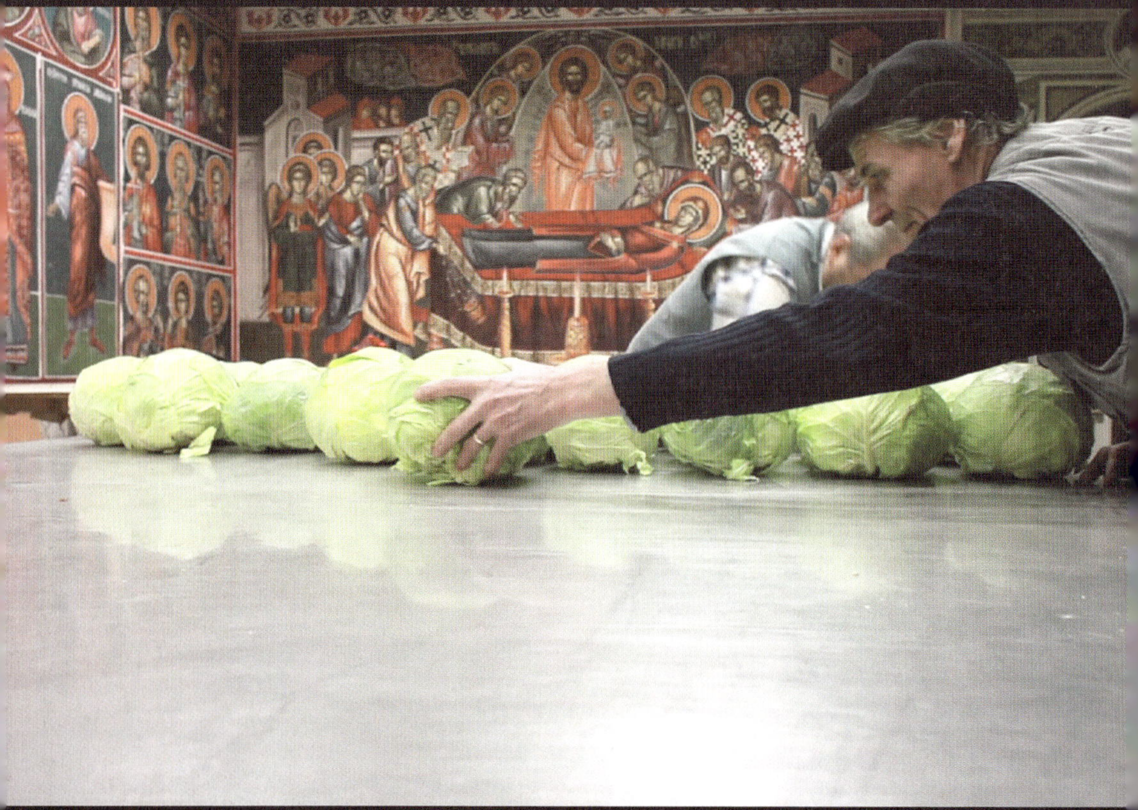

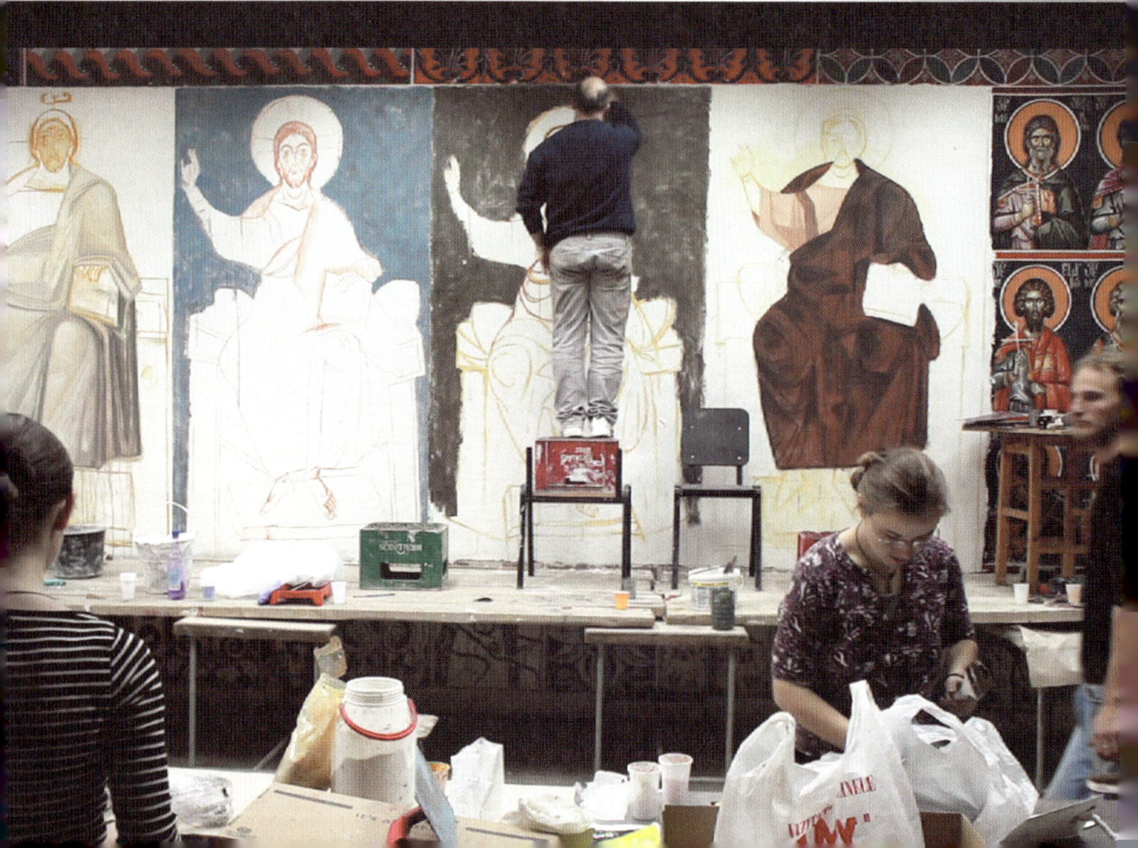

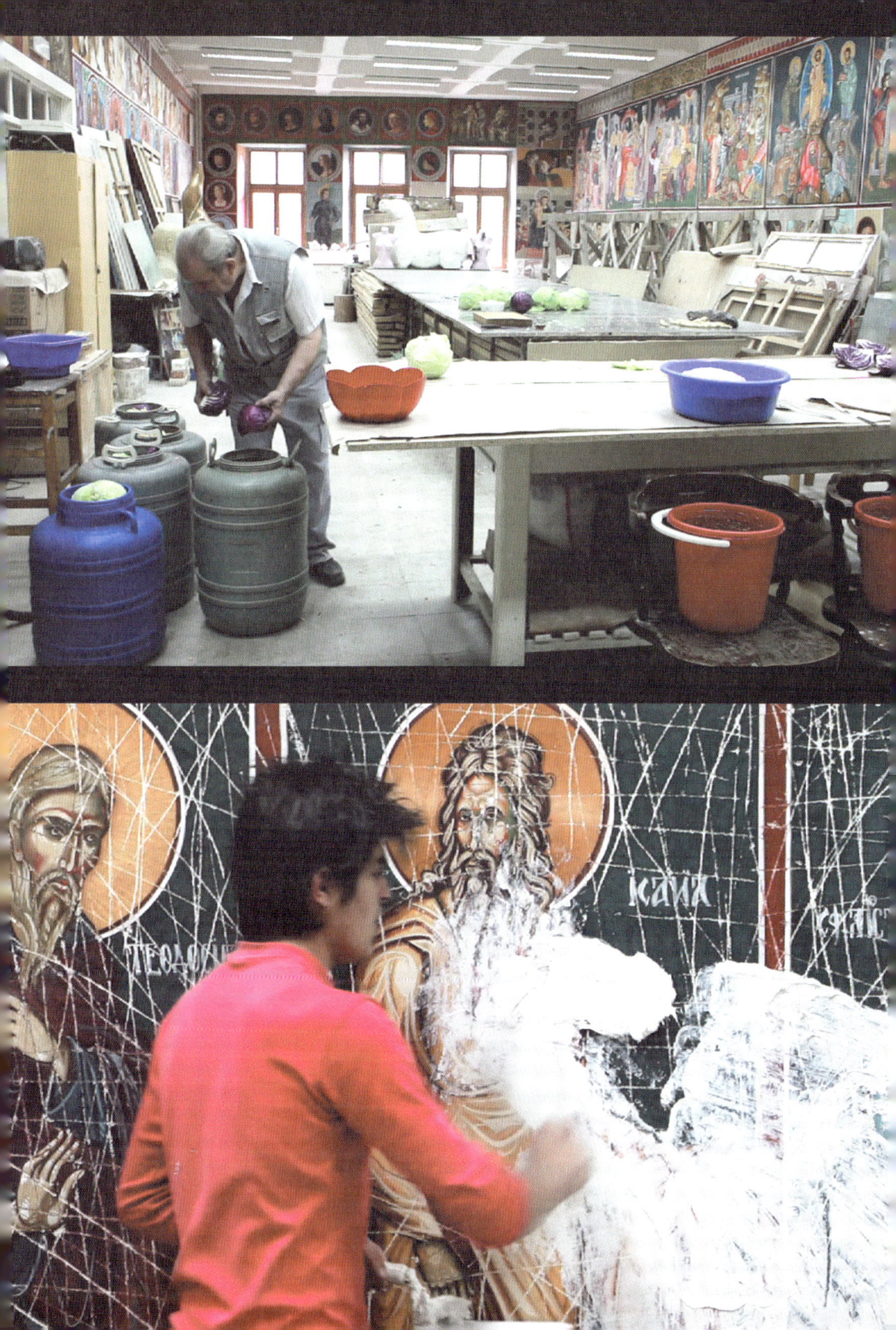

Realizată cu ocazia unei expoziții personale la Galeria Plan B din Cluj, această lucrare a avut ca punct de plecare cercetarea aforismelor lui Brâncuși și a fost prezentată împreună cu filmul *The Cabbage Process* – un comentariu alegoric asupra persistenței artei ca meșteșug în instituțiile românești de învățămînt superior. În contextul standardizării și profesionalizării educației artistice ca urmare a procesului Bologna, tradiția producerii verzei murate de către Nea Aurică în cadrul secției de Artă murală a Universității Naționale de Arte din București, documentată în cea din urmă lucrare, poate fi privită drept o modalitate alternativă de a construi un spațiu social comun, o practică relațională într-o instituție conservatoare. În ambele lucrări, Alexandra Croitoru dezvoltă o reflecție ironică asupra condiției precare a artistului și a învățămîntului artistic autohton, formulînd o subtilă critică instituțională. Ambele proiecte pun în discuție noțiunea de tradiție și perpetuarea valorilor artistice în cadrul unui sistem educațional în mare parte încă tributar transmiterii unor deprinderi și cunoștințe standardizate. Aforismele lui Brâncuși reprezintă o parte semnificativă a cultului artistului de geniu construit în România. Aforismul inscripționat pe fațada clădirii, care părea a-i servi sculptorului drept paleativ psihologic în atelierul său parizian[1], funcționează ca o lecție de carieră lăsată de Brâncuși urmașilor și a fost consacrat, în diverse formule, de multe publicații dedicate sculptorului. Textul, care a apărut pentru cîteva luni ca motto al celei mai importante comunități artistice din Cluj, a fost realizat de studenți, viitori artiști. Asumînd rolul unor simpli executanți care îndeplinesc o muncă necalificată, aceștia devin "sclavi" ai artei datorită unor conjuncturi sociale nefavorabile. Precaritatea condiției reale a tinerilor artiști este astfel subliniată prin contrast cu tonul optimist al aforismului brâncușian, care poate fi citit ca o rețetă a succesului.

Aforismul inserat în publicația expoziției provine chiar din transcrierea notițelor lui Brâncuși din arhiva Centrului Pompidou, notițe care de altfel conțin și o versiune a primului aforism. Scrisă de mînă pe un carton volant multiplicat prin fotocopiere, această versiune secundă a aceluiași aforism este pusă în circulație pe canale informale asemeni unui samizdat în cadrul discursului dominant, evidențiind astfel practicile de excluziune active în cadrul acestui discurs și limitările sale. Asumarea personală a acestui text, sugerată de scrisul de mînă și statutul său marginal, contrastează cu impersonala, monumentala și, în acest context, cinica inscripție de pe fațada clădirii, care afirmă autonomia creatoare a artistului. Împreună, cele două versiuni ale textului formează astfel un contra-monument. Diferența marcată de statut și de vizibilitate dintre cele două versiuni ale textului se referă și la procesul de istoricizare selectivă a aforismelor lui Brâncuși, punînd sub semnul întrebării toată această aură a învățăturii "marelui artist" care ne este transmisă pe canalele oficiale.

---

1 Ionel Jianou, *Brancusi*, Arted, 1963.

Produced for a solo exhibition at Galeria Plan B in Cluj, the work sets out from research into Brancusi's aphorisms and was presented along with the film *The Cabbage Process*, an allegorical commentary on the persistence of art as a craft in Romanian higher education. In the context of the standardisation and professionalisation of artistic education as a result of the Bologna process, Aurică's tradition of making pickled cabbage in the Mural Art department of the Bucharest National University of Arts, documented in the film, can be viewed as an alternative mode of constructing a common social space, a relational practice within a conservative institution. In both works, Alexandra Croitoru develops an ironic reflection on the precarious condition of the Romanian artist and artistic education, formulating a subtle institutional critique. Both projects bring into question the notion of tradition and the perpetuation of artistic values within an educational system largely based on the passing down of standardised skills and knowledge.

Brancusi's aphorisms represent a significant part of the cult of the artist as genius that has been constructed in Romania. The one inscribed on the front of the building, which seemed to serve the sculptor as a psychological palliative in his Parisian studio[1], functions as a career lesson passed down by Brancusi to his successors and has been consecrated in various forms by numerous books on the sculptor. The text, which for a few months served as the motto of the most important artistic community in Cluj, was realised by students, future artists. Taking on the role of mere executants performing unqualified labour, they become "slaves" of art due to unfavourable social circumstances. The precarity of the real circumstances of young artists is thereby emphasised through its contrast with the optimistic tone of Brancusi's aphorism, which can be read as a recipe for success.

The aphorism inserted into the exhibition publication comes from a transcription of Brancusi's notes from the archive of the Pompidou Centre, notes which also contain a version of the first aphorism. Handwritten on a loose piece of paper and photocopied, the second version of the same aphorism was circulated by informal means, like a samizdat text within the framework of the dominant discourse, thereby throwing into relief the practices of exclusion at work within this discourse and its limitations. The personal vouching for the text suggested by the handwriting and its marginal status contrast with the impersonal, monumental and, in this context, cynical inscription on the front of the building, which asserts the artist's creative autonomy. Together, the two versions of the text thereby form a counter-monument. The marked difference in status and visibility between the two versions of the text also refers to the process of selective historicising of Brancusi's aphorisms, and throws into question the whole aura of the teachings of the "great artist" passed down to us by official channels.

____

1 Ionel Jianou, *Brancusi*, Arted, 1963.

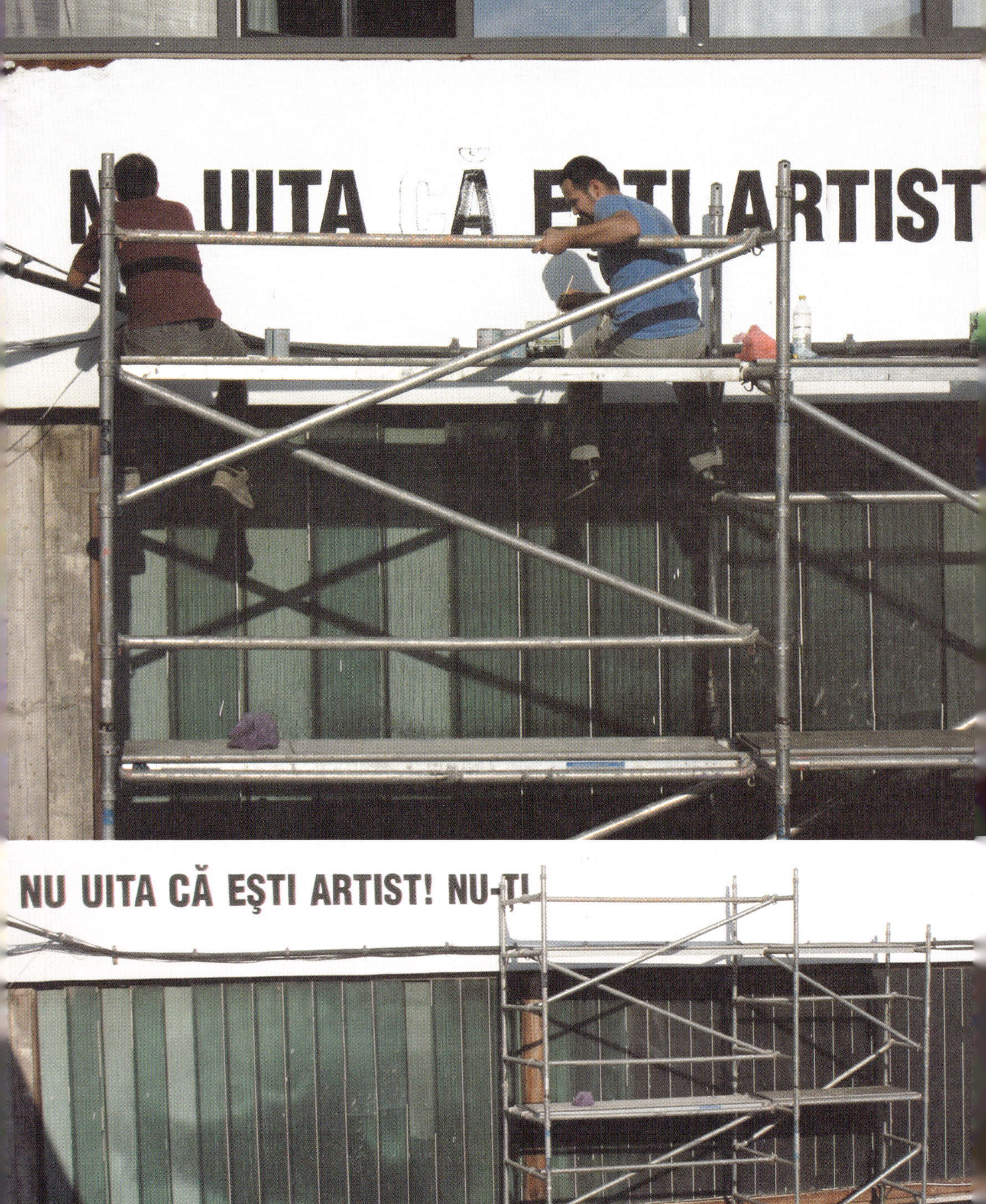
NU UITA CĂ EŞTI ARTIST
NU UITA CĂ EŞTI ARTIST! NU-TI

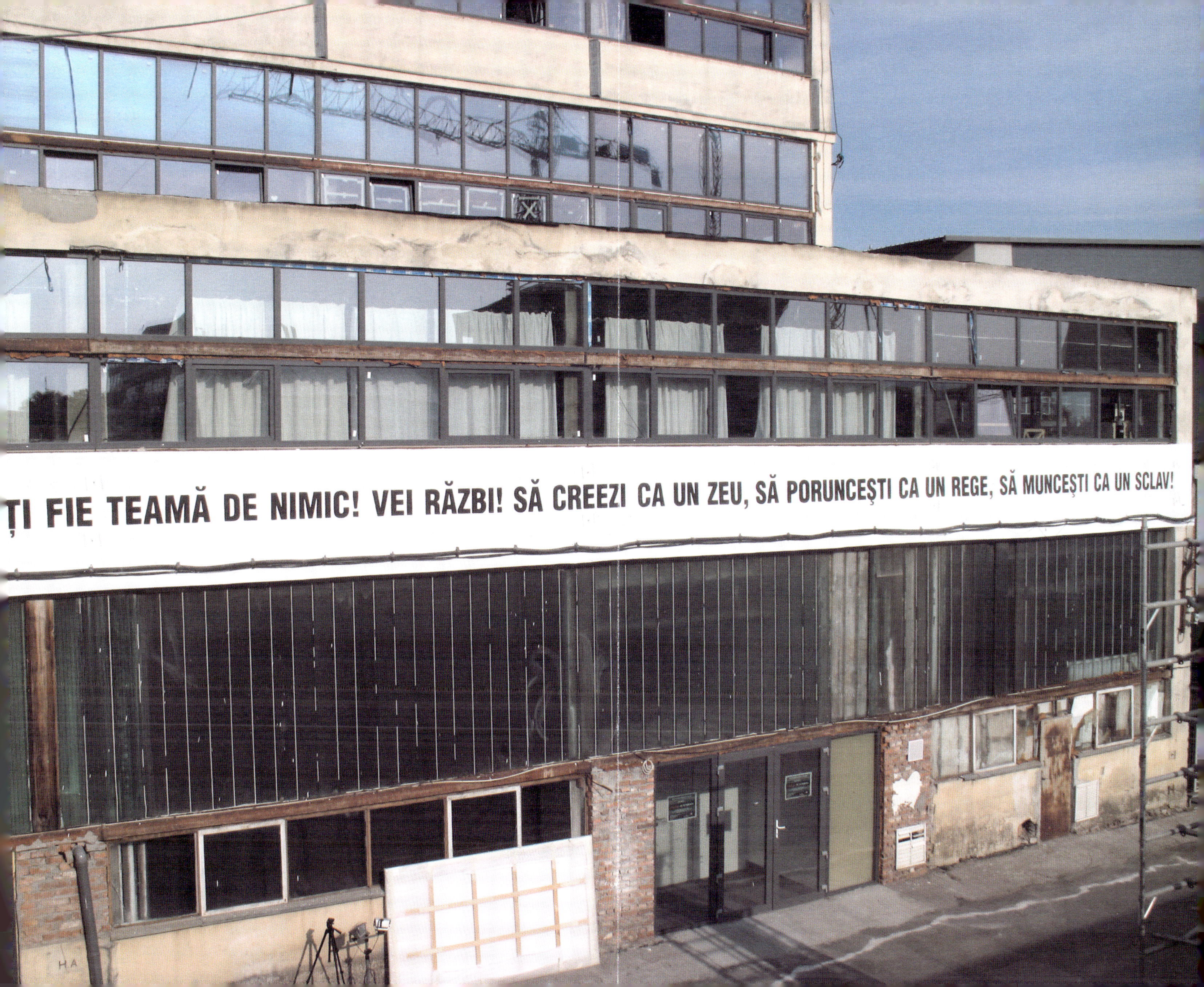

ȚI FIE TEAMĂ DE NIMIC! VEI RĂZBI! SĂ CREEZI CA UN ZEU, SĂ PORUNCEȘTI CA UN REGE, SĂ MUNCEȘTI CA UN SCLAV!

SUNT ZEUL CARE SE
SINUCIDE,
REGELE CARE SE CACĂ
PE COROANĂ,
SCLAVUL CARE ÎȘI CAUTĂ
UN STĂPÂN.

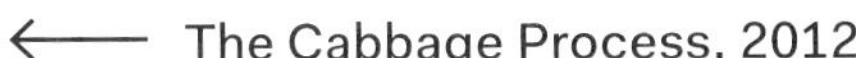

⟵ The Cabbage Process, 2012

Video, 35'49''

⟵ Nu uita că ești artist! Nu-ți pierde curajul, nu-ți fie teamă de
nimic! Vei răzbi! Să creezi ca un zeu, să poruncești ca un rege, să
muncești ca un sclav!, 2012

Intervenție pe fațada Fabricii de Pensule realizată de studenți ai Universității de Artă și Design
Cluj, 25 m x 1.50 m

Do not forget you are an artist! Do not lose heart, do not be afraid
of anything! You will prevail! Create like a god, command like a
king, work like a slave!, 2012

Intervention on the façade of the Paintbrush Factory in Cluj realized by students of the Cluj Art
and Design University, 25 m x 1.50 m

⟵ Sînt zeul care se sinucide, regele care se cacă pe coroană, sclavul
care își caută un stăpîn, 2012

Insert în publicația expoziției, 10,5 x 15 cm

I am the god who commits suicide, the king who shits on the
crown, the slave in search of a master, 2012

Insert in the exhibition publication, 10,5 x 15 cm

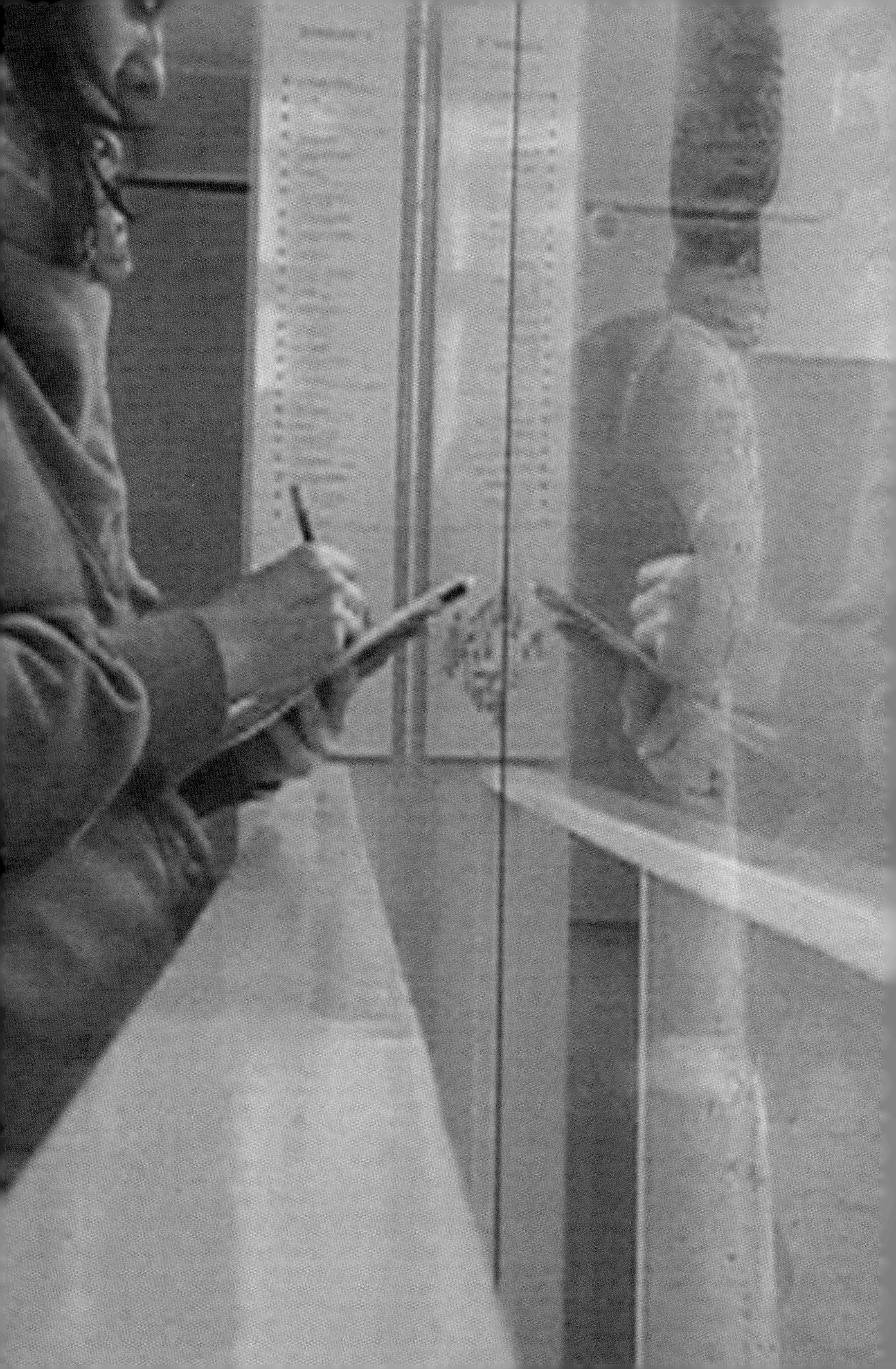

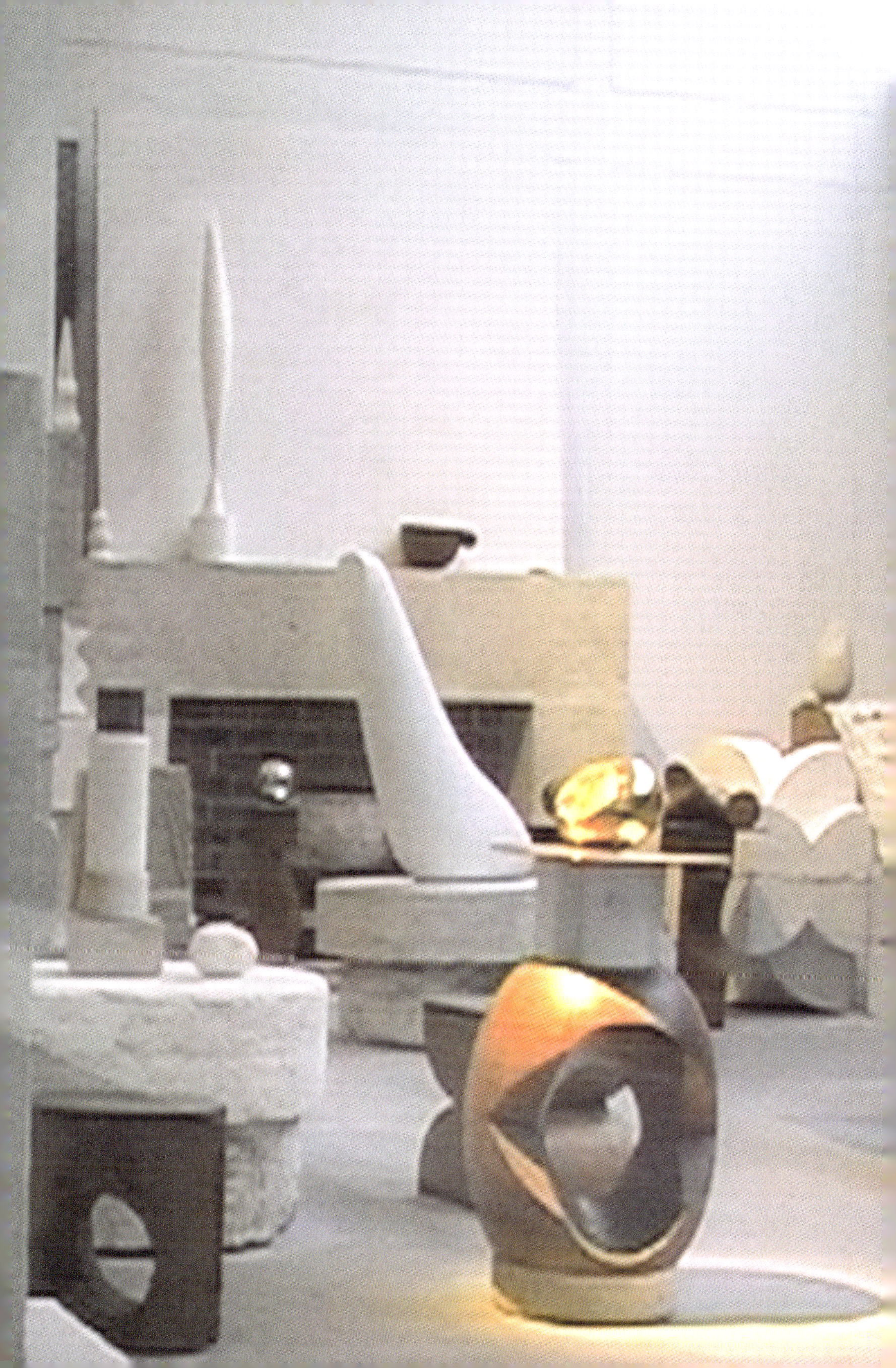

Bravo to Brancusi, bravo to Romania! He was Romanian and there was nothing they could do to change that!

05.03.2011

We shouldn't let them steal our culture and legacy. He is, was and will remain a <u>Romanian</u>. Don't forget that, all you who pass through here... He is one of ours... but they take the praise for this studio... The real cultural legacy is in our souls, the souls of Romanians everywhere...

02.02.2011

I'm proud to be Romanian! May God preserve all us Romanians wherever we are in the world and let us not forget: we are beautiful, intelligent, talented, to the envy of many. Be proud to be Romanian.

We thank God that there existed among us Romanians people to do us honour. Eternal glory.

07.04.2011

Bravo pentru Brănești, bravo pentru
România! A fost român, n-au cum să
mai schimbe asta! 05.03.2011
–
N-ar trebui să-i lăsăm să ne fure cultura
și moștenirea. Este, a fost și va rămâne
un român. Nu uitați asta, voi toți ai
care treceți pe aici... E de-al nostru...
doar că ai să lucrolă cu acest atelier...
Adevărata moștenire culturală e în
sufletele noastre, ale românilor de
pretutindeni... 02 02 2014
–
Sunt mândru că sunt român! Să ne
ocrotească Dumnezeu pe toți românii
oriunde ne-am afla pe mapamond și
să nu uităm! Suntem frumoși, inteligenți,
talentați, spre invidia multora. Fii mândru
că ești român.
–
Mulțumim lui Dțeu că au existat între
noi românii oameni care ne fac asta,
Glorie eterna. 07 04 2014

We thank you, thank you, thank you! You made men of us...

The works of Brancusi enchanted me to the point of tears. It's painful that the great artists of the Romanian people live and lived and suffered in exile.

Look on every page to see how many proud Romanians there are. P. S. We are not all gypsies and beggars!

18.09.2011

Nous ne sommes pas tous voleurs et tzigans.

18.09.2011

A pity that this museum isn't in Romania!

02.10.2011

Brancusi is one of the examples that prove that Romanians are not all criminals and gypsies. What a pity that in Paris and New York his works are more appreciated than in his home country. I rejoiced at this museum, the same as I rejoiced to see a statue of Eminescu on a street in Paris.

10.10.2011

Mulțumim, mulțumim, mulțumim! Ne-ai topit sufletul...

— Lucrările lui B m-au sedus până la lacrimi. E dureros că marii artiști ai neamului românesc trăiesc și au trăit și suferit în exil.

— Uitați-vă pe toate paginile și vedeți câți români mândri sunt. P.S. Nu suntem toți numai țigani și cerșetori! 18.09 2011

— Nous ne sommes pas tous voleurs et tzigans. 18,09,2011

— Păcat că nu este acest muzeu în Ro! 0? 10.2011

— Brâncuși este unul dintre exemplele care demonstrează că românii nu sînt toți infractori sau țigani. Păcat că la Paris sau NY, operele lui sînt mai apreciate decât în țară. M-a bucurat acest muzeu la fel cum m-am bucurat să văd pe o stradă din Paris, statuia lui Eminescu.
                                    10.10 2011

BRANCUSI ROMANIAN

07.04.2012

Brother Constantin, the legacy you have left us is food for our souls.

I don't know whether to call you Mr. Brancusi or *Bădie* Brancusi, to me you are a titan who has greatly enraptured the French people and Romanians like me who have seen all the works in your studio amid tears, many, many tears.

Constantin Brancusi, Romanians have an inferiority complex, particularly when they travel outside the home country. Your work has a therapeutic role for Romanians. Each is comforted when he enters here, and his soul is flooded with pride... national pride. What would we do without you, Brancusi?

27.04.2012

Brancusi = universality = Romania

We are proud of the creative genius of the Romanian people!

29.04.2012

BRÂNCUȘI ROMÂN   5.04.2012

— Frate Constantine, moștenirea pe care
ne-ai lăsat-o este hrana sufletelor
noastre

— Nu știu cum să-ți spun "Dle
Brâncuși" sau "Bădie B" pentru mine
ești un titan care ai bucurat mult
poporul francez și pe românii cu mine
care au văzut toate operele din atelier
printre lacrimi, multe, multe lacrimi.

— C. B, românii au un sentiment de
inferioritate, în special atunci când
călătoresc în afara țării. Opera ta are
un rol terapeutic pentru români
fiecare dintre ei este mângâiat când
vatră aici, iar sufletul îi este inundat
de mândrie ... națională.
   Ce ne facem fără tine. B?

   27.04.2012

— B = universalitate = Ro
— Suntem mândri de geniul creator al
poporului român! 29.04.12

What an elevating joy to be Romanian, to be part of Brancusi's family! And your soul soars for joy, pride and gratitude!

08.2012

We are enchanted by the talent of this great Romanian!

22.08.2012

I invite you to Romania, to Targu Jiu to experience in the Romanian style Brancusi's work!

08.2012

A year and a half ago I abandoned my home country at the age of 27 and I live in Germany trying to battle with foreigners' mentalities about Romanians, sometimes even feeling ashamed of being Romanian... With tears of joy in my eyes today I am proud to be Romanian! I bow before this great talent.

08.2012

Next to his works I can feel happy to be Romanian. In the midst of the Romanian people, NO. Thank you France! P.S. Absolutely enchanted to discover that the genius played golf...

02.09.2012

Ce bucurie înălțătoare, să fii
român, să fii de-al lui B!
Să sufletul ți-l înalță de bucurie,
mândrie și recunoștință! aug 2012
- Suntem încântați de talentul acestui
mare român! 22.08.2012
- Vă invit în Ro, la Tg. Jiu să simțiți
românește opera lui B! aug 2012
-
De un an și jumătate mi-au
părăsit țara la vârsta de 27 ani și
trăiesc în Germania încercând să lupt
cu mentalitățile străinilor despre
români, uneori chiar gândindu-mă că
sunt româncă... Cu lacrimi de bucurie
în ochi sunt astăzi mândră ca sunt
româncă! Plecăciune în fața acestui
mare talent. aug 2012
- Lângă operele sale pot să mă simt
fericit că sunt român. În mijlocul
poporului român, NU. Mulțumim Franța!
P.S. Absolut încântat să descopăr ca geniul
încă golt... 02.sept.2012

We thank you Brancusi for having existed, because you are a true ambassador of Romania.

17.01.2013

Constantin! Can we Romanians hold out any longer!? Can we still go on?

A Romanian who makes me feel good that I was born in Romania. An initiate, an artist who understood something of what we humans call life!

An Oltenian from Gorj who made Romania known throughout the world! Bravo to him and our thanks.

13.02.2013

Bravo Brancusi, Romania is proud of you!

A unique moment when you feel like shouting to everybody that you are Romanian like Brancusi, you have reason to be proud for a moment at least.

24.02.2013

Unfortunately I'm very dissatisfied because the text is not in Romanian at the entrance. Also, the Romanian flag should be at the entrance.

Îți mulțumim Brâncuși că ai existat
pentru că ești un adevărat ambasador
al României 17.01.2013

Constantine! Oare noi românii o să mai
rezistăm!? Mai putem?

Tu român care mă faci să mă simt
bine că sunt născută în România, Un
inițiat, un artist care a înțeles ceva din
ceea ce noi oamenii numim viață!

Un oltean plecat din Gorj care a
făcut Ro cunoscută în lume! Bravo
îți mulțumim   13.02.2013

Bravo B, Ro se mândrește cu tine!

Un moment unic în care îți vine
să le strigi tuturor că tu ești român
ca și B, ai de ce să fii mândru
pentru un moment măcar, 24.02.2013

Din păcate sunt f nemulțumit pt că
nu este sens în românia de intrare. Și
pus steagul României la intrare

I am proud to be Romanian. Brancusi is the emblem of Romania!!!

11.02.2012

Bravo! We are Romanians, the descendants of the Dacians!!!

20.06.2013

I love French people's love for art and I appreciate that they opened such a space dedicated to one of our sculptors. I hate that they have made him one of their own.

10.04.2013

Very nice! Cristi sends you greetings and is trying to bring you back to your homeland!

10.10.2012

A true Dacian!

14.09.2012

This is an invitation to visit Romania and Hobita Village where Brancusi was born.

19.09.2012

Infinite gratitude and admiration for a complete artist. We thank you for the impressive legacy you have left us, Constantin Brancusi! It is our wish that all these will remain for eternity. It is our hope that you will return once more to your home in Romania.

24.08.2012

Mă mândresc ca sunt româncă , B este
emblema României !!!   11.02.2012 / 16

– Bravo ! Noi suntem români, urmașii
dacilor !!!   20.06.2013 / 21

– Iubesc inițiativa francezilor pt artă și
apreciez să fac un asemenea spațiu
dedicat unui sculptor de-al nostru.
Vrăsc să această să devenit de-al lor.

   10.04.2013 / 20

– Foarte frumos ! Cristi + H transmite salutări
și încearcă să te aducă în țară !

   10.10.2012 / 19

– Un dac adevărat !   14.09.2012 / 19

– This is an invitation to visit Roumanie
And Hobița Village where B Was born.

   14.09.2012 / 19

– Recunoștiață și admirație infinită pentru
un artist complet. Mulțumim pentru impresionanta
moștenire pe care ne-ai lăsat-o. C.B.! Ne
dorim ca toate astea să rămână în
eternitate. Sperăm să revii din nou acasă,
în România ta. 24.08.2012 / 19

Performance-ul realizat la Atelierul Brâncuși din Centrul Georges Pompidou și lucrarea rezultată în urma sa prelungesc interesul Alexandrei Croitoru pentru cadrele discursive și manifestările ideologice care circumscriu raportarea diferită la opera lui Constantin Brâncuși în România și în afara sa. Ambele lucrări explorează clivajul dintre contemplarea estetică a operei de artă înțeleasă drept creație autonomă și politizarea sa inevitabilă ca artefact cultural. Prin adîncirea acestei tensiuni, ele problematizează totodată conceptele de cosmpolitanism și transculturalitate.

Ideea acestui performance a pornit de la experiența descrisă de Richard Serra într-un interviu cu Friedrich Teja Bach: în 1964, în timpul unui stagiu la Paris, în fiecare zi timp de patru luni, artistul a mers în atelierul lui Brâncuși și a desenat după sculpturi, încercînd să le înțeleagă. Alexandra Croitoru reia acest gest, acompaniindu-l însă cu cel al transcrierii mesajelor lăsate de vizitatori în caietele de impresii ale atelierului. Dacă Serra era interesat de aspectul formal și de caracteristicile estetice ale sculpturii, performance-ul artistei asumă bruiajul datorat patosului naționalist ce înconjoară subiectul Brâncuși în contextul românesc. Simpla copiere executată de Croitoru denotă mai curînd servilismul dogmatic, iar repetiția mecanică a acelorași procedee de figurație vizuală conduce, în cele din urmă, la golirea de semnificații a formei artistice. Facilitată de acest exercițiu de multiplicare a imaginii artistice deopotrivă în sfera artei și în afara sa, raportarea la opera lui Brâncuși iese inevitabil din sfera specifică artei. Politizarea ei se relevă cu claritate în caietele de impresii transcrise de Alexandra Croitoru. Opțiunea pentru reconstituirea selectivă a unei arhive textuale paralele celei vizuale asociate sculpturilor lui Brâncuși exprimă interesul artistei pentru cadrele discursive implicite ce condiționează și reglementează circulația, semnificația și efectele acestor imagini. Fragmentele textuale alese ilustrează frecvența asocierilor lui Brâncuși cu cultura națională în detrimentul oricăror considerații estetice sau asocieri artistice. Brâncuși reprezintă un motiv de mîndrie națională, fiind capabil să contracareze reprezentările marginalizante și xenofobe ale românilor vehiculate de mass-media occidentală; el trebuie "repatriat" în mod simbolic.

⟵ I wanted to draw from them in order to understand them, 2014

Performance, 60'

⟵ Livres d'Or, 2014

Creion pe hîrtie A4 [Pencil on A4 paper]
(foto: Marius Poput)

The performance at the Brancusi Studio in the Georges Pompidou Centre and the piece resulting therefrom are an extension of Alexandra Croitoru's interest in the discursive frameworks and ideological manifestations that circumscribe the different relationships to Brancusi's work inside and outside Romania. Both works explore the rift between the aesthetic contemplation of the artwork understood as autonomous creation and its inevitable politicisation as cultural artefact. At the same time, by heightening this tension they problematise the concepts of cosmopolitanism and the trans-cultural. The idea for the performance arose from the experience described by Richard Serra in an interview with Friedrich Teja Bach: in 1964, during his stay in Paris, the artist went to Brancusi's studio every day for four months and draw from the sculptures in an attempt to understand them. Alexandra Croitoru repeated this act, but accompanying it with that of transcribing the messages written in the studio visitors' book. If Serra was interested in the formal and aesthetic qualities of the sculpture, the Romanian artist's performance embraces the white noise produced by the nationalist pathos surrounding Brancusi in the Romanian context. The mere act of copying performed by Croitoru sooner denotes dogmatic servility, and the mechanical repetition of the same procedures of visual figuration ultimately leads to the artistic form being emptied of meaning. Facilitated by this exercise of multiplying the artistic image both inside and outside the field of art, the relationship with the work of Brancusi inevitably leaves the artworld. Its unavoidable politicisation is clearly revealed in the visitors' books transcribed by Alexandra Croitoru. The choice of selectively reconstructing a textual archive parallel to the visual archive associated with the sculptures of Brancusi expresses the artist's interest in the implicit discursive frameworks that condition and regulate the circulation, meaning and effects of the images. The textual fragments selected illustrate the frequency of the association of Brancusi with the national culture to the detriment of any aesthetic considerations or artistic associations. Brancusi represents a motive for national pride, capable of counteracting the marginalising and xenophobic representations of Romanians spread by the Western mass media; he must be symbolically "repatriated."

Text
Cristian Nae

Traducere [Translation]
Alistair Ian Blyth

Corectură [Proofreading]
George State

Graphic Design
Nona Inescu